John Henry Newman

Maxims of the kingdom of heaven

John Henry Newman

Maxims of the kingdom of heaven

ISBN/EAN: 9783741143441

Manufactured in Europe, USA, Canada, Australia, Japa

Cover: Foto ©Thomas Meinert / pixelio.de

Manufactured and distributed by brebook publishing software (www.brebook.com)

John Henry Newman

Maxims of the kingdom of heaven

MAXIMS

OF THE

KINGDOM OF HEAVEN.

Nihil obstat :
>J. C. ROBERTSON,
>>*Censor deputatus.*

Imprimatur :
>✠ HENRICUS EDUARDUS.
>>*Archiep. Westmonast.*

Die 21 *Junii,* 1872.

MAXIMS

OF THE

KINGDOM OF HEAVEN.

Second Edition,

ENLARGED AND RE-ARRANGED FOR
MEDITATION AND REFERENCE.

LONDON:
R. WASHBOURNE, 18, PATERNOSTER ROW.
1873.

Google

NOTE TO THE FIRST EDITION.

The following collection of passages from the Holy Scriptures has been put into my hands by the compiler to carry through the press. I could not but gladly avail myself of the opportunity, which a friend thus presented to me, of having a share, however small, in a work directed, in so pious a spirit, towards the promotion among Catholics of an habitual reverent meditation upon the sacred words of Him who spake as " man never did speak."

J. H. N.

1860.

1 CHRIST. My son, hear my words, words most sweet, exceeding all the learning of the philosophers, and of the wise men of this world. My words are spirit and life, and not to be estimated by the sense of man . . .

3 It is I who have taught the prophets from the beginning, and even till now I cease not to speak to all; but many are deaf to my voice, and hard.

5 Write my words in thy heart, and think diligently on them; for they will be very necessary in time of temptation. What thou understandest not when thou readest, thou shalt know in the day of visitation.

FOLLOWING OF CHRIST.

Book iii., chap. 3rd.

DEDICATION.

To MARY, the ever Blessed and Glorious Virgin, Mother of God, are dedicated these selections from the written Word:

Mary, who ever kept God's Word in holy silence and prudence, pondering it in her heart:

Mary, whose sole testimony sufficed to establish the truth that the Word was made flesh and dwelt among us, and whose prayer will ever be most lovingly applied to form Christ in our hearts:

Mary, who is heard even if God's time is "not yet come," as when she said: "Son, they have no wine":

Mary, whose humility resembling that of Jesus, sought not her own glory, but remained "full of grace" under the shadow of the Most High:

Mary, whose compassion is as great now, as when,

standing at the foot of the cross, the sword pierced her Immaculate Heart, and when by a supreme charity as mother of us all she accepted S. John for her son in the stead of her divine Jesus.

O Mother of Him who will at the last day come in great power and majesty to judge the living and the dead by the Gospel's holy law, pray for us, that, rejecting the false maxims of a world at enmity with God, we may die to it, and to ourselves, and so, the Spirit of Jesus may alone live in us and direct us, to the Glory of God the Father. Amen.

MAXIMS

OF THE

KINGDOM OF HEAVEN.

ACKNOWLEDGMENT OF SIN.

6 My God, I am confounded and ashamed to lift up my face to thee: for our iniquities are multiplied over our heads, and our sins are grown up even unto heaven. — 1 Esdras ix.

2 ... In thy sight no man living shall be justified. — Ps. cxlii.

33 Thou art just in all things that have come upon us: because thou hast done truth, but we have done wickedly. — 2 Esdras ix.

20 If I would justify myself, my own mouth shall condemn me. If I would shew myself innocent, He shall prove me wicked. — Job ix.

27 ... I have sinned, and indeed I have offended, and I have not received what I have deserved. — Job xxxiii.

6 We have sinned with our fathers: we have acted unjustly, we have wrought iniquity. — Ps. cv.

9 Who can say: My heart is clean, I am pure from sin. — Prov. xx.

13 He that hideth his sins, shall not prosper: but he that shall confess, and forsake them, shall obtain mercy. — Prov. xxviii.

21 There is no just man upon earth, that doth good, and sinneth not. — Eccles. vii.

25 ... We have sinned against the Lord our God, we and our fathers from our youth even to this day ... — Jer. iii.

9 I will bear the wrath of the Lord, because I have sinned against him ... — Micheas vii.

28 ... Thou hast executed true judgments in all the things that thou hast brought upon us ... — Daniel iii.

29 For we have sinned, and committed iniquity, departing from thee: and we have trespassed in all things.

12 Our iniquities are multiplied before thee, and our sins have testified against us: for our wicked doings are with us, and we have known our iniquities, — Isaias lix.

13 In sinning and lying against the Lord: and we have turned away so that we went not after our God, but spoke calumny and transgression: we have conceived, and uttered from the heart, words of falsehood.

5 I have acknowledged my sin to thee, and my injustice I have not concealed. — Ps. xxxi.

Acknowledgment of Sin.

I said I will confess against myself my injustice to the Lord; and thou hast forgiven the wickedness of my sin.

8 O Lord, to us belongeth confusion of face, to our princes, and to our fathers that have sinned; — Dan. ix.

9 But to thee, the Lord our God, mercy and forgiveness, for we have departed from thee:

10 And we have not hearkened to the voice of the Lord our God, to walk in his law, which he set before us by his servants the prophets.

21 ... Father, I have sinned against heaven, and before thee, I am not now worthy to be called thy son. — S. Luke xv.

13 And the publican standing afar off would not so much as lift up his eyes towards heaven; but struck his breast, saying: O God, be merciful to me a sinner. — S. Luke xviii.

15 A faithful saying, and worthy of all acceptation, that Christ Jesus came into this world to save sinners, of whom I am the chief. — 1 Tim. i.

31 If we would judge ourselves, we should not be judged. — 1 Cor. xi.

8 If we say that we have no sin; we deceive ourselves, and the truth is not in us. — 1 S. John i.

9 If we confess our sins; he is faithful

and just to forgive us our sins, and to cleanse us from all iniquity.

AFFLICTION.

16 Thus saith the Lord: Let thy voice cease from weeping, and thine eyes from tears.: for there is a reward for thy work . . .   Jer. xxxi.

11 . . . I will chastise thee in judgment, that thou mayest not seem to thyself innocent.   Jer. xxx.

15 Call upon me in the day of trouble: I will deliver thee, and thou shalt glorify me.   Ps. xlix.

18 . . . It is the Lord: Let him do what is good in his sight.   1 Kings iii.

7 If I shall walk in the midst of tribulation, thou wilt quicken me . . .   Ps. cxxxvii.

6 Nothing upon earth is done without a cause, and sorrow doth not spring out of the ground.   Job. v.

21 . . . We deserve to suffer these things, because we have sinned against our brother, seeing the anguish of his soul, when he besought us, and we would not hear: therefore is this affliction come upon us.   Gen. xlii.

17 Blessed is the man whom God correcteth: refuse not therefore the chastising of the Lord.   Job. v.

18 For he woundeth, and cureth: he striketh, and his hands shall heal.

Affliction.

5 He hath chastised us for our iniquities: and he will save us for his own mercy. — Tobias xiii.

20 Many are the afflictions of the just; but out of them all will the Lord deliver them. — Ps. xxxiii.

12 Thou hast corrected man for iniquity. — Ps. xxxviii.

7 Thou hast made us to be a contradiction to our neighbours: and our enemies have scoffed at us. — Ps. lxxix.

1 In my trouble I cried to the Lord: and he heard me. — Ps. cxix.

5 They that sow in tears shall reap in joy. — Ps. cxxv.

6 Going they went and wept, casting their seeds;

7 But coming they shall come with joyfulness, carrying their sheaves.

11 My son, reject not the correction of the Lord: and do not faint when thou art chastised by him. — Prov. iii.

12 For whom the Lord loveth, he chastiseth . . .

1 O how good and sweet is thy Spirit, O Lord, in all things. — Wisd. xii.

2 And therefore thou chastiseth them that err, by little and little: and admonishest them, and speakest to them concerning the things wherein they offend: that leaving their wickedness, they may believe in thee, O Lord.

13 God is compassionate and merciful, and will forgive sins in the day of tribulation. — Eccles. ii.

26 The mercy of God is beautiful in the time of affliction, as a cloud of rain in the time of drought. — Eccles. xxxv.

19 Wo is me for my destruction, my wound is very grievous. But I said: truly this is my own evil, and I will bear it. — Jer. x.

18 He that feareth the Lord, will receive his discipline. — Eccles. xxxii.

18 Thou hast chastised me, and I was instructed. — Jer. xxxi.

33 He hath not willingly afflicted, nor cast off the children of men. — Lament. iii.

28 For as it was your mind to go astray from God; so when you return again you shall seek him ten times as much. — Baruch iv.

29 For he that hath brought evils upon you, shall bring you everlasting joy again with your salvation.

1 In their affliction they will rise early to me: Come, and let us return to the Lord. — Osee vi.

2 For he hath taken us, and he will heal us: he will strike, and he will cure us.

7 The Lord is good, and giveth strength in the day of trouble: and knoweth them that hope in him. — Nahum i.

13 For it is a token of great goodness when sinners are not suffered to go on in their ways for a long time, but are presently punished. — 2 Mach. vi.

Affliction.

30 O Lord, who hast the holy knowledge, thou knowest manifestly that whereas I might be delivered from death, I suffer grievous pains in body: but in soul am well content to suffer these things because I fear thee.

2 ... Every branch that beareth fruit, he will purge it, that it may bring forth more fruit. — S. John xv.

5 Blessed are they that mourn: for they shall be comforted. — S. Matt. v.

21 Blessed are ye that weep now: for you shall laugh. — S. Luke vi.

33 In the world you shall have distress: but have confidence; I have overcome the world. — S. John xvi.

21 ... Through many tribulations we must enter into the kingdom of God. — Acts xiv.

3 But we glory also in tribulations, knowing that tribulation worketh patience: — Rom. v.

4 And patience trial: and trial hope.

18 For I reckon, that the sufferings of this present time are not worthy to be compared with the glory to come, that shall be revealed in us. — Rom. viii.

5 For as the sufferings of Christ abound in us; so also by Christ doth our comfort abound. — 2 Cor. i.

7 ... Knowing that as you are partakers of the sufferings, so shall you be also of the consolation.

32 But whilst we are judged, we are chastised by the Lord; that we be not condemned with this world.   1 Cor. xi.

17 For our present tribulation, which is momentary and light, worketh for us above measure exceedingly an eternal weight of glory.   2 Cor. iv.

4 ... I exceedingly abound with joy in all our tribulation.   2 Cor. vii.

9 ... I glory in my infirmities, that the power* of Christ may dwell in me.   2 Cor. xii.

10 Therefore, I take pleasure in my infirmities, in reproaches, in necessities, in persecutions, in distresses for Christ's sake. For when I am weak, then am I powerful.

8 In all things we suffer tribulation; but are not distressed: we are straitened, but are not destitute.   2 Cor. iv.

6 And you became followers of us, and of the Lord; receiving the word in much tribulation, with joy of the Holy Ghost.   1 Thess. i.

3 That no man should be moved in these tribulations: for yourselves know, that we are appointed thereunto.   1 Thess. iii.

34 You both had compassion on them that were in bands, and took with joy the being stripped of your goods, knowing that you have a better and a lasting substance.   Heb. x.

* See note in GOD OUR STRENGTH.

Affliction.

12 If we suffer, we shall also reign with him...   2 Tim. ii.

4 You have not yet resisted unto blood, striving against sin.   Heb. xii.

5 And you have forgotten the consolation, which speaketh to you as unto children, saying: My son, neglect not the discipline of the Lord: neither be thou wearied whilst thou art rebuked by him.

6 For whom the Lord loveth, he chasteneth; and he scourgeth every son whom he receiveth.

7 Persevere under chastisement. God dealeth with you as with sons; for what son is there, whom the father doth not correct?

8 But if you be without chastisement, whereof all are made partakers; then are you bastards, and not sons.

9 Moreover, we have had, indeed, for our instructors, the fathers of our flesh; and we reverenced them: shall we not much more obey the Father of Spirits, and live?

10 And they indeed, for a few days, chastised us according to their own pleasure; but he, for our profit, that we might be partakers of his holiness.

11 Now no chastisement for the present seemeth to bring with it joy, but sorrow: but afterwards it will yield to them that are

exercised by it, the most peaceable fruit of justice.

1 Christ, therefore, having suffered in the flesh, be you also armed with the same thought: for he that hath suffered in the flesh, hath ceased from sins: 1 S. Pet. iv.

2 That now, as to the rest of his time in the flesh, he may live not after the desires of men, but according to the will of God.

13 Rejoice, being partakers of the sufferings of Christ; that when his glory shall be revealed, you may also be glad with exceeding joy.

19 Those whom I love, I rebuke and chastise... Apoc. iii.

13 And one of the ancients answered, and said to me: Who are these that are clothed in white robes: and whence are they come? Apoc. vii.

14 And I said to him: My lord, thou knowest. And he said to me: These are they who are come out of great tribulation, and have washed their robes, and have made them white in the blood of the Lamb.

15 Therefore, they are before the throne of God, and serve him day and night in his temple: and he that sitteth on the throne shall dwell over them.

16 They shall not hunger, nor thirst any more; neither shall the sun fall on them, nor any heat:

17 For the Lamb, which is in the midst of the throne, shall rule them, and shall lead them to the fountains of the waters of life; and God shall wipe away all tears from their eyes.

4 ... And death shall be no more; nor mourning, nor crying, nor sorrow shall be any more, for the former things are passed away.   Apoc. xxi.

ALMSGIVING.

7 If one of thy brethren that dwelleth within the gates of thy city in the land which the Lord thy God will give thee, come to poverty: thou shalt not harden thy heart, nor close thy hand,   Deut. xv.

8 But shalt open it to the poor man ...

10 Thou shalt give to him: neither shalt thou do anything craftily in relieving his necessities: that the Lord thy God may bless thee at all times, and in all things to which thou shalt put thy hand.

11 There will not be wanting poor in the land of thy habitation; therefore I command thee to open thy hand to thy needy and poor brother, that liveth in the land.

7 Give alms out of thy substance; and turn not away thy face from any poor person, for so it shall come to pass that the face of the Lord shall not be turned from thee.   Tobias iv.

8 According to thy ability be merciful.

9 If thou have much give abundantly: if thou have little take care even so to bestow willingly a little.

2 Blessed is he that understandeth concerning the needy and the poor: the Lord will deliver him in the evil day.   Ps. xl.

3 The Lord preserve him and give him life, and make him blessed upon the earth: and deliver him not up to the will of his enemies.

4 The Lord help him on his bed of sorrow: thou hast turned all his couch in his sickness.

21 ... He that sheweth mercy to the poor, shall be blessed.   Prov. xiv.

17 He that hath mercy on the poor, lendeth to the Lord; and he will repay him.   Prov. xix.

13 He that stoppeth his ear against the cry of the poor, shall also cry himself and shall not be heard.   Prov. xxi.

27 He that giveth to the poor, shall not want: he that despiseth his entreaty, shall suffer indigence.   Prov. xxviii.

33 Water quencheth a flaming fire, and alms resisteth sins: Ecclus. iii.

34 And God provideth for him that sheweth favour: he remembereth him afterwards, and in the time of his fall he shall find a sure stay.

Almsgiving.

1 Son, defraud not the poor of alms, and turn not away thy eyes from the poor. Ecclus. iv.

2 Despise not the hungry soul; and provoke not the poor in his want.

3 Afflict not the heart of the needy, and defer not to give to him that is in distress.

4 Reject not the petition of the afflicted: and turn not away thy face from the needy.

5 Turn not away thy eyes from the poor for fear of anger: and leave not to them that ask of thee to curse thee behind thy back.

6 For the prayer of him that curseth thee in the bitterness of his soul, shall be heard: for he that made him will hear him.

10 Neglect not to pray, and to give alms. Ecclus. vii.

36 Stretch out thy hand to the poor, that thy expiation and thy blessing may be perfected.

1 If thou do good, know to whom thou dost it, and there shall be much thanks for thy good deeds. Ecclus. xii.

2 Do good to the just, and thou shalt find great recompense: and if not of him, assuredly of the Lord.

4 Give to the merciful and uphold not the sinner . . .

28 . . . After thou hast given, upbraid not.

13 Do good to thy friend before thou die, Ecclus. xiv,

and according to thy ability stretching out thy hand give to the poor.

18 The alms of a man is as a signet with him, and shall preserve the grace of a man as the apple of the eye. Ecclus. xvii.

15 Shut up alms in the heart of the poor, and it shall obtain help for thee against all evil. Ecclus. xxix.

16 Better than the shield of the mighty, and better than the spear:

17 It shall fight for thee against thy enemy.

7 Deal thy bread to the hungry, and bring the needy and the harbourless into thy house: and when thou shalt see one naked, cover him, and despise not thy own flesh. Isaias lviii.

8 Then shall thy light break forth as the morning, and thy health shall speedily arise, and thy justice shall go before thy face, and the glory of the Lord shall gather thee up.

9 Then shalt thou call, and the Lord shall hear: thou shalt cry, and he shall say: Here I am . . .

24 Wherefore, O King, let my counsel be acceptable to thee, and redeem thou thy sins with alms, and thy iniquities with works of mercy to the poor . . . Dan. iv.

41 And Jesus sitting over against the treasury, beheld how the people cast money into the treasury: and many that were rich cast in much. S. Mark xii.

Almsgiving.

42 And there came a certain poor widow, and she cast in two mites, which make a farthing.

43 And calling his disciples together, he saith to them: Amen I say to you, this poor widow hath cast in more than all they who have cast into the treasury.

44 For they all did cast in of their abundance; but she of her want cast in all she had, even her whole living.

1 Take heed that you do not your justice* before men, that you may be seen by them: otherwise you shall not have a reward of your Father, who is in heaven. — S. Matt. vi.

2 Therefore, when thou dost an almsdeed, sound not a trumpet before thee, as the hypocrites do in the synagogues and in the streets, that they may be honoured by men. Amen I say to you, they have received their reward.

3 But when thou dost alms, let not thy left hand know what thy right hand doth.

4 That thy alms may be in secret, and thy Father who seeth in secret will repay thee.

11 ... He that hath two coats, let him give to him that hath none; and he that hath meat, let him do in like manner. — S. Luke iii.

* *I.e.* Fasting, prayer, and alms-deeds, which ought to be performed, not out of ostentation, or a view to please men, but solely to please God.

30 Give to every one that asketh thee. . . . S. Luke vi.

38 Give, and it shall be given to you: good measure, and pressed down, and shaken together, and running over, shall they give into your bosom, for with the same measure that you shall mete withal, it shall be measured to you again.

33 Sell what you possess, and give alms. S. Luke xii. Make to yourselves bags which grow not old, a treasure in heaven which faileth not: where the thief approacheth not, nor the moth corrupteth.

34 For where your treasure is, there will your heart be also.

16 Do not forget to do good and to impart: for by such sacrifices God's favour is obtained. Heb. xiii.

35 Remember the word of the Lord Jesus, Acts xx. how he said: It is more blessed to give, than to receive.

12 If the will be forward, it is accepted according to that which a man hath, not according to that which he hath not. 2 Cor. viii.

6 Now this I say: He who soweth sparingly, shall also reap sparingly: and he who soweth in blessings, shall also reap blessings. 2 Cor. ix.

7 Every one as he hath determined in his heart, not with sadness, or of necessity: for God loveth a cheerful giver.

Almsgiving.

8 And God is able to make all grace abound in you; that ye always having all sufficiency in all things, may abound in every good work.

9 As it is written: He hath dispersed abroad, he hath given to the poor: his justice remaineth for ever.

10 Now he that administereth seed to the sower, will both give you bread to eat, and will multiply your seed, and increase the growth of the fruits of your justice:

11 That being enriched in all things, you may abound unto all bountifulness, which causeth through us thanksgiving to God.

16 If any of the faithful have widows, let him relieve them. . . .   1 Tim. v.

15 If a brother or sister be naked, and want daily food: S. James ii.

16 And one of you say to them: Go in peace, be you warmed and filled: yet give them not those things that are necessary for the body, what shall it profit?

17 He that hath the substance of this world, and shall see his brother in need, and shall shut up his bowels from him: how doth the charity of God abide in him?   1 S. John iii.

18 My little children, let us not love in word, nor in tongue, but in deed, and in truth.

Maxims.

AMBITION.

6 IF his pride mount up even to heaven, Job xx.
and his head touch the clouds.

7 In the end, he shall be destroyed like a
dung-hill, and they that had seen him, shall
say: Where is he?

24 They are lifted up for a little while Job xxiv.
and shall not stand, and shall be brought
down as all things, and shall be taken away,
and as the tops of the ears of corn they shall
be broken.

11 ... They shall leave their riches to Ps. xlviii.
strangers:

12 And their sepulchres shall be their
houses for ever. Their dwelling places to all
generations: they have called their lands by
their names.

8 Wo to you that join house to house Isaias v.
and lay field to field, even to the end of the
place: shall you alone dwell in the midst of
the earth?

16 Thy arrogancy hath deceived thee, and Jer. xlix.
the pride of thy heart: O thou that dwellest
in the clefts of the rock, and endeavourest
to lay hold on the height of the hill: but
though thou shouldst make thy nest as high
as an eagle, I will bring thee down from
thence saith the Lord.

9 Wo to him that gathereth together an Habac.
evil covetousness to his house, that his nest ii.
may be on high, and thinketh he may be
delivered out of the hand of evil.

10 Thou hast devised confusion to thy
house, thou hast cut off many people, and
thy soul hath sinned.

12 Wo to him that buildeth a town with
blood, and prepareth a city by iniquity.

5 As wine deceiveth him that drinketh it:
so shall the proud man be, and he shall not
be honoured: who hath enlarged his desire
like hell: and is himself like death, and he
is never satisfied: but will gather together
unto him all nations, and heap together unto
him all people.

2 They have coveted fields, and taken Mich. ii.
them by violence, and houses they have
forcibly taken away: and oppressed a man
and his house, a man and his inheritance.

3 Therefore thus saith the Lord: Behold,
I devise an evil against this family: from
which you shall not withdraw your necks,
and you shall not walk haughtily, for this
is a very evil time.

25 And he (Jesus) said to them: The S. Luke
kings of the gentiles lord it over them; and xxii.
they that have power over them, are called
beneficent.

26 But you not so: but he who is the greatest among you, let him be as the least: and he that is the leader, as he that serveth.

27 ... I am in the midst of you as he serveth.

ANGELS.

20 BEHOLD I will send my Angel, who shall go before thee and keep thee in thy journey, and bring thee into the place that I have prepared. — Exodus xxiii.

21 Take notice of him, and hear his voice, and do not think him one to be contemned: for he will not forgive when thou hast sinned, and my name is in him.

18 The chariot of God is attended by ten thousands: thousands of them that rejoice. The Lord is among them in Sina, in the holy place. — Ps. lxvii.

11 He hath given his angels charge over thee: to keep thee in all thy ways. — Ps. xc.

12 In their hands they shall bear thee up: lest thou dash thy foot against a stone.

2 I will sing praise to thee in the sight of the angels. — Ps. cxxxvii.

6 Thou hast made him (man) a little less than the angels. — Ps. viii.

4 Who makest thy angels spirits: and thy ministers a burning fire. — Ps. ciii.

8 The Angel of the Lord shall encamp round about them that fear him: and shall deliver them. — Ps. xxxiii.

9 ... The Angel of his presence saved them. — Isaias lxiii.

22 My God hath sent his Angel, and hath shut up the mouths of the lions, and they have not hurt me. — Dan. vi.

13 And he (Jesus) was in the desert forty days, and forty nights: and was tempted by Satan, and he was with beasts, and the angels ministered to him. — S. Mark i.

53 Thinkest thou that I cannot ask my Father and he will give me presently more than twelve legions of angels? — S. Matt. xxvi.

43 And there appeared unto him an angel from heaven strengthening him. — S. Luke xxii.

39 ... The harvest is the end of the world and the reapers are the angels. — S. Matt. xiii.

27 Then shall he send his angels, and shall gather together his elect from the four winds, from the uttermost part of the earth to the uttermost part of heaven. — S. Mark xiii.

41 The son of man shall send his angels and they shall gather out of his kingdom all scandals, and them that work iniquity. — S. Matt. xiii.

51 ... Amen, amen, I say to you, you shall see the heaven opened, and the angels of God ascending and descending upon the Son of man. — S. John i.

22 And it came to pass that the beggar died and was carried by the angels into Abraham's bosom.*   S. Luke xvi.

11 ... Now I know in very deed that the Lord hath sent his Angel.   Acts xii.

23 For an angel of God, whose I am, and whom I serve, stood by me this night.   Acts xxvii.

14 Are they not all ministering spirits, sent to minister for them, who shall receive the inheritance of salvation.   Heb. i.

ANGER.

8 CEASE from anger, and leave rage.   Ps. xxxvi.

29 ... He that is impatient, exalteth his folly.   Prov. xiv.

1 A mild answer breaketh wrath: but a harsh word stirreth up fury.   Prov. xv.

4 A peaceable tongue is a tree of life: but that which is immoderate, shall crush the spirit.

14 ... A spirit that is easily angered, who can bear?   Prov. xviii.

19 He that is impatient, shall suffer damage ...   Prov. xix.

19 It is better to dwell in a wilderness, than with a quarrelsome and passionate woman.   Prov. xxi.

* The place of rest, where the souls of the Saints resided, till Christ had opened heaven by His death.

Anger.

21 As coals are to burning coals, and wood to fire, so an angry man stirreth up strife. — Prov. xxvi.

33 ... He that provoketh wrath, bringeth forth strife. — Prov. xxx.

20 Hast thou seen a man hasty to speak? folly is rather to be looked for than his amendment. — Prov. xxix.

22 A passionate man provoketh quarrels: and he that is easily stirred up to wrath, shall be more prone to sin.

35 Be not as a lion in thy house, terrifying them of thy household, and oppressing them that are under thee. — Ecclus. iv.

10 Be not quickly angry: for anger resteth in the bosom of a fool. — Ecclus. vii.

22 A hot soul is a burning fire, it will never be quenched, till it devour something. — Ecclus. xxiii.

33 Anger and fury are both of them abominable, and the sinful man shall be subject to them. — Ecclus. xxvii.

3 Man to man reserveth anger, and doth he seek remedy of God? — Ecclus. xxviii.

4 He hath no mercy on a man like himself, and doth he entreat for his own sins?

5 He that is but flesh, nourisheth anger, and doth he ask forgiveness of God? who shall obtain pardon for his sins?

6 Remember thy last things, and let enmity cease.

8 Remember the fear of God, and be not angry with thy neighbour.

9 Remember the covenant of the most High, and overlook the ignorance of thy neighbour.

22 I say to you, that whosoever is angry with his brother, shall be in danger of the judgment . . .   S. Matt. v.

26 Be angry, and sin not. Let not the sun go down upon your anger.   Ephes. iv.

27 Give not place to the devil.

31 Let all bitterness and anger and indignation, and clamour, and blasphemy be put away from you, with all malice.

19 . . . And let every man be swift to hear, but slow to speak, and slow to anger.   S. James i.

20 For the anger of man worketh not the justice of God.

AVOID EVIL COMPANIONSHIP.

7 Sanctify yourselves, and be ye holy, because I am the Lord your God.   Lev. xx.

26 . . . Depart from the tents of these wicked men, and touch nothing of theirs, lest you be involved in their sins.   Numb. xvi.

1 Blessed is the man who hath not walked in the counsel of the ungodly, nor stood in the way of sinners.   Ps. i.

Avoid Evil Companionship.

10 My son, if sinners shall entice thee, consent not to them. — Prov. i.

15 Walk not thou with them, restrain thy foot from their paths.

16 For they sleep not except they have done evil: and their sleep is taken away unless they have made some to fall. — Prov. iv.

14 Be not delighted in the paths of the wicked, neither let the way of evil men please thee.

15 Flee from it, pass not by it: go aside, and forsake it.

16 That thou mayest be delivered from the strange woman, and from the stranger, who softeneth her words: — Prov. ii.

17 And forsaketh the guide of her youth,

18 And hath forgotten the covenant of her God: for her house inclineth unto death, and her paths to hell.

19 None that go in unto her, shall return again, neither shall they take hold of the paths of life.

5 Her feet go down into death, and her steps go in as far as hell. — Prov. v.

8 Remove thy way far from her, and come not nigh the doors of her house.

9 Give not thy honour to strangers, and thy years to the cruel.

3 . . . Write it upon the tables of thy heart. — Prov. vii.

4 Say to wisdom: Thou art my sister: and call prudence thy friend,

5 That she may keep thee from the woman that is not thine, and from the stranger who sweeteneth her words.

10 ... Talkative and wandering,

11 Not bearing to be quiet, nor able to abide still at home,

12 Now abroad, now in the streets, now lying in wait near the corners.

3 He that joineth himself to harlots, will be wicked. Rottenness and worms shall inherit him, and he shall be lifted up for a greater example, and his soul shall be taken away out of the number.   *Ecclus. xix.*

3 Look not upon a woman that hath a mind for many: lest thou fall into her snares.   *Ecclus. ix.*

6 Give not thy soul to harlots in any point: lest thou destroy thyself and thy inheritance.

11 Many by admiring the beauty of another man's wife, have become reprobate, for her conversation burneth as fire.

27 I have found a woman more bitter than death, who is the hunter's snare, and her heart is a net, and her hands are bands. He that pleaseth God shall escape from her: but he that is a sinner, shall be caught by her.   *Eccles. vii.*

23 ... Reproofs of instruction are the way of life: *Prov. vi.*

24 That they may keep thee from the evil woman, and from the flattering tongue of the stranger.

25 Let not thy heart covet her beauty, be not caught with her winks.

35 Take heed to thyself of a mischievous man, for he worketh evils: lest he bring upon thee reproach for ever.   Ecclus. xi.

5 ... The counsels of the wicked are deceitful.   Prov. xii.

1 Seek not to be like evil men, neither desire to be with them.   Prov. xxiv.

19 Contend not with the wicked, nor seek to be like the ungodly:

20 For evil men have no hope of things to come, and the lamp of the wicked shall be put out.

17 Number not thyself among the multitude of the disorderly.   Ecclus. vii.

28 Who will trust him that hath no rest, and that lodgeth wheresoever the night taketh him, as a robber well appointed, that skippeth from city to city.   Ecclus. xxxvi.

14 The discourse of sinners is hateful, and their laughter is at the pleasures of sin.   Ecclus. xxvii.

16 Behold I send you as sheep in the midst of wolves. Be ye therefore wise as serpents and simple* as doves.   S. Matt. x.

* That is harmless, plain, sincere, and without guile.

11 ... Holy Father, keep them in thy S. John
name, whom thou hast given me. xvii.

15 I pray not that thou shouldst take
them out of the world, but that thou shouldst
keep them from evil.

17 Now I beseech you, brethren, to mark Rom.
them who make dissensions and offences xvi.
contrary to the doctrines which you have
learnt, and to avoid them.

33 Be not seduced: evil communications 1 Cor.
corrupt good manners. xv.

BACKSLIDERS.

15 ... He forsook God who made him, Deut.
and departed from God his Saviour. xxxii.

9 And the Lord was angry with Solomon, 3 Kings
because his mind was turned away from the xi.
Lord the God of Israel, who had appeared
to him twice.

13 O Lord, the hope of Israel: all that Jer.
forsake thee shall be confounded: they that xvii.
depart from thee, shall be written in the
earth: because they have forsaken the Lord,
the vein of living waters.

2 ... If you forsake him, he will forsake 2 Parali.
you. xv.

19 Thy own wickedness shall reprove thee, Jer. ii.
and thy apostacy shall rebuke thee. Know
thou, and see that it is an evil and a bitter

Backsliders. 29

thing for thee, to have left the Lord thy God, and that my fear is not with thee, saith the Lord the God of hosts.

13 My people have done two evils. They have forsaken me, the fountain of living waters, and have digged to themselves cisterns, broken cisterns, that can hold no water.

6 Thou hast forsaken me, saith the Lord, Jer. xv. thou art gone backward: and I will stretch out my hand against thee, and I will destroy thee: I am weary of entreating thee.

6 ... Thou hast forgotten the law of thy Osee iv. God, I also will forget thy children.

12 Because iniquity hath abounded, the S. Matt. charity of many shall grow cold. xxiv.

12 Take heed, brethren, lest perhaps there Heb. iii. be in any of you an evil heart of unbelief, to depart from the living God.

21 For it had been better for them not to 2 S. Pet. have known the way of justice, than after ii. they have known it, to turn back from that holy commandment which was delivered to them.

17 ... Take heed, lest being led aside by 2 S. Pet. the error of the unwise, you fall from your iii. own steadfastness.

BLESSED VIRGIN.

48 ... BEHOLD, from henceforth all gene-   S. Luke
rations shall call me blessed.*   i.

14 The Lord God said to the serpent ... Gen. iii.

15 I will put enmities between thee and
the woman, and thy seed and her seed: she
shall crush thy head, and thou shalt lie in
wait for her heel.†

1 And there shall come forth a rod out of   Isaias
the root of Jesse, and a flower shall rise up   xi.
out of his root.

14 ... Behold a virgin shall conceive, and   Isaias
bear a son, and his name shall be called   vii.
Emmanuel.‡

26 ... The Angel Gabriel was sent from   S. Luke
God into a city of Galilee, called Nazareth,   i.

27 To a virgin espoused to a man whose
name was Joseph, of the house of David; and
the virgin's name was Mary.

28. And the Angel being come in, said
unto her: Hail, full of grace, the Lord is
with thee: Blessed art thou among women.

29 And when she had heard, she was

---

* These words are a prediction of that honour which the church in all ages should pay to the Blessed Virgin.

† For it is by her seed Jesus Christ, that the woman crushes the serpent's head.

‡ Which being interpreted is, God with us.

troubled at his saying, and thought within herself what manner of salutation this should be.

30 And the Angel said to her: Fear not, Mary; for thou hast found grace with God:

31 Behold, thou shalt conceive in thy womb, and shalt bring forth a Son; and thou shalt call his name Jesus.

32 He shall be great, and shall be called the Son of the most High: and the Lord God shall give unto him the throne of David his father: and he shall reign in the house of Jacob for ever.

33 And of his kingdom there shall be no end.

34 And Mary said to the Angel: How shall this be done, because I know not man?

35 And the Angel answering, said to her: The Holy Ghost shall come upon thee, and the power of the most High shall overshadow thee. And therefore also the Holy which shall be born of thee, shall be called the Son of God.

38 And Mary said: Behold the handmaid of the Lord: be it done to me according to thy word.

39 And Mary rising up in those days, went into the mountainous country with haste, into a city of Juda.

40 And she entered into the house of Zachary, and saluted Elizabeth.

41 And it came to pass; that when Elizabeth heard the salutation of Mary, the infant leaped in her womb: and Elizabeth was filled with the Holy Ghost:

42 And she cried out with a loud voice, and said: Blessed art thou among women; and blessed is the fruit of thy womb.

43 And whence is this to me, that the mother of my Lord should come to me?

44 For behold, as soon as the voice of thy salutation sounded in my ears, the infant in my womb leaped for joy.

45 And blessed art thou that hast believed, because those things shall be accomplished that were spoken to thee by the Lord.

46 And Mary said: My soul doth magnify the Lord:

47 And my spirit hath rejoiced in God my Saviour.

48 Because he hath regarded the humility of his handmaid: for, behold, from henceforth all generations shall call me blessed.

49 For he that is mighty hath done great things to me: and holy is his name.

56 And Mary abode with her (cousin Elizabeth) about three months: and she returned to her own house.

1 And it came to pass in those days there went out a decree from Cæsar Augustus; that the whole world should be enrolled.   S. Luke ii.

4 And Joseph also went up from Galilee out of the city of Nazareth into Judea, to the city of David, which is called Bethlehem: because he was of the house and family of David.

5 To be enrolled with Mary his espoused wife who was with child.

6 And it came to pass that when they were there, her days were accomplished, that she should be delivered.

7 And she brought forth her first-born* son, and wrapped him up in swaddling clothes, and laid him in a manger: because there was no room for them in the inn.

22 And after the days of her purification according to the law of Moses were accomplished, they carried him to Jerusalem, to present him to the Lord.

25 And behold, there was a man in Jerusalem named Simeon, and this man was just and devout, waiting for the consolation of Israel; and the Holy Ghost was in him.

34 And Simeon . . . said to Mary . . .

35 And thy own soul a sword shall pierce, that out of many hearts thoughts may be revealed.

---

* The meaning is, not that she had afterward any other child, but it is a way of speech among the Hebrews to call them also the first-born who are the only children.

1 ... Behold, there came wise men from   S. Matt.
the East to Jerusalem.   ii.

11 And going into the house, they found
the child with Mary his mother ...

16 They (the shepherds) came with haste: S. Luke
and they found Mary, and Joseph, and the   ii.
infant lying in a manger.

13 And after (the wise men) were de-   S. Matt.
parted, behold an angel of the Lord ap-   ii.
peared in sleep to Joseph, saying: Arise,
and take the child and his mother, and fly
into Egypt: and be there until I shall tell
thee.

42 And when he (Jesus) was twelve years   S. Luke
old they went up to Jerusalem, according to   ii.
the custom of the feast.

43 And after they had fulfilled the days,
when they returned, the child Jesus remained in Jerusalem; and his parents knew
it not.

45 And not finding him, they returned
into Jerusalem, seeking him.

46 And it came to pass, that after three
days they found him in the temple, sitting in
the midst of the doctors, hearing them, and
asking them questions.

48 ... And his mother said to him: Son,
why hast thou done so to us? behold, thy
father and I have sought thee sorrowing.

49 And he said to them: How is it that

you sought me? did you not know, that I must be about my Father's business?

51 And he went down with them to Nazareth: and was subject to them: And his mother kept all these words in her heart.

5 ... Whatsoever he shall say to you, do ye. S. John ii.

25 Now there stood by the cross of Jesus, his mother, and his mother's sister, Mary of Cleophas, and Mary Magdalen. S. John xix.

26 When Jesus, therefore, saw his mother and the disciple standing, whom he loved, he saith to his mother: Woman, behold thy son.

27 After that, he saith to the disciple: Behold thy mother. And from that hour the disciple took her to his own.

BLESSINGS OF GOD'S SERVANTS.

15 HE shall cry to me, and I will hear him: I am with him in tribulation, I will deliver him, and I will glorify him. Ps. xc.

16 I will fill him with length of days; and will show him my salvation ...

12 Let all them be glad that hope in thee: they shall rejoice for ever, and thou shalt dwell in them. And all they that love thy name shall glory in thee. Ps. v.

13 For thou wilt bless the just.

28 The Lord loveth judgment, and will not forsake his saints: they shall be preserved for ever. — Ps. xxxvi.

40 The Lord will help them and deliver them: and he will rescue them from the wicked, and save them, because they have hoped in him.

9 I will hear what the Lord God will speak in me: for he will speak peace unto his people: And unto his saints and unto them that are converted to the heart. — Ps. lxxxiv.

29 The children of thy servants shall continue: and their seed shall be directed for ever. — Ps. ci.

3 Blessed are they that keep judgment, and do justice at all times. — Ps. cv.

4 To the righteous a light is risen up in darkness: he is merciful, and compassionate and just. — Ps. cxi.

7 The just shall be in everlasting remembrance: he shall not fear the evil hearing.

28 The expectation of the just is joy . . . — Prov. x.

8 The just is delivered out of distress: and the wicked shall be given up for him. — Prov. xi.

30 The fruit of the just man is a tree of life: and he that gaineth souls, is wise.

29 . . . The Lord will hear the prayers of the just. — Prov. xv.

22 The Lord is only for them that wait upon him in the way of truth and justice. — Ecclus. xxxiv.

7 The just that walketh in his simplicity, shall leave behind him blessed children. — Prov. xx.

16 The just shall live for evermore: and their reward is with the Lord, and the care of them with the most High. — Wisd. v.

13 All thy children shall be taught of the Lord: and great shall be the peace of thy children. — Isaias liv.

23 My elect shall not labour in vain, nor bring forth in trouble: for they are the seed of the blessed of the Lord, and their posterity with them. — Isaias lxv.

38 And they shall be my people, and I will be their God. — Jer. xxxii.

39 And I will give them one heart, and one way, that they may fear me all days: and that it may be well with them, and with their children after them.

40 And I will make an everlasting covenant with them, and will not cease to do them good: and I will give my fear in their heart, that they may not revolt from me.

26 If any man minister to me, let him follow me: and where I am, there also shall my minister be. If any man minister to me, him will my Father honour. — S. John xii.

22 Being made free from sin, and become servants to God, you have your fruit unto sanctification, and the end life everlasting. — Rom. vi.

16 The Spirit himself giveth testimony to our spirit, that we are the sons of God. — Rom. viii.

17 And if sons, heirs also: heirs indeed of God, and joint heirs with Christ: yet so if we suffer with him, that we may also be glorified with him.

BLESSINGS OF GOD'S TEACHING.

20 BLESS God at all times: and desire of him to direct thy ways, and that all thy counsels may abide in him. — Tobias iv.

12 Blessed is the man whom thou shalt instruct, O Lord: and shalt teach him out of thy law. — Ps. xciii.

11 Conduct me, O Lord, in thy way, and I will walk in thy truth . . . — Ps. lxxxv.

8 . . . Make the way known to me, wherein I should walk: for I have lifted up my soul to thee. — Ps. cxlii.

5 Direct me in thy truth and teach me: for thou art God my Saviour. — Ps. xxiv.

23 With the Lord shall the steps of a man be directed, and he shall like well his way. — Ps. xxxvi.

24 When he shall fall, he shall not be bruised, for the Lord putteth his hand under him.

3 . . . He set my feet upon a rock, and directed my steps. — Ps. xxxix.

Blessings of God's Teaching.

3 Lay open thy works to the Lord: and thy thoughts shall be directed. — Prov. xvi.

9 The heart of man disposeth his way: but the Lord must direct his steps.

17 Thus saith the Lord thy redeemer, the Holy One of Israel: I am the Lord thy God that teach thee profitable things, that govern thee in the way that thou walkest. — Isaias xlviii.

27 All things are delivered to me by my Father. And no one knoweth the Son, but the Father: neither doth any one know the Father, but the Son, and he to whom it shall please the Son to reveal him. — S. Matt. xi.

6 I have manifested thy name to the men whom thou hast given me out of the world... — S. John xvii.

26 I have made known thy name to them, and will make it known; that the love, wherewith thou hast loved me, may be in them, and I in them.

12 Now we have received not the spirit of this world, but the Spirit that is of God: that we may know the things that are given us from God. — 1. Cor. ii.

5 And the Lord direct your hearts in the charity of God, and the patience of Christ. — 2 Thess. iii.

17 That the God of our Lord Jesus Christ, the Father of glory, may give unto you the spirit of wisdom and of revelation, in the knowledge of him. — Ephes. i.

CALLING (GENERAL)—*See* VOCATION (RELIGIOUS).

29 O EARTH, earth, earth, hear the word of the Lord. — Jer. xxii.

2 Speak to all the congregation of Israel, and thou shalt say to them: Be ye holy, because I the Lord your God am holy. — Lev. xix.

1 Come near, ye Gentiles, and hearken, ye people: let the earth hear, and all that is therein, the world, and everything that cometh forth of it. — Isaias xxxiv.

13 Hear, you that are far off, what I have done, you that are near, know my strength. — Isaias xxxiii.

16 (Jesus said:) A certain man made a great supper, and invited many. — S. Luke xiv.

17 And he sent his servant at supper time to say to them that were invited, that they should come, for now all things are ready.

18 And they began all at once to make excuse. The first said to him: I have bought a farm, and I must needs go out and see it: I pray thee, have me excused.

19 And another said: I have bought five yoke of oxen, and I go to try them: I pray thee, hold me excused.

20 And another said: I have married a wife, and therefore I cannot come.

21 And the servant returning told these things to his lord. Then the master of the house being angry, said to his servant. Go out quickly into the streets, and lanes of the city: and bring in hither the poor, and the feeble, and the blind, and the lame.

22 And the servant said: Lord, it is done as thou hast commanded, and yet there is room.

23 And the Lord said to the servant: Go out into the highways and hedges; and compel them to come in, that my house may be filled.

24 But I say unto you, that none of those men, that were called, shall taste my supper.

17 As the Lord hath distributed to every one, as God hath called every one, so let him walk: and so in all churches I teach.   1 Cor. vii.

26 For see your vocation, brethren, that there are not many wise according to the flesh, not many mighty, not many noble: 1 Cor. i.

27 But the foolish things of the world hath God chosen, that he may confound the wise: and the weak things of the world hath God chosen, that he may confound the strong:

28 And the mean things of the world, and the things that are contemptible hath God chosen and things that are not, that he might destroy the things that are:

29 That no flesh should glory in his sight.

30 But of him are you in Christ Jesus, who of God is made unto us wisdom, and justice, and sanctification, and redemption.

1 I therefore, a prisoner in the Lord, beseech you that you walk worthy of the vocation in which you are called. — Ephes. iv.

6 And having different gifts, according to the grace that is given us, either prophecy (to be used) according to the rule of faith: — Rom. xii.

7 Or ministry, in ministering; or he that teacheth, in doctrine.

8 He that exhorteth in exhorting, he that giveth with simplicity, he that ruleth with carefulness, he that sheweth mercy with cheerfulness.

11 Wherefore also we pray always for you that our God would make you worthy of his calling, and fulfil all the good pleasure of his goodness and the work of faith in power. — 2 Thess. i.

10 The God of all grace, who hath called us unto his eternal glory in Christ Jesus, after you have suffered a little, will himself perfect, and confirm, and establish you. — 1 S. Pet. v.

CALUMNY.

16 Thou shalt not bear false witness against thy neighbour. — Ex. xx.

13 Thou shalt not calumniate thy neighbour ...   Lev. xix.

18 A man that beareth false witness against his neighbour, is like a dart and a sword and a sharp arrow.   Prov. xxv.

11 ... The mouth that belieth, killeth the soul.   Wisd. i.

13 Devise not a lie against thy brother: neither do the like against thy friend.   Ecclus. vii.

28 A lying witness shall perish ...   Prov. xxi.

28 Be not witness without cause against thy neighbour ...   Prov. xxiv.

14 ... Neither calumniate any man ...   S. Luke iii.

11 Blessed are you when men shall ... speak all that is evil against you, untruly, for my sake.   S. Matt. v.

44 ... Pray for them that persecute and calumniate you.

CARNAL MIND.

21 ... THE imagination and thought of man's heart are prone to evil from his youth.   Gen. viii.

9 The heart is perverse above all things, and unsearchable, who can know it?   Jer. xvii.

3 Son of man, these men have placed their uncleannesses in their hearts, and have set up before their face the stumbling-block of their iniquity: and shall I answer when they inquire of me?   Ezech. xiv.

35 ... An evil man out of an evil treasure S. Matt.
bringeth forth evil things. xii.

21 For from within out of the heart of S. Mark
men proceed evil thoughts, adulteries, forni- vii.
cations, murders,

22 Thefts, covetousness, wickedness, deceit, lasciviousness, an evil eye, blasphemy, pride, foolishness.

23 All these evil things come from within, and defile a man.

22 Do penance therefore from this thy Acts
wickedness, and pray to God, if perhaps this viii.
thought of thy heart may be forgiven thee.

18 I know that there dwelleth not in me, Rom.
that is to say, in my flesh, that which is vii.
good ...

5 They that are according to the flesh, Rom.
mind the things that are of the flesh ... viii.

8 And they who are in the flesh, cannot please God.

13 If you live according to the flesh, you shall die ...

14 The sensual man* perceiveth not these 1. Cor.
things that are of the Spirit of God: for it ii.
is foolishness to him, and he cannot understand: because it is spiritually examined.

* The sensual man is either he who is taken up with sensual pleasures, with carnal and worldly affections, or he who measureth Divine mysteries by natural reason, sense, and human wisdom only. Now such a man has little or no notion of the things of God.

17 The flesh lusteth against the spirit, and   Gal. v.
the spirit against the flesh; for these are
contrary one to another: so that you do not
the things that you would.

19 Now the works of the flesh are manifest: which are, fornication, uncleanness, immodesty, luxury,

20 Idolatry, witchcraft, enmities, contentions, emulations, wrath, quarrels, dissensions, sects,

21 Envy, murders, drunkenness, revellings, and such like; of the which I foretell you as I have foretold to you, that they who do such things shall not obtain the kingdom of God.

8 What things a man shall sow, those also   Gal. vi.
shall he reap. For he that soweth in his
flesh, of the flesh also shall reap corruption:
but he, that soweth in the Spirit, of the
Spirit shall reap life everlasting.

CHARITY, OR LOVE TO NEIGHBOUR.

16 SEE thou never do to another what   Tobias
thou would'st hate to have done to thee by   iv.
another.

12 ... Charity covereth all sins.   Prov. x.

21 If thy enemy be hungry, give him to   Prov.
eat: if he thirst, give him water to drink.   xxv.

29 Say not: I will do to him as he hath done to me: I will render to every one according to his work. Prov. xxiv.

6 Remember not any injury done thee by thy neighbour, and do thou nothing by deeds of injury. Ecclus. x.

2 Forgive thy neighbour if he hath hurt thee: and then shall thy sins be forgiven to thee when thou prayest. Ecclus. xxviii.

10 Hast thou heard a word against thy neighbour? let it die within thee . . . Ecclus. xix.

18 Love thy neighbour and be joined to him with fidelity. Ecclus. xxvii.

39 . . . Thou shalt love thy neighbour as thyself. S. Matt. xxii.

31 As you would that men should do to you, do you also to them in like manner. S. Luke vi.

32 And if you love them that love you, what thanks are to you? for sinners also love those that love them.

33 And if you do good to them who do good to you; what thanks are to you? for sinners also do this.

34 And if you lend to them of whom you hope to receive: what thanks are to you? for sinners also lend to sinners, for to receive as much.

35 But love ye your enemies; do good, and lend, hoping for nothing thereby: and your reward shall be great, and you shall be

Charity, or Love to Neighbour. 47

the sons of the Highest; for he is kind to
the unthankful, and to the evil.

24 And he said to them: Take heed S. Mark
what you hear. In what measure you shall iv.
mete, it shall be measured to you again, and
more shall be given to you.

34 A new commandment I give unto S. John
you: That you love one another, as I have xiii.
loved you, that you also love one another.

35 By this shall all men know that you
are my disciples, if you have love one for
another.

17 These things I command you, that S. John
you love one another.   xv.

8 Before all things have a constant mutual 1 S. Pet.
charity among yourselves: for charity cover- iv.
eth a multitude of sins.

9 Now concerning fraternal charity, we 1 Thess.
have no need to write to you: for your- iv.
selves have learned of God to love one
another.

10 ... But we entreat you, brethren, that
you abound more.

10 Loving one another with brotherly Rom. xii.
love; in honour preventing* one another.

10 The love of the neighbour worketh no Rom.
evil. Love, therefore, is the fulfilling of the xiii.
law.

* Preferring one another by a charity stronger than our self-
love.

13 ... By charity of the spirit serve one another. — Gal. v.

14 For all the law is fulfilled in one sentence: Thou shalt love thy neighbour as thyself.

2 Bear ye one another's burdens; and so shall you fulfil the law of Christ. — Gal. vi.

32 And be ye kind one to another, merciful, forgiving one another, even as God hath forgiven you in Christ. — Ephes. iv.

2 And walk in love, as Christ also hath loved us ... — Ephes. v.

12 And may the Lord multiply you, and make you abound in charity towards each other and towards all men. — 1 Thess. iii.

1 Let fraternal charity abide in you. — Heb xiii.

8 If then you fulfil the royal law, according to the Scriptures: Thou shalt love thy neighbour as thyself; you do well. — S. James ii.

10 He that loveth his brother, abideth in the light, and there is no scandal in him. — 1 S. John ii.

11 For this is the declaration, which you have heard from the beginning, that you should love one another. — 1 S. John iii.

14 We know that we have passed from death to life: because we love the brethren ...

7 Dearly beloved, let us love one another: for charity is of God. And every — 1 S. John iv.

Charity, or Love to Neighbour. 49

one that loveth, is born of God, and knoweth God.

12 ... If we love one another, God abideth in us, and his charity is perfected in us.

2 In this we know that we love the children of God, when we love God, and keep his commandments.   1 S. John v.

1 If I speak with the tongues of men and of angels, and have not charity, I am become as sounding brass, or a tinkling cymbal.   1 Cor. xiii.

2 And if I should have prophecy, and should know all mysteries, and all knowledge : and if I should have all faith, so that I could remove mountains, and have not charity, I am nothing.

3 And if I should distribute all my goods to feed the poor, and if I should deliver my body to be burned, and have not charity, it profiteth me nothing.

4 Charity is patient, is kind : charity envieth not, dealeth not perversely, is not puffed up,

5 Is not ambitious, seeketh not her own, is not provoked to anger, thinketh no evil,

6 Rejoiceth not in iniquity, but rejoiceth with the truth :

7 Beareth all things, believeth all things, hopeth all things, endureth all things.

8 Charity never faileth:

13 And now there remain, faith, hope, and charity, these three: but the greatest of these is charity.

CHARITY TO NEIGHBOUR (FURTHER DUTIES AND COUNSELS OF).

4 If thou meet thy enemy's ox, or ass going astray, bring it back to him.   Exod. xxiii.

5 If thou see the ass of him that hateth thee lie underneath his burden, thou shalt not pass by, but shalt lift him up with him.

21 Thou shalt not molest a stranger, nor afflict him: for yourselves also were strangers in the land of Egypt.   Exod. xxii.

1 Thou shalt not pass by, if thou seest thy brother's ox, or his sheep go astray; but thou shalt bring them back to thy brother.   Deut. xxii.

2 And if thy brother be not nigh, or thou know him not: thou shalt bring them to thy house, and they shall be with thee until thy brother seek them, and receive them.

3 Thou shalt do in like manner with his ass, and with his raiment, and with everything that is thy brother's, which is lost: if thou find it, neglect it not as pertaining to another.

10 If at any time thou come to fight against a city, thou shalt first offer it peace.   Deut. xx.

19 When thou hast besieged a city a long

time, and hath compassed it with bulwarks to take it, thou shalt not cut down the trees that may be eaten of, neither shalt thou spoil the country round about with axes . . .

19 When thou hast reaped the corn in thy field, and hast forgot and left a sheaf, thou shalt not return to take it away: but thou shalt suffer the stranger, and the fatherless and the widow to take it away: that the Lord thy God may bless thee in all the works of thy hands. *Deut. xxiv.*

20 If thou have gathered the fruit of thy olive trees, thou shalt not return to gather whatsoever remaineth on the trees: but shalt leave it for the stranger, for the fatherless and the widow.

21 If thou make the vintage of thy vineyard, thou shalt not gather the clusters that remain, but they shall be for the stranger, the fatherless, and the widow.

35 If thy brother be impoverished and weak of hand, and thou receive him as a stranger and sojourner and he live with thee, *Lev. xxv.*

36 Take not usury of him nor more than thou gavest: fear thy God that thy brother may live with thee.

25 If thou lend money to any of my people that is poor, that dwelleth with thee, thou shalt not be hard upon them as an extortioner, nor oppress them with usuries. *Exod. xxii.*

9 Deliver him that suffereth wrong out of the hand of the proud: and be not faint-hearted in thy soul.   Ecclus. iv.

38 Be not wanting in comforting them that weep, and walk with them that mourn.   Ecclus. vii.

39 Be not slow to visit the sick: for by these things thou shalt be confirmed in love.

9 Thus saith the Lord of hosts, saying: Judge ye true judgment, and shew ye mercy and compassion every man to his brother.   Zach. vii.

12 All things, therefore, whatsoever you would that men should do to you, do you also to them, for this is the law and the prophets.   S. Matt. vii.

44 I say to you, Love your enemies, do good to them that hate you: and pray for them that persecute and calumniate you.   S. Matt. v.

46 For if you love those that love you, what reward shall you have? do not even the publicans the same?

9 Let love be without dissimulation . . .   Rom. xii.

8 Owe no man anything, but to love one another.   Rom. xiii.

2 Fulfil ye my joy, that you be of one mind, having the same charity, being of one accord, agreeing in sentiment.   Philip. ii. xxii.

2 With all humility, and mildness, with patience, supporting one another in charity.   Ephes. iv.

8 . . . Having compassion one of another,   1 S. Pet. iii.

being lovers of the brotherhood, merciful, modest, humble.

11 For this is the declaration, which you have heard from the beginning, that you should love one another. — 1 S. John iii.

CHILDREN (DUTIES OF).

16 Honour thy father and mother, as the Lord thy God hath commanded thee, that thou mayest live a long time, and it may be well with thee in the land, which the Lord thy God will give thee. — Deut. v.

3 Let every one fear his father, and his mother ... — Lev. xix.

3 ... Thou shalt honour thy mother all the days of her life. — Tobias iv.

1 Hear, ye children, the instruction of a father, and attend that you may know prudence. — Prov. iv.

1 A wise son maketh the father glad: but a foolish son is the sorrow of his mother. — Prov. x.

1 My son, keep my words, and lay up my precepts with thee. — Prov. vii.

1 My son, forget not my law, and let thy heart keep my commandments.

2 For they shall add to thee length of days, and years of life and peace. — Prov. iii.

20 My son, keep the commandments of thy father, and forsake not the law of thy mother. — Prov. vi.

1 A wise son heareth the doctrine of his father: but he that is a scorner, heareth not when he is reproved. — Prov. xiii.

15 ... No good shall come to the deceitful son. ... — Prov. xiv.

20 A wise son maketh a father joyful: but the foolish man despiseth his mother. — Prov. xv.

26 He that afflicteth his father, and chaseth away his mother, is infamous and unhappy. — Prov. xix.

20 He that curseth his father, and mother, his lamp shall be put out in the midst of darkness. — Prov. xx.

22 ... Despise not thy mother when she is old. — Prov. xxiii.

25 Let thy father, and thy mother be joyful, and let her rejoice that bore thee.

2 Children, hear the judgment of your father, and so do that you may be saved. — Ecclus. iii.

3 For God hath made the father honourable to the children: and seeking the judgment of the mother, hath confirmed it upon the children.

5 He that honoureth his mother is as one that layeth up a treasure.

6 He that honoureth his father shall have joy in his own children, and in the day of his prayer he shall be heard.

7 He that honoureth his father, shall enjoy a long life: and he that obeyeth the father, shall be a comfort to his mother.

Children (Duties of).

8 He that feareth the Lord, honoureth his parents, and will serve them as his masters that brought him into the world.

9 Honour thy father, in work and word, and all patience.

10 That a blessing may come upon thee from him, and his blessing may remain in the latter end.

11 The father's blessing establisheth the houses of the children: but the mother's curse rooteth up the foundation.

14 Son, support the old age of thy father, and grieve him not in his life;

15 And if his understanding fail, have patience with him, and despise him not when thou art in thy strength: for the relieving of the father shall not be forgotten.

17 And in justice thou shalt be built up, and in the day of affliction thou shalt be remembered: and thy sins shall melt away as the ice in the fair warm weather.

18 Of what an evil fame is he that forsaketh his father: and he is cursed of God that angereth his mother.

3 ... Why do you also transgress the commandment of God for your tradition? For God said:

4 Honour thy father and mother: And: He that shall curse father or mother, let him die the death.

S. Matt. xv.

5 But you say: Whosoever shall say to father or mother, The gift* whatsoever proceedeth from me, shall profit thee.

6 And he shall not honour his father or his mother: and you have made void the commandment of God for your tradition.

4 ... Make a return of duty to ... parents: for this is acceptable before God.   1 Tim. v.

20 Children, obey your parents in all things: for this is well pleasing to the Lord.   Col. iii.

1 Children, obey your parents in the Lord: for this is just.   Ephes. vi.

2 Honour thy father and thy mother, which is the first commandment with a promise.

3 That it may be well with thee, and thou mayest be long-lived upon earth.

CHILDHOOD (DUTIES TOWARDS).

11 ... Thou shalt read the words of this law before all Israel, in their hearing.   Deut. xxxi.

12 ... Both men and women, children

---

* That is, the offering that I shall make to God, shall be instead of that which should be expended for thy profit. This tradition of the Pharisees was calculated to enrich themselves; by exempting children from giving any farther assistance to their parents, if they once offered to the temple and the priests, that which should have been the support of their parents. But this was a violation of the law of God, and of nature, which our Saviour here condemns.

and strangers, that are within thy gates: that hearing they may learn, and fear the Lord your God, and keep, and fulfil all the words of this law.

13 That their children also, who are now ignorant, may hear, and fear the Lord their God ...

14 ... Suffer the little children to come to me, and forbid them not: for of such is the kingdom of God. — S. Mark x.

36 Whosoever shall receive one such child as this in my name, receiveth me: and whosoever shall receive me, receiveth not me, but him that sent me. — S. Mark ix.

6 He that shall scandalize* one of these little ones that believe in me, it were better for him that a mill-stone were hanged about his neck, and that he were drowned in the depth of the sea. — S. Matt. xviii.

10 Take heed that you despise not one of these little ones: for I say to you, that their Angels in heaven always see the face of my Father who is in heaven.

CHRIST OUR LIFE.

12 He that hath the Son, hath life; he that hath not the Son, hath not life. — 1 S. John v.

* That is, shall put a stumbling-block in their way, and cause them to fall into sin.

4 In him was life, and the life was the light of men. — S. John i.

12 As many as received him, he gave them power to be made the sons of God, to them that believe in his name.

12 ... Jesus spoke to them, saying: I am the light of the world: he that followeth me, walketh not in darkness, but shall have the light of life. — S. John viii.

10 ... I am come that they may have life, and may have it more abundantly. — S. John x.

57 He that eateth my flesh, and drinketh my blood, abideth in me, and I in him. — S. John vi.

64 ... The words that I have spoken to you, are spirit and life.*

24 Amen, amen I say unto you, that he who heareth my word, and believeth him that sent me, hath life everlasting; and cometh not into judgment, but is passed from death to life. — S. John v.

4 Abide in me: and I in you. As the branch cannot bear fruit of itself, unless it abide in the vine, so neither can you, unless you abide in me. — S. John xv.

5 I am the vine; you the branches: he that abideth in me, and I in him, the same beareth much fruit: for without me you can do nothing.

* By proposing to you a heavenly sacrament, in which you shall receive, in a wonderful manner, spirit, grace, and life in its very fountain.

7 If you abide in me, and my words abide in you, you shall ask whatever you will, and it shall be done unto you.

19 Yet a little while: and the world seeth me no more. But you see me: because I live, and you shall live. — S. John xiv.

20 In that day you shall know that I am in my Father, and you in me, and I in you.

1 There is now therefore no condemnation to them that are in Christ Jesus, who walk not according to the flesh. — Rom. viii.

2 For the law of the spirit of life, in Christ Jesus, hath delivered me from the law of sin and of death.

9 ... Now if any man have not the Spirit of Christ, he is none of his.

10 And if Christ be in you; the body indeed is dead because of sin, but the spirit liveth because of justification.

19 ... That I may live to God; with Christ I am nailed to the cross. — Gal. ii.

20 And I live, now not I; but Christ liveth in me. And that I live now in the flesh: I live in the faith of the Son of God, who loved me, and delivered himself for me.

8 Now if we be dead with Christ, we believe that we shall live also together with Christ. — Rom. vi.

11 A faithful saying. For if we be dead with him, we shall live also with him. — 2 S. Tim. ii.

6 As therefore you have received Jesus Christ the Lord, walk ye in him.   Coloss. ii.

7 Rooted and built up in him, and confirmed in the faith, as also you have learned, abounding in him in thanksgiving.

17 He, who is joined to the Lord, is one spirit.*   1 Cor. vi.

5 ... Know you not your ownselves, that Christ Jesus is in you? unless perhaps you be reprobates.   2 Cor. xiii.

26 The mystery, which hath been hidden from ages and generations, but now is made manifest to his saints,   Coloss. i.

27 To whom God would make known the riches of the glory of this mystery among the Gentiles, which is Christ, in you the hope of glory.

4 When Christ shall appear, who is your life; then shall you also appear with him in glory.   Coloss. iii.

15 Sanctify the Lord Christ in your hearts ...   1 S. Pet. iii.

9 By this hath the charity of God appeared towards us, because God hath sent his only begotten Son into the world, that we may live by him.   1 S. John iv.

5 Whosoever keepeth his word, the charity of God is truly perfect in him; and by this we know that we are in him.   1 S. John ii.

* 2 Cor. v. 17.

6 He that saith he abideth in him, ought himself also to walk, even as he walked.

6 Whosoever abideth in him, sinneth not:* and whosoever sinneth, hath not seen him, nor known him. — 1 S. John iii.

24 And he that keepeth his commandments, abideth in him, and he in him. And in this we know that he abideth in us, from the Spirit which he hath given us.

28 And now, little children, abide in him; that when he shall appear, we may have confidence, and not be confounded by him at his coming. — 1 S. John ii.

CHURCH (PASTORS).

6 They shall be holy to their God, and shall not profane his name: for they offer the burnt-offering of the Lord, and the bread of their God, and therefore they shall be holy. — Lev. xxi.

10 The high-priest, that is to say, the priest, is the greatest among his brethren upon whose head the oil of unction hath been poured and whose hands have been consecrated for the priesthood, and who hath been vested with the holy vestments . . .

8 To Levi also he said: Thy perfection, and thy doctrine be to thy holy man, whom thou hast proved in the temptation, and judged at the waters of contradiction. — Deut. xxxiii.

* *Viz.*, mortally.

9 Who hath said to his father, and to his mother: I do not know you; and to his brethren: I know you not, and their own children they have not known. These have kept thy word, and observed thy covenant.

5 Blessed is he whom thou hast chosen, and taken to thee: he shall dwell in thy courts. — Ps. lxiv.

26 ... Blessed be he that cometh in the name of the Lord ... — Ps. cxvii.

7 How beautiful upon the mountains are the feet of him that bringeth good tidings, and that preacheth peace: of him that sheweth forth good, that preacheth salvation, that saith to Sion: Thy God shall reign! — Isaias lii.

8 The voice of thy watchmen: they have lifted up their voice, they shall praise together: for they shall see eye to eye when the Lord shall convert Sion.

7 So thou, O son of man, I have made thee a watchman to the house of Israel: therefore thou shalt hear the word from my mouth, and shalt tell it them from me. — Ezech. xxxiii.

19 And (Jesus) saith to them: Come ye after me, and I will make you to be fishers of men. — S. Matt. iv.

40 He that receiveth you, receiveth me: and he that reciveth me, receiveth him that sent me. — S. Matt. x.

Church (Pastors).

15 Jesus saith to them : But whom do you say that I am ? S. Matt. xvi.

16 Simon Peter answered and said : Thou art Christ the Son of the living God.

17 And Jesus answering, said to him : Blessed art thou, Simon Bar-Jona : because flesh and blood hath not revealed it to thee, but my Father who is in heaven.

18 And I say to thee : That thou art Peter ;* and upon this rock I will build my

---

* "Thou art Peter . . ." &c. As S. Peter, by Divine revelation, here made a solemn profession of his faith in the divinity of Christ ; so in recompense of this faith and profession, our Lord here declares to him the dignity to which he is pleased to raise him. Viz., that he, to whom he had already given the name of Peter, signifying a rock, should be a rock indeed, of invincible strength, for the support of the building of the church ; in which building he should be, next to Christ himself, the chief foundation stone, in quality of chief pastor, ruler, and governor ; and should have accordingly all fulness of ecclesiastical power, signified by the keys of the kingdom of heaven. Ibid. "Upon this rock," &c. The words of Christ to Peter, spoken in the vulgar language of the Jews which our Lord made use of, were the same as if he had said in English, Thou art a Rock, and upon this rock I will build my church. So that, by the plain course of the words, Peter is here declared to be the rock, upon which the church was to be built : Christ himself being the principal foundation and founder of the same. Where also note, that Christ, by building his house, that is his church, upon a rock, has thereby secured it against all storms and floods, like the wise builder (S. Matt. vii., 24th and 25th verses), against which the gates of hell, &c., can never prevail.

church, and the gates of hell shall not prevail against it.

19 And I will give to thee the keys of the kingdom of heaven. And whatsoever thou shalt bind upon earth, it shall be bound also in heaven: and whatsoever thou shalt loose* on earth, it shall be loosed also in heaven.

15 And he said to (his apostles): Go ye into the whole world, and preach the gospel to every creature. S. Mark xvi.

3 Go: Behold I send you as lambs among wolves. S. Luke x.

5 Into whatsoever house you enter, first say: Peace be to this house:

6 And if the son of peace be there, your peace shall rest upon him: but if not, it shall return to you.

16 He that heareth you, heareth me: and he that despiseth you, despiseth me. And he that despiseth me, despiseth him that sent me.

35 ... Behold, I say to you, lift up your eyes, and see the countries, for they are white already to harvest. S. John iv.

36 And he that reapeth receiveth wages, and gathereth fruit unto everlasting life.

---

* "Loose on earth." The loosing the bands of temporal punishments due to sins, is called an Indulgence, the power of which is here granted.

16 You have not chosen me: but I have S. John
chosen you; and have appointed you, that xv.
you should go, and should bring forth fruit,
and your fruit should remain: that whatsoever you shall ask of the Father in my
name, he may give it you.

14 Whosoever shall not receive you, nor S. Matt.
hear your words; going forth out of that x.
house or city, shake off the dust from your
feet.

15 Amen I say to you, it shall be more
tolerable for the land of Sodom and Gomor-
rha in the day of judgment, than for that
city.

21 And he said to them again: Peace be S. John
to you. As the Father hath sent me, I also xx.
send you.

22 When he had said this, he breathed on
them: and he said to them: Receive ye the
Holy Ghost.

23 Whose sins you shall forgive, they are
forgiven them: and whose sins you shall
retain they are retained.*

15 ... Jesus saith to Simon Peter: Simon S. John
son of John, lovest thou me more than xxi.
these? He saith to him: Yea, Lord, thou

---

* Verse 23. See here the commission, stamped by the broad seal of heaven, by virtue of which the pastors of Christ's church absolve repenting sinners upon their confession.

knowest that I love thee. He saith to him: eed my lambs.

16 He saith to him again: Simon son of John, lovest thou me? He saith to him: Yea, Lord, thou knowest that I love thee. He saith to him: Feed my lambs.

17 He saith to him the third time: Simon son of John, lovest thou me? Peter was grieved, because he said to him the third time, Lovest thou me? And he said to him: Lord, thou knowest all things; thou knowest that I love thee. He said to him: Feed my sheep.*

16 And the eleven disciples went into Galilee, unto the mountain where Jesus had appointed them.   S. Matt. xxviii.

18 And Jesus coming, spoke to them, saying: All power † is given me in heaven and in earth.

---

* Verse 17. Our Lord had promised the spiritual supremacy to S. Peter (S. Matt. xvi., 9th verse). And here He fulfils that promise, by charging him with the superintending of all His sheep, without exception: and consequently of His whole flock, that is, of His whole church.

† "All power." See here the warrant and commission of the apostles and their successors, the bishops and pastors of Christ's church. He received from His Father all power in heaven and in earth: and in virtue of this power He sends them even as His Father sent Him (S. John xx., 21st verse) to teach not one, but all nations: and instruct them in all truths: and that He may assist them effectually in the execution of this commission, He

19 Go ye, therefore, and teach all nations; baptizing them in the name of the Father, and of the Son, and of the Holy Ghost.

20 Teaching them to observe all things whatsoever I have commanded you; and behold, I am with you all days, even to the consummation of the world.*

8 You shall receive the power of the Holy Ghost coming upon you, and you shall be witnesses unto me in Jerusalem, and in all Judea, and Samaria, and even to the uttermost parts of the earth. — Acts i.

4 ... Our Lord Jesus Christ ... — Rom. i.

5 By whom we have received grace and apostleship for obedience to the faith in all nations for his name.

15 How shall they preach unless they be sent? — Rom. x.

14 But Peter standing in the midst of the eleven, lifted up his voice, and spoke to them: Ye men of Judea, and all you that dwell in Jerusalem, be this known to you, and with your ears receive my words.† — Acts ii.

41 They therefore that received his word

promises to be with them (not for three or four hundred years) but all days, even to the consummation of the world.

* How then could the Catholic church ever go astray: having always with her pastors, as is here promised, Christ himself, who is the way, the truth, and the life (S. John xiv.)?

† 15th to 40th verse inclusive, Acts ii.

were baptized: and there was added in that day about three thousand souls.

12 And by the hands of the apostles were many signs and wonders wrought among the people ... Acts v.

13 But of the rest no man durst join himself unto them; but the people magnified them.

34 And Peter opening his mouth, said: In very deed I perceive that God is no respecter of persons. Acts x.

36 God sent his word to the children of Israel, preaching peace by Jesus Christ (he is Lord of all):

42 And he commanded us to preach to the people, and to testify that it is he who was appointed by God to be judge of the living and of the dead.

44 While Peter was yet speaking these words, the Holy Ghost fell on all them that heard the word.

45 And the faithful of the circumcision, who came with Peter, were astonished, for that the grace of the Holy Ghost was poured out on the gentiles also.

4 But Peter began and declared to them the matter in order. Acts xi.

13 He told us how (Cornelius) had seen an angel in his house standing and saying to him: Send to Joppe: and call hither Simon, who is surnamed Peter,

Church (Pastors).

14 Who shall speak to thee words whereby thou shalt be saved, and all thy house.

15 And when I began to speak, the Holy Ghost fell upon them, as upon us also in the beginning.

1 And some coming down from Judea, taught the brethren: That except you be circumcised after the manner of Moses, you cannot be saved.   *Acts xv.*

6 And the apostles and ancients assembled to consider this matter.

7 And when there had been much disputing, Peter rising up said to them: Men brethren, you know that in former days God made choice among us, that by my mouth the gentiles should hear the word of the gospel and believe.

8 And God who knoweth the hearts, gave testimony, giving unto them the Holy Ghost as unto us.

32 And it came to pass, that Peter, as he passed through visiting all, came to the saints who dwelt at Lydda.   *Acts ix.*

19 For God indeed was in Christ reconciling the world to himself, not imputing to them their sins, and he hath placed in us the word of reconciliation.   *2 Cor. v.*

20 We are, therefore, ambassadors for Christ, God as it were exhorting by us. For Christ we beseech you, be ye reconciled to God.

4 But we will give ourselves continually to prayer, and to the ministry of the word. — Acts vi.

9 For we are God's coadjutors: you are God's husbandry, you are God's building. — 1 Cor. iii.

4 But as we were approved of God, that the gospel should be committed to us; even so we speak, not as pleasing men, but God, who proveth our hearts. — 1 Thess. ii.

8 For if also I should boast somewhat more of our power, which the Lord hath given us unto edification, and not for your destruction; I should not be ashamed. — 2 Cor. x.

10 ... What I forgave, if I have forgiven anything, for your sakes have I done it in the person of Christ. — 2 Cor. ii.

14 (You) ... Received me as an angel of God, even as Christ Jesus. — Gal. iv.

CHURCH (DUTIES OF THE FAITHFUL).

12 He that will be proud, and refuse to obey the commandment of the priest, who ministereth at that time to the Lord thy God, and the decree of the judge, that man shall die, and thou shalt take away the evil from Israel. — Deut. xvii.

4 He commanded also the people that dwelt in Jerusalem, to give to the priests, and the Levites their portion, that they might attend to the law of the Lord. — 2 Paralp. xxxi.

20 And all the multitude of the children of Israel going out from the presence of Moses,   Ex. xxxv.

21 Offered first fruits to the Lord with a most ready and devout mind, to make the work of the tabernacle of the testimony. Whatsoever was necessary to the service, and to the holy vestments.

9 And the people rejoiced, when they promised their offerings willingly: because they offered them to the Lord with all their heart . . .   1 Paralip. xxix.

13 Now therefore our God we give thanks to thee, and we praise thy glorious name.

14 . . . All things are thine : and we have given thee what we received of thy hand.

7 The lips of the priest shall keep knowledge, and they shall seek the law at his mouth : because he is the angel of the Lord of hosts.   Malach. ii.

31 With all thy soul fear the Lord, and reverence his priests.   Ecclus. vii.

32 With all thy strength love him that made thee : and forsake not his ministers.

33 Honour God with all thy soul, and give honour to the priests . . .

34 Give them their portion, as it is commanded thee . . .

12 Give to the most High according to what he hath given to thee, and with a good   Ecclus. xxxv.

eye do according to the ability of thy hands.

17 Keep thy foot, when thou goest into the house of God, and draw near to hear. For much better is obedience, than the victims of fools, who know not what evil they do. — Eccles. iv.

15 And I will give you pastors according to my own heart, and they shall feed you with knowledge and doctrine. — Jer. iii.

20 Amen, amen, I say to you, he that receiveth whomsoever I send, receiveth me: and he that receiveth me, receiveth him that sent me. — S. John xiii.

37 ... The harvest, indeed, is great, but the labourers are few. — S. Matt. ix.

38 Pray ye, therefore, the Lord of the harvest, that he send forth labourers into his harvest.

14 Go, show yourselves to the priests. And it came to pass, that as they went, they were made clean. — S. Luke xvii.

15 If thy brother shall offend against thee, go and reprove him between thee and him alone. If he shall hear thee, thou shalt gain thy brother. — S. Matt. xviii.

16 But if he will not hear thee, take with thee one or two more, that in the mouth of two or three witnesses every word may stand.

17 And if he will not hear them, tell the church. And if he will not hear the church,

let him be to thee as the heathen and the publican.

6 Let him who is instructed in the word, communicate to him, who instructeth him, in all good things. — Gal. vi.

11 If we have sown unto you spiritual things, is it a great matter if we reap your carnal things? — 1 Cor. ix.

14 So also the Lord ordained that they who preach the gospel, should live of the gospel.

14 You have done well, in communicating to my tribulation. — Phil. iv.

17 Not that I seek the gift: but I seek the fruit that may abound to your account.

18 ... The things you sent, an odour of sweetness, an acceptable sacrifice, pleasing to God.

1 Let a man so look upon us as the ministers of Christ, and the dispensers of the mysteries of God. — 1 Cor. iv.

1 Be ye followers of me, as I also am of Christ. — 8 Cor. xi.

16 Nevertheless, whereunto we are come, that we be of the same mind, let us also continue in the same rule. — Phil. iii.

3 Careful to keep the unity of the Spirit in the bond of peace. — Ephes. iv.

4 One body, and one Spirit: as you are called in one hope of your vocation.

5 One Lord, one faith, one baptism.

6 One God and Father of all, who is above all, and through all, and in us all.

12 And we beseech you, brethren, to know them who labour among you, and are over you in the Lord, and admonish you: 1 Thess. v.

13 That you esteem them more abundantly in charity for their work's sake. Have peace with them.

16 That you also be subject to such, and to every one that worketh with us, and laboureth.   1 Cor. xvi.

17 Let the priests who rule well be esteemed worthy of double honour: especially they who labour in the word and doctrine.   1 Tim. v.

7 Remember your prelates, who have spoken to you the word of God; considering well the end of their conversation, imitate their faith.   Heb. xiii.

17 Obey your prelates, and be subject to them. For they watch as being to render an account of your souls: that they may do this with joy, and not with grief: for this is not expedient for you.

18 Pray for us.

14 Is any man sick among you? Let him bring in the priests of the church, and let them pray over him, anointing him with oil in the name of the Lord.   S. James v.

15 And the prayer of faith shall save the

sick man; and the Lord shall raise him up: and if he be in sins, they shall be forgiven him.

16 Confess therefore, your sins one to another;* and pray for one another, that you may be saved.

COMMANDMENTS.

4 HEAR, O Israel, the Lord our God is one Lord. Deut. vi.

5 Thou shalt love the Lord thy God with thy whole heart, and with thy whole soul, and with thy whole strength.

6 And these words which I command thee this day, shall be in thy heart:

7 And thou shalt tell them to thy children, and thou shalt meditate upon them sitting in thy house, and walking on thy journey, sleeping and rising.

47 For they are not commanded you in vain, but that every one should live in them... Deut. xxxii.

1 And the Lord spoke all these words: Ex. xx.

2 I am the Lord thy God, who brought thee out of the land of Egypt, and out of the house of bondage.

* To those whom God hath appointed, and who by their ordination and jurisdiction, have received the power of remitting sins in His name.

3 Thou shalt not have strange Gods before me.

4 Thou shalt not make to thyself a graven thing, nor the likeness of any thing that is in heaven above, or in the earth beneath, nor of those things that are in the waters under the earth.

5 Thou shalt not adore them, nor serve them: I am the Lord thy God, mighty, jealous, visiting the iniquity of the fathers upon the children, unto the third and fourth generation of them that hate me:

6 And shewing mercy unto thousands to them that love me, and keep my commandments.

7 Thou shalt not take the name of the Lord thy God in vain: for the Lord will not hold him guiltless that shall take the name of the Lord his God in vain.

8 Remember that thou keep holy the sabbath day.

9 Six days shalt thou labour, and shalt do all thy works.

10 But on the seventh day is the sabbath of the Lord thy God: thou shalt do no work on it, thou nor thy son, nor thy daughter, nor thy man-servant, nor thy maid-servant, nor thy beast, nor the stranger that is within thy gates.

11 For in six days the Lord made heaven

and earth, and the sea, and all things that are in them, and rested on the seventh day: therefore the Lord blessed the seventh day, and sanctified it.

12 Honour thy father and thy mother, that thou mayest be long-lived upon the land which the Lord thy God will give thee.

13 Thou shalt not kill.

14 Thou shalt not commit adultery.

15 Thou shalt not steal.

16 Thou shalt not bear false witness against thy neighbour.

17 Thou shalt not covet thy neighbour's house: neither shalt thou desire his wife, nor his servant, nor his hand-maid, nor his ox, nor his ass, nor anything that is his.

11 This commandment, that I command thee this day is not above thee, nor far off from thee: Deut. xxx.

12 Nor is it in heaven, that thou shouldst say: Which of us can go up to heaven to bring it unto us, that we may hear and fulfil it in work?

14 But the word is very nigh unto thee, in thy mouth and in thy heart, that thou mayest do it.

19 I call heaven and earth to witness this day, that I have set before you life and death, blessing and cursing. Choose there-

fore life, that both thou and thy seed may live.

16 He that shall steal a man and sell him, being convicted of the guilt, shall be put to death. Ex. xxi.

20 He that striketh his bondman or bondwoman with a rod, and they die under his hands, shall be guilty of the crime.

14 Thou shalt not speak evil of the deaf, nor put a stumbling-block before the blind; but thou shalt fear the Lord thy God, because I am the Lord. Lev. xix.

33 If a stranger dwell in your land, and abide among you, do not upbraid him.

34 But let him be among you as one of the same country: and you shall love him as yourselves ... I am the Lord your God.

17 Do not afflict your countrymen, but let every one fear his God: because I am the Lord your God. Lev. xxv.

39 Know therefore this day, and think in thy heart that the Lord he is God in heaven above, and in the earth beneath, and there is no other. Deut. iv.

40 Keep his precepts and commandments, which I command thee: that it may be well with thee, and thy children after thee, and thou mayest remain a long time upon the land, which the Lord thy God will give thee.

8 I the Lord, this is my name: I will not Isaias

give my glory to another, nor my praise to graven things. — xlii.

18 ... I am the Lord, and there is no other. — Isaias xlv.

19 I have not spoken in secret, in a dark place of the earth: I have not said to the seed of Jacob: Seek me in vain.

I am the Lord that speak justice, that declare right things.

8 The law of the Lord is unspotted, converting souls. — Ps. xviii.

18 ... He that keepeth the law is blessed. — Prov. xxix.

9 He that turneth away his ears from hearing the law, his prayer shall be an abomination. — Prov. xxviii.

14 God made man from the beginning, and left him in the hand of his own counsel. — Ecclus. xv.

15 He added his commandments and precepts.

16 If thou wilt keep his commandments and perform acceptable fidelity for ever, they shall preserve thee.

12 Who hath continued in his commandment, and hath been forsaken? or who hath called upon him, and he despised him. — Ecclus. ii.

37 ... There is nothing sweeter than to have regard to the commandments of the Lord. — Ecclus. xxiii.

38 It is great glory to follow the Lord:

for length of days shall be received from him.

14 Place thy treasure in the command-ments of the most High, and it shall bring thee more profit than gold. Ecclus. xxix.

10 Who is wise, and he shall understand these things? prudent, and he shall know these things? for the ways of the Lord are right, and the just shall walk in them: but the transgressors shall fall in them. Osee xiv.

17 Do not think I am come to destroy the law, or the prophets. I am not come to destroy, but to fulfil. S. Matt. v.

18 For amen I say unto you, till heaven and earth pass, one jot, or one tittle shall not pass of the law, till all be fulfilled.

19 Whosoever, therefore shall break one of these least commandments, and shall teach men so, he shall be called the least in the kingdom of heaven: but whosoever shall do and teach, the same shall be called great in the kingdom of heaven.

17 It is easier for heaven and earth to pass, than one tittle of the law to fail. S. Luke xvi.

36 Master, which is the great command-ment in the law? S. Matt. xxii.

37 Jesus said to him: Thou shalt love the Lord thy God with thy whole heart, and with thy whole soul, and with thy whole mind.

38 This is the greatest and the first commandment.

39 ... And the second is like to this: Thou shalt love thy neighbour as thyself.

40 On these two commandments dependeth the whole law and the prophets.

17 ... If thou wilt enter into life, keep the commandments.   S. Matt. xix.

18 He said to him: Which? and Jesus said: Thou shalt do no murder. Thou shalt not commit adultery: Thou shalt not steal: Thou shalt not bear false witness:

19 Honour thy father and thy mother: and, Thou shalt love thy neighbour as thyself.

17 If you know these things, you shall be blessed if you do them.   S. John xiii.

15 If you love me keep my commandments.   S. John xiv.

21 He that hath my commandments, and keepeth them: he it is that loveth me. And he that loveth me, shall be loved of my Father: and I will love him, and will manifest myself to him.

12 This is my commandment, that you love one another, as I have loved you.   S. John xv.

14 You are my friends, if you do the things that I command you.

10 If you keep my commandments, you shall abide in my love; as I also have kept

my Father's commandments, and do abide in his love.

50 And I know that his commandment is life everlasting. The things therefore that I speak; even as the Father said unto me, so do I speak. — S. John xii.

10 ... When you shall have done all these things that are commanded you, say: We are unprofitable* servants; we have done that which we ought to do. — S. Luke xvii.

13 Not the hearers of the law are just before God: but the doers of the law shall be justified. — Rom. ii.

12 Wherefore the law indeed is holy, and the commandment holy, and just, and good. — Rom. vii.

5 Now the end of the commandment is charity from a pure heart, and a good conscience, and an unfeigned faith. — 1 Tim. i.

6 From which things some going astray, are turned aside to vain talk.

3 By this we know that we have known him,† if we keep his commandments. — 1 S. John ii.

4 He who saith that he knoweth him, and

---

* Unprofitable servants. Because our service is of no profit to our master; and He justly claims it as our bounden duty. But though we are unprofitable to Him, our serving Him is not unprofitable to us: for He is pleased to give by His grace a value to our good works, which, in consequence of His promise, entitles them to an eternal reward.

† Jesus Christ the Just.

keepeth not his commandments, is a liar, and the truth is not in him.

3 For this is the charity of God, that we keep his commandments: and his commandments are not heavy. — 1 S. John v.

22 And whatsoever we shall ask, we shall receive of him: because we keep his commandments, and do those things which are pleasing in his sight. — 1 S. John iii.

23 And this is his commandment: that we should believe in the name of his Son Jesus Christ; and love one another, as he hath given commandment unto us.

CONFIDENCE IN GOD.

6 Do manfully, and be of good heart: fear not, nor be ye dismayed at their sight: for the Lord thy God he himself is thy leader, and will not leave thee nor forsake thee. — Deut. xxxi.

3 If armies in camp should stand together against me, my heart shall not fear. If a battle should rise up against me, in this will I be confident. — Ps. xxvi.

7 The Lord God is my helper, therefore am I not confounded: therefore have I set my face as a most hard rock, and I know that I shall not be confounded. — Isaias l.

8 He is near that justifieth me, who will contend with me?

9 Behold, the Lord God is my helper:
who is he that shall condemn me? ...

8 It is good to confide in the Lord, rather Ps. cxvii.
than to have confidence in man.

5 Have confidence in the Lord with all Prov. iii.
thy heart, and lean not upon thy own prudence.

7 Blessed be the man that trusteth in the Jer. xvii.
Lord, and the Lord shall be his confidence.

7 I will look towards the Lord, I will wait Mich.
for God my Saviour: my God will hear me. vii.

4 ... The Lord will hear me when I Ps. iv.
shall cry unto him.

11 ... Christ Jesus our Lord. Ephes. iii.

12 In whom we have boldness and access
with confidence by the faith of him.

12 ... I know whom I have believed, 2 Tim. i.
and I am certain that he is able to keep that
which I have committed unto him, against
that day.

35 Do not therefore lose your confidence, Heb. x.
which hath a great reward.

CONTENT.

16 BETTER is a little to the just, than the Ps. xxxvi.
great riches of the wicked.

16 Better is a little with the fear of the Prov. xv.
Lord, than great treasures without content.

18 The life of a labourer that is content Ecclus.
xl.

with what he hath, shall be sweet, and in it thou shalt find a treasure.

14 ... Be content with your pay.   S. Luke iii.

8 Having food, and wherewith to be 1 Tim. vi. covered, with these we are content.

11 ... For I have learned, in whatsoever Philip. iv. state I am, to be content therewith.

12 I know both how to be brought low, and I know how to abound: (everywhere, and in all things I am instructed), both to be full, and to be hungry; both to abound, and to suffer need.

5 Let your manners be without covetous- Heb. xiii. ness, contented with such things as you have: for he hath said: I will not leave thee, neither will I forsake thee.

6 Godliness with contentment is great 1 Tim. vi. gain.

CONTENTION.

20 O how great is the multitude of thy Ps. xxx. sweetness, O Lord, which thou hast hidden for them that fear thee! Which thou hast wrought for them that hope in thee, in the sight of the sons of men.

21 Thou shalt hide them, in the secret of thy face, from the disturbance of men. Thou shalt protect them in thy tabernacle from the contradiction of tongues.

8 Let there be no quarrel, I beseech thee, between me and thee, and between my herdsmen and thy herdsmen: for we are brethren. — Gen. xiii.

10 Among the proud there are always contentions. — Prov. xiii.

1 Better is a dry morsel with joy, than a house full of victims with strife. — Prov. xvii.

3 It is an honour for a man to separate himself from quarrels: but all fools are meddling with reproaches. — Prov. xx.

8 The things which thy eyes have seen, utter not hastily in a quarrel: lest afterwards thou mayest not be able to make amends, when thou hast dishonoured thy friend. — Prov. xxv.

25 He that boasteth, and puffeth up himself, stirreth up quarrels ... — Prov. xxviii.

10 Refrain from strife, and thou shalt diminish thy sins. — Ecclus. xxviii.

11 For a passionate man kindleth strife, and a sinful man will trouble his friends, and bring in debate in the midst of them that are at peace.

16 In the quarrels of the proud is the shedding of blood: and their cursing is a grievous hearing. — Ecclus. xxvii.

32 ... [Jesus asked his disciples]: What did you treat of in the way? — S. Mark ix.

33 But they held their peace, for in the way they had disputed among themselves which of them should be greatest.

Contention. 87

24 And there was also a strife amongst them, which of them should seem to be greater. — S. Luke xxii.

33 God is not the God of dissension, but of peace ... — 1 Cor. xiv.

14 ... Contend not in words, for it is to no profit, but to the subverting of the hearers. — 2 Tim. ii.

16 Where envying and contention is, there is inconstancy, and every evil work. — S. James iii.

1 From whence are wars and contentions among you? Come they not hence, from your concupiscences, which war in your members? — S. James iv.

2 You covet, and have not: you kill, and envy, and cannot obtain: you contend, and war: and you have not, because you ask not:

3 You ask, and receive not; because you ask amiss; that you may consume it in your concupiscences.

CONVERSION.

37 HEAR me, O Lord, hear me: that this people may learn that thou art the Lord God, and that thou hast turned their heart again. — 3 Kings xviii.

8 O God of hosts, convert us ... — Ps. lxxix.

5 Convert us, O God our Saviour .... — Ps. lxxxiv.

18 ... Convert me, and I shall be converted: for thou art the Lord my God. — Jer. xxxi.

40 Let us search our ways, and seek, and return to the Lord. — Lament. iii.

15 Turn away from evil and do good: seek after peace and pursue it. — Ps. xxxiii.

8 Delay not to be converted to the Lord, and defer it not from day to day. — Ecclus. v.

21 Turn to the Lord, and forsake thy sins. — Ecclus. xvii.

23 Return to the Lord, and turn away from thy injustice, and greatly hate abomination.

28 How great is the mercy of the Lord, and his forgiveness to them that turn to him!

5 To depart from iniquity is that which pleaseth the Lord, and to depart from injustice, is an entreaty for sins. — Ecclus. xxxv.

22 Be converted to me, and you shall be saved, all ye ends of the earth: for I am God, and there is no other. — Isaias xlv.

6 ... Be converted, and depart from your idols, and turn away your faces from all your abominations. — Ezech. xiv.

7 Let the wicked forsake his way, and the unjust man his thoughts, and let him return to the Lord, and he will have mercy on him, and to our God: for he is bountiful to forgive. — Isaias lv.

7 And I will give them a heart to know me, that I am the Lord: and they shall be my people, and I will be their God: because — Jer. xxiv.

they shall return to me with their whole heart.

23 Is it my will that a sinner should die, saith the Lord God, and not that he should be converted from his ways and live? — Ezech. xviii.

27 When the wicked turneth himself away from his wickedness, which he hath wrought, and doeth judgment, and justice: he shall save his soul alive.

31 Cast away from you all your transgressions, by which you have transgressed, and make to yourselves a new heart, and a new spirit: and why will you die, O house of Israel?

32 For I desire not the death of him that dieth, saith the Lord God, return ye, and live.

12 ... Be converted to me with all your heart, in fasting, and in weeping, and in mourning. — Joel ii.

13 And rend your hearts, and not your garments, and turn to the Lord your God: for he is gracious and merciful, patient and rich in mercy, and ready to repent of the evil.

14 Who knoweth but he will return, and forgive, and leave a blessing behind him ...

6 Therefore turn thou to thy God: keep mercy and judgment, and hope in thy God always. — Osee xii.

2 Return, O Israel, to the Lord thy God: Osee xiv.
for thou hast fallen down by thy iniquity.

15 Hate evil, and love good, and establish Amos v.
judgment, in the gate ...

7 ... Return to me, and I will return to Malach.
you, saith the Lord of hosts. iii.

3 Amen I say to you, unless you be con- S. Matt.
verted, and become as little children, you xviii.
shall not enter into the kingdom of heaven.

15 For the heart of this people is grown S. Matt.
gross, and with their ears they have been xiii.
dull of hearing, and their eyes they have
shut: lest at any time they should see with
their eyes, and hear with their ears, and understand with their hearts, and be converted,
and I should heal them.

26 To you first God raising up his Son, Acts iii.
hath sent him to bless you: that every one
may convert himself from his wickedness.

19 Be penitent, therefore, and be converted, that your sins may be blotted out.

8 Draw nigh to God, and he will draw S. James
nigh to you. Cleanse your hands, ye sin- iv.
ners: and purify your hearts, ye double
minded.

25 You were as sheep going astray: but 1 S. Peter
you are now converted to the shepherd and ii.
bishop of your souls.

19 My brethren, if any of you err from the S. James
truth, and one convert him: v.

20 He must know, that he who causeth a sinner to be converted from the error of his way, shall save his soul from death, and shall cover a multitude of sins.

COVETOUSNESS.

7 SURELY man passeth as an image: yea, and he is disquieted in vain. He storeth up: and he knoweth not for whom he shall gather these things. — Ps. xxxviii.

2 Treasures of wickedness shall profit nothing: but justice shall deliver from death. — Prov. x.

11 Trust not in iniquity, and covet not robberies ... — Ps. lxi.

19 The ways of every covetous man destroy the souls of the possessors. — Prov. i.

6 He that gathereth treasures by a lying tongue, is vain and foolish, and shall stumble upon the snares of death. — Prov. xxi.

5 Lift not up thy eye to riches which thou canst not have ... — Prov. xxiii.

8 He that heapeth together riches by usury and loan, gathereth them for him that will be bountiful to the poor. — Prov. xxviii.

26 God hath given to a man that is good in his sight, wisdom and knowledge, and joy: but to the sinner he hath given vexation, and superfluous care, to heap up and to gather together, and to give it to him that hath — Eccles. ii.

pleased God: but this also is vanity, and a fruitless solicitude of the mind.

9 A covetous man shall not be satisfied with money: and he that loveth riches shall reap no fruit from them: so this also is vanity.   Eccles. v.

36 Let not thy hand be stretched out to receive, and shut when thou shouldst give.   Ecclus. iv.

1 Set not thy heart upon unjust possessions, and say not: I have enough to live on: for it shall be of no service in the time of vengeance and darkness.   Ecclus. v.

9 Nothing is more wicked than the covetous man...   Ecclus. x.

10 There is not a more wicked thing than to love money: for such a one setteth even his own soul to sale: because while he liveth he hath cast away his bowels.

18 There is one that is enriched by living sparingly, and this is the portion of his reward.   Ecclus. xi.

19 In that he saith: I have found me rest, and now I will eat of my goods alone:

20 And he knoweth not what time shall pass, and that death approacheth, and that he must leave all to others, and shall die.

4 He that gathereth together by wronging his own soul, gathereth for others, and another will squander away his goods in rioting.   Ecclus. xiv.

9 The eye of the covetous man is insa-

tiable in his portion of iniquity: he will not be satisfied till he consume his own soul, drying it up.

5 He that loveth gold, shall not be justified; and he that followeth after corruption, shall be filled with it. — Ecclus. xxxi.

6 Many have been brought to fall for gold, and the beauty thereof hath been their ruin.

17 For the iniquity of his covetousness I was angry, and I struck him: I hid my face from thee, and was angry: and he went away wandering in his own heart. — Isaias lvii.

9 Wo to him that gathereth together an evil covetousness to his house, that his nest may be on high, and thinketh he may be delivered out of the hand of evil. — Habac. ii.

19 Lay not up for yourselves treasures on earth: where the rust, and the moth consume, and where thieves dig through, and steal. — S. Matt. vi.

20 But lay up for yourselves treasures in heaven: where neither the rust nor the moth doth consume, and where thieves do not dig through, nor steal.

21 For where thy treasure is, there is thy heart also.

15 And he said to them: Take heed and beware of all covetousness: for a man's life doth not consist in the abundance of things which he possesseth. — S. Luke xii.

16 And he spoke a similitude to them, saying: The land of a certain rich man brought forth plenty of fruits:

17 And he thought within himself, saying: What shall I do, because I have not where to lay up together my fruits?

18 And he said: This will I do: I will pull down my barns, and will build greater: and into them I will gather all things that are grown to me, and my goods.

19 And I will say to my soul: Soul, thou hast much goods laid up for many years, take thy rest, eat, drink, make good cheer.

20 But God said to him: Thou fool, this night do they require thy soul of thee; and whose shall those things be, which thou hast provided?

21 So is he that layeth up treasure for himself, and is not rich towards God.

13 No servant can serve two masters, for either he will hate the one, and love the other: or he will hold to the one, and despise the other. You cannot serve God and mammon. S. Luke xvi.

14 Now the Pharisees, who were covetous, heard all these things: and they derided him.

3 ... Covetousness, let it not so much as be named among you, as it becometh saints; Ephes. v.

5 For know ye this, and understand, that no ... covetous person (which is a serving

of idols), hath any inheritance in the Kingdom of Christ, and of God.

10 For the desire of money is the root of all evils ; which some coveting have erred from the faith, and have entangled themselves in many sorrows. — 1 S. Tim. vi.

DEATH.

23 ... Yesterday for me, and to-day for thee. — Ecclus. xxxviii.

27 ... It is appointed for men once to die, and after this, the judgment. — Heb. ix.

19 In the sweat of thy face shalt thou eat bread till thou return to the earth, out of which thou wast taken : for dust thou art, and into dust thou shalt return. — Gen. iii.

1 ... Thus saith the Lord God: Give charge concerning thy house, for thou shalt die, and not live. — 4 Kings xx.

5 ... O Lord, make me know my end, and what is the number of my days : that I may know what is wanting to me. — Ps. xxxviii.

5 The days of man are short, and the number of his months is with thee : thou hast appointed his bounds which cannot be passed. — Job xiv.

23 For behold short years pass away, and I am walking in a path by which I shall not return. — Job xvi.

17 There the wicked cease from tumult, Job iii.
and the wearied in strength are at rest.

32 The just hath hope in his death. Prov. xiv.

22 The death of the wicked is very Ps.
evil . . . xxxiii.

29 O that they would be wise and would Deut.
understand, and would provide for their last xxxii.
end.

4 Though I should walk in the midst of Ps.
the shadow of death, I will fear no evils, for xxii.
thou art with me. Thy rod and thy staff,
they have comforted me.

15 Precious in the sight of the Lord is Ps. cxv.
the death of his saints.

2 (Better) . . . is the day of death than Eccles.
the day of one's birth. vii.

12 Seek not death in the error of your Wisd. i.
life, neither procure ye destruction by the
works of your hands.

13 For God made not death, neither hath
he pleasure in the destruction of the living.

1 The souls of the just are in the hands Wisd. iii.
of God, and the torment of death shall not
touch them.

2 In the sight of the unwise they seemed
to die: and their departure was taken for
misery.

3 And their going away from us, for utter
destruction: but they are in peace.

4 And though in the sight of men they

suffered torments, their hope is full of immortality.

7 The just man, if he be prevented with death, shall be in rest. — Wisd. iv.

10 He pleased God and was beloved, and living among sinners he was translated.

11 He was taken away lest wickedness should alter his understanding, or deceit beguile his soul.

12 For the bewitching of vanity obscureth good things, and the wandering of concupiscence overturneth the innocent mind.

13 Being made perfect in a short space, he fulfilled a long time:

14 For his soul pleased God: therefore he hastened to bring him out of the midst of iniquities: but the people see this, and understand not, nor lay up such things in their hearts.

16 The just that is dead, condemneth the wicked that are living, and youth soon ended, the long life of the unjust.

13 With him that feareth the Lord, it shall go well in the latter end, and in the day of his death he shall be blessed. — Ecclus. i.

5 Fear not the sentence of death. Remember what things have been before thee, and what shall come after thee: this sentence is from the Lord upon all flesh. — Ecclus. xli.

8 It is not in man's power to stop the Eccles.
spirit, neither hath he power in the day of viii.
death . . .

16 Give ye glory to the Lord your God, Jer. xiii.
before it be dark, and before your feet stumble upon the dark mountains : you shall look for light, and he will turn it into the shadow of death, and into darkness. |

1 The just perisheth, and no man layeth Isaias
it to heart, and men of mercy are taken lvii.
away, because there is none that understandeth; for the just man is taken away from before the face of evil.

11 Weep but a little for the dead, for he Ecclus.
is at rest. xxii.

29 Now thou dost dismiss thy servant, O S. Luke
Lord, according to thy word in peace. ii.

42 And (the penitent thief) said to Jesus: S. Luke
Lord, remember me when thou shalt come xxiii.
into thy kingdom.

43 And Jesus said to him : Amen I say to thee, this day thou shalt be with me in paradise.

25 He that believeth in me although he S. John
be dead, shall live. xi.

26 And every one that liveth, and believeth in me, shall not die for ever.

59 . . . Lord Jesus, receive my spirit. Acts vii.

22 As in Adam all die, so also in Christ 1 Cor.
all shall be made alive. xv.

Death.

10 ... Who hath indeed destroyed death, and hath enlightened life and incorruption by the gospel. — 2 S. Tim. i.

56 Now the sting of death is sin ... — 1 Cor. xv.

57 But thanks be to God, who hath given us the victory through our Lord Jesus Christ.

1 For we know that if our earthly house of this habitation be dissolved, that we have a building of God, a house not made with hands, eternal in heaven. — 2 Cor. v.

4 For we also, who are in this tabernacle, do groan being burdened: because we would not be unclothed, but clothed over; that what is mortal may be swallowed up by life.

5 Now he, that maketh us for this very thing, is God, who hath given us the pledge of the Spirit.

6 Therefore, having always confidence, knowing that, while we are in the body, we are absent from the Lord:

8 We are confident, I say, and have a good will to be absent rather from the body, and to be present with the Lord.

9 And therefore we labour, whether absent or present, to please him.

21 For to me, to live is Christ: and to die is gain: — Phil. i.

22 And if to live in the flesh, this is to me the fruit of labour; and what I shall choose, I know not.

23 But I am straitened between two: having a desire to be dissolved, and to be with Christ, being by much the better:

24 But to remain in the flesh is necessary for you.

14 Forasmuch then as the children were partakers of flesh and blood, he also (Jesus) himself in like manner partook of the same: that, through death, he might destroy him who had the empire of death, that is to say, the devil;   Heb. ii.

15 And might deliver them, who through the fear of death were all their life-time subject to slavery.

9 There remaineth, therefore, a rest for the people of God.   Heb. iv.

10 For he who is entered into his rest, he also hath rested from his own works, as God from his.

11 Let us hasten, therefore, to enter into that rest . . .

13 And I heard a voice from heaven, saying to me: Write: Blessed are the dead, who die in the Lord.* From henceforth now, saith the Spirit, that they may rest from their labours; for their works follow them.   Apoc. xiv.

17 . . . Fear not. I am the first and the last.   Apoc. i.

* It is understood of the martyrs who die for the Lord.

18 And alive, and was dead, and behold I am living for ever and ever, and have the keys of death and hell.

DECEIT AND LYING.

11 ... You shall not lie, neither shall any man deceive his neighbour.   Lev. xix.

7 Thou shalt fly lying ...   Ex. xxiii.

24 ... Deceitful men shall not live out half their days.   Ps. liv.

4 The wicked are alienated from the womb, they have gone astray from the womb, they have spoken false things.   Ps. lvii.

4 ... He that trusteth to lies feedeth the winds ...   Prov. x.

9 The dissembler with his mouth deceiveth his friend ...   Prov. xi.

13 He that walketh deceitfully, revealeth secrets: but he that is faithful, concealeth the thing committed to him by his friend.

19 ... A hasty witness, frameth a lying tongue.   Prov. xii.

27 The deceitful man shall not find gain: but the substance of a just man shall be precious gold.

13 ... Deceitful souls go astray in sins ...   Prov. xiii.

17 ... The crafty man is hateful.   Prov. xiv.

25 ... The double dealer uttereth lies.

4 The evil man obeyeth an unjust tongue: and the deceitful hearkeneth to lying lips. — Prov. xvii.

5 A false witness shall not be unpunished: and he that speaketh lies shall not escape. — Prov. xix.

17 The bread of lying is sweet to a man: but afterwards his mouth shall be filled with gravel. — Prov. xx.

28 ... Deceive not any man with thy lips. — Prov. xxiv.

28 A deceitful tongue loveth not truth: and a slippery mouth worketh ruin. — Prov. xxvi.

5 The holy spirit of discipline will flee from the deceitful ... — Wisd. i.

30 In no wise speak against the truth, but be ashamed of the lie of thy ignorance. — Ecclus. iv.

14 Be not willing to make any manner of lie: for the custom thereof is not good. — Ecclus. vii.

11 Winnow not with every wind; and go not into every way: for so is every sinner proved by a double tongue. — Ecclus. v.

26 A lie is a foul blot in a man, and yet it will be continually in the mouth of men without discipline. — Ecclus. xx.

27 A thief is better than a man that is always lying: but both of them shall inherit destruction.

28 The manners of lying men are without honour: and their confusion is with them without ceasing.

20 Thou shalt not bear false witness. — S. Luke xviii.

Deceit and Lying.

44 You are of your father, the devil; and the desires of your father you will do ... He stood not in the truth; because truth is not in him. When he speaketh a lie, he speaketh of his own: for he is a liar, and the father thereof. — S. John viii.

25 Wherefore, putting away lying, speak ye the truth every man with his neighbour: for we are members one of another. — Ephes. iv.

10 He that will love life, and see good days, let him refrain his tongue from evil, and his lips that they speak no guile. — 1 S. Peter iii.

1 Wherefore, laying aside all malice, and all guile, and dissimulations. — 1 S. Peter ii.

9 Lie not one to another ... — Col. iii.

8 ... All liars, their portion shall be in the pool burning with fire and brimstone: which is the second death. — Apoc. xxi.

22 Who is a liar, but he who denieth that Jesus is the Christ? — 1 S. John ii.

DESPAIR.

12 We have no hopes: for we will go after our own thoughts, and we will do every one according to the perverseness of his evil heart. — Jer. xviii.

18 And I said: My end, and my hope is perished from the Lord. — Lament. iii.

5 And [Judas] casting down the pieces of silver in the temple, he departed: and went and hanged himself with a halter.   S. Matt. xxvii.

11 And they blasphemed the God of heaven, because of their pains and wounds, and did not penance from their works.   Apoc. xvi.

DETACHMENT.

7 ... ARISE, and fear not.   S. Matt.
8 And they lifting up their eyes, saw no one, but only Jesus.   xvii.

37 He that loveth father or mother more than me, is not worthy of me: and he that loveth son or daughter more than me, is not worthy of me.   S. Matt. x.

29 This therefore I say, brethren: the time is short: it remaineth that they also who have wives, be as if they had none: 1 Cor. vii.

30 And they that weep, as though they wept not; and they that rejoice, as if they rejoiced not; and they that buy, as though they possessed not.

31 And they that use this world, as if they used it not: for the fashion of this world passeth away.

DETRACTION.

24 ... TAKE heed thou speak not anything harshly against Jacob.   Gen. xxxi.

5 Thou hast loved malice more than goodness: and iniquity rather than to speak righteousness. — Ps. li.

6 Thou hast loved all the words of ruin, O deceitful tongue.

7 Therefore will God destroy thee for ever: he will pluck thee out, and remove thee from thy dwelling place: and thy root out of the land of the living.

19 Thy mouth hath abounded with evil, and thy tongue framed deceits. — Ps. xlix.

20 Sitting thou didst speak against thy brother, and didst lay a scandal against thy mother's son: 21 these things hast thou done, and I was silent.

Thou thoughtest unjustly that I shall be like to thee: but I will reprove thee, and set before thy face.

16 Thou shalt not be a detractor nor a whisperer among the people … — Lev. xix.

24 Remove from thee a froward mouth, and let detracting lips be far from thee. — Prov. iv.

9 … The detractor is the abomination of men. — Prov. xxiv.

15 Lie not in wait, nor seek after wickedness in the house of the just, nor spoil his rest.

16 For a just man shall fall seven times, and shall rise again: but the wicked shall fall down into evil.

21 My son, fear the Lord, and the king: and have nothing to do with detractors.

23 The north wind driveth away rain, as doth a sad countenance a backbiting tongue. — Prov. xxv.

22 Do not apply thy heart to all words that are spoken: lest perhaps thou hear thy servant reviling thee. — Eccles. vii.

23 For thy conscience knoweth that thou also hast often spoken evil of others.

11 If a serpent bite in silence, he is nothing better that backbiteth secretly. — Eccles. x.

10 Hast thou heard a word against thy neighbour? let it die within thee. — Ecclus. xix.

11 ..: Refrain your tongue from detraction, for an obscure speech shall not go for nought ... — Wisd. i.

15 The whisperer and the double-tongued is accursed: for he hath troubled many that were at peace. — Ecclus. xxviii.

45 ... An evil man out of the evil treasure (of his heart) bringeth forth that which is evil. For out of the abundance of the heart the mouth speaketh. — S. Luke vi.

1 If I speak with the tongues of men, and of angels, and have not charity, I am become as sounding brass, or a tinkling cymbal. — 1 Cor. xiii.

2 Speak evil of no man ... — Titus iii.

15 If you bite and devour one another: take heed you be not consumed one of another. — Gal. v.

Detraction.

11 Detract not one another, my brethren. S. James
He that detracteth his brother, or he that iv.
judgeth his brother, detracteth the law, and
judgeth the law ...

10 ... Now is come salvation, and Apoc.
strength, and the kingdom of our God, and xii.
the power of his Christ: because the accuser
of our brethren is cast forth, who accused
them before our God day and night.

DISCOURAGEMENT.

20 I CRY to thee, and thou hearest me Job xxx.
not: I stand up and thou dost not regard me.

4 Thy words have confirmed them that Job iv.
were staggering ...

5 But now the scourge is come upon thee,
and thou faintest: it hath touched thee, and
thou art troubled.

6 Where is thy fear, thy fortitude, thy
patience, and the perfection of thy ways?

3 Strengthen ye the feeble hands, and Isaias
confirm the weak knees. xxxv.

4 Say to the faint-hearted: Take courage
... God himself will come and will save you.

10 Who is there among you that feareth Isaias l.
the Lord, that heareth the voice of his servant, that hath walked in darkness, and hath
no light? Let him hope in the name of the
Lord, and lean upon his God.

17 ... It was now dark, and Jesus was not come unto them.   S. John vi.

8 For we would not have you ignorant, brethren, of our tribulation, which came to us in Asia, that we were pressed out of measure above our strength, so that we were weary even of life.   2 Cor. i.

13 Wherefore I pray you not to faint at my tribulations for you, which is your glory.   Ephes. iii.

14 For this cause I bow my knees to the Father of our Lord Jesus Christ.

16 That he would grant you, according to the riches of his glory, to be strengthened by his Spirit with might unto the inward man.

DISOBEDIENCE.

9 BE not rebellious against the Lord ...   Num. xiv.

23 Because it is like the sin of witchcraft to rebel: and like the crime of idolatry to refuse to obey.   1 Kings xv.

15 If you will not hearken to the voice of the Lord, but will rebel against his words, the hand of the Lord shall be upon you, and upon your fathers.   1 Kings xii.

14 And they hearkened not, but hardened their necks like to the neck of their fathers, who would not obey the Lord their God.   4 Kings xvii.

17 ... Because thou ... hast eaten of the tree whereof I commanded thee, that   Gen. iii.

thou shouldst not eat, cursed is the earth in thy work . . .

21 . . . Because thou hast not been obedient to the Lord . . . 3 Kings xiii.

22 . . . Thy dead body shall not be brought into the sepulchre of thy fathers.

19 . . . By the disobedience of one man many were made sinners . . . Rom. v.

2 . . . And every . . . disobedience received a just recompense of reward. Heb. ii.

DIVINE THREATENINGS.

24 THE Lord thy God is a consuming fire, a jealous God. Deut. iv.

17 The Lord your God he is the God of gods, and the Lord of lords, a great God, and mighty and terrible, who accepteth no person nor taketh bribes. Deut. x.

6 The Lord trieth the just and the wicked . . . Ps. x.

7 He shall rain snares upon sinners: fire and brimstone and storms of winds shall be the portion of their cup.

27 For behold they that go far from thee shall perish . . . Ps. lxxii.

10 For yet a little while, and the wicked shall not be: and thou shalt seek his place, and shalt not find it. Ps. xxxvi.

18 He shall be punished for all that he Job xx.

did, and yet shall not be consumed: according to the multitude of his devices so also shall he suffer.

16 Cursed be he that honoureth not his father and mother.   Deut. xxvii.

17 Cursed be he that removeth his neighbour's land-marks.

18 Cursed be he that maketh the blind to wander out of his way.

19 Cursed be he that perverteth the judgment of the stranger, of the fatherless, and the widow.*

21 ... They are cursed who decline from thy commandments.   Ps. cxviii.

20 The wicked shall perish. And the enemies of the Lord, presently after they shall be honoured and exalted, shall come to nothing, and vanish like smoke.   Ps. xxxvi.

28 ... The unjust shall be punished, and the seed of the wicked shall perish.

12 But my people heard not my voice: and Israel hearkened not to me.   Ps. lxxx.

13 So I let them go according to the desires of their heart: they shall walk in their own inventions.

24 That which the wicked feareth, shall come upon him ...   Prov. x.

27 ... The years of the wicked shall be shortened.

* See Deut. xxviii., 15th and following verses.

28 ... The hope of the wicked shall perish.

29 Fear to them that work evil.

3 ... The deceitfulness of the wicked shall destroy them.   Prov. xi.

13 He that rendereth evil for good, evil shall not depart from his house.   Prov. xvii.

10 The wicked shall be punished according to their own devices: who have neglected the just, and have revolted from the Lord.   Wisd. iii.

19 Humble thy spirit very much: for the vengeance on the flesh of the ungodly is fire and worms.   Ecclus. vii.

3 There is no good for him that is always occupied in evil, and that giveth no alms ...   Ecclus. xii.

27 ... He that loveth danger shall perish in it.   Ecclus. iii.

9 The inheritance of the children of sinners shall perish, and with their posterity shall be a perpetual reproach.   Ecclus. xli.

14 Wo to them that are of a double heart, and to wicked lips, and to the hands that do evil, and to the sinner that goeth on the earth two ways.   Ecclus. ii.

15 Wo to them that are faint-hearted, and who believe not God: and therefore shall not be protected by him.

16 Wo to them that have lost patience, and that have forsaken the right ways, have gone aside into crooked ways.

17 And what will they do, when the Lord shall begin to examine?

11 The lofty eyes of man are humbled, and the haughtiness of men shall be made to stoop: and the Lord alone shall be exalted in that day. Isaias ii.

12 Because the day of the Lord of hosts shall be upon every one that is proud and high-minded, and upon every one that is arrogant, and he shall be humbled.

11 Wo to the wicked unto evil: for the reward of his hands shall be given him. Isaias iii.

20 Wo to you that call evil good, and good evil: that put darkness for light, and light for darkness: that put bitter for sweet, and sweet for bitter. Isaias v..

22 Wo to you that are mighty to drink wine, and stout men at drunkenness.

23 That justify the wicked for gifts, and take away the justice of the just from him.

1 And I turned, and lifted up my eyes: and I saw, and behold a volume flying: Zach. v.

3 ... This is the curse, that goeth forth over the face of the earth: for every thief shall be judged as is there written: and every one that sweareth in like manner shall be judged by it.

4 ... And it shall come to the house of the thief, and to the house of him that sweareth falsely by my name: and it shall

remain in the midst of his house, and shall consume it, with the timber thereof, and the stones thereof.

1 Wo to them that make wicked laws: Isaias x. and when they write, write injustice.

2 To oppress the poor in judgment, and do violence to the cause of the humble of my people: that widows might be their prey, and that they might rob the fatherless.

3 What will you do in the day of visitation, and of the calamity which cometh from afar? To whom will ye flee for help? and where will ye leave your glory?

9 Behold, the day of the Lord shall come, Isaias a cruel day, and full of indignation, and of xiii. wrath, and fury, to lay the land desolate, and to destroy the sinners thereof out of it.

11 And I will visit the evils of the world, and against the wicked for their iniquity, and I will make the pride of infidels to cease, and will bring down the arrogancy of the mighty.

15 Wo to you that are deep of heart, to Isaias hide your counsel from the Lord: and their xxix. works are in the dark, and they say: Who seeth us, and who knoweth us?

1 Wo to thee that spoilest, shalt not thou Isaias thyself also be spoiled? and thou that xxxiii. despisest, shall not thyself also be despised? when thou shall have made an end of spoil-

ing, thou shalt be spoiled: when being wearied thou shalt cease to despise, thou shalt be despised.

13 Wo to him that buildeth up his house by injustice, and his chambers not in judgment: that will oppress his friend without cause, and will not pay him his wages. — Jer. xxii.

1 Wo to the pastors, that destroy and tear the sheep of my pasture, saith the Lord. — Jer. xxiii.

2 If you will not hear, and if you will not lay it to heart, to give glory to my name, saith the Lord of hosts: I will send poverty upon you, and I will curse your blessings, yea, I will curse them: because you have not laid it to heart. — Malach. ii.

30 Every one shall die for his own iniquity... — Jer. xxxi.

5 And I will come to you in judgment, and will be a speedy witness against sorcerers, and adulterers, and false swearers, and them that oppress the hireling in his wages, the widows and the fatherless: and oppress the stranger, and have not feared me, saith the Lord of hosts. — Malach. iii.

4 Hear this, you that crush the poor, and make the needy of the land to fail. — Amos viii.

11 ... The day of the Lord is great and very terrible: and who can stand it? — Joel ii.

1 For behold the day shall come kindled as a furnace: and all the proud, and all that — Malach. iv.

do wickedly shall be stubble; and the day that cometh shall set them on fire, saith the Lord of hosts, it shall not leave them root, nor branch.

10 Every tree, therefore, that yieldeth not good fruit, shall be cut down, and cast into the fire. — S. Matt. iii.

6 If any one abide not in me: he shall be cast forth as a branch, and shall wither, and they shall gather him up, and cast him into the fire, and he burneth. — S. John xv.

49 So shall it be at the end of the world. The angels shall go out, and shall separate the wicked from among the just. — S. Matt. xiii.

30 And the unprofitable servant cast ye out into the exterior darkness. There shall be weeping and gnashing of teeth. — S. Matt. xxv.

48 If that evil servant should say in his heart: My lord is long a coming: — S. Matt. xxiv.

49 And shall begin to strike his fellow-servants, and shall eat, and drink with drunkards:

50 The lord of that servant shall come in a day that he hopeth not, and at an hour that he knoweth not:

51 And shall separate him, and appoint his portion with the hypocrites. There shall be weeping and gnashing of teeth.

31 It is a fearful thing to fall into the hands of the living God. — Heb. x.

6 Who will render to every man according to his works. — Rom. ii.

8 To them that are contentious, and who obey not the truth, but give credit to iniquity, wrath and indignation.

9 Tribulation and anguish upon every soul of man that doeth evil...

9 Be not deceived: Neither fornicators, nor idolaters, nor adulterers, — 1 Cor. vi.

10 Nor the effeminate, nor sodomites, nor thieves, nor the covetous, nor drunkards, nor railers, nor extortioners, shall possess the kingdom of God.

25 He that doeth an injury shall receive for that which he hath done unjustly; for there is no respect of persons with God. — Col. iii.

12 The countenance of the Lord is against them that do evil things. — 1 S. Peter iii.

18 And if the just man shall scarcely be saved, where shall the wicked and the sinner appear? — 1 S. Peter iv.

25 See that you refuse not him who speaketh. For if they escaped not who refused him that spoke upon earth, much more shall not we, who turn away from him that speaketh to us from heaven. — Heb. xii.

7 But the heavens and the earth, which are now, by the same word are kept in store, reserved unto fire against the day of judgment, and perdition of wicked men. — 2 S. Peter iii.

8 When the wicked shall spring up as Ps. xci.
grass, and all the workers of iniquity shall
appear: That they may perish for ever and
ever.

DUTY TOWARDS RULERS.

15 By me kings reign, and lawgivers de- Prov.
cree just things. viii.

28 ... The prince of thy people thou Ex. xxii.
shalt not curse.

21 My son, fear the Lord and the king: Prov.
and have nothing to do with detractors. xxiv.

21 ... Render to Cæsar the things that S. Matt.
are Cæsar's: and to God, the things that are xxii.
God's.

5 ... Thou shalt not speak evil of the Acts
prince of thy people. xxiii.

1 Let every soul be subject to higher Rom.
powers: for there is no power but from God: xiii.
and those that are, are ordained of God.

2 Therefore he that resisteth the power,
resisteth the ordinance of God; and they
that resist, purchase to themselves damnation.

3 For rulers are not a terror to the good
work, but to the evil. Wilt thou then not
be afraid of the power? Do that which is
good: and thou shalt have praise from the
same.

4 For he is the minister of God to thee, for good. But if thou do that which is evil, fear: for he beareth not the sword in vain. For he is the minister of God: an avenger to execute wrath upon him that doeth evil.

5 Wherefore be subject of necessity, not only for wrath, but also for conscience-sake.

6 For therefore also you pay tribute: for they are the ministers of God, serving unto this purpose.

7 Render therefore to all their dues. Tribute, to whom tribute is due: custom to whom custom: fear to whom fear: honour to whom honour.

13 Be ye subject, therefore, to every human creature, for God's sake; whether it be to the king, as excelling;   1 S. Peter ii.

14 Or to governors, as sent by him for the punishment of evil doers, and for the praise of the good:

15 For so is the will of God, that by doing well, you may silence the ignorance of foolish men.

17 Honour all men: love the brotherhood: fear God: honour the king.

ENVY.

30 ... Envy is the rottenness of the bones.   Prov. xiv.

Envy.

1 Be not emulous of evil doers; nor envy them that work iniquity. — Ps. xxxvi.

7 Envy not the man who prospereth in his way; the man who doth unjust things.

8 ... Have no emulation to do evil.

16 Envy not the glory and riches of a sinner: for thou knowest not what his ruin shall be. — Ecclus. ix.

31 Envy not the unjust man, and do not follow his ways. — Prov. iii.

17 Let not thy heart envy sinners: but be thou in the fear of the Lord all the day long. — Prov. xxiii.

1 Instead of a friend become not an enemy to thy neighbour: for an evil man shall inherit reproach and shame, so shall every sinner that is envious and double-tongued. — Ecclus. vi.

8 The eye of the envious is wicked: and he turneth away his face, and despiseth his own soul. — Ecclus. xiv.

24 By the envy of the devil, death came into the world:

25 And they follow him that are of his side. — Wisd. ii.

9 The patriarchs, through envy, sold Joseph in Egypt ... — Acts vii.

10 (Pilate), knew that the chief priests had delivered (Jesus) up out of envy. — S. Mark xv.

12 Cain, who was of the wicked one, and killed his brother. And wherefore did he — 1 S. John iii.

kill him? Because his own works were wicked: and his brother's just.

5 ... To envy doth the spirit covet which dwelleth in you. — S. James iv.

13 Let us walk honestly as in the day ... Not in contention and envy. — Rom. xiii.

3 Whereas there is among you envying and contention, are you not carnal, and walk according to man? — 1 Cor. iii.

4 ... Charity envieth not ... — 1 Cor. xiii.

EXAMPLE OF CHRIST.

6 I HAVE given my body to the strikers, and my cheeks to them that plucked them: I have not turned away my face from them that rebuked me, and spit upon me. — Isaias l.

50 ... Friend, whereto art thou come? ... — S. Matt. xxvi.

48 And Jesus said to him: Judas, dost thou betray the son of man with a kiss? — S. Luke xxii.

7 He was offered because it was his own will ... — Isaias liii.

9 ... If any man have not the Spirit of Christ, he is none of his. — Rom. viii.

14 Whosoever are led by the Spirit of God, they are the sons of God.

29 For whom he foreknew, he also predestinated to be made conformable to the

Example of Christ.

image of his Son: that he might be the first-born among many brethren.*

6 He that saith he abideth in him, ought himself also to walk, even as he walked.   1 S. John ii.

24 Then Jesus said to his disciples: If any man will come after me, let him deny himself, and take up his cross, and follow me.   S. Matt. xvi.

35 And rising very early, going out he went into a desert place: and there he prayed.   S. Mark i.

23 And having dismissed the multitude, he went up into a mountain alone to pray. And when it was evening he was there alone.   S. Matt. xiv.

12 ... And he passed the whole night in the prayer of God.   S. Luke vi.

43 ... And being in an agony, he prayed the longer.   S. Luke xxii.

16 ... And he went into the synagogue according to his custom on the sabbath day ...   S. Luke iv.

31 ... There he taught them on the sabbath days.

25 ... Is not this he whom they seek to kill?   S. John vii.

---

* That is, God hath preordained that all his elect should be conformable to the image of his Son. We must not here offer to dive into the secrets of God's eternal election: only firmly believe that all our "Good," in time, and eternity, flows "Originally" from God's free goodness; and all our evil from man's free will.

26 And behold he speaketh openly, and they say nothing to him ...

34 A new commandment I give unto you: That you love one another, as I have loved you, that you also love one another. — S. John xiii.

13 You call me Master, and Lord: and you say well, for so I am.

14 If then I, being your Lord and Master, have washed your feet; you also ought to wash one another's feet.

15 For I have given you an example, that as I have done to you, so you do also.

27 ... I am in the midst of you, as he that serveth. — S. Luke xxii.

25 ... You know that the princes of the gentiles lord it over them: and they that are the greater, exercise power upon them. — S. Matt. xx.

26 It shall not be so among you, but whosoever will be the greater among you, let him be your minister:

27 And he that will be first among you, shall be your servant.

28 Even as the Son of Man is not come to be ministered unto, but to minister, and his life to give a redemption for many.

16 In this we have known the charity of God, because he hath laid down his life for us: and we ought to lay down our lives for the brethren. — 1 S. John iii.

32 ... He was led as a sheep to the — Acts viii.

slaughter: and like a lamb without voice before his shearer, so openeth he not his mouth.*

12 And when he was accused by the chief priests and ancients, he answered nothing.   S. Matt. xxvii.

14 And he answered him (Pilate) to never a word: so that the governor wondered exceedingly.

5 Let this mind be in you, which was also in Christ Jesus: Phil. ii.

6 Who being in the form of God, thought it not robbery, to be equal with God:

7 But emptied himself,† taking the form of a servant, being made in the likeness of men, and in habit found as a man.

8 He humbled himself, becoming obedient unto death: even to the death of the cross.

2 Walk in love, as Christ also hath loved us, and hath delivered himself for us, an oblation and a sacrifice to God, for an odour of sweetness.   Ephe. v.

11 ... The chalice which my Father hath given me, shall I not drink it?   S. John xviii.

33 ... They crucified him ...   S. Luke xxiii.

34 And Jesus said: Father, forgive them, for they know not what they do.

---

* Isaias liii. 7.
† Made himself as of no account.

46 ... Father, into thy hands I commend my spirit ...

4 I have glorified thee on the earth: I have finished the work which thou gavest me to do. S. John xvii.

1 Christ therefore having suffered in the flesh, be you also armed with the same thought: for he that hath suffered in the flesh, hath ceased from sins. 1 S. Peter iv.

21 For unto this are you called: because Christ also suffered for us, leaving you an example that you should follow his steps; 1 S. Peter ii.

22 Who did no sin, neither was guile found in his mouth;

26 ... Holy, innocent, undefiled, separated from sinners ... Heb. vii.

23 Who, when he was reviled, did not revile: when he suffered he threatened not: but delivered himself to him that judged him unjustly. 1 S. Peter ii.

1 ... Let us run by patience to the fight proposed to us: Heb. xii.

2 Looking on Jesus the author and finisher of faith, who having joy set before him, endured the cross, despising the shame, and now sitteth at the right hand of the throne of God.

3 Think diligently upon him that endured such opposition from sinners against

himself: that you be not wearied, fainting in your minds.

2 ... We know, that, when he shall appear, we shall be like to him: because we shall see him as he is. — 1 S. John iii.

3 And every man that hath this hope in him, sanctifieth himself, as he also is holy.

18 But we all beholding the glory of the Lord with face uncovered, are transformed into the same image from glory to glory, as by the Spirit of the Lord. — 2 Cor. iii.

EXCUSES IN SINS.

12 AND Adam said: The woman, whom thou gavest me to be my companion, gave me of the tree, and I did eat. — Gen. iii.

13 And the Lord God said to the woman: Why hast thou done this? And she answered: The serpent deceived me, and I did eat.

4 Incline not my heart to evil words; to make excuses in sins. — Ps. cxl.

17 The just is first accuser of himself ... — Prov. xviii.

9 And the Lord said to Cain: Where is thy brother Abel? And he answered, I know not: am I my brother's keeper? — Gen. iv.

21 A sinful man will flee reproof, and will find an excuse according to his will. — Ecclus. xxxii.

15 ... You are they that justify yourselves before men: but God knoweth your hearts ...   S. Luke xvi.

20 If our heart reprehend us, God is greater than our heart, and knoweth all things.   1 S. John iii.

EXHORTATION TO KINGS AND PRINCES.

12 ... The throne is established by justice.   Prov. xvi.

17 God hath overturned the thrones of proud princes, and hath set up the meek in their stead.   Ecclus. x.

28 Mercy and truth preserve the king, and his throne is strengthened by clemency.   Prov. xx.

16 A prince void of prudence shall oppress many by calumny: but he that hateth covetousness, shall prolong his days.   Prov. xxviii.

12 A prince that gladly heareth lying words, hath all his servants wicked.   Prov. xxix.

8 Open thy mouth for the dumb, and for the causes of all the children that pass.   Prov. xxxi.

9 ... Decree that which is just, and do justice to the needy and poor.

8 Oppression troubleth the wise, and shall destroy the strength of his heart.   Ecclus. vii.

4 Power is given you by the Lord, and strength by the most High, who will examine your works, and search out your thoughts.   Wisd. vi.

5 Because being ministers of his kingdom,

you have not judged rightly, nor kept the law of justice, nor walked according to the will of God.

6 Horribly and speedily will he appear to you: for a most severe judgment shall be for them that bear rule.

7 For to him that is little, mercy is granted: but the mighty shall be mightily tormented.

8 For God will not except any man's person, neither will he stand in awe of any man's greatness: for he hath made the little and the great, and he hath equally care of all.

9 But a greater punishment is ready for the more mighty.

22 If then your delight be in thrones and sceptres, O ye kings of the people, love wisdom, that you may reign for ever.

23 Love the light of wisdom, all ye that bear rule over peoples.

26 Now the multitude of the wise is the welfare of the whole world: and a wise king is the upholding of a people.

1 God of my fathers, and Lord of mercy, Wisd. ix. who hast made all things with thy word.

4 Give me wisdom, that sitteth by thy throne.

10 Send her out of thy holy heaven, and from the throne of thy majesty, that she may be with me, and may labour with me, that I may know what is acceptable with thee.

12 So shall my works be acceptable, and I shall govern thy people justly.

8 ... He that ruleth with carefulness.   Rom. xii.

EXHORTATION TO MASTERS.

22 HURT not the servant that worketh faithfully, nor the hired man that giveth thee his life.   Ecclus. vii.

43 Afflict him not by might, but fear thy God.   Lev. xxv.

26 ... Take heed of them of thy household.   Ecclus. xxxii.

18 Turn not away thy eyes from them when thou makest them free: because he hath served thee six years according to the wages of a hireling: that the Lord thy God may bless thee in all the works that thou dost.   Deut. xv.

23 Let a wise servant be dear to thee as thy own soul; defraud him not of liberty, nor leave him needy.   Ecclus. vii.

31 If thou have a faithful servant, let him be to thee as thy own soul: treat him as a brother ...   Ecclus. xxxiii.

1 Masters, do to your servants that which is just and equal, knowing that you also have a master in heaven.   Col. iv.

9 Forbearing threatenings: knowing, that the Lord both of them and you is in heaven: and there is no respect of persons with him.   Ephes. vi.

EXHORTATION TO MEN.

19 I know that he will command his children, and his household after him to keep the way of the Lord, and do judgment and justice ... — Gen. xviii.

8 I will, therefore, that men pray in every place, lifting up pure hands, without anger and strife, — 1 S. Tim. ii.

14 Let our men, also, learn to excel in good works for necessary uses that they be not unfruitful. — S. Titus iii.

16 If any of the faithful have widows, let him relieve them. — 1 S. Tim. v.

2 That the aged men be sober, chaste, prudent, sound in faith, in charity, in patience. — S. Titus ii.

6 Young men in like manner exhort that they be sober.

5 ... Subject to the ancients ... — 1 S. Peter v.

EXHORTATION TO PARENTS.

19 ... The father shall make thy truth known to the children. — Isaias xxxviii.

13 ... I will judge his house for ever, for iniquity, because he knew that his sons did wickedly, and did not chastise them. — 1 Kings iii.

11 Command your children, that they do justice and alms-deeds, and that they be mindful of God, and bless him at all times in truth, and with all their power.   Tobias xiv.

4 ... Declaring the praises of the Lord, and his powers, and his wonders which he hath done.   Ps. lxxvii.

5 ... How great things he commanded our fathers, that they should make the same known to their children; 6 that another generation might know them. The children that should be born and should rise up, and declare them to their children.

7 That they may put their hope in God, and may not forget the works of God: and may seek his commandments.

15 Folly is bound up in the heart of a child, and the rod of correction shall drive it away.   Prov. xxii.

15 The rod and reproof give wisdom: but the child that is left to his own will bringeth his mother to shame.   Prov. xxix.

18 Chastise thy son, despair not ...   Prov. xix.

17 Instruct thy son, and he shall refresh thee, and shall give delight to thy soul.   Prov. xxix.

24 The father of the just rejoiceth greatly ...   Prov. xxiii.

1 Rejoice not in ungodly children, if they be multiplied: neither be delighted in them, if the fear of God be not with them.   Ecclus. xvi.

Exhortation to Parents.

2 Trust not to their life, and respect not their labours.

4 It is better to die without children, than to leave ungodly children.

1 He that loveth his son, frequently chastiseth him. — Ecclus. xxx.

8 A horse not broken becometh stubborn, and a child left to himself will become headstrong.

9 Give thy son his way, and he shall make thee afraid . . .

11 Give him not liberty in his youth, and wink not at his devices.

12 Bow down his neck while he is young, . . . lest he grow stubborn, and regard thee not, and so be a sorrow of heart to thee.

3 A son ill taught is the confusion of the father: and a foolish daughter shall be to his loss. — Ecclus. xxii.

2 He that instructeth his son, shall be praised in him, and shall glory in him, in the midst of them of his household. — Ecclus. xxx.

4 His father is dead, and he is as if he were not dead: for he hath left one behind him that is like himself.

5 While he lived he saw and rejoiced in him: and when he died he was not sorrowful . . .

14 Suffer the little children to come unto — S. Mark x.

me, and forbid them not. For of such is the kingdom of God.

4 Fathers, provoke not your children to anger: but bring them up in the discipline and correction of the Lord.   Ephes. vi.

21 Fathers, provoke not your children to indignation: lest they be discouraged.   Col. iii.

8 If any man have not care of his own, and especially of those of his house, he hath denied the faith, and is worse than an infidel.   1 Tim. v.

14 ... Neither ought the children to lay up for the parents, but the parents for the children.   2 Cor. xii.

EXHORTATION TO PRIESTS.

1 CRY, cease not, lift up thy voice like a trumpet, and shew my people their wicked doings, and the house of Jacob their sins.   Isaias lviii.

30 And the Levites are to stand in the morning to give thanks, and to sing praises to the Lord: and in like manner in the evening.   1 Paralip. xxiii.

1 Behold now, bless ye the Lord, all ye servants of the Lord: Who stand in the house of the Lord, in the courts of the house of our God.   Ps. cxxxiii.

2 In the nights lift up your hands to the holy places, and bless ye the Lord.

28 Take heed to yourselves, and to the whole flock, wherein the Holy Ghost hath   Acts xx.

placed your bishops, to rule the church of God, which he hath purchased with his own blood.

2 Feed the flock of God which is among you, taking care of it not by constraint, but willingly according to God: not for filthy lucre's sake, but voluntarily: *1 S. Peter v.*

4 And when the prince of pastors shall appear, you shall receive a never-fading crown of glory.

11 But thou, O man of God, ... pursue justice, piety, faith, charity, patience, meekness. *1 S. Tim. vi.*

12 Fight the good fight of faith: lay hold on eternal life whereunto thou art called, and hast confessed a good confession before many witnesses.

14 Keep the commandment without spot, blameless, unto the coming of our Lord Jesus Christ.

3 Giving no offence to any one, that our ministry be not blamed: *2 Cor. vi.*

4 But in all things let us exhibit ourselves as the ministers of God, in much patience, in tribulation, in necessities, in distresses,

5 In stripes, in prisons, in seditions, in labours, in watchings, in fastings,

6 In chastity, in knowledge, in long suffering, in sweetness, in the Holy Ghost, in charity unfeigned,

7 In the word of truth, in the power of God; by the armour of justice, on the right hand, and on the left,

8 Through honour and dishonour, through infamy and good name; as seducers, and yet speaking truth; as unknown, and yet known;

9 As dying, and behold, we live; as chastised, and not killed;

10 As sorrowful, yet always rejoicing; as needy, yet enriching many; as having nothing, and possessing all things.

12 Let no man despise thy youth: but be thou an example to the faithful, in word, in conversation, in charity, in faith, in chastity.   1 S. Tim. iv.

13 ... Attend to reading, to exhortation, and to doctrine.

14 Neglect not the grace which is in thee, which was given thee by prophecy, with the imposition of the hands of the priesthood.

15 Meditate on these things: be wholly in these things; that thy proficiency may be manifest to all.

16 Attend to thyself and to doctrine: be earnest in them: for in doing this thou shalt both save thyself and them that hear thee.

14 Keep the good deposited in trust to thee by the Holy Ghost, who dwelleth in us.   2 S. Tim. i.

3 Labour as a good soldier of Christ Jesus.   2 S. Tim. ii.

Exhortation to Priests.

4 No man, being a soldier to God, entangleth himself with worldly business; that he may please him to whom he hath engaged himself.

15 Carefully study to present thyself approved unto God, a workman that needeth not to be ashamed, rightly handling the word of truth.

16 But shun profane and vain speeches: for they grow much towards impiety.

22 Flee thou youthful desires; and pursue justice, faith, charity, and peace, with those who call on the Lord from a pure heart.

23 And avoid foolish and unlearned questions; knowing that they beget strifes.

24 But the servant of the Lord must not wrangle, but be gentle towards all men, fit to teach, patient.

25 With modesty admonishing those who resist the truth: if at any time God give them repentance to know the truth,

26 And they recover themselves from the snares of the devil, by whom they are held captives at his will.

8 It is a faithful saying: and of these things I will have thee to affirm earnestly: that they who believe in God may be careful to excel in good works. These things are good and profitable to men. *Titus iii.*

1 I charge thee before God and Jesus *2 Tim. iv.*

Christ, who shall judge the living and the dead, by his coming, and his kingdom:

2 Preach the word, be instant in season, out of season, reprove, entreat, rebuke with all patience and doctrine.

5 Be thou vigilant; labour in all things; do the work of an evangelist;* fulfil thy ministry. Be sober.

7 In all things show thyself an example of good works, in doctrine, in integrity, in gravity, — Titus ii.

8 Sound speech, unblamable; that he who is on the contrary part may be afraid, having no evil to say of us.

EXHORTATION TO WOMEN.

16 ... Thou shalt be under thy husband's power, and he shall have dominion over thee. — Gen. iii.

2 A virtuous woman rejoiceth her husband, and shall fulfil the years of his life in peace. — Ecclus. xxvi.

10 Who shall find a valiant woman? far, and from the uttermost coasts is the price of her. — Prov. xxxi.

11 The heart of her husband trusteth in her, and he shall have no need of spoils.

---

* A diligent preacher of the gospel.

12 She will render him good, and not evil, all the days of her life.

27 She hath looked well to the paths of her house, and hath not eaten her bread idle.

28 Her children rose up, and called her blessed: her husband, and he praised her.

30 Favour is deceitful, and beauty is vain; the woman that feareth the Lord, she shall be praised.

31 Give her of the fruit of her hands: and let her works praise her in the gates.

13 Admonishing her to honour her father Tobias x. and mother-in-law, to love her husband, to take care of the family, to govern the house, and to behave herself irreprehensibly.

4 A diligent woman is a crown to her hus- Prov. band: and she that doth things worthy of xii. confusion, is as rottenness in his bones.

24 As everlasting foundations upon a Ecclus. solid rock, so the commandments of God in xxvi. the heart of a holy woman.

17 Her discipline is the gift of God.

18 Such is a wise and silent woman, and there is nothing so much worth as a well-instructed soul.

34 Let women keep silence in the churches: 1 Cor. for it is not permitted to them to speak, but xiv. to be subject, as also the law saith.

35 But if they would learn anything, let

them ask their husbands at home. For it is a shame for a woman to speak in the church.

11 Let the woman learn in silence, with all subjection.   1 Tim. ii.

12 I suffer not a woman to teach, nor to use authority over the man; but to be in silence.

9 In like manner women also in decent apparel: adorning themselves with modesty and sobriety, not with plaited hair, or gold, or pearls, or costly attire,

10 But as it becometh women professing godliness, with good works.

11 ... Chaste, not slanderers, but sober, faithful in all things.   1 Tim. iii.

3 The aged women, in like manner, in holy attire; not false accusers, not given to much wine: teaching well.   Titus ii.

4 That they may teach the young women to be wise, to love their husbands, to love their children,

5 To be discreet, chaste, sober, having a care of the house, gentle, obedient to their husbands, that the word of God be not blasphemed.

FAITH.

20 ... Believe in the Lord your God, and you shall be secure: believe his prophets, and all things shall succeed well.   2 Paralip. xx.

Faith.

34 ... That which is agreeable to him.   Ecclus. i.

35 ... Is faith and meekness ...

28 He that believeth God, taketh heed to the commandments ...   Ecclus. xxxii.

22 Seek not the things that are too high for thee, and search not into things that are above thy ability ...   Ecclus. iii.

23 For it is not necessary for thee to see with thy eyes those things that are hid.

25 For many things are shewn to thee above the understanding of men.

16 He that believeth, and is baptized, shall be saved: but he that believeth not, shall be condemned.   S. Mark xvi.

29 ... According to your faith, be it done unto you.   S. Matt. ix.

23 ... I do believe, Lord; help thou my unbelief.   S. Mark ix.

22 ... Take courage, daughter: thy faith hath made thee whole.   S. Matt. ix.

28 ... O woman, great is thy faith: be it done to thee as thou wilt.   S. Matt. xv.

5 And when Jesus saw their faith, he saith to the sick of the palsy: Son, thy sins are forgiven thee.   S. Mark ii.

50 ... Thy faith hath made thee safe: go in peace.   S. Luke vii.

22 All things whatsoever you shall ask in prayer, believing, you shall receive.   S. Matt. xxi.

5 And the Apostles said to the Lord: Increase our faith. — S. Luke xvii.

6 And the Lord said: If you had faith like to a grain of mustard-seed, you might say to this mulberry-tree; be thou rooted up, and be thou transplanted into the sea: and it would obey you.

22 And Jesus saith to him: If thou canst believe, all things are possible to him that believeth. — S. Mark ix.

14 As Moses lifted up the serpent in the desert, so must the Son of man be lifted up: — S. John iii.

15 That whosoever believeth in him, may not perish, but may have life everlasting.

47 Amen, amen, I say unto you: He that believeth in me, hath everlasting life. — S. John vi.

26 And every one that liveth, and believeth in me, shall not die for ever. — S. John xi.

44 ... He that believeth in me, doth not believe in me, but in him that sent me. — S. John xii.

46 I am come a light into the world: that whosoever believeth in me, may not remain in darkness.

1 Let not your heart be troubled. You believe in God, believe also in me. — S. John xiv.

12 ... Amen, amen, I say to you, he that believeth in me, the works that I do, he also shall do, and greater than these shall he do.

13 Because I go to the Father ...

29 ... Because thou hast seen me, S. John Thomas, thou hast believed: blessed are xx. they that have not seen, and have believed.

17 ... The just man liveth by faith.   Rom. i.

1 Therefore being justified by faith, let us Rom. v. have peace with God through our Lord Jesus Christ.

22 Hast thou faith? Have it to thyself Rom. before God.   xiv.

20 ... But thou standest by faith: be Rom. xi. not high-minded, but fear.

2 ... If I should have all faith, so that I 1 Cor. could remove mountains, and have not xiii. charity, I am nothing.

6 In Christ Jesus neither circumcision Gal. v. availeth anything, nor uncircumcision; but faith, that worketh by charity.

7 We walk by faith and not by sight.   2 Cor. v.

18 While we look not at the things which 2 Cor. iv. are seen, but at the things which are not seen. For the things which are seen, are temporal: but the things which are not seen, are eternal.

26 You are all the children of God by Gal. iii. faith, in Christ Jesus.

19 Having faith and a good conscience, 1 Tim. i. which some rejecting have made shipwreck concerning the faith.

8 By grace you are saved through faith, Ephes. ii.

and that not of yourselves, for it is the gift of God.

6 Without faith it is impossible to please God. For he that cometh to God, must believe that he is, and is a rewarder of them that seek him. — Heb. xi.

16 In all things taking the shield of faith, wherewith you may be able to extinguish all the fiery darts of the most wicked one. — Ephes. vi.

7 That the trial of your faith, much more precious than gold (which is tried by the fire) may be found unto praise, and glory, and honour, at the appearing of Jesus Christ. — 1 S. Peter i.

8 Whom having not seen you love: In whom also now, though you see him not, you believe; and believing, shall rejoice with an unspeakable and glorified joy:

9 Receiving the end of your faith, even the salvation of your souls.

14 ... If a man say he hath faith, but hath not works? Shall faith be able to save him? — S. James ii.

17 Faith, if it have not works, is dead in itself.

26 For as the body without the spirit is dead, so also faith without works is dead.

FAMILY UNION.

1 BEHOLD how good, and how pleasant it is for brethren to dwell together in unity. — Ps. cxxxii.

Family Union.

24 So (Joseph) sent away his brethren, and at their departing said to them: Be not angry in the way. — Gen. xlv.

21 Fear not: I will feed you and your children. And he comforted them, and spoke gently and mildly. — Gen. l.

19 A brother that is helped by his brother, is like a strong city . . . — Prov. xviii.

1 With three things my spirit is pleased, which are approved before God, and men: — Ecclus. xxv.

2 The concord of brethren, and the love of neighbours, and man and wife that agree well together.

4 If (thy brother) sin against thee seven times in a day, and seven times in a day be converted unto thee, saying, I repent: forgive him. — S. Luke xvii.

FASTING.

11 Know ye that the Lord will hear your prayers, if you continue with perseverance in fastings and prayers in the sight of the Lord. — Judith iv.

8 Prayer is good with fasting and alms, more than to lay up treasures of gold. — Tobias xii.

3 Why have we fasted, and thou hast not regarded: have we humbled our souls, and thou hast not taken notice? Behold in the day of your fast your own will is found, and you exact of all your debtors. — Isaias lviii.

4 Behold you fast for debates and strife,

and strike with the fist wickedly. Do not fast as you have done until this day, to make your cry heard on high.

5 ... When you fasted, and mourned ... did you keep a fast unto me?   Zach. vii.

31 A man that fasteth for his sins, and doth the same again, what doth his humbling himself profit him? Who will hear his prayer?   Ecclus. xxxiv.

12 Now therefore saith the Lord: Be converted to me with all your heart, in fasting and in weeping and in mourning.   Joel ii.

5 And the men of Ninive believed in God: and they proclaimed a fast, and put on sackcloth from the greatest to the least.   Jonas iii.

9 Who can tell if God will turn, and forgive: and will turn away from his fierce anger, and we shall not perish?

14 Then came to (Jesus) the disciples of John, saying: Why do we and the Pharisees fast often, but thy disciples do not fast?   S. Matt. ix.

15 And Jesus said to them: Can the children of the bridegroom mourn, as long as the bridegroom is with them? but the days will come when the bridegroom shall be taken away from them, and then they shall fast.

16 And when you fast, be not, as the hypocrites, sad: for they disfigure their faces, that they may appear unto men to fast. Amen   S. Matt. vi.

I say to you, they have received their reward.

17 But thou, when thou fastest, anoint thy head, and wash thy face;

18 That thou appear not to men to fast, but to thy Father, who is in secret: and thy Father who seeth in secret, will reward thee.

2 And as they were ministering to the Lord, and fasting, the Holy Ghost said to them: Separate me Saul and Barnabas, for the work whereunto I have taken them. *Acts xiii.*

3 Then they fasting and praying, and imposing their hands upon them, sent them away.

22 And when they had ordained to them priests in every church, and had prayed with fasting, they commended them to the Lord, in whom they believed. *Acts xiv.*

FATHERLESS AND WIDOWS.

14 ... Thou wilt be a helper to the orphan. *Ps. ix. (bis.)*

18 (God) doth judgment to the fatherless and the widow, loveth the stranger, and giveth him food and raiment. *Deut. x.*

22 You shall not hurt a widow or an orphan. *Ex. xxii.*

23 If you hurt them they will cry out to me, and I will hear their cry:

24 And my rage shall be enkindled, and I will strike you with the sword, and your wives shall be widows, and your children fatherless.

9 The Lord keepeth the strangers, he will support the fatherless and the widow . . .   Ps. cxlv.

10 Touch not the bounds of little ones: and enter not into the field of the fatherless.   Prov. xxiii.

10 Oppress not the widow, and the fatherless, and the stranger, and the poor . . .   Zach. vii.

17 (The Lord) will not despise the prayers of the fatherless: nor the widow, when she poureth out her complaint.   Ecclus. xxxv.

18 Do not the widow's tears run down the cheek, and her cry against him that causeth them to fall?

19 For from the cheek they go up even to heaven, and the Lord that heareth will not be delighted with them.

11 Leave thy fatherless children: I will make them live: and thy widows shall hope in me.   Jer. xlix.

4 And Judith . . . was a widow now three years and six months.   Judith viii.

5 And she made herself a private chamber in the upper part of her house, in which she abode shut up with her maids,

6 And she wore hair-cloth upon her loins, and fasted all the days of her life, except the sabbaths, and new-moons, and the feasts of the house of Israel.

8 And she was greatly renowned among all, because she feared the Lord very much, neither was there any one that spoke an ill word of her.

37 And (Anna) was a widow until four- S. Luke
score and four years; who departed not ii.
from the temple, by fasting and prayers
serving night and day.

14 Wo to you scribes and Pharisees, hypo- S. Matt.
crites: because you devour the houses of xxiii.
widows, praying long prayers. For this you
shall receive the greater judgment.

3 Honour widows who are widows in- 1 Tim.
deed. v.

4 But if any widow have children, or grandchildren; let her learn first to govern her own house, and to make a return of duty to her parents: for this is acceptable before God.

5 But she that is a widow indeed, and desolate, let her trust in God, and continue in supplications and prayers night and day.

6 For she that liveth in pleasures, is dead while she is living.

7 And this give in charge, that they may be blameless.

9 Let a widow be chosen* not under threescore years of age, who hath been the wife of one husband,

* As deaconess.

10 Having testimony of her good works, if she have brought up children, if she have exercised hospitality, if she have washed the saints' feet, if she have ministered to them that suffer tribulation, if she have diligently followed every good work.

11 But the younger widows avoid. For when they have grown wanton in Christ, they will marry;

12 Having damnation, because they have made void their first faith.*

13 And withal being idle, they learn to go about from house to house: and are not only idle, but tattlers also, and busy-bodies, speaking things which they ought not.

14 I will, therefore, that the younger should marry, bear children, be mistresses of families, give no occasion to the adversary to speak evil.

15 For some are already turned aside after satan.

27 Religion clean and undefiled before *S. James* God and the Father, is this: to visit the fatherless and widows in their tribulations: and to keep one's self unspotted from this world.

* Their vow, by which they had engaged themselves to Christ.

FEAR OF GOD.*

13 ... Fear God, and keep his com- Eccles.
mandments: for this is all man. xii.

24 Fear the Lord and serve him in truth 1 Kings
and with your whole heart, for you have seen xii.
the great works he hath done among you.

28 ... Behold the fear of the Lord, that Job
is wisdom: and to depart from evil, is un- xxviii.
derstanding.

10 The fear of the Lord is holy, enduring Ps. xviii.
for ever and ever ...

10 Fear the Lord, all ye saints: for there Ps. xxxiii.
is no want to them that fear him.

13 His soul shall dwell in good things: Ps. xxiv.
and his seed shall inherit the land.

13 He hath blessed all that fear the Lord, Ps. cxiii.
both little and great.

1 Blessed are all they that fear the Lord; Ps.
that walk in his ways. cxxvii.

19 (The Lord) Will do the will of them Ps.
that fear him: and he will hear their prayer, cxliv.
and save them.

11 The Lord taketh pleasure in them that Ps.
fear him: and in them that hope in his cxlvi.
mercy.

10 The fear of the Lord is the beginning Prov. ix.
of wisdom ...

* Filial fear.

26 In the fear of the Lord is confidence of strength, and there shall be hope for his children. Prov. xiv.

27 The fear of the Lord is a fountain of life, to decline from the ruin of death.

6 ... By the fear of the Lord men depart from evil. Prov. xvi.

11 The fear of the Lord is honour, and glory, and gladness, and a crown of joy. Ecclus. i.

12 The fear of the Lord shall delight the heart, and shall give joy, and gladness, and length of days.

16 The fear of the Lord is the beginning of wisdom, and was created with the faithful in the womb, it walketh with chosen women, and is known with the just and faithful.

19 It shall go well with him that feareth the Lord, and in the days of his end he shall be blessed.

22 The fear of the Lord is a crown of wisdom, filling up peace and the fruit of salvation.

27 The fear of the Lord driveth out sin.

7 Ye that fear the Lord, wait for his mercy: and go not aside from him, lest ye fall. Ecclus. ii.

8 Ye that fear the Lord, believe him; and your reward shall not be made void.

9 Ye that fear the Lord, hope in him; and mercy shall come to you for your delight.

10 Ye that fear the Lord love him, and your hearts shall be enlightened.

18 They that fear the Lord, will not be incredulous to his word: and they that love him will keep his way.

20 They that fear the Lord, will prepare their hearts, and in his sight will sanctify their souls.

21 They that fear the Lord, keep his commandments, and will have patience even until his visitation.

25 The fear of the Lord is the glory of the rich, and of the honourable, and of the poor. — Ecclus. x.

1 He that feareth God, will do good... Ecclus. xv.

18 ... The fear of God is all wisdom ... Ecclus. xix.

16 The fear of God is the beginning of his love: and the beginning of faith is to be fast joined unto it. — Ecclus. xxv.

1 No evils shall happen to him that feareth the Lord, but in temptation God will keep him, and deliver him from evils. — Ecclus. xxxiii.

17 The soul of him that feareth the Lord is blessed. — Ecclus. xxxiv.

19 The eyes of the Lord are upon them that fear him, he is their powerful protector, and strong stay, a defence from the heat, and a cover from the sun at noon. — Ecclus. xxxiv.

20 A preservation from stumbling, and a help from falling; he raiseth up the soul,

and enlighteneth the eyes, and giveth health, and life, and blessing.

27 There is no want in the fear of the Lord, and it needeth not to seek for help. — Ecclus. xl.

6 ... The fear of the Lord is his treasure. — Isaias xxxiii.

13 Sanctify the Lord of hosts himself; and let him be your fear, and let him be your dread.
14 And he shall be a sanctification to you ... — Isaias viii.

9 ... Salvation shall be to them that fear thy name ... — Mich. vi.

7 Because for this end thou hast put thy fear in our hearts, to the intent that we should call upon thy name ... — Baruch. iii.

5 ... Fear ye him, who after he hath killed, hath power to cast into hell: Yea, I say to you, fear him. — S. Luke xii.

50 His mercy is from generation unto generations, to them that fear him. — S. Luke i.

26 Men brethren, sons of the race of Abraham, and whosoever among you fear God, to you the word of this salvation is sent. — Acts xiii.

35 In every nation, he that feareth him, and worketh justice, is acceptable to him. — Acts x.

1 ... Let us cleanse ourselves from all defilement of the flesh and of the spirit, perfecting sanctification in the fear of God. — 2 Cor. vii.

18 The time is come ... to render a reward to thy servants the prophets, and to the saints, and to them that fear thy name, little and great ... — Apoc. xi.

4 Who shall not fear thee, O Lord, and magnify thy name? For thou only art holy. — Apoc. xv.

FLATTERY.'

17 They say to them that blaspheme me: The Lord hath said: You shall have peace: and to every one that walketh in the perverseness of his own heart, they have said: No evil shall come upon you. — Jer. xxiii.

12 ... O my people, they that call thee blessed, the same deceive thee, and destroy the way of thy steps. — Isaias iii.

10 There is no truth in their mouth: their heart is vain.' — Ps. v.

11 Their throat is an open sepulchre: they dealt deceitfully with their tongues ...

3 ... With deceitful lips, and with a double heart have they spoken. — Ps. xi.

6 Better are the wounds of a friend, than the deceitful kisses of an enemy. — Prov. xxvii.

22 ... His words are smoother than oil, and the same are darts. — Ps. liv.

15 An enemy speaketh sweetly with his lips, but in his heart he lieth in wait, to throw thee into a pit. — Ecclus. xii.

18 An enemy hath tears in his eyes, and

while he pretendeth to help thee, will undermine thy feet.

26 In the sight of thy eyes he will sweeten his mouth, and will admire thy words : but at the last he will writhe with his mouth, and on thy words he will lay a stumbling-block : — Ecclus. xxvii.

27 I have hated many things, but not like him, and the Lord will hate him.

3 The sinner is praised in the desires of his soul: and the unjust man is blessed. — Ps. ix.

4 They that forsake the law, praise the wicked man . . . — Prov. xxviii.

24 They that say to the wicked man: Thou art just : shall be cursed by the people, and the tribes shall abhor them. — Prov. xxiv.

25 They that rebuke him, shall be praised: and a blessing shall come upon them.

5 A man that speaketh to his friend with flattering and dissembling words, spreadeth a net for his feet. — Prov. xxix.

26 When a rich man hath been deceived, he hath many helpers : he hath spoken proud things, and they have justified him. — Ecclus. xiii.

28 The rich man spoke, and all held their peace, and what he said they extol even to the clouds.

16 . . . Admiring persons for gain's sake. — S. Jude.

18 . . . Pleasing speeches, and good words, seduce the hearts of the innocent. — Rom. xvi.

21 And upon a day appointed, Herod — Acts xii.

Flattery.

being arrayed in kingly apparel, sat in the judgment-seat, and made an oration to them.

22 And the people made acclamation saying: It is the voice of a god, and not of a man.

23 And forthwith an Angel of the Lord struck him, because he had not given the honour to God: and being eaten up by worms, he gave up the ghost.

FOOLS.

8 He that deviseth to do evils, shall be called a fool. — Prov. xxiv.

12 The wicked life of a wicked fool is worse than death. — Ecclus. xxii.

15 The way of a fool is right in his own eyes ... — Prov. xii.

20 ... A friend of fools shall become like to them. — Prov. xiii.

3 In the mouth of a fool is the rod of pride ... — Prov. xiv.

9 A fool will laugh at sin ...

24 ... The folly of fools, is imprudence.

2 ... The mouth of fools, bubbleth out folly. — Prov. xv.

5 A fool laugheth at the instruction of his father ...

25 A foolish son is the anger of the father: and the sorrow of the mother that bore him. — Prov. xvii.

27 It is the folly of a man to hearken at the door: and a wise man will be grieved with the disgrace. — Ecclus. xxi.

29 The heart of fools is in their mouth: and the mouth of wise men is in their heart.

6 The fool will speak foolish things, and his heart will work iniquity, to practise hypocrisy, and speak to the Lord deceitfully, and to make empty the soul of the hungry, and take away drink from the thirsty. — Isaias xxxii.

15 ... The number of fools is infinite. — Eccles. i.

26 Every one that heareth these my words, and doth them not, shall be like a foolish man that built his house upon the sand, — S. Matt. vii.

27 And the rain fell, and the floods came, and the winds blew, and they beat upon that house, and it fell, and great was the fall thereof.

3 The five foolish (virgins), having taken their lamps, did not take oil with them. — S. Matt. xxv.

19 ... Soul, thou hast much goods laid up for many years, take thy rest, eat, drink, make good cheer. — S. Luke xii.

20 But God said to him: Thou fool ...*

22 Professing themselves to be wise they became fools. — Rom. i.

23 And they changed the glory of the

---

* See end of 20th and following verses in Covetousness.

incorruptible God, into the likeness of the image of a corruptible man, and of birds and of four-footed beasts and of creeping things.

FORGIVENESS OF INJURIES.

12 Forgive us our debts, as we also forgive our debtors. — S. Matt. vi.

2 Forgive thy neighbour if he hath hurt thee: and then shall thy sins be forgiven to thee when thou prayest. — Ecclus. xxviii.

11 The learning of a man is known by patience: and his glory is to pass over wrongs. — Prov. xix.

37 ... Forgive, and you shall be forgiven. — S. Luke vi.

14 For if you will forgive men their offences, your heavenly Father will also forgive you your offences. — S. Matt. vi.

15 But if you will not forgive men, neither will your Father forgive you your offences.

23 If therefore thou offer thy gift at the altar, and there thou remember that thy brother hath anything against thee; — S. Matt. v.

24 Leave there thy gift before the altar, and first go to be reconciled to thy brother, and then come and offer thy gift.

44 ... Love your enemies: do good to them that hate you: and pray for them that persecute and calumniate you:

45 That you may be the children of your Father, who is in heaven: who maketh his sun to rise upon the good and bad, and raineth upon the just and the unjust.

21 Then came Peter unto him, and said: Lord, how often shall my brother offend against me, and I forgive him? till seven times?

S. Matt. xviii.

22 Jesus said to him: I say not to thee, till seven times: but till seventy times seven times?

23 Therefore is the kingdom of heaven likened to a king, who would take an account of his servants.

24 And when he had begun to take the account, one was brought to him, that owed him ten thousand talents.

25 And as he had not wherewith to pay it, his lord commanded that he should be sold, and his wife and children, and all that he had, and payment to be made.

26 But that servant falling down, besought him saying: Have patience with me, and I will pay thee all.

27 And the lord of that servant, being moved with compassion, let him go, and forgave him the debt.

28 But when that servant was gone out, he found one of his fellow-servants that owed him a hundred pence, and laying hold of

him, he throttled him, saying: Pay what thou owest:

29 And his fellow-servant, falling down, besought him, saying: Have patience with me, and I will pay thee all.

30 And he would not: but went and cast him into prison, till he should pay the debt.

31 Now his fellow-servants seeing what was done, were very much grieved: and they came, and told their lord all that was done.

32 Then his lord called him; and said to him: Thou wicked servant, I forgave thee all the debt, because thou besought me:

33 Shouldest not thou then have had compassion also on thy fellow-servant, even as I had compassion on thee?

34 And his lord being angry, delivered him to the torturers, until he should pay all the debt.

35 So also shall my heavenly Father do to you, if you forgive not every one his brother from your hearts.

21 Be not overcome by evil, but overcome evil by good. Rom. xii.

9 Grudge, not, brethren, one against another, that you may not be judged. Behold the judge standeth before the door. S. James v.

31 Let all bitterness and anger, and indignation and clamour, and blasphemy be put away from you, with all malice. Ephes. iv.

32 And be ye kind one to another, merciful, forgiving one another, even as God hath forgiven you in Christ.

15 ... Lest any root of bitterness spring- Heb. xii.
ing up do hinder, and by it many be defiled.

FRATERNAL REPROOF.

17 Thou shalt not hate thy brother in Lev. xix.
thy heart, but reprove him openly, lest thou
incur sin through him.

23 ... Reproofs of instruction are the Prov. vi.
way of life.

5 The just man shall correct me in mercy, Ps. cxl.
and shall reprove me ...

8 ... Rebuke a wise man, and he will Prov.
love thee. ix.

23 He that rebuketh a man, shall after- Prov.
wards find favour with him, more than he xxviii.
that by a flattering tongue deceiveth him.

17 The way of life to him that observeth Prov. x.
correction...

1 He that loveth correction, loveth know- Prov.
ledge: but he that hateth reproof is foolish. xii.

18 ... He that yieldeth to reproof, shall Prov.
be glorified. xiii.

5 ... He that regardeth reproofs shall Prov. xv.
become prudent.

31 The ear that heareth the reproofs of
life, shall abide in the midst of the wise.

6 It is better to be rebuked by a wise man, than to be deceived by the flattery of fools. — Ecclus. vii.

28 ... A man that is prudent and well instructed will not murmur when he is reproved ... — Ecclus. x.

7 Before thou enquire blame no man: when thou hast enquired, reprove justly. — Ecclus. xi.

13 Reprove a friend, lest he may not have understood, and say I did it not: or if he did it, that he may do it no more.

14 Reprove thy neighbour, for it may be he hath not said it: and if he hath said it, that he may not say it again.

17 For who is there that hath not offended with his tongue? Admonish thy neighbour before thou threaten him. — Ecclus. xix.

1 How much better it is to reprove, than to be angry ... — Ecclus. xx.

3 Take heed to yourselves. If thy brother sin against thee, reprove him: and if he do penance, forgive him. — S. Luke xvii.

15 But if thy brother shall offend against thee, go, and rebuke him between thee and him alone. If he shall hear thee, thou shalt gain thy brother. — S. Matt. xviii.

14 And I myself, also, my brethren, am assured of you, that you also are full of love, replenished with all knowledge, so that you are able to admonish one another. — Rom. xv.

1 If a man be overtaken in any fault, Gal. vi.
you, who are spiritual, instruct such a one in
the spirit of meekness, considering thyself,
lest thou also be tempted.

14 And we beseech you, brethren, rebuke 1 Thess.
the unquiet . . . v.

11 And have no fellowship with the un- Ephes. v.
fruitful works of darkness, but rather reprove
them.

13 Exhort one another every day, whilst Heb. iii.
it is called to-day; lest any of you be hardened by the deceitfulness of sin.

2 For in many things we all offend . . . S. James iii.

FRATERNAL SYMPATHY.

48 My eye hath run down with streams Lament.
of water, for the destruction of the daughter iii.
of my people.

17 But if you will not hear this, my soul Jer. xiii.
shall weep in secret for your pride: weeping
it shall weep, and my eyes shall run down
with tears, because the flock of the Lord
is carried away captive.

3 It is better to go to the house of mourn- Eccles.
ing, than to the house of feasting: for in that vii.
we are put in mind of the end of all, and the
living thinketh what is to come.

38 Be not wanting in comforting them Ecclus.
that weep, and walk with them that mourn. vii.

39 Be not slow to visit the sick: for by these things thou shalt be confirmed in love.

17 ... We have piped to you, and you have not danced: we have lamented, and you have not mourned.   S. Matt. xi.

15 Rejoice with them that rejoice, weep with them that weep.   Rom. xii.

2 Bear ye one another's burdens: and so you shall fulfil the law of Christ.   Gal. vi.

8 ... Having compassion one of another ...   1 S. Peter iii.

14 ... Comfort the feeble-minded, support the weak, be patient towards all men.   1 Thess. v.

3 Remember them that are in bands, as if you were bound with them; and them that are afflicted, as being yourselves also in the body.   Heb. xiii.

FRIENDSHIP.

18 ... Thou shalt love thy friend as thyself. I am the Lord.   Lev. xix.

10 Thy own friend, and thy father's friend forsake not ...   Prov. xxvii.

29 Practise not evil against thy friend, when he hath confidence in thee.   Prov. iii.

12 He that despiseth his friend is mean of heart ...   Prov. xi.

13 ... He that is faithful, concealeth the thing committed to him by his friend.

26 He that neglecteth a loss for the sake Prov. xii.
of a friend, is just . . .

17 He that is a friend loveth at all times: Prov.
and a brother is proved in distress. xvii.

18 As he is guilty that shooteth arrows, Prov.
and lances unto death: xxvi.

19 So is the man that hurteth his friend deceitfully: and when he is taken, saith: I did it in jest.

7 If thou wouldst get a friend, try him be- Ecclus.
fore thou takest him, and do not credit him vi.
easily.

8 For there is a friend for his own occasion, and he will not abide in the day of thy trouble.

9 And there is a friend that turneth to enmity: and there is a friend that will disclose hatred, and strife, and reproaches.

10 And there is a friend a companion at the table, and he will not abide in the day of distress.

11 A friend if he continue steadfast, shall be to thee as thyself, and shall act with confidence among them of thy household.

14 A faithful friend is a strong defence: and he that hath found him, hath found a treasure.

15 Nothing can be compared to a faithful friend, and no weight of gold and silver is able to countervail the goodness of his fidelity.

16 A faithful friend is the medicine of life and immortality: and they that fear the Lord, shall find him.

17 He that feareth God, shall likewise have good friendship: because according to him shall his friend be.

14 Forsake not an old friend, for the new will not be like to him.   Ecclus. ix.

15 A new friend is as new wine: it shall grow old, and thou shalt drink it with pleasure.

8 A friend shall not be known in prosperity, and an enemy shall not be hidden in adversity.   Ecclus. xii.

9 In the prosperity of a man, his enemies are grieved: and a friend is known in his adversity.

12 Blessed is he that findeth a true friend, and that declareth justice to an ear that heareth.   Ecclus. xxv.

15 Admonish thy friend: for there is often a fault committed.   Ecclus. xix.

16 And believe not every word. There is one that slippeth with the tongue, but not from his heart.

13 Do good to thy friend before thou die, and according to thy ability stretching out thy hand give to the poor.   Ecclus. xiv.

6 Forget not thy friend in thy mind, and be not unmindful of him in thy riches.   Ecclus. xxxvii.

15 Be continually with a holy man, whomsoever thou shalt know to observe the fear of God.

16 Whose soul is according to thine own soul: and who, when thou shalt stumble in the dark, will be sorry for thee.

13 Greater love than this no man hath, S. John that a man lay down his life for his friends. xv.

14 You are my friends, if you do the things that I command you ...

15 ... I have called you friends ...

GENERAL PRECEPTS AND EXHORTATION.

8 I WILL shew thee, O man, what is good, Mich. vi. and what the Lord requireth of thee: verily, to do judgment, and to love mercy, and to walk solicitous* with thy God.

35 Do not any unjust thing in judgment, Lev. xix. in rule, in weight, or in measure.

1 Thou shalt not receive the voice of a Ex. xxiii. lie: neither shalt thou join thy hand to bear false witness for a wicked person.

12 Six days shalt thou work: the seventh day thou shalt cease, that thy ox and thy ass may rest: and the son of thy handmaid and the stranger may be refreshed.

8 Keep my precepts and do them. I am Lev. xx. the Lord that sanctify you.

* Anxiously or carefully.

4 Follow the Lord your God, and fear him, and keep his commandments, and hear his voice: him you shall serve, and to him you shall cleave. — Deut. xiii.

16 The fathers shall not be put to death for the children, nor the children for the fathers, but every one shall die for his own sin. — Deut. xxiv.

17 Thou shalt not pervert the judgment of the stranger nor of the fatherless, neither shalt thou take away the widow's raiment for a pledge.

7 Make thyself affable to the congregation of the poor, and humble thy soul to the ancient, and bow thy head to a great man. — Ecclus. iv.

22 Pride was not made for men: nor wrath for the race of women. — Ecclus. x.

18 Judge of the disposition of thy neighbour by thyself. — Ecclus. xxxi.

13 Kindle not the coals of sinners by rebuking them lest thou be burnt with the flame of the fire of their sins. — Ecclus. viii.

10 My son, meddle not with many matters . . . — Ecclus. xi.

25 . . . He that undertaketh many things shall fall into judgment . . . — Ecclus. xxix.

7 Offend not against the multitude of a city, neither cast thyself in upon the people, — Ecclus. vii.

8 Nor bind sin to sin: for even in one thou shalt not be unpunished.

25 Go to the side of the holy age, with them that live and give praise to God.   Ecclus. xvii.

14 Talk not much with a fool, and go not with him that hath no sense.   Ecclus. xxii.

1 Have they made thee ruler? be not lifted up: be among them as one of them.   Ecclus. xxxii.

2 Have care of them, and so sit down, and when thou hast acquitted thyself of all thy charge take thy place.

3 That thou mayest rejoice for them ...

18 Remember thy father and thy mother, for thou sittest in the midst of great men: Ecclus. xxiii.

19 Lest God forget thee in their sight ...

30 There is no wisdom, there is no prudence, there is no counsel against the Lord.   Prov. xxi.

2 Blessed is the man ... that keepeth his hands from doing any evil.   Isaias lvi.

9 ... Judge ye true judgment, and shew ye mercy and compassion every man to his brother.   Zach. vii.

10 And oppress not the widow, and the fatherless, and the stranger, and the poor: and let not a man devise evil in his heart against his brother.

12 The night is past, and the day is at hand. Let us therefore cast off the works of darkness, and put on the armour of light.   Rom. xiii.

13 Let us walk honestly as in the day: not in rioting and drunkenness, not in

chambering and impurities, not in contention and envy.

9 And this I pray, that your charity may more and more abound in knowledge and in all understanding: [Philip i.]

10 That you may approve the better things, that you may be sincere and without offence unto the day of Christ.

11 Filled with the fruit of justice through Jesus Christ, unto the glory and praise of God.

1 Know also this, that, in the last days, shall come on dangerous times. [2 Tim. iii.]

2 Men shall be lovers of themselves, covetous, haughty, proud, blasphemers, disobedient to parents, ungrateful, wicked,

3 Without affection, without peace, slanderers, incontinent, unmerciful, without kindness,

4 Traitors, stubborn, puffed up, and lovers of pleasures more than of God:

5 Having an appearance indeed, of godliness, but denying the power thereof. Now these avoid.

6 For of this sort are they who creep into houses, and lead captive silly women laden with sins, who are led away with divers desires:

7 Ever learning, and never attaining to the knowledge of the truth.

8 But now put you also all away: anger, Col. iii.
indignation, malice, blasphemy, filthy speech
out of your mouth.

13 Bearing with one another, and forgiving
one another, if any have a complaint against
another. Even as the Lord hath forgiven
you, so do you also.

2 With all humility, and mildness, with Ephes.
patience, supporting one another in charity. iv.

1 Wherefore, laying aside all malice, and 1 S. Peter
all guile, and dissimulations, and envies, and ii.
all detractions.

5 Giving all diligence, join with your faith 2 S. Peter
virtue; and with virtue, knowledge; i.

6 And with knowledge, abstinence; and
with abstinence, patience; and with patience,
piety;

7 And with piety, brotherly love; and
with brotherly love, charity.

8 For if these things be with you, and
abound, they will make you to be neither
empty, nor unfruitful in the knowledge of
our Lord Jesus Christ.

9 For he that hath not these things with
him, is blind, and groping, forgetting his
being purged from his old sins.

GOD.

20 ... Thou canst not see my face: for man shall not see me and live. — Ex. xxxiii.

6 I am the Lord, and I change not ... — Malach. iii.

6 ... I am the first, and I am the last, and besides me there is no God. — Isaias xliv.

9 ... The Lord our God is holy. — Ps. xcviii.

18 The Lord shall reign for ever and ever. — Ex. xv.

27 His dwelling is above, and underneath are the everlasting arms. — Deut. xxxiii.

11 Who is like to thee, among the strong, O Lord? who is like to thee, glorious in holiness, terrible and praiseworthy, doing wonders? — Ex. xv.

13 In thy mercy thou hast been a leader to the people, which thou hast redeemed: and in thy strength thou hast carried them to thy holy habitation.

6 ... O the Lord, the Lord God, merciful and gracious, patient and of much compassion, and true, — Ex. xxxiv.

7 Who keepest mercy unto thousands: who takest away iniquity, and wickedness, and sin, and no man of himself is innocent before thee. Who renderest the iniquity of the fathers to the children, and to the grandchildren, unto the third and fourth generation.

10 The Lord is the true God: he is the living God, and the everlasting king: at his wrath the earth shall tremble, and the nations shall not be able to abide his threatening. — Jer. x.

18 He doth judgment to the fatherless and the widow, loveth the stranger, and giveth him food and raiment. — Deut. x.

3 He hath loved the people, all the saints are in his hand: and they that approach to his feet, shall receive of his doctrine. — Deut. xxxiii.

9 He will keep the feet of the saints, and the wicked shall be silent in darkness, because no man shall prevail by his own strength. — 1 Kings ii.

17 The Lord is just in all his ways: and holy in all his works. — Ps. cxliv.

14 O Lord God of Israel, there is no God like thee in heaven nor in earth: who keepest covenant and mercy with thy servants, that walk before thee with all their hearts. — 2 Paralip. vi.

6 ... O Lord, the God of truth. — Ps. xxx.

14 ... To thee is the poor man left: thou wilt be a helper to the orphan. — Ps. ix.

5 For thou, O Lord, art sweet and mild: and plenteous in mercy to all that call upon thee. — Ps. lxxxv.

8 The Lord is just, and hath loved justice: his countenance hath beheld righteousness. — Ps. x.

God.

15 Thou, O Lord, art a God of compassion, and merciful, patient, and of much mercy, and true. — Ps. lxxxv.

7 Who keepeth truth for ever: who executeth judgment for them that suffer wrong: who giveth food to the hungry. — Ps. cxlv.

The Lord looseth them that are fettered: 8 the Lord enlighteneth the blind.

The Lord lifteth up them that are cast down: the Lord loveth the just:

9 The Lord keepeth the strangers, he will support the fatherless and the widow . . .

20 . . . Wisdom and fortitude are his. — Dan. ii.

12 Mercy and wrath are with him. He is mighty to forgive, and to pour out indignation. — Ecclus. xvi.

13 According as his mercy is, so his correction judgeth a man according to his works.

14 The sinner shall not escape in his rapines, and the patience of him that sheweth mercy shall not be put off.

1 Thou, our God, art gracious and true, patient, and ordering all things in mercy. — Wisd. xv.

16 . . . Thou, O Lord, art our father, our redeemer, from everlasting is thy name. — Isaias lxiii.

18 . . . O most mighty, great, and powerful, the Lord of hosts is thy name: — Jer. xxxii.

19 Great in counsel, and incomprehensible in thought: whose eyes are open upon all the ways of the children of Adam, to render

unto every one according to his ways, and according to the fruit of his devices.

18 Who is a God like to thee, who takest away iniquity, and passest by the sin of the remnant of thy inheritance? ...   Mich. vii.

13 Thy eyes are too pure to behold evil, and thou canst not look on iniquity.   Hab. i.

9 ... Father, who art in heaven ...   S. Matt. vi.

45 ... Who maketh his sun to rise upon the good, and bad, and raineth upon the just and the unjust.   S. Matt. v.

18 ... None is good but one, that is God.   S. Mark x.

49 ... And holy is his name.   S. Luke i.

18 No man hath seen God at any time: the only-begotten Son who is in the bosom of the Father, he hath declared him.   S. John i.

24 God is a spirit: and they that adore him, must adore him in spirit and in truth.   S. John iv.

30 I and the Father are one.   S. John x.

9 ... He that seeth me, seeth the Father also ...   S. John xiv.

13 ... The Son of his love,   Coloss. i.

15 Who is the image of the invisible God, the first-born of every creature.

8 ... God is charity.   1 S. John iv.

3 ... Father of mercies, and the God of all comfort.   2 Cor. i.

5 ... God is light, and in him there is no 1 S. John
darkness.   i.

17 ... Father of lights, with whom there   S. James
is no change, nor shadow of alteration.   i.

17 The king of ages, immortal, invisible   1 Tim. i.
...

16 Who only hath immortality, and in-   1 Tim.
habiteth light inaccessible, whom no man   vi.
hath seen, nor can see, to whom be honour
and empire everlasting.   Amen.|

GOD (COMPASSION OF).

13 As a father hath compassion on his   Ps. cii.
children, so hath the Lord compassion on
them that fear him:

14 For he knoweth our frame. He remembereth that we are dust.

3 (The Lord) healeth the broken of heart,   Ps.
and bindeth up their bruises.   cxlvi.

3 The bruised reed he shall not break,   Isaias
and the smoking flax he shall not quench ...   xlii.

11 He shall feed his flock like a shepherd: Isaias
he shall gather together the lambs with his xl.
arm, and shall take them up in his bosom,
and he himself shall carry them that are
with young.

35 Jesus wept.   S. John xi.

28 Come to me, all you that labour, and   S. Matt.
are burdened, and I will refresh you.   xi.

14 And he coming forth saw a great mul- S. Matt.
titude, and had compassion on them, and xiv.
healed their sick.

36 ... He had compassion on them: S. Matt.
because they were distressed, and lying like ix.
sheep that have no shepherd.

2 I have compassion on the multitude, for S. Mark
behold they have now been with me, three viii.
days, and have nothing to eat.

41 And when he drew near, seeing the S. Luke
city, he wept over it. xix.

40 And there came a leper to him, be- S. Mark
seeching him, and kneeling down, said to i.
him: If thou wilt; thou canst make me
clean.

41 And Jesus having compassion on him,
stretched forth his hand; and touching him,
saith to him: I will. Be thou made clean.

49 ... Lord, come down before that my S. John
son die. iv.

50 Jesus saith to him: Go thy way, thy
son liveth ...

23 And Jesus went about all Galilee, S. Matt.
teaching in their synagogues, and preaching iv.
the gospel of the kingdom: and healing all
manner of sickness, and every infirmity,
among the people.

15 ... And many followed him, and he S. Matt.
healed them all. xii.

12 And when he came nigh to the gate of S. Luke
vii.

the city (called Naim), behold a dead man was carried out, the only son of his mother; and she was a widow: and much people of the city was with her.

13 And when the Lord saw her, he had compassion on her, and said to her: Weep not.

14 And he came near and touched the bier. (And they that carried it, stood still.) And he said: Young man, I say to thee, arise.

15 And he that was dead, sat up, and began to speak. And he delivered him to his mother.

11 ... The Lord is merciful and compassionate.   S. James v.

GOD CREATOR.

1 IN the beginning God created heaven, and earth.   Gen. i.

27 God created man to his own image ...

3 ... He made us, and not we ourselves.   Ps. xcix.

24 ... I am the Lord, that make all things, that alone stretch out the heavens, that establish the earth, and there is none with me.   Isaias xliv.

6 Thou thyself, O Lord, alone, thou hast made heaven, and the heaven of heavens, and all the host thereof: the earth and all things that are in it: the seas and all that   2 Esdras ix.

are therein: and thou givest life to all these things, and the host of heaven adoreth thee.

3 ... Holy, holy, holy, the Lord God of hosts, all the earth is full of his glory. — Isaias vi.

3 His glory covered the heavens, and the earth is full of his praise. — Habac. iii.

4 The works of God are perfect, and all his ways are judgments ... — Deut. xxxii.

7 He stretched out the north over the empty space, and hangeth the earth upon nothing. — Job xxvi.

2 The heavens show forth the glory of God, and the firmament declareth the work of his hands. — Ps. xviii.

3 Day to day uttereth speech, and night to night sheweth knowledge.

4 There are no speeches nor languages, where their voices are not heard.

26 In the beginning, O Lord, thou foundest the earth: and the heavens are the works of thy hands. — Ps. ci.

27 They shall perish but thou remainest: and all of them shall grow old like a garment: and as a vesture thou shalt change them, and they shall be changed.

28 But thou art always the self-same, and thy years shall not fail.

5 Thou hast given me, O Lord, a delight in thy doings: and in the works of thy hands I shall rejoice. — Ps. xci.

10 Let all thy works, O Lord, praise thee; and let thy saints bless thee. — Ps. cxliv.

11 They shall speak of the glory of thy kingdom: and shall tell of thy power.

7 He set his eye upon their hearts to shew the greatness of his works. — Ecclus. xvii.

12 He that maketh the earth by his power, that prepareth the world by his wisdom, and stretcheth out the heavens by his knowledge. — Jer. x.

13 At his voice he giveth a multitude of waters in the heaven, and lifteth up the clouds from the ends of the earth: he maketh lightnings for rain, and bringeth forth the wind out of his treasures.

26 ... By his magnificence the clouds run hither and thither. — Deut. xxxiii.

1 He that liveth for ever created all things together. God only shall be justified, and he remaineth an invincible king for ever. — Ecclus. xviii.

2 Who is able to declare his works?

3 For who shall search out his glorious acts?

4 And who shall shew forth the power of his majesty? or who shall be able to declare his mercy?

5 Nothing may be taken away, nor added, neither is it possible to find out the glorious works of God.

1 In the beginning was the Word, and the Word was with God, and the Word was God. — S. John i.

2 The same was in the beginning with God.

3 All things were made by him: and without him was made nothing that was made.

16 For in him were all things created in heaven, and on earth, visible, and invisible, whether thrones, or dominations, or principalities, or powers: all things were created by him, and in him: Coloss. i.

17 And he is before all, and by him all things consist.

3 ... Great and wonderful are thy works, O Lord God Almighty: just and true are thy ways, O King of ages.   Apoc. xv.

GOD'S HATRED.

7 ... I ABHOR the wicked.   Exod. xxiii.

16 The Lord thy God ... hateth all injustice.   Deut. xxv.

15 He that justifieth the wicked, and he that condemneth the just, both are abominable before God.   Prov. xvii.

7 Thou hatest all the workers of iniquity: thou wilt destroy all that speak a lie. The bloody and the deceitful man the Lord will abhor.   Ps. v.

32 Every mocker is an abomination to the Lord...   Prov. iii.

5 Every proud man is an abomination to the Lord ...   Prov. xvi.

10 Diverse weights and diverse measures, both are abominable before God.   Prov. xx.

22 Lying lips are an abomination to the Lord.   Prov. xii.

17 (The Lord hateth) Haughty eyes, a lying tongue, hands that shed innocent blood.   Prov. vi.

18 A heart that deviseth wicked plots, feet that are swift to run into mischief,

19 A deceitful witness that uttereth lies, and him that soweth discord among brethren.

13 ... I hate arrogance and pride, and every wicked way, and a mouth with a double tongue.   Prov. viii.

9 To God the wicked and his wickedness are hateful alike.   Wisd. xiv.

17 Let none of you imagine evil in your hearts against his friend: and love not a false oath: for all these are the things that I hate, saith the Lord.   Zach. viii.

4 Do not commit this abominable thing (idolatry), which I hate.   Jer. xliv.

4 ... We know that an idol is nothing in the world, and that there is no God, but one.   1 Cor. viii.

30 Detracters, hateful to God.   Rom. i.

GOD'S LOVE.*

10 My father and my mother have left me : but the Lord hath taken me up. Ps. xxvi.

25 Thou lovest all things that are, and hatest none of the things which thou hast made: for thou didst not appoint, or make anything hating it. Wisd. xi.

26 And how could anything endure, if thou wouldst not? or be preserved, if not called by thee?

27 But thou sparest all : because they are thine, O Lord, who lovest souls.

13 In thy mercy thou hast been a leader to the people which thou hast redeemed : and in thy strength thou hast carried them to thy holy habitation. Ex. xv.

31 In the wilderness (as thou hast seen) the Lord thy God hath carried thee, as a man is wont to carry his little son, all the way you have come, until you came to this place. Deut. i.

9 ... In his love, and in his mercy he redeemed them, and he carried them and lifted them up all the days of old. Isaias lxiii.

17 The Lord thy God in the midst of thee is mighty, he will save : he will rejoice over thee with gladness, he will be silent in his love, he will be joyful over thee in praise. Soph. iii.

* See Jesus Saviour.

13 Give praise, O ye heavens, and rejoice, O earth, ye mountains, give praise with jubilation: because the Lord hath comforted his people, and will have mercy on his poor ones. — Isaias xlix.

13 As one whom the mother caresseth, so will I comfort you, and you shall be comforted in Jerusalem. — Isaias lxvi.

5 ... I will not leave thee, neither will I forsake thee. — Heb. xiii.

12 I, I myself will comfort you ... — Isaias li.

15 Can a woman forget her infant, so as not to have pity on the son of her womb? and if she should forget, yet will not I forget thee. — Isaias xlix.

4 Even to your old age I am the same, and to your grey hairs I will carry you: I have made you, and I will bear, I will carry, and I will save. — Isaias xlvi.

16 Behold, I have graven thee in my hands ... — Isaias xlix.

3 ... Yea, I have loved thee with an everlasting love, therefore have I drawn thee, taking pity on thee. — Jer. xxxi

15 I will feed my sheep: and I will cause them to lie down, saith the Lord God. — Ezech. xxxiv.

16 I will seek that which was lost: and that which was driven away, I will bring again: and I will bind up that which was broken, and I will strengthen that which was

weak, and that which was fat and strong I will preserve: and I will feed them in judgment.

4 I will draw them with the cords of Adam, with the bands of love . . . Osee xi.

14 I will deliver them out of the hand of death. I will redeem them from death: O death, I will be thy death, O hell, I will be thy bite . . . Osee xiii.

8 . . . He that toucheth you, toucheth the apple of my eye. Zech. ii.

16 God so loved the world, as to give his only begotten Son; that whosoever believeth in him, may not perish, but may have life everlasting. S. John iii.

17 For God sent not his Son into the world, to judge the world, but that the world may be saved by him.

9 As the Father hath loved me, I also have loved you. Abide in my love. S. John xv.

27 The Father himself loveth you, because you have loved me, and have believed that I came out from God. S. John xvi.

8 God commendeth his charity towards us: because when as yet we were sinners, according to the time, Rom. v.

9 Christ died for us . . .

32 He that spared not even his own Son: but delivered him up for us all, how hath he not also, with him, given us all things? Rom. viii.

God's Love.

38 For I am sure that neither death, nor life, nor angels, nor principalities, nor powers, nor things present, nor things to come, nor might,

39 Nor height, nor depth, nor any other creature shall be able to separate us from the love of God, which is in Christ Jesus our Lord.

4 God, who is rich in mercy, for his exceeding charity wherewith he loved us, — Ephes. ii.

5 Even when we were dead in sins, hath quickened us together in Christ (by whose grace you are saved).

1 Behold what manner of charity the Father hath bestowed upon us, that we should be called, and should be the sons of God ... — 1 S. John iii.

16 In this we have known the charity of God, because he hath laid down his life for us ...

9 By this hath the charity of God appeared towards us, because God hath sent his only begotten Son into the world, that we may live by him. — 1 S. John iv.

10 In this is charity: not as though we had loved God, but because he hath first loved us, and sent his Son to be a propitiation for our sins.

11 My dearest, if God hath so loved us; we ought also to love one another.

16 And we have known and have believed

the charity, which God hath to us: God is charity . . .

GOD (MERCY OF).

6 SHEWING mercy unto thousands to them that love me, and keep my commandments. — Ex. xx.

12 . . . I am holy, saith the Lord, and I will not be angry for ever. — Jer. iii.

11 Shall I not spare Ninive, that great city, in which there are more than a hundred and twenty thousand persons, that know not how to distinguish between their right hand and their left, and many beasts? — Jonas iv.

2 . . . When thou art angry, thou wilt remember mercy. — Hab. iii.

18 The Lord is patient and full of mercy . . . — Numb. xiv.

10 . . . Mercy shall encompass him that hopeth in the Lord. — Ps. xxxi.

5 He loveth mercy and judgment; the earth is full of the mercy of the Lord. — Ps. xxxii.

9 The Lord is sweet to all: and his tender mercies are over all his works. — Ps. cxliv.

8 The Lord is compassionate and merciful: long suffering and plenteous in mercy. — Ps. cii.

11 For according to the height of the heaven above the earth: he hath strengthened his mercy towards them that fear him.

17 The mercy of the Lord is from eternity and unto eternity upon them that fear him.

God (Mercy of).

8 Let the mercies of the Lord give glory to him: and his wonderful works to the children of men. Ps. cvi.

23 According to his greatness, so also is his mercy with him. Ecclus. ii.

12 The compassion of man is towards his neighbour: but the mercy of God is upon all flesh. Ecclus. xviii.

13 He hath mercy, and teacheth, and correcteth, as a shepherd doth his flock.

18 The Lord waiteth that he may have mercy on you: and therefore shall he be exalted sparing you . . . Isaias xxx.

7 For a small moment have I forsaken thee, but with great mercies will I gather thee. Isaias liv.

8 In a moment of indignation have I hid my face a little while from thee, but with everlasting kindness have I had mercy on thee, said the Lord thy Redeemer.

32 For if he hath cast off, he will also have mercy, according to the multitude of his mercies. Lament. iii.

33 For he hath not willingly afflicted, nor cast off the children of men.

50 His mercy is from generation unto generations, to them that fear him. S. Luke i.

4 Who will have all men to be saved, and to come to the knowledge of the truth. 1 Tim. ii.

9 The Lord delayeth not his promise, as 2 Peter iii.

some imagine : but beareth patiently for your sake, not willing that any should perish, but that all should return to penance.

GOD (PRESENCE OF).

24 SHALL a man be hid in secret places, and I not see him, saith the Lord? do not I fill heaven and earth, saith the Lord? — Jer. xxiii.

22 There is no darkness, and there is no shadow of death, where they may be hid who work iniquity. — Job xxxiv.

7 Whither shall I go from thy spirit? or whither shall I flee from thy face? — Ps. cxxxviii.

12 Darkness shall not be dark to thee, and night shall be light as the day: the darkness thereof, and the light thereof are alike to thee.

21 The Lord beholdeth the ways of man, and considereth all his steps. — Prov. v.

3 The eyes of the Lord in every place behold the good and the evil. — Prov. xv.

11 Hell and destruction are before the Lord: how much more the hearts of the children of men?

2 All the ways of man are open to his eyes: the Lord is the weigher of spirits. — Prov. xvi.

16 Say not: I shall be hidden from God, and who shall remember me from on high? — Ecclus. xvi.

17 In such a multitude I shall not be

known: for what is my soul in such an immense creation?

20 In all these things the heart is senseless: and every heart is understood by him.

19 For the wisdom of God is great, and he is strong in power, seeing all men without ceasing.   Ecclus. xv.

13 Their ways are always before him, they are not hidden from his eyes.   Ecclus. xvii.

28 ... The eyes of the Lord are far brighter than the sun, beholding round about all the ways of men, and the bottom of the deep, and looking into the hearts of men, into the most hidden parts.   Ecclus. xxiii.

29 For all things were known to the Lord God, before they were created: so also after they were perfected he beholdeth all things.

28 For in him we live, and we move, and we are.   Acts xvii.

GOD OUR PROTECTOR.

14 BECAUSE he hoped in me I will deliver him: I will protect him because he hath known my name ...   Ps. xc.

12 ... I am God.   Isaias xliii.

13 And from the beginning I am the same, and there is none that can deliver out of my hand: I will work, and who shall turn it away?

31 ... The Lord giveth safety.   Prov. xxi.

10 ... The Lord preserveth the souls of his saints, he will deliver them out of the hand of the sinner.   Ps. xcvi.

7 The Lord keepeth thee from all evil: may the Lord keep thy soul.   Ps. cxx.

3 For the Lord will not leave the rod of sinners upon the lot of the just; that the just may not stretch forth their hands to iniquity.   Ps. cxxiv.

22 Say not: I will return evil: wait for the Lord, and he will deliver thee.   Prov. xx.

GOD (PROVIDENCE OF).

21 His eyes are upon the ways of men, and he considereth all their steps.   Job xxxiv.

16 My lots are in thy hands ...   Ps. xxx.

7 The Lord maketh poor and maketh rich, he humbleth and he exalteth.   1 Kings ii.

7 ... Men and beasts thou wilt preserve, O Lord.   Ps. xxxv.

8 Who covereth the heaven with clouds, and prepareth rain for the earth: Ps. cxlvi.
Who maketh grass to grow on the mountains, and herbs for the service of men.

9 Who giveth to beasts their food: and to the young ravens that call upon him.

27 All expect of thee that thou give them food in season.   Ps. ciii.

28 What thou givest to them they shall

God (Providence of).

gather up: When thou openest thy hand, they shall all be filled with good.

29 But if thou turnest away thy face, they shall be troubled: thou shalt take away their breath, and they shall fail, and shall return to their dust.

13 Every man that eateth and drinketh, and seeth good of his labour, this is the gift of God. — Eccles. iii.

14 Good things and evil, life and death, poverty and riches are from God. — Ecclus. xi.

24 The steps of man are guided by the Lord . . . — Prov. xx.

28 The Lord loveth judgment and will not forsake his saints: they shall be preserved for ever. — Ps. xxxvi.

29 Are not two sparrows sold for a farthing: and not one of them shall fall on the ground without your Father. — S. Matt. x.

30 But the very hairs of your head are all numbered.

31 Fear not therefore: better are you than many sparrows.

35 When I sent you without purse and scrip and shoes, did you want anything? — S. Luke xxii.

36 But they said: Nothing . . .

31 Be not solicitous therefore, saying: What shall we eat, or what shall we drink, or wherewith shall we be clothed? — S. Matt. vi.

32 For after all these things do the

heathens seek. For your Father knoweth
that you have need of all these things.

25 ... It is he who giveth to all life, and Acts xvii.
breath, and all things:

26 And hath made of one all mankind, to
dwell upon the whole face of the earth, determining appointed times, and the limits of
their habitation.

27 That they should seek God ...

28 And we know that to them that love Rom.
God, all things work together unto good, to viii.
such as according to his purpose are called
to be saints.

GOD OUR STRENGTH.

9 THE eyes of the Lord behold all the 2 Paralip.
earth, and give strength to those who with a xvi.
perfect heart trust in him.

29 The strength of the upright is the way Prov. x.
of the Lord ...

17 ... The Lord strengtheneth the just. Ps. xxxvi.

7 The Lord is good, and giveth strength Nahum i.
in the day of trouble: and knoweth them
that hope in him.

10 Fear not, for I am with thee: turn not Isaias
aside, for I am thy God: I have strength- xli.
ened thee, and have helped thee, and the
right hand of my just One hath upheld thee.

9 ... My grace is sufficient for thee: for 2 Cor. xii.

power is made perfect* in infirmity. Gladly therefore will I glory in my infirmities, that the power of Christ may dwell in me.

10 ... For when I am weak, then am I powerful.

16 ... Though our outward man is cor- 2 Cor. iv.
rupted: yet the inward man is renewed day by day.

13 I can do all things in him who strength- Philip
eneth me.   iv.

5 Not that we are sufficient to think any- 2 Cor. iii.
thing of ourselves, as of ourselves; but our sufficiency is from God.

3 God is faithful, who will strengthen and 2 Thess.
keep you from evil.   iii.

10 Finally, brethren, be strengthened in Ephes.
the Lord, and in the might of his power.   vi.

11 Put you on the armour of God, that you may be able to stand against the deceits of the devil.

12 For our wrestling is not against flesh and blood: but against principalities and powers, against the rulers of the world of this darkness, against the spirits of wickedness in the high places.

---

* The strength and power of God more perfectly shines forth in our weakness and infirmity; as the more weak we are of ourselves, the more illustrious is His grace in supporting us, and giving us the victory under all trials and conflicts.

GOD (TRUTH OF).

6 ... I AM the way, and the truth, and the life ...   S. John xiv.

10 All the ways of the Lord are mercy and truth ...   Ps. xxiv.

13 ... He shall judge the world with justice, and the people with his truth.   Ps. xcv.

19 ... The father shall make thy truth known to the children.   Isaias xxxviii.

6 ... O the Lord, the Lord God, merciful and gracious, patient, and of much compassion, and true.   Ex. xxxiv.

7 Who keepeth truth for ever ...   Ps. cxlv.

2 ... I will show forth thy truth with my mouth to generation and generation.   Ps. lxxxviii.

15 ... Mercy and truth shall go before thy face.

151 ... All thy ways are truth ...   Ps. cxviii.

160 The beginning of thy words is truth ...

6 ... Thou hast redeemed me, O Lord, the God of truth.   Ps. xxx.

14 And the Word was made flesh, and dwelt among us; (and we saw his glory, the glory as of the only-begotten of the Father,) full of grace and truth.   S. John i.

33 He that hath received his testimony hath set to his seal that God is true.   S. John iii.

17 Sanctify them in truth. Thy word is truth.   S. John xvii.

6 ... It is the Spirit which testifieth, that 1 S. John
Christ is the truth.   v.

3 ... Just and true are thy ways, O king Apoc. xv.
of ages.

GOOD COUNSEL.

24 My son, do thou nothing without coun- Ecclus.
sel, and thou shalt not repent when thou hast xxxii.
done.

6 Be in peace with many, but let one of Ecclus.
a thousand be thy counsellor.   vi.

36 If thou see a man of understanding, go
to him early in the morning, and let thy foot
wear the steps of his doors.

15 ... He that is wise hearkeneth unto Prov. xii.
counsels.

7 The lips of the wise shall disperse Prov. xv.
knowledge ...

12 The just considereth seriously the Prov. xxi.
house of the wicked, that he may withdraw
the wicked from evil.

9 ... The good counsels of a friend are Prov.
sweet to the soul.   xxvii.

7 Consult not with him that layeth a snare Ecclus.
for thee, and hide thy counsel from them xxxvii.
that envy thee.

8 Every counsellor giveth out counsel, but
there is one that is a counsellor for himself.

9 Beware of a counsellor. And know
before what need he hath: for he will devise to his own mind.

12 Treat not with a man without religion concerning holiness, nor with an unjust man concerning justice, nor with a woman touching her of whom she is jealous, nor with a coward concerning war, nor with a merchant about traffic, nor with a buyer of selling, nor with an envious man of giving thanks,

13 Nor with the ungodly of piety, nor with the dishonest of honesty, nor with the field labourer of every work,

14 ... Nor with an idle servant of much business: give no heed to these in any matter of counsel.

15 But be continually with a holy man whomsoever thou shalt know to observe the fear of God,

16 Whose soul is according to thine own soul: and who, when thou shalt stumble in the dark, will be sorry for thee,

17 And establish within thyself a heart of good counsel: for there is no other thing of more worth to thee than it.

18 The soul of a holy man discovereth sometimes true things, more than seven watchmen that sit in a high place to watch.

19 But above all these things pray to the most High, that he may direct thy way in truth.

20 In all thy works let the true word go before thee, and steady counsel before every action.

GOOD EXAMPLE AND EDIFICATION.

16 So let your light shine before men, that they may see your good works, and glorify your Father who is in heaven. — S. Matt. v.

15 I have given you an example, that as I have done to you, so you do also. — S. John xiii.

19 Let us follow after the things that are of peace: and keep the things that are of edification one towards another. — Rom. xiv.

2 Let every one of you please his neighbour for his good, unto edification. — Rom. xv.

11 Wherefore comfort one another, and edify one another, as you also do. — 1 Thess. v.

29 Let no evil speech proceed from your mouth; but that which is good to the edification of faith, that it may administer grace to the hearers. — Ephes. iv.

21 For we forecast what may be good not only before God, but also before men. — 2 Cor. viii.

22 From all appearance of evil refrain yourselves. — 1 Thess. v.

15 For so is the will of God, that by doing well, you may put to silence the ignorance of foolish men. — 1 S. Peter ii.

10 Always bearing about in our body the dying of Jesus; that the life also of Jesus may be made manifest in our bodies. — 2 Cor. iv.

GOOD WORKS.

9 ... From Me is thy fruit found. — Osee xiv.

38 Work your work before the time, and he will give you your reward in his time. — Ecclus. li.

27 Decline from evil and do good, and dwell for ever and ever. — Ps. xxxvi.

5 ... The beginning of a good way, is to do justice: and this is more acceptable with God, than to offer sacrifices. — Prov. xvi.

1 Lord, who shall dwell in thy tabernacle? or who shall rest in thy holy hill? — Ps. xiv.

2 He that walketh without blemish, and worketh justice.

14 Remember me, O my God, for this thing, and wipe not out my kindnesses, which I have done relating to the house of my God, and his ceremonies. — 2 Esdras xiii.

1 He that feareth God will do good ... — Ecclus. xv.

15 I was an eye to the blind, and a foot to the lame. — Job xxix.

16 I was the father of the poor: and the cause which I knew not, I searched out most diligently.

15 Turn away from evil and do good ... — Ps. xxxiii.

3 Judge for the needy and fatherless: do justice to the humble and the poor. — Ps. lxxxi.

27 Do not withhold him from doing good — Prov. iii.

who is able: and if thou art able, do good thyself also.

15 My son, in thy good deeds, make no complaint, and when thou givest any thing, add not grief by an evil word. — Ecclus. xviii.

17 Eat thy bread with the hungry and the needy, and with thy garments cover the naked. — Tobias iv.

17 Learn to do well: seek judgment, relieve the oppressed, judge for the fatherless, defend the widow. — Isaias i.

15 For the fruit of good labours is glorious ... — Wis. iii.

20 Lay up for yourselves treasures in heaven; where neither the rust nor the moth doth consume, and where thieves do not break through, nor steal. — S. Matt. vi.

21 For where thy treasure is, there is thy heart also.

33 ... By the fruit the tree is known. — S. Matt. xii.

17 Every good tree yieldeth good fruit ... — S. Matt. vii.

6 He spoke also this parable: A certain man had a fig-tree planted in his vineyard, and he came seeking fruit on it, and found none. — S. Luke xiii.

7 And he said to the dresser of the vineyard: Behold, these three years I come seeking fruit on this fig-tree, and I find none.

Cut it down therefore; why cumbereth it the ground?

5 I am the vine; you the branches: he that abideth in me, and I in him, the same beareth much fruit: for without me you can do nothing. — S. John xv.

8 In this is my Father glorified: that you bring forth very much fruit and become my disciples.

12 Having your conversation good among the gentiles: that whereas they speak against you as evil doers, they may by the good works, which they shall behold in you, glorify God in the day of visitation. — 1 S. Peter ii.

5 But there arose some of the sect of the Pharisees that believed, saying: They must be circumcised, and be commanded to observe the law of Moses. — Acts xv.

16 ... By the works of the law no flesh shall be justified ... — Gal. ii.

11 Other foundation no man can lay, but that which is laid; which is Christ Jesus. — 1 Cor. iii.

12 Now if any man build upon this foundation,* gold, silver, precious stones, wood, hay, stubble:

13 Every man's work shall be manifest: for the day of the Lord shall declare it, because it shall be revealed in fire: and the

* The foundation is Christ and His doctrine; or the true faith in Him, working through charity ...

fire shall try every man's work, of what sort it is.

14 If any man's work abide, which he hath built thereupon, he shall receive a reward.

31 Cornelius, thy prayer is heard, and thy alms are had in remembrance in the sight of God. — Acts x.

10 Glory and honour and peace to every one that worketh good . . . — Rom. ii.

8 . . . Every man shall receive his own reward according to his own labour. — 1 Cor. iii.

9 And in doing good, let us not fail: for in due time we shall reap, not failing. — Gal. vi.

10 For we are his workmanship, created in Christ Jesus in good works, which God hath prepared that we should walk in them. — Ephes. ii.

11 Filled with the fruit of justice through Jesus Christ, unto the glory and praise of God. — Philip. i.

14 (Jesus Christ) Who gave himself for us, that he might redeem us from all iniquity, and purify unto himself a people acceptable, pursuing good works. — Titus ii.

8 It is a faithful saying: and these things I will have thee to affirm constantly: that they, who believe in God, may be careful to excel in good works. These things are good and profitable to men. — Titus iii.

6 That the communication of thy faith may be made evident in the acknowledgment — Philem.

of every good work, that is in you in Christ Jesus.

10 God is not unjust, that he should forget your work, and the love which you have shewn in his name, you who have ministered, and do minister to the saints. Heb. vi.

11 And we desire that every one of you shew forth the same carefulness to the accomplishing of hope unto the end.

24 And let us consider one another to provoke unto charity and to good works. Heb. x.

10 That you may walk worthy of God, in all things pleasing: being fruitful in every good work, and increasing in the knowledge of God. Coloss. i.

25 . . . A doer of the work; this man shall be blessed in his deed. S. James i.

24 Do you see that by works a man is justified, and not by faith only? S. James ii.

17 To him, therefore, who knoweth to do good, and doeth it not, to him it is sin. S. James iv.

10 Wherefore, brethren, labour the more, that by good works you may make sure your vocation and election. For doing these things, you shall not sin at any time. 2 S. Peter i.

GRACE.

12 GOD loveth mercy and truth: the Lord will give grace and glory. Ps. lxxxiii.

Grace. 203

34 ... To the meek he will give grace.   Prov. iii.

9 ... Among the just grace shall abide.   Prov. xiv.

2 He that is good shall draw grace from the Lord ...   Prov. xii.

18 The grace of our Lord Jesus Christ be with your spirit.   Gal. vi.

2 Grace to you and peace be accomplished in the knowledge of God, and of Christ Jesus our Lord.   2 S. Peter i.

16 Of his fulness we all have received, and grace for grace.   S. John i.

17 For the law was given by Moses, grace and truth came by Jesus Christ.

24 Being justified freely by his grace, through the redemption that is in Jesus Christ.   Rom. iii.

21 That as sin hath reigned to death: so also grace might reign by justice unto life everlasting, through Jesus Christ our Lord.   Rom. v.

23 The wages of sin, is death. But the grace of God, life everlasting, in Christ Jesus our Lord.   Rom. vi.

1 And we helping do exhort you, that you receive not the grace of God in vain.   2 Cor. vi.

10 As every man hath received grace, ministering the same one to another: as good stewards of the manifold grace of God.   1 S. Peter iv.

6 To the praise and glory of his grace by which he made us acceptable through his beloved Son.   Ephes. i.

7 In whom we have redemption through his blood, the remission of sins, according to the riches of his grace.

7 That he might shew in the ages to come the abundant riches of his grace, in goodness upon us in Christ Jesus.   Ephes. ii.

8 For by grace are you saved through faith, and that not of yourselves, for it is the gift of God;

9 Not of works,* that no man may glory.

24 Grace be with all them that love our Lord Jesus Christ in incorruption.   Ephes. vi.

12 That the name of our Lord Jesus Christ may be glorified in you, and you in him, according to the grace of our God, and of the Lord Jesus Christ.   2 Thess. i.

14 Now the grace of our Lord hath abounded exceedingly with faith and love which is in Christ Jesus.   1 Tim. i.

1 Thou therefore my son be strong in the grace which is in Christ Jesus.   2 Tim. ii.

11 For the grace of God our Saviour hath appeared to all men.   Titus ii.

12 Instructing us that, denying ungodliness and worldly desires, we should live soberly, and justly, and godly in this world.

7 Being justified by his grace we may be heirs according to hope of life everlasting.   Titus iii.

* Not of works as of our own growth, or from ourselves, but as from the grace of God.

28 Therefore we, receiving an immoveable kingdom, have grace, whereby let us serve, pleasing God with fear and reverence. — Heb. xii.

6 ... God resisteth the proud and giveth grace to the humble. — S. James iv.

18 But grow in grace and in the knowledge of our Lord and Saviour Jesus Christ. To him be glory both now and unto the day of eternity. — 2 S. Peter iii.

15 Now our Lord Jesus Christ himself, and God our Father, who hath loved us, and hath given us everlasting consolation, and good hope in grace,

16 Exhort your hearts, and confirm you in every good work and word. — 2 Thess. ii.

13 The grace of our Lord Jesus Christ, and the charity of God, and the communication of the Holy Ghost be with you all. Amen. — 2 Cor. xiii.

4 Grace be unto you, and peace from him that is, and that was, and that is to come, and from the seven spirits which are before his throne. — Apoc. i.

HATRED.

17 THOU shalt not hate thy brother in thy heart ... — Lev. xix.

12 Hatred stirreth up strifes ... — Prov. x.

18 Lying lips hide hatred ...

17 It is better to be invited to herbs with love : than to a fatted calf with hatred. — Prov. xv.

26 He that covereth hatred deceitfully, his malice shall be laid open in the public assembly. — Prov. xxvi.

22 You shall be hated by all men for my name's sake. — S. Matt. x.

44 ... Do good to them that hate you ... — S. Matt. v.

3 For we ourselves also were some time unwise, incredulous, erring, slaves to divers desires and pleasures, living in malice and envy, hateful, and hating one another. — Titus iii.

9 He that saith he is in the light, and hateth his brother, is in darkness, even until now. — 1 S. John ii.

11 He that hateth his brother is in darkness, and walketh in darkness, and knoweth not whither he goeth : because the darkness hath blinded his eyes.

10 In this the children of God are manifest and the children of the devil. Whosoever is not just, is not of God, nor is he that loveth not his brother. — 1 S. John iii.

12 As Cain, who was of the wicked one, and killed his brother. And wherefore did he kill him ? Because his own works were wicked : and his brother's just.

14 ... He that loveth not, abideth in death.

15 Whosoever hateth his brother, is a murderer. And you know that no murderer hath eternal life abiding in himself.

8 He that loveth not, knoweth not God: for God is charity.

1 S. John iv.

20 If any man say, I love God, and hateth his brother, he is a liar. For he that loveth not his brother whom he seeth, how can he love God, whom he seeth not?

HATRED OF REPROOF.

17 ... He that forsaketh reproofs goeth astray.

Prov. x.

1 ... He that hateth reproof is foolish.

Prov. xii.

18 Poverty and shame to him that refuseth instruction ...

Prov. xiii.

5 A fool laugheth at the instruction of his father ...

Prov. xv.

10 Instruction is grievous to him who forsaketh the way of life: he that hateth reproof shall die.

12 A corrupt man loveth not one that reproveth him: nor will he go to the wise.

32 He that rejecteth instruction, despiseth his own soul: but he that yieldeth to reproof possesseth understanding.

7 He that hateth to be reproved walketh in the trace of a sinner ...

Ecclus. xxi.

14 He that is not wise in good, will not be taught.

10 They have hated him that rebuketh in Amos v.
the gate : and have abhorred him that speaketh perfectly.

HATRED OF SIN.

10 You that love the Lord, hate evil: Ps. xcvi.
the Lord preserveth the souls of his saints,
he will deliver them out of the hand of the
sinner.

53 A fainting hath taken hold of me, be- Ps.
cause of the wicked that forsake thy law. cxviii.

128 ... I have hated all wicked ways.

163 I have hated and abhorred iniquity;
but I have loved thy law.

21 Have I not hated them, O Lord, that Ps.
hated thee : and pined away because of thy cxxxviii.
enemies ?

3 Three sorts my soul hateth, and I am Ecclus.
greatly grieved at their life : xxv.

4 A poor man that is proud : a rich man
that is a liar: an old man that is a fool, and
doting.

7 My mouth shall meditate truth, and my Prov.
lips shall hate wickedness. viii.

13 The fear of the Lord hateth evil ...

9 ... Hating that which is evil, cleaving Rom. xii.
to that which is good.

HEAVEN.

3 Glorious things are said of thee, O city of God. Ps. lxxxvi.

4 From the beginning of the world they have not heard, nor perceived with the ears: the eye hath not seen, O God, besides thee, what things thou hast prepared for them that wait for thee. Isaias lxiv.

13 Thy kingdom is a kingdom of all ages: and thy dominion endureth throughout all generations. Ps. cxliv.

6 Lift up your eyes to heaven, and look down to the earth beneath: for the heavens shall vanish like smoke, and the earth shall be worn away like a garment, and the inhabitants thereof shall perish in like manner: but my salvation shall be for ever, and my justice shall not fail. Isaias li.

10 And the redeemed of the Lord shall return, and shall come into Sion with praise, and everlasting joy shall be upon their heads: they shall obtain joy and gladness, and sorrow and mourning shall flee away. Isaias xxxv.

17 For behold I create new heavens, and a new earth: and the former things shall not be in remembrance, and they shall not come upon the heart. Isaias lxv.

18 But you shall be glad and rejoice for

ever in these things, which I create: for behold I create Jerusalem rejoicing, and the people thereof joy.

19 And I will rejoice in Jerusalem, and joy in my people, and the voice of weeping shall no more be heard in her, nor the voice of crying.

19 Thou shalt no more have the sun for thy light by day, neither shall the brightness of the moon enlighten thee: but the Lord shall be unto thee for an everlasting light, and thy God for thy glory. — Isaias lx.

20 Thy sun shall go down no more, and thy moon shall not decrease: for the Lord shall be unto thee for an everlasting light, and the days of thy mourning shall be ended.

21 And thy people shall be all just, they shall inherit the land for ever, the branch of my planting, the work of my hand to glorify me.

22 The least shall become a thousand, and a little one a most strong nation: I the Lord will suddenly do this thing in its time.

32 Fear not, little flock, for it hath pleased your Father to give you a kingdom. — S. Luke xii.

2 In my Father's house there are many mansions. If not, I would have told you, because I go to prepare a place for you. — S. John xiv.

24 Father, I will that where I am, they also whom thou hast given me may be with — S. John xvii.

me: that they may see my glory which thou hast given me, because thou hast loved me before the foundation of the world.

9 ... Eye hath not seen, nor ear heard, neither hath it entered into the heart of man, what things God hath prepared for them that love him.   1 Cor. ii.

10 When that which is perfect is come, that which is in part shall be done away.   1 Cor. xiii.

12 We see now through a glass in a dark manner: but then face to face. Now I know in part: but then I shall know even as I am known.

13 And we look for new heavens and a new earth, according to his promise, in which justice dwelleth.   2 S. Peter iii.

14 Wherefore, dearly beloved, waiting for those things, be diligent that you may be found before him unspotted and blameless in peace.

3 And every one that hath this hope in him, sanctifieth himself, as he also is holy.   1 S. John iii.

9 After this I saw a great multitude, which no man could number, of all nations, and tribes, and peoples, and tongues: standing before the throne, and in sight of the Lamb, clothed with white robes, and palms in their hands: Apoc. vii.

10 And they cried with a loud voice, say-

ing: Salvation to our God, who sitteth upon the throne, and to the Lamb.

4 And God shall wipe away all tears from their eyes: and death shall be no more, nor mourning, nor crying, nor sorrow shall be any more, for the former things are passed away. *Apoc. xxi.*

5 And he that sat on the throne, said: Behold, I make all things new. And he said to me: Write, for these words are most faithful and true.

6 And he said to me: It is done: I am alpha and omega: the beginning and the end. To him that thirsteth I will give of the fountain of the water of life, freely.

7 He that shall overcome shall possess these things, and I will be his God: and he shall be my son.

9 And there came one of the seven angels, ... saying: Come, and I will shew thee the bride, the wife of the Lamb.

10 And he took me up in spirit to a great and high mountain: and he shewed me the holy city Jerusalem coming down out of heaven from God.

22 And I saw no temple therein. For the Lord God Almighty is the temple thereof, and the Lamb.

23 And the city hath no need of the sun, nor of the moon, to shine in it, for the glory

Heaven.

of God hath enlightened it, and the Lamb is the lamp thereof.

24 And the nations shall walk in the light of it: and the kings of the earth shall bring their glory and honour into it.

25 And the gates thereof shall not be shut by day: for there shall be no night there.

26 And they shall bring the glory and honour of the nations into it.

27 There shall not enter into it any thing defiled, or that worketh abomination, or maketh a lie, but they that are written in the book of life of the Lamb.

3 And there shall be no curse any more: but the throne of God and of the Lamb shall be in it, and his servants shall serve him.   Apoc. xxii.

4 And they shall see his face: and his name shall be on their foreheads.

5 And night shall be no more: and they shall not need the light of a lamp, nor the light of the sun, for the Lord God shall enlighten them, and they shall reign for ever and ever.

6 And he said to me: These words are most faithful and true . . .

20 He that giveth testimony of these things saith, Surely I come quickly: Amen. Come, Lord Jesus.

HELL.

18 The wicked shall be turned into hell, all the nations that forget God. — Ps. ix.

14 The sinners in Sion are afraid, trembling hath seized upon the hypocrites. Which of you can dwell with devouring fire? which of you shall dwell with everlasting burnings? — Isaias xxxiii.

33 For Topheth is prepared from yesterday, prepared by the king deep and wide. The nourishments thereof is fire and much wood: the breath of the Lord as a torrent of brimstone kindling it. — Isaias xxx.

41 ... Depart from me, you cursed, into everlasting fire which was prepared for the devil and his angels. — S. Matt. xxv.

46 And these shall go into everlasting punishment ...

51 ... Appoint his portion with the hypocrites. There shall be weeping and gnashing of teeth. — S. Matt. xxiv.

42 If thy hand scandalize thee,* cut it off: it is better for thee to enter into life, maimed, than having two hands to go into hell, into unquenchable fire: — S. Mark ix.

43 Where their worm dieth not, and the fire is not extinguished.

44 And if thy foot scandalize thee, cut it

---

* See note to S. Matt. v., 29th v., in Sin.

off. It is better for thee to enter lame into life everlasting, than having two feet, to be cast into the hell of unquenchable fire:

45 Where their worm dieth not, and the fire is not extinguished.

46 And if thy eye scandalize thee, pluck it out. It is better for thee with one eye to enter into the kingdom of God, than having two eyes, to be cast into the hell of fire:

47 Where their worm dieth not, and the fire is not extinguished.

11 The smoke of their torments shall ascend up for ever and ever: neither have they rest day nor night: who have adored the beast.   Apoc. xiv.

15 And whosoever was not found written in the book of life, was cast into the pool of fire.   Apoc. xx.

6 And the angels, who kept not their principality but forsook their own habitation, he hath reserved under darkness in everlasting chains, unto the judgment of the great day.   S. Jude.

HOLINESS OF CONDUCT.*

20 UNLESS your justice abound more than that of the Scribes and Pharisees, you shall not enter into the kingdom of heaven.   S. Matt. v.

* See Perfection.

28 In the path of justice is life . . .   Prov. xii.

19 They that fear the Lord, will seek after the things that are well pleasing to him: and they that love him, shall be filled with his law.   Ecclus. ii.

15 Health of the soul in holiness of justice, is better than all gold and silver . . .   Ecclus. xxx.

10 Say to the just man that it is well, for he shall eat the fruit of his doings.   Isaias iii.

17 And the work of justice shall be peace, and the service of justice quietness, and security for ever.   Isaias xxxii.

74 That being delivered from the hand of our enemies, we may serve him without fear.   S. Luke i.

75 In holiness and justice before him, all our days.

14 . . . Holiness: without which no man shall see God.   Heb. xii.

3 . . . He calleth his own sheep by name, and leadeth them out.   S. John x.

4 And when he hath let out his own sheep, he goeth before them: and the sheep follow him, because they know his voice.

1 Be ye therefore followers of God, as most dear children.   Ephes. v.

27 Let your conversation be worthy of the gospel of Christ . . .   Philip. i.

4 As he chose us in him before the foundation of the world, that we should be holy and unspotted in his sight in charity.   Ephes. i.

13 To confirm your hearts without blame, in holiness, before God and our Father, at the coming of our Lord Jesus Christ with all his saints. — 1 Thess. iii.

12 We testified to every one of you that you would walk worthy of God, who hath called you unto his kingdom and glory. — 1 Thess. ii.

1 For the rest therefore, brethren, we pray and beseech you in the Lord Jesus, that as you have received of us, how you ought to walk, and to please God, so also you would walk, that you may abound the more. — 1 Thess. iv.

23 And may the God of peace himself sanctify you in all things: that your whole spirit, and soul, and body, be preserved blameless in the coming of our Lord Jesus Christ. — 1 Thess. v.

2 Speak evil of no man, not to be litigious, but gentle: showing all mildness towards all men. — Titus iii.

12 Put ye on therefore, as the elect of God, holy, and beloved, the bowels of mercy, benignity, humility, modesty, patience. — Coloss. iii.

16 Because it is written: you shall be holy, for I am holy. — 1 S. Peter i.

17 ... Converse in fear during the time of your sojourning here.

18 Knowing that you were not redeemed with corruptible things as gold or silver, from

your vain conversation of the tradition of your fathers:

19 But with the precious blood of Christ, as of a lamb unspotted and undefiled.

HOLY COMMUNION.

27 LABOUR not for the meat which perisheth, but for that which endureth unto life everlasting, which the son of man will give you. For him hath God, the Father, sealed. — S. John vi.

3 ... On the tenth day of this month let every man take a lamb by their families and houses.

5 And it shall be a lamb without blemish ...

6 ... The whole multitude of the children of Israel shall sacrifice it in the evening.

8 They shall eat the flesh ... And unleavened bread ... — Exodus xii.

6 (Elias) looked, and behold there was at his head a hearth-cake ...

7 ... Arise, eat: for thou hast yet a great way to go.

8 And he arose, and eat, and drank, and walked in the strength of that food* forty days and forty nights, unto the mount of God. — 3 Kings xix.

* This bread, with which Elias was fed in the wilderness, was a figure of the bread of life which we receive in the Blessed

5 Thou hast prepared a table before me, against them that afflict me ... and my chalice which inebriateth me, how goodly is it! — Ps. xxii.

20 ... Thou didst feed thy people with the food of angels, and gavest them bread from heaven prepared without labour: having in it all that is delicious, and the sweetness of every taste. — Wisd. xvi.

5 Come, eat my bread, and drink the wine which I have mingled for you. — Prov. ix.

29 They that eat me shall yet hunger: and they that drink me shall yet thirst. — Ecclus. xxiv.

3 ... I sat down under his shadow, whom I desired: and his fruit was sweet to my palate. — Cant. ii.

4 He brought me into the cellar of wine, he set in order charity in me.

16 My beloved to me, and I to him who feedeth among the lilies.

25 I have inebriated the weary soul: and I have filled every hungry soul. — Jer. xxxi.

17 For what is the good thing of him, and what is his beautiful thing, but the corn of the elect, and wine springing forth virgins? — Zach. ix.

Sacrament: by the strength of which we are to be supported in our journey through the wilderness of this world till we come to the true mountain of God, and His vision in a happy eternity.

11 For from the rising of the sun even to the going down, my name is great among the Gentiles, and in every place there is sacrifice, and there is offered to my name a clean oblation: for my name is great among the Gentiles, saith the Lord of hosts. — Malach. i.

4 The Lord hath sworn, and he will not repent: Thou art a priest for ever according to the order of Melchisedech. — Ps. cix.

18 Melchisedech the king of Salem, bringing forth bread and wine, for he was the priest of the most high God. — Gen. xiv.

15 Verily thou art a hidden God, the God of Israel the saviour. — Isaias xlv.

23 ... They shall call his name Emmanuel, which being interpreted is, God with us. — S. Matt. i.

21 ... If I shall touch only his garment, I shall be healed. — S. Matt. ix.

11 Give us this day our supersubstantial bread. — S. Matt. vi.

32 Then Jesus said to them: Amen, amen, I say to you: Moses gave you not bread from heaven, but my Father giveth you the true bread from heaven. — S. John vi.

33 For the bread of God, is that which cometh down from heaven, and giveth life to the world.

34 They said therefore unto him: Lord, give us always this bread.

35 And Jesus said to them: I am the bread of life, he that cometh to me shall not hunger; and he that believeth in me, shall never thirst.

48 I am the bread of life.

49 Your fathers did eat manna in the desert, and are dead.

50 This is the bread which cometh down from heaven: that if any man eat of it, he may not die.

51 I am the living bread, which came down from heaven.

52 If any man eat of this bread, he shall live for ever: and the bread that I will give, is my flesh for the life of the world.

53 The Jews therefore strove among themselves, saying: How can this man give us his flesh to eat?

54 Then Jesus said to them: Amen, amen, I say unto you: Except you eat* the flesh of the Son of man, and drink his blood, you shall not have life in you.

55 He that eateth my flesh, and drinketh

---

* To receive the body and blood of Christ, is a divine precept, insinuated in this text: which the faithful fulfil, though they receive but in one kind; because in one kind they receive both body and blood, which cannot be separated from each other. Hence, eternal life is here promised to the worthy receiving, though but in one kind.

my blood, hath everlasting life: and I will raise him up in the last day.

56 For my flesh is meat indeed: and my blood is drink indeed:

57 He that eateth my flesh, and drinketh my blood, abideth in me, and I in him.

58 As the living Father hath sent me, and I live by the Father: so he that eateth me, the same also shall live by me.

59 This is the bread that came down from heaven. Not as your fathers did eat manna, and are dead. He that eateth this bread, shall live for ever.

61 Many, therefore, of his disciples hearing it, said: This saying is hard, and who can hear it?

67 After this many of his disciples went back; and walked no more with him.

68 Then Jesus said to the twelve: Will you also go away?

69 And Simon Peter answered him: Lord, to whom shall we go? thou hast the words of eternal life.

70 And we have believed, and have known that thou art the Christ the Son of God.

1 ... Jesus knowing that his hour was come, that he should pass out of this world to the Father: having loved his own who were in the world, he loved them unto the end. S. John xiii.

14 And when the hour was come, he sat S. Luke
down and the twelve apostles with him.   xxii.

15 And he said to them: with desire I
have desired to eat this pasch with you before I suffer.

16 For I say to you, that from this time
I will not eat it, till it be fulfilled in the kingdom of God.

19 ... Do this for a commemoration of
me.*

26 And whilst they were at supper, Jesus S. Matt.
took bread, and blessed, and broke: and   xxvi.
gave to his disciples, and said: Take ye,
and eat: This is my body.

27 And taking the chalice he gave thanks:
and gave to them, saying: Drink ye all of
this.

28 For this is my blood of the new testament, which shall be shed for many for the
remission of sins.

34 One of the soldiers with a spear opened S. John
his side, and immediately there came out   xix.
blood and water.

7 ... Christ our pasch, is sacrificed.   1 Cor. v.

16 The Chalice of benediction, which we 1 Cor. x.
bless, is it not the communion of the blood

---

* It is the manner that He Himself hath commanded, of commemorating and celebrating His death, by offering in sacrifice, and receiving in the Sacrament, that body and blood by which we were redeemed.

of Christ? And the bread, which we break, is it not the partaking of the body of the Lord?

17 Because the bread is one, all we, being many, are one body, who partake of that one bread.*

30 For we are members of his body, of his flesh, and of his bones. Ephes. v.

29 ... Stay with us, because it is towards evening, and the day is now far spent. And he went in with them. S. Luke xxiv.

30 And it came to pass, whilst he was at table with them, he took bread, and blessed and brake, and gave to them.

31 And their eyes were opened, and they knew him: and he vanished out of their sight.

35 And they told what things were done in the way: and how they knew him in the breaking of bread.

23 I have received of the Lord that which also I delivered unto you, that the Lord Jesus, the same night in which he was betrayed, took bread, 1 Cor. xi.

24 And giving thanks, broke, and said: Take ye and eat: this is my body which shall be delivered for you: this do for the commemoration of me.

25 In like manner also the chalice, after he had supped, saying: This chalice is the

* See Note of Douay Version.

Holy Communion.

new testament in my blood: this do ye, as often as you shall drink, for the commemoration of me.

26 For as often as you shall eat this bread, and drink this chalice, you shall show the death of the Lord, until he come.

27 Therefore, whosoever shall eat this bread, or drink the chalice of the Lord unworthily, shall be guilty of the body and blood of the Lord.

28 But let a man prove himself: and so let him eat of that bread, and drink of the chalice.

29 For he that eateth and drinketh unworthily, eateth and drinketh judgment to himself, not discerning the body of the Lord.

30 Therefore are there many infirm and weak among you, and many sleep.

HOLY JOY.

15 THE voice of rejoicing and of salvation is in the tabernacles of the just. Ps. cxvii.

7 I will bring them into my holy mount, and will make them joyful in my house of prayer... Isaias lvi.

1 My heart hath rejoiced in the Lord... 1 Kings ii.

7 The light of thy countenance, O Lord, is signed upon us: thou hast given gladness in my heart. Ps. iv.

3 I will be glad and rejoice in thee: I will sing to thy name, O thou most high. — Ps. ix.

16 I will rejoice in thy salvation...

11 Thou hast made known to me the ways of life, thou shalt fill me with joy with thy countenance: at thy right hand are delights even to the end. — Ps. xv.

7 Thou art my refuge from the trouble which hath encompassed me: my joy, deliver me from them that surround me. — Ps. xxxi.

11 Be glad in the Lord, and rejoice, ye just, and glory, all ye right of heart.

21 For in him our heart shall rejoice: and in his holy name we have trusted. — Ps. xxxii.

4 Delight in the Lord, and he will give thee the requests of thy heart. — Ps. xxxvi.

9 My soul shall rejoice in the Lord; and shall be delighted in his salvation. — Ps. xxxiv.

11 ... Let my heart rejoice that it may fear thy name. — Ps. lxxxv.

14 We are filled in the morning with thy mercy: and we have rejoiced, and are delighted all our days. — Ps. lxxxix.

15 We have rejoiced for the days in which thou hast humbled us: for the years in which we have seen evils.

21 Whatsoever shall befall the just man, it shall not make him sad... — Prov. xii.

15 It is joy to the just to do judgment... — Prov. xxi.

3 You shall draw waters with joy out of the Saviour's fountains. — Isaias xii.

47 My spirit hath rejoiced in God my Saviour. — S. Luke i.

24 ... Ask, and you shall receive: that your joy may be full. — S. John xvi.

11 These things I have spoken to you, that my joy may be in you, and your joy may be filled. — S. John xv.

28 Thou hast made known to me the ways of life: Thou shalt make me full of joy with thy countenance. — Acts ii.

4 Rejoice in the Lord always: again, I say, rejoice. — Philip. iv.

16 Always rejoice. — 1 Thes. v.

12 Rejoicing in hope: patient in tribulation; instant in prayer. — Rom. xii.

13 But if you partake of the suffering of Christ rejoice; that when his glory shall be revealed, you may also be glad with exceeding joy. — 1 S. Peter iv.

8 Whom having not seen you love: in whom also now, though you see him not, you believe: and believing shall rejoice with joy unspeakable and glorified. — 1 S. Peter i.

HOLY SPIRIT INDWELLING.

12 ... Thou shalt dwell in them ... — Ps. v.

9 I will hear what the Lord God will speak in me: for he will speak peace unto — Ps. lxxxiv.

his people: and unto his saints: and unto them that are converted to the heart.

11 ... Where is he that brought them up out of the sea, with the shepherds of his flock? Where is he that put in the midst of them the spirit of his holy One? — Isaias lxiii.

2 The Spirit of the Lord shall rest upon him: the spirit of wisdom, and of understanding, the spirit of counsel, and of fortitude, the spirit of knowledge, and of godliness. — Isaias xi.

3 And he shall be filled with the spirit of the fear of the Lord ...

27 And I will put my Spirit in the midst of you: and I will cause you to walk in my commandments, and to keep my judgments and do them. — Ezech. xxxvi.

16 And I will ask the Father, and he shall give you another Paraclete,* that he may abide with you for ever.† — St. John xiv.

17 The Spirit of truth, whom the world cannot receive, because it seeth him not, nor knoweth him: but you shall know him; because he shall abide with you, and shall be in you.

* That is, comforter, or also an advocate; inasmuch as by inspiring prayer, He prays, as it were, in us, and pleads for us.

† For ever. Hence it is evident that this Spirit of truth was not only promised to the apostles, but also to their successors, through all generations.

18 I will not leave you orphans: I will come to you.

26 When the Paraclete cometh, whom I will send you from the Father, the Spirit of truth, who proceedeth from the Father, he shall give testimony of me. — S. John xv.

14 He shall glorify me: because he shall receive of mine, and shall show it to you. — S. John xvi.

9 You are not in the flesh, but in the spirit, if so be that the Spirit of God dwell in you. — Rom. viii.

11 And if the Spirit of him that raised up Jesus from the dead, dwell in you; he that raised up Jesus Christ from the dead, shall quicken also your mortal bodies, because of his Spirit that dwelleth in you.

14 Whosoever are led by the Spirit of God, they are the sons of God.

3 ... And no man can say, the Lord Jesus, but by the Holy Ghost. — 1 Cor. xii.

4 Now there are diversities of graces, but the same Spirit;

5 And there are diversities of ministries, but the same Lord.

6 And there are diversities of operations, but the same God, who worketh all in all.

7 And the manifestation of the Spirit is given to every man unto profit.

8 To one indeed, by the Spirit, is given the word of wisdom: and to another the

word of knowledge, according to the same Spirit.

9 To another, faith in the same Spirit: to another, the graces of healing in one Spirit.

10 To another, the working of miracles: to another, prophecy: to another, the discerning of spirits: to another, divers kinds of tongues: to another, interpretations of speeches.

11 But all these things one and the same Spirit worketh, dividing to everyone according as he will.

16 Know you not that you are the temple of God, and that the Spirit of God dwelleth in you? 1 Cor. iii.

22 Who also hath sealed us, and given the pledge of the Spirit in our hearts. 2 Cor. i.

19 Or know you not, that your members are the temple of the Holy Ghost, who is in you, whom you have from God; and you are not your own? 1 Cor. vi.

16 ... For you are the temple of the living God: as God saith: I will dwell in them and walk among them, and I will be their God, and they shall be my people. 2 Cor. vi.

22 The fruit of the Spirit is, charity, joy, peace, patience, benignity, goodness, longanimity, Galat. v.

23 Mildness, faith, modesty, continency, chastity ...

25 If we live in the Spirit, let us also walk in the Spirit.

HOPE.

5 HOPE confoundeth not: because the charity of God is poured forth in our hearts, by the Holy Ghost who is given to us. — Rom. v.

9 In peace in the selfsame I will sleep, and I will rest: — Ps. iv.

10 For thou, O Lord, singularly hast settled me in hope.

2 Have mercy on me, O God, have mercy on me: for my soul trusteth in thee: and in the shadow of thy wings will I hope, until iniquity pass away. — Ps. lvi.

11 My children, behold the generations of men: and know ye that no one hath hoped in the Lord, and hath been confounded. — Ecclus. ii.

10 If thou lose hope being weary in the day of distress, thy strength shall be diminished. — Prov. xxiv.

31 They that hope in the Lord shall renew their strength, they shall take wings as eagles, they shall run and not be weary, they shall walk and not faint. — Isaias xl.

8 Rejoice not, thou mine enemy, over me, because I am fallen: I shall arise; when I sit in darkness, the Lord is my light. — Mich. vii.

6 Turn thou to thy God: keep mercy and judgment, and hope in thy God always. — Osee x.

24 For we are saved by hope. But hope that is seen, is not hope. For what a man seeth, why doth he hope for? — Rom. viii.

25 But if we hope for that which we see not: we wait for it with patience.

13 Now the God of hope fill you with all joy and peace in believing: that you may abound in hope, and in the power of the Holy Ghost. — Rom. xv.

18 ... Hold fast the hope set before us. — Heb. vi.

19 Which we have as an anchor of the soul, sure and firm ...

13 Wherefore having the loins of your mind girt up, being sober, hope perfectly for that grace which is offered to you at the revelation of Jesus Christ. — 1 S. Peter i.

21 (You) who through him are faithful in God, who raised him up from the dead, and hath given him glory, that your faith and hope might be in God.

15 Sanctify the Lord Christ in your hearts, being ready always to satisfy every one that asketh you a reason of that hope which is in you. — 1 S. Peter iii.

6 ... Hold fast the confidence and glory of hope unto the end. — Heb. iii.

13 Looking for the blessed hope and coming of the glory of the great God and our Saviour Jesus Christ. — Titus ii.

HOSPITALITY.

20 Where is he? Why have you let the man go? Call him that he may eat bread.   Exodus ii.

31 ... Come in, thou blessed of the Lord: why standest thou without? I have prepared the house, and a place for the camels.   Gen. xxiv.

32 The stranger did not stay without, my door was open to the traveller.   Job xxxi.

7 Deal thy bread to the hungry, and bring the needy and the harbourless into thy house...   Isaias lviii.

29 And the Levite that hath no other part nor possession with thee, and the stranger and the fatherless and the widow, that are within thy gates, shall come, and shall eat and be filled: that the Lord thy God may bless thee in all the works of thy hands that thou shalt do.   Deut. xiv.

41 He that receiveth a prophet in the name of a prophet, shall receive the reward of a prophet: and he that receiveth a just man in the name of a just man, shall receive the reward of a just man.   S. Matt. x.

42 And whosoever shall give to drink to one of these little ones a cup of cold water only in the name of a disciple, amen I say to you, he shall not lose his reward.

12 ... When thou makest a dinner or a supper, call not thy friends, nor thy brethren, nor thy kinsmen, nor thy neighbours who are rich: lest perhaps they also invite thee again, and a recompense be made to thee. *S. Luke xiv.*

13 But when thou makest a feast, call the poor, the maimed, the lame, and the blind.

14 And thou shalt be blessed, because they have not wherewith to make thee recompense: for recompense shall be made thee at the resurrection of the just.

13 ... Pursuing hospitality. *Rom. xii.*

7 Receive one another, as Christ also hath received you unto the honour of God. *Rom. xv.*

2 Hospitality do not forget, for by this some, being not aware of it, have entertained angels. *Heb. xiii.*

9 Using hospitality towards one another without murmuring. *1 S. Peter iv.*

HUMAN RESPECT.

2 Thou shalt not follow the multitude to do evil: neither shalt thou yield in judgment, to the opinion of the most part, to stray from the truth. *Ex. xxiii.*

2 How long will you judge unjustly: and accept the persons of the wicked? *Ps. lxxxi.*

25 He that feareth man, shall quickly fall ... *Prov. xxix.*

24 For thy soul be not ashamed to say Ecclus.
the truth. iv.

25 For there is a shame that bringeth
sin . . .

27 Reverence not thy neighbour in his
fall:

28 And refrain not to speak in the time of
salvation. Hide not thy wisdom in her
beauty.

32 Every one therefore that shall confess S. Matt.
me before men, I will also confess him before x.
my Father who is in heaven.

33 But he that shall deny me before men,
I will also deny him before my Father, who
is in heaven.

26 He that shall be ashamed of me and S. Luke
of my words, of him shall the Son of man ix.
be ashamed, when he shall come in his
majesty, and that of his Father, and of the
holy angels.

42 However many . . . did not confess S. John
him . . . xii.

43 For they loved the glory of men, more
than the glory of God.

10 With the heart, we believe unto jus- Rom. x.
tice; but with the mouth, confession is made
unto salvation.

9 King (Herod) was struck sad: yet be- S. Matt.
cause of his oath, and for them that sat with xiv.
him at table . . .

10 He sent, and beheaded John in the prison.

11 There is no respect of persons with God. — Rom. ii.

17 ... Who without respect of persons, judgeth according to every one's work ... — 1 S. Peter i.

12 ... If we deny him, he also will deny us. — 2 Tim. ii.

1 My brethren, have not the faith of our Lord Jesus Christ of glory with respect of persons. — S. James ii.

2 For if there shall come into your assembly a man having a golden ring, in fine apparel, and there shall come in also a poor man in mean attire,

3 And you have respect to him that is clothed with the fine apparel, and shall say to him: Sit thou here well: but say to the poor man: Stand thou there, or sit under my footstool:

4 Do you not judge within yourselves, and are become judges of unjust thoughts?

9 If you have respect to persons, you commit sin, being reproved by the law as transgressors.

HUMILITY.

22 ... I WILL be little in my own eyes ... — 2 Kings vi.

Humility.

28 For thou wilt save the humble people; but wilt bring down the eyes of the proud. — Ps. xvii.

29 He that hath been humbled, shall be in glory: and he that shall bow down his eyes, he shall be saved. — Job. xxii.

4 Whosoever is a little one, let him come to me. — Prov. ix.

6 The Lord is the keeper of little ones: I was humbled, and he delivered me. — Ps. cxiv.

18 He hath had regard to the prayer of the humble: and he hath not despised their petition. — Ps. ci.

2 . . . Where humility is, there also is wisdom. — Prov. xi.

33 . . . Humility goeth before glory. — Prov. xv.

4 The fruit of humility is the fear of the Lord, riches and glory and life. — Prov. xxii.

4 Seek not of the Lord a pre-eminence, nor of the king the seat of honour. — Ecclus. vii.

20 The greater thou art, the more humble thyself in all things, and thou shalt find grace before God. — Ecclus. iii.

21 For great is the power of God alone, and he is honoured by the humble.

9 Humble thyself to God, and wait for his hands. — Ecclus. xiii.

15 For thus saith the High and the Eminent that inhabiteth eternity: and his name is Holy, who dwelleth in the high and holy place, and with a contrite and humble spirit: — Isaias lvii.

to revive the spirit of the humble, and to revive the heart of the contrite.

2 ... To whom shall I have respect, but to him that is poor and little, and of a contrite spirit, and that trembleth at my words. — Isaias lxvi.

3 Blessed are the poor in spirit: for theirs is the kingdom of heaven. — S. Matt. v.

29 Take up my yoke upon you, and learn of me, because I am meek, and humble of heart; and you shall find rest to your souls. — S. Matt. xi.

15 Amen I say to you, whosoever shall not receive the kingdom of God as a little child, shall not enter into it. — S. Mark x.

48 ... He that is the lesser among you all, he is the greater. — S. Luke ix.

26 He that is the greater among you, let him become as the younger: and he that is the leader, as he that serveth. — S. Luke xxii.

27 ... I am in the midst of you, as he that serveth.

21 In that same hour he rejoiced* in the Holy Ghost, and said: I confess to thee, O Father, Lord of heaven and earth, that thou hast hid these things from the wise and prudent, and hast revealed them to little ones. Yea, Father, for so it hath seemed good in thy sight. — S. Luke x.

---

* That is: according to His humanity, He rejoiced in the Holy Ghost, and gave thanks to His eternal Father.

3 Let nothing be done through strife, nor by vain-glory: but in humility, let each esteem others better than themselves.* — Philip. ii.

5 ... And do ye all insinuate humility one to another: for God resisteth the proud, but to the humble he giveth grace. — 1 S. Peter v.

6 Be you humbled, therefore, under the mighty hand of God; that he may exalt you in the time of visitation.

HYPOCRISY.

5 THE praise of the wicked is short, and the joy of the hypocrite but for a moment. — Job. xx.

8 For what is the hope of the hypocrite if through covetousness he take by violence, and God deliver not his soul? — Job. xxvii.

9 Will God hear his cry, when distress shall come upon him?

10 Or can he delight himself in the Almighty, and call upon God at all times?

13 ... The hope of the hypocrite shall perish. — Job. viii.

36 Be not incredulous to the fear of the Lord: and come not to him with a double heart. — Ecclus. i.

37 Be not a hypocrite in the sight of men, and let not thy lips be a stumbling block to thee.

* See 5th to 8th v. inclusive.

38 Watch over them, lest thou fall, and bring dishonour upon thy soul,

39 And God discover thy secrets, and cast thee down in the midst of the congregation.

40 Because thou camest to the Lord wickedly, and thy heart is full of guile and deceit.

19 He that seeketh the law, shall be filled with it: and he that dealeth deceitfully, shall meet with a stumbling-block therein. — Ecclus. xxxii.

24 There is one that submitteth himself exceedingly with a great lowliness: and there is one that casteth down his countenance, and maketh as if he did not see that which is unknown: — Ecclus. xix.

25 And if he be hindered from sinning for want of power, if he shall find opportunity to do evil, he will do it.

15 Wo to you that are deep of heart, to hide your counsel from the Lord: and their works are in the dark, and they say: Who seeth us, and who knoweth us? — Isaais xxix.

3 And why seest thou the mote that is in thy brother's eye; and seest not the beam that is in thy own eye? — S. Matt. vii.

4 Or how sayest thou to thy brother: Let me cast the mote out of thy eye; and behold a beam is in thy own eye?

5 Thou hypocrite, cast out first the beam

out of thy own eye, and then shalt thou see to cast out the mote out of thy brother's eye.

24 Blind guides, who strain out a gnat and swallow a camel. — S. Matt. xxiii.

25 Wo to you scribes and Pharisees, hypocrites: because you make clean the outside of the cup and of the dish: but within you are full of rapine and uncleanness.

26 Thou blind Pharisee, first make clean the inside of the cup and of the dish, that the outside may become clean.

27 Wo to you, scribes and Pharisees, hypocrites: because you are like to whited sepulchres, which outwardly appear to men beautiful, but within are full of dead men's bones, and of all filthiness:

28 So you also outwardly indeed appear to men just; but inwardly you are full of hypocrisy and iniquity.

33 You serpents, generation of vipers, how will you flee from the judgment of hell?

6 ... Well did Isaias prophecy of you, hypocrites, as it is written: This people honoureth me with their lips, but their heart is far from me. — S. Mark vii.

42 Wo to you Pharisees, because you tithe mint and rue and every herb: and pass over judgment, and the charity of God. Now these things you ought to have done, and not to leave the other undone. — S. Luke xi.

26 Wo to you when men shall bless you: S. Luke
For according to these things did their vi.
fathers to the false prophets.

1 ... Beware ye of the leaven of the S. Luke
Pharisees, which is hypocrisy. xii.

2 For there is nothing covered, that shall
not be revealed: nor hidden, that shall not
be known.

3 For whatsoever things you have spoken
in darkness, shall be published in the light:
and that which you have spoken in the ear
in the chambers, shall be proclaimed on the
house-tops.

46 Beware of the scribes, who desire to S. Luke
walk in long robes, and love salutations in xx.
the market-place, and the first chairs in
the synagogues, and the chief rooms at
feasts.

47 Who devour the houses of widows,
feigning long prayer. These shall receive
greater damnation.

2 Speaking lies in hypocrisy, and having 1 Tim. iv.
their conscience seared.

1 ... I know thy works, that thou hast Apoc. iii.
the name of being alive: and thou art dead.

IGNORANCE OF GOD.

25 ... THE ignorant teach ye freely. 1 Esdras vii.
21 The lips of the just teach many: but Prov. x.

they that are ignorant, shall die in the want of understanding.

3 The ox knoweth his owner, and the ass his master's crib: but Israel hath not known me, and my people hath not understood. — Isaias i.

13 Therefore is my people led away captive, because they had not knowledge ... — Isaias v.

22 For my foolish people have not known me: they are foolish and senseless children: they are wise to do evils, but to do good they have no knowledge. — Jer. iv.

6 My people have been silent, because they had no knowledge: because thou hast rejected knowledge, I will reject thee, that thou shalt not do the office of priesthood to me ... — Osee iv.

34 ... Father, forgive them, for they know not what they do. — S. Luke xxiii.

19 ... Neither me do you know, nor my Father: if you did know me, perhaps you would know my Father also. — S. John viii.

4 He who saith that he knoweth him, and keepeth not his commandments, is a liar, and the truth is not in him. — 1 S. John ii.

8 He that loveth not, knoweth not God ... — 1 S. John iv.

3 For to know thee is perfect justice: and to know thy justice and thy power, is the root of immortality.* — Wis. xv.

* See also Ephes. iv. 18, in Character of the Wicked.

IGNORANCE OF AND UNCERTAINTY OF FUTURE EVENTS.

1 Boast not for to-morrow, for thou knowest not what the day to come may bring forth. — Prov. xxvii.

7 Because (man) is ignorant of things past, and things to come he cannot know by any messenger. — Eccles. viii.

1 ... There are just men and wise men, and their works are in the hand of God: and yet man knoweth not whether he be worthy of love, or hatred: — Eccles. ix.

2 But all things are kept uncertain for the time to come, because all things equally happen to the just and to the wicked, to the good and to the evil, to the clean and to the unclean, to him that offereth victims, and to him that despiseth sacrifices. As the good is, so also is the sinner: as the perjured, so he also that sweareth truth.

3 This is a very great evil among all things that are done under the sun, that the same things happen to all men: whereby also the hearts of the children of men are filled with evil, and with contempt while they live, and afterwards they shall be brought down to hell.

11 ... The race is not to the swift, nor

the battle to the strong, nor bread to the wise, nor riches to the learned, nor favour to the skilful: but time and chance in all.

13 ... Behold, now you that say: To-day or to-morrow we will go into such a city, and there we will spend a year, and will traffic, and make our gain. — S. James iv.

14 Whereas you know not what shall be on the morrow.

7 ... It is not for you to know the times or moments, which the Father hath put in his own power. — Acts i.

7 ... What I do, thou knowest not now, but thou shalt know hereafter. — S. John xiii.

INDISCRETION.

17 Let not thy mouth be accustomed to indiscreet speech: for therein is the word of sin. — Ecclus. xxiii.

22 Open not thy heart to every man: lest he repay thee with an evil turn, and speak reproachfully to thee. — Ecclus. viii.

17 He that discloseth the secret of a friend loseth his credit, and shall never find a friend to his mind. — Ecclus. xxviii.

18 Love thy neighbour, and be joined to him with fidelity.

19 But if thou discover his secrets, follow no more after him.

20 For as a man that destroyeth his friend, so also is he that destroyeth the friendship of his neighbour.

1 Repeat not the word which thou hast heard, and disclose not the thing that is secret. Ecclus. xlii.

INGRATITUDE.

13 HE that rendereth evil for good, evil shall not depart from his house. Prov. xvii.

21 A sinner attributeth to himself the goods of his surety: and he that is of an unthankful mind will leave him that delivered him. Ecclus. xxix.

14 A little city, and few men in it: there came against it a great king, and invested it and built bulwarks round about it, and the siege was perfect. Eccles. ix.

15 Now there was found in it a man poor and wise, and he delivered the city by his wisdom, and no man afterward remembered that poor man.

INGRATITUDE TO GOD.

6 Is this the return thou makest to the Lord, O foolish and senseless people? is not he thy father, that hath possessed thee, and made thee, and created thee? Deut. xxxii.

47 Because thou didst not serve the Lord Deut. xxviii.

thy God with joy and gladness of heart, for the abundance of all things:

48 Thou shalt serve thy enemy whom the Lord will send upon thee, in hunger, and thirst, and nakedness, and in want of all things: and he shall put an iron yoke upon thy neck, till he consume thee.

16 (You) have said: No, but we will flee to horses: therefore shall you flee. And we will mount upon swift ones: therefore shall they be swifter that shall pursue after you.   Isaias xxx.

1 ... My beloved* had a vineyard on a hill in a fruitful place.   Isaias v.

2 And he fenced it in, and picked the stones out of it, and planted it with the choicest wines, and built a tower in the midst thereof, and set up a wine press therein: and he looked that it should bring forth grapes, and it brought forth wild grapes.

11 And you made a ditch between the two walls for the water of the old pool: and you have not looked up to the maker thereof, nor regarded him even at a distance, that wrought it long ago.   Isaias xxii.

31 ... Why then have my people said: We are revolted, we will come to thee no more.   Jer. ii.

* "My cousin." So the prophet calls Christ, as being of his family and kindred, by descending from the house of David.

32 ... My people hath forgotten me days without number.

3 O my people, what have I done to thee, or in what have I molested thee? answer thou me. Mich. vi.

6 And they shall say to him: What are these wounds in the midst of thy hands? And he shall say: With these I was wounded in the house of them that loved me. Zach. xiii.

37 Jerusalem, Jerusalem, thou that killest the prophets, and stonest them that are sent unto thee, how often would I have gathered thy children, as the hen doth gather her chickens under her wings, and thou wouldest not! S. Matt. xxiii.

17 ... Were not ten made clean? and where are the nine? S. Luke xvii.

18 There is no one found to return and give glory to God, but this stranger.

46 Some of them went to the Pharisees, and told them the things that Jesus had done. S. John xi.

53 From that day therefore they devised to put him to death.

14 You denied the Holy one and the Just, and desired a murderer to be granted unto you. Acts iii.

INNOCENCE.

29 ... BEHOLD the Lamb of God, behold him who taketh away the sin of the world. — S. John i.

6 I will wash my hands among the innocent: and will compass thy altar, O Lord. — Ps. xxv.

33 God who hath girt me with strength: and made my way blameless. — Ps. xvii.

13 He will not deprive of good things them that walk in innocence ... — Ps. lxxxiii.

30 The innocent shall be saved, and he shall be saved by the cleanness of his hands. — Job. xxii.

1 Blessed is the man who hath not walked in the counsel of the ungodly, nor stood in the way of sinners, nor sat in the chair of pestilence.

2 But his will is in the law of the Lord, and on his law he shall meditate day and night. — Ps. i.

37 Keep innocence, and behold justice; for there are remnants for the peaceable man. — Ps. xxxvi.

INTEMPERANCE.

20 BE not in the feasts of great drinkers ... — Prov. xxiii.

11 ... He that is delighted in passing his time over wine, leaveth a reproach in his strong holds. — Prov. xii.

1 Wine is a luxurious thing, and drunkenness riotous: whosoever is delighted therewith shall not be wise.   Prov. xx.

17 He that loveth good cheer, shall be in want: he that loveth wine, and fat things, shall not be rich.   Prov. xxi.

21 Because they that give themselves to drinking, and that club together shall be consumed; and drowsiness shall be clothed in rags.   Prov. xxiii.

29 Who hath wo? whose father hath wo? who hath contentions? who falls into pits? who hath wounds without cause? who hath redness of eyes?

30 Surely they that pass their time in wine, and study to drink off their cups.

31 Look not upon the wine when it is yellow, when the colour thereof shineth in the glass: it goeth in pleasantly.

32 But in the end, it will bite like a snake, and will spread abroad poison like a basilisk.

33 Thy eyes shall behold strange women, and thy heart shall utter perverse things.

34 And thou shall be as one sleeping in the midst of the sea, and as a pilot fast asleep, when the stern is lost.

7 He that keepeth the law is a wise son: but he that feedeth gluttons, shameth his father.   Prov. xxviii.

Intemperance.

1 A workman that is a drunkard shall not be rich ...   Ecclus. xix.

30 Challenge not them that love wine: for wine hath destroyed very many.   Ecclus. xxxi.

32 Be not greedy in any feasting, and pour not out thyself upon any meat: Ecclus. xxxvii.

33 For in many meats there will be sickness, and greediness will turn to choler.

34 By surfeiting many have perished: but he that is temperate shall prolong life.

11 Wo to you that rise up early in the morning to follow drunkenness, and to drink till the evening, to be inflamed with wine.   Isaias v.

12 The harp, and the lyre, and the timbrel, and the pipe, and wine are in your feasts: and the work of the Lord you regard not, nor do you consider the works of his hands.

11 Fornication, and wine, and drunkenness, take away the understanding.   Osee iv.

13 ... Let us eat, and drink; for to-morrow we shall die.   Isaias xxii.

14 And the voice of the Lord of hosts was revealed in my ears: Surely this iniquity shall not be forgiven you till you die, saith the Lord God of hosts.

34 Take heed to yourselves, lest perhaps your hearts be overcharged with surfeiting and drunkenness and the cares of this life: and that day come upon you suddenly.   S. Luke xxi.

35 For as a snare shall it come upon all that sit upon the face of the whole earth.

18 Be not drunk with wine, wherein is luxury . . .   Ephes. v.

7 Neither become ye idolaters, as some of them: as it is written: The people sat down to eat and drink, and rose up to play.   1 Cor. x.

18 For many walk, of whom I have told you often (and now tell you weeping) that they are enemies of the cross of Christ;   Philip. iii.

19 Whose end is destruction: whose God is their belly: and whose glory is in their shame: who mind earthly things.

JESUS SAVIOUR.

8 DROP down dew, ye heavens, from above, and let the clouds rain the just: let the earth be opened, and bud forth a saviour: and let justice spring up together: I the Lord have created him.   Isaias xlv.

6 . . . Behold I have given thee to be the light of the Gentiles, that thou mayest be my salvation even to the farthest part of the earth.   Isaias xlix.

2 Unto you that fear my name the Sun of justice shall arise, and health in his wings . . .   Malach. iv.

21 This is the way, walk ye in it: and go not aside, neither to the right hand, nor to the left.   Isaias xxx.

4 Surely he hath borne our infirmities, and carried our sorrows: and we have thought him as it were a leper, and as one struck by God and afflicted. — Isaias liii.

5 But he was wounded for our iniquities, he was bruised for our sins: the chastisement of our peace was upon him, and by his bruises we are healed.

11 Behold the Lord hath made it to be heard in the ends of the earth, tell the daughter of Sion: Behold, thy Saviour cometh: behold his reward is with him, and his work before him. — Isaias lxii.

6 In those days shall Juda be saved, and Israel shall dwell confidently: and this is the name that they shall call him: The Lord our just one. — Jer. xxiii.

2 ... He is like a refining fire, and like the fuller's herb. — Malach. iii.

9 Rejoice greatly, O daughter of Sion, shout for joy, O daughter of Jerusalem: Behold thy king will come to thee, the just and saviour: he is poor, and riding upon an ass, and upon a colt the foal of an ass. — Zach. ix.

21 ... Thou shalt call his name Jesus. For he shall save his people from their sins. — S. Matt. i.

11 This day is born to you a Saviour, who is Christ the Lord. — S. Luke ii.

21 And in his name the Gentiles shall hope. — S. Matt. xii.

10 For the son of man is come to seek and to save that which was lost. — S. Luke xix.

79 To enlighten them that sit in darkness, and in the shadow of death: to direct our feet into the way of peace. — S. Luke i.

42 ... We ourselves have heard him, and know that this is indeed the Saviour of the world. — S. John iv.

28 Come to me, all you that labour, and are burdened, and I will refresh you. — S. Matt. xi.

12 ... They that are in health need not a physician, but they that are sick. — S. Matt. ix.

13 ... I am not come to call the just but sinners.

56 The son of man came not to destroy souls, but to save ... — S. Luke ix.

9 I am the door. By me if any man enter in, he shall be saved: and he shall go in, and go out, and shall find pastures. — S. John x.

11 I am the good shepherd. The good shepherd giveth his life for his sheep.

14 I am the good shepherd; I know mine, and mine know me.

6 ... I am the way, and the truth, and the life. No man cometh to the Father, but by me. — S. John xiv.

32 And I, if I be lifted up from the earth, will draw all things to myself. — S. John xii.

47 ... I came not to judge the world, but to save the world.

Jesus Saviour.

37 All that the Father giveth me shall come to me;* and him that cometh to me I will not cast out. — S. John vi.

1 Jesus spoke, and lifting up his eyes to heaven, he said: Father, the hour is come, glorify thy Son, that thy Son may glorify thee. — S. John xvii.

2 As thou hast given him power over all flesh, that he may give eternal life to all whom thou hast given him.

3 Now this is eternal life: That they may know thee, the only true God, and Jesus Christ, whom thou hast sent.

10 He that believeth in the Son of God, hath the testimony of God in himself... — 1 S. John v.

11 And this is the testimony, that God hath given to us eternal life. And this life is in his Son.

12 Neither is there salvation in any other. For there is no other name under heaven given to men, whereby we must be saved. — Acts iv.

43 To him all the prophets give testimony, that by his name all receive remission of sins, who believe in him. — Acts x.

5 ... Who is over all things, God blessed for ever. Amen. — Rom. ix.

---

* Not by compulsion, nor by laying the free will under any necessity, but by the strong and sweet motions of His heavenly grace.

19 ... Let every one depart from iniquity who nameth the name of the Lord. — 2 Tim. ii.

12 Giving thanks to God the Father, who hath made us worthy to be partakers of the lot of the saints in light, — Coloss. i.

13 Who hath delivered us from the power of darkness, and hath translated us into the kingdom of the Son of his love,

14 In whom we have redemption through his blood, the remission of sins.

18 And he is the head of the body, the church, who is the beginning, the first-born from the dead: that in all things, he may hold the primacy:

19 Because in him, it hath well pleased the Father, that all fulness should dwell:

20 And through him to reconcile all things unto himself, making peace through the blood of his cross, both as to the things on earth, and the things that are in heaven.

5 For there is one God, and one mediator* of God and men, the man Christ Jesus: — 1 Tim. ii.

* Christ is the one and only mediator of redemption: who gave Himself, as the apostle writes in the following verse, "redemption for all." He is also the only mediator, who stands in need of no other to recommend His petitions to the Father. But this is not against our seeking the prayers and intercessions, as well of the faithful upon earth, as of the saints and angels in heaven, for obtaining mercy, grace, and salvation through Jesus Christ. As St. Paul himself often desired the help of the prayers of the faithful, without injury to the mediatorship of Jesus Christ.

Jesus Saviour.

6 Who gave himself a redemption for
all . . .

9 And being consummated, he became Heb. v.
the cause of eternal salvation to all that
obey him.

24 For he that continueth for ever, hath Heb. vii.
an everlasting priesthood,

25 Whereby he is able also to save for
ever, them that come to God by him : always
living to make intercession for us.

8 Jesus Christ: yesterday, and to-day : Heb. xiii.
and the same for ever.

10 If, when we were enemies, we were re- Rom. v.
conciled to God by the death of his Son :
much more being reconciled, shall we be
saved by his life.

JUDGE NOT.

1 JUDGE not, that you may not be S. Matt.
judged. vii.

2 For with what judgment you judge, you
shall be judged : and with what measure you
mete, it shall be measured to you again.

37 Judge not, and you shall not be S. Luke
judged. Condemn not, and you shall not vi.
be condemned . . .

7 . . . He that is without sin among you, S. John
let him first cast a stone . . . viii.

13 Who art thou who judgest thy neigh- S. James
bour ? . . . iv.

1 And there were ... some that told [Jesus] of the Galileans, whose blood Pilate had mingled with their sacrifices. — S. Luke xiii.

2 And he answering said to them : Think you that these Galileans were sinners above all the men of Galilee, because they suffered such things ?

4 Or those eighteen upon whom the tower fell in Siloe and slew them : think you that they also were debtors above all the men that dwelt in Jerusalem ?

5 No, I say to you: but except you do penance you shall all likewise perish.

1 Wherefore thou art inexcusable, O man, whosoever thou art that judgest : for wherein thou judgest another, thou condemnest thyself. For thou dost the same thing which thou judgest. — Rom. ii.

3 And thinkest thou this, O man, that judgest them who do such things, and dost the same, that thou shalt escape the judgment of God ?

4 Who art thou that judgest another man's servant ? To his own lord he standeth or falleth. And he shall stand: for God is able to make him stand. — Rom. xiv.

10 But thou, why judgest thou thy brother ? or thou, why dost thou despise thy brother ? For we shall all stand before the judgment-seat of Christ.

12 So, then, every one of us shall render account to God for himself.

13 Let us not, therefore, judge one another any more . . .

3 . . . To me, it is a very small thing to be judged by you, or by man's day: but neither do I judge mine own self. — 1 Cor. iv.

4 For I am not conscious to myself of anything, yet am I not hereby justified: but he that judgeth me, is the Lord.

5 Therefore judge not before the time; until the Lord come, who both will bring to light the hidden things of darkness, and will make manifest the counsels of the hearts: and then shall every man have praise from God.

JUST JUDGMENTS OF GOD.

23 THE Lord will reward every one, according to his justice, and his faithfulness. — 1 Kings xxvi.

10 I am the Lord who search the heart, and prove the reins: who give to every one according to his way, and according to the fruit of his devices. — Jer. xvii.

29 . . . Know ye that there is a judgment. — Job xix.

13 . . . The Almighty will look into the causes of every one. — Job xxxv.

10 The wickedness of sinners shall be brought to nought: and thou shalt direct — Ps. vii.

the just: the searcher of hearts and reins is God.

4 ... God is faithful and without iniquity, he is just and right. — Deut. xxxii.

7 Who keepeth truth for ever: who executeth judgment for them that suffer wrong ... — Ps. cxlv.

8 ... I have seen those who work iniquity, and sow sorrows, and reap them, — Job iv.

9 Perishing by the blast of God, and consumed by the spirit of his wrath.

7 Thou hast not given water to the weary, thou hast withdrawn bread from the hungry. — Job xxii.

10 Therefore art thou surrounded with snares, and sudden fear troubleth thee.

10 Many are the scourges of the sinner, but mercy shall encompass him that hopeth in the Lord. — Ps. xxxi.

17 The countenance of the Lord is against them that do evil things: to cut off the remembrance of them from the earth. — Ps. xxxiii.

75 I know, O Lord, that thy judgments are equity: and in thy truth thou hast humbled me. — Ps. cxviii.

17 ... God shall judge both the just and the wicked, and then shall be the time of everything. — Eccles. iii.

28 For it is easy before God in the day of death to reward every one according to his ways. — Ecclus. xi.

18 Before man is life and death, good Ecclus.
and evil, that which he shall choose shall be xv.
given him.

14 And all things that are done, God will Eccles.
bring to judgment for every error, whether it xii.
be good or evil.

16 The Lord will not accept any person Ecclus.
against a poor man, and he will hear the xxxv.
prayer of him that is wronged.

23 And he will repay vengeance to the Gentiles, till he have taken away the multitude of the proud, and broken the sceptres of the unjust.

24 Till he have rendered to men according to their deeds: and according to the works of Adam, and according to his presumption.

25 Till he have judged the cause of his people, and he shall delight the just with his mercy.

11 Because sentence is not speedily pro- Eccles.
nounced against the evil, the children of men viii.
commit evils without any fear.

12 But though a sinner do evil a hundred times, and by patience be borne withal, I know from thence that it shall be well with them that fear God, who dread his face.

11 For he will render to a man his work, Job
and according to the ways of every one he xxxiv.
will reward them.

47 That servant who knew the will of his S. Luke
lord, and prepared not himself, and did not   xii.
according to his will, shall be beaten with
many stripes.

48 But he that knew not and did things
worthy of stripes shall be beaten with few
stripes . . .

2 For we know that the judgment of God Rom. ii.
is according to truth against them that do
such things.

4 Or despisest thou the riches of his goodness, and patience, and long-suffering? knowest thou not that the benignity of God leadeth thee to penance?

5 But according to thy hardness and impenitent heart, thou treasurest up to thyself wrath, against the day of wrath, and revelation of the just judgment of God,

6 Who will render to every man according to his works.

12 For whosoever have sinned without the law, shall perish without the law: and whosoever have sinned in the law, shall be judged by the law.

13 For not the hearers of the law are just before God; but the doers of the law shall be justified.

8 What things a man shall sow, those also Gal. vi.
shall he reap. For he that soweth in his flesh, of the flesh also shall reap corruption.

But he, that soweth in the Spirit, of the Spirit shall reap life everlasting.

8 That which bringeth forth thorns and briars, is reprobate, and very near unto a curse, whose end is to be burnt. *Heb. vi.*

22 See then the goodness and the severity of God : towards them indeed that are fallen, the severity ; but towards thee, the goodness of God, if thou abide in goodness, otherwise thou also shalt be cut off. *Rom. xi.*

33 O the depth of the riches, of the wisdom and of the knowledge of God ! How incomprehensible are his judgments, and how unsearchable his ways !

9 The Lord knoweth how to deliver the godly out of temptation, but to reserve the unjust unto the day of judgment to be tormented. *2 S. Peter ii.*

10 He that shall lead into captivity, shall go into captivity: he that shall kill by the sword, must be killed by the sword . . . *Apoc. xiii.*

11 He that hurteth, let him hurt still : * and he that is filthy, let him be filthy still : and he that is just, let him be justified still : and he that is holy, let him be sanctified still. *Apoc. xxii.*

* It is not an exhortation, or licence to go on in sin ; but an intimation, that how far soever the wicked may proceed, their progress shall quickly end, and then they must expect to meet with proportionable punishments.

14 Blessed are they that wash their robes in the blood of the Lamb: that they may have a right to the tree of life, and may enter in by the gates into the city.

12 Behold, I come quickly, and my reward is with me, to render to every man according to his works.

JUSTICE.

1 Thus saith the Lord: keep ye judgment, and do justice: for my salvation is near to come, and my justice to be revealed. — Isaias lvi.

12 ... Deliver him that is oppressed by violence out of the hand of the oppressor ... — Jer. xxi.

33 Strive for justice for thy soul, and even unto death fight for justice, and God will overthrow thy enemies for thee. — Ecclus. iv.

3 Thus saith the Lord: Execute judgment and justice, and deliver him that is oppressed out of the hand of the oppressor: and afflict not the stranger, the fatherless, and the widow, nor oppress them unjustly ... — Jer. xxii.

LAST JUDGMENT.

27 The Son of man shall come in the glory of his Father with his angels: and then will he render to every man according to his works. — S. Matt. xvi.

27 As lightning cometh out of the east, and appeareth even into the west: so shall also the coming of the Son of man be. *S. Matt. xxiv.*

36 But of that day and hour no one knoweth, no not the angels of heaven, but the Father alone.

36 Watch ye therefore, praying at all times, that you may be accounted worthy to escape all these things that are to come, and to stand before the Son of man. *S. Luke xxi.*

31 When the Son of man shall come in his majesty, and all the angels with him, then shall he sit upon the seat of his majesty: *S. Matt. xxv.*

32 And all nations shall be gathered together before him, and he shall separate them one from another, as the shepherd separateth the sheep from the goats:

33 And he shall set the sheep on his right hand, but the goats on his left.

34 Then shall the king say to them that shall be on his right hand: Come, ye blessed of my Father, possess you the kingdom prepared for you from the foundation of the world.

35 For I was hungry, and you gave me to eat: I was thirsty, and you gave me to drink: I was a stranger, and you took me in:

36 Naked, and you covered me: sick, and you visited me: I was in prison, and you came to me.

37 Then shall the just answer him, saying: Lord, when did we see thee hungry, and fed thee; thirsty, and gave thee drink?

38 And when did we see thee a stranger, and took thee in? or naked, and covered thee?

39 Or when did we see thee sick or in prison, and came to thee?

40 And the king, answering, shall say to them: Amen I say to you, as long as you did it to one of these my least brethren, you did it to me.

41 Then he shall say to them also that shall be on his left hand: Depart from me, you cursed, into everlasting fire which was prepared for the devil and his angels.

42 For I was hungry, and you gave me not to eat: I was thirsty, and you gave me not to drink.

43 I was a stranger, and you took me not in: naked, and you covered me not: sick and in prison, and you did not visit me.

44 Then they also shall answer him, saying: Lord, when did we see thee hungry or thirsty, or a stranger, or naked, or sick, or in prison, and did not minister to thee?

45 Then he shall answer them, saying: Amen I say to you, as long as you did it not to one of these least, neither did you do it to me.

46 And these shall go into everlasting punishment: but the just, into life everlasting.

22 ... The Father ... hath given all judgment to the Son.   S. John v.

23 That all men may honour the Son as they honour the Father ...

27 And he hath given him power to do judgment, because he is the Son of man.

10 For we must all appear before the judgment-seat of Christ, that every one may receive the proper things of the body, according as he hath done, whether it be good or evil.   2 Cor. v.

2 For yourselves know perfectly, that the day of the Lord shall so come, as a thief in the night.   1 Thess. v.

7 ... When the Lord Jesus shall be revealed from heaven with the angels of his power: 2 Thess. i.

8 In a flame of fire yielding vengeance to them who know not God, and who obey not the Gospel of our Lord Jesus Christ.

9 Who shall suffer eternal punishment in destruction, from the face of the Lord and from the glory of his power:

10 When he shall come to be glorified in his saints, and to be made wonderful in all them who have believed ...

10 The day of the Lord shall come as a thief, in which the heavens shall pass away with great violence, and the elements shall be melted with heat, and the earth and the works which are in it shall be burnt up. 2 S. Peter iii.

14 . . . Behold, the Lord cometh with thousands of his saints, S. Jude.

15 To execute judgment upon all . . .

7 Behold, he cometh with the clouds, and every eye shall see him, and they also that pierced him. And all the tribes of the earth shall bewail themselves because of him. Apoc. i.

15 And the kings of the earth, and the princes, and the tribunes, and the rich, and the strong, and every bondman, and every freeman hid themselves in the dens, and in the rocks of the mountains: Apoc. vi.

16 And they say to the mountains and the rocks: Fall upon us, and hide us from the face of him that sitteth upon the throne, and from the wrath of the Lamb:

17 For the great day of their wrath is come: and who shall be able to stand?

18 And the nations were angry; and thy wrath is come, and the time of the dead, that they should be judged, and that thou shouldest render reward to thy servants the prophets and to the saints, and to them that fear thy name, little and great, and shouldest destroy them who have corrupted the earth. Apoc. xi.

Last Judgment.

11 And I saw a great white throne, and one sitting upon it, from whose face the earth and heaven fled away, and there was no place found for them. — Apoc. xx.

12 And I saw the dead, great and small, standing in the presence of the throne, and the books were opened: and another book was opened, which is the book of life: and the dead were judged by those things which were written in the books, according to their works.

13 And the sea gave up the dead, that were in it, and death and hell gave up their dead, that were in them: and they were judged every one according to their works.

14 And hell and death were cast into the pool of fire. This is the second death.

LENDING AND BORROWING.

7 THE rich ruleth over the poor: and the borrower is servant to him that lendeth. — Prov. xxii.

33 Make not thyself poor by borrowing to contribute to feasts when thou hast nothing in thy purse: for thou shalt be an enemy to thy own life. — Ecclus. xviii.

7 If one of thy brethren that dwelleth within the gates of thy city in the land which the Lord thy God will give thee, come to — Deut. xv.

poverty: thou shalt not harden thy heart, nor close thy hand,

8 But shalt open it to the poor man, thou shalt lend him, that which thou perceivest he hath need of.

25 ... Thou shalt not be hard upon them as an extortioner, nor oppress them with usuries.   Exod. xxii.

21 The sinner shall borrow, and not pay again: but the just sheweth mercy and shall give.   Ps. xxxvi.

26 He sheweth mercy and lendeth all the day long; and his seed shall be in blessing.

5 Acceptable is the man that sheweth mercy and lendeth: he shall order his words with judgment.   Ps. cxi.

1 He that sheweth mercy, lendeth to his neighbour ...   Ecclus. xxix.

2 Lend to thy neighbour in the time of his need, and pay thou thy neighbour again in due time.

3 Keep thy word, and deal faithfully with him: and thou shalt always find that which is necessary for thee.

4 Many have looked upon a thing lent as a thing found, and have given trouble to them that helped them.

5 Till they receive, they kiss the hands of the lender, and in promises they humble their voice:

6 But when they should repay, they will ask time, and will return tedious and murmuring words, and will complain of the time:

7 And if he be able to pay, he will stand off, he will scarce pay one half, and will count it as if he had found it:

8 But if not, he will defraud him of his money, and he shall get him for an enemy without cause:

9 And he will pay him with reproaches and curses, and instead of honour and good turn will repay him injuries.

10 Many have refused to lend, not out of wickedness, but they were afraid to be defrauded without cause.

11 But yet towards the poor be thou more hearty, and delay not to show him mercy.

12 Help the poor because of the commandment: and send him not away empty-handed because of his poverty.

26 Recover thy neighbour according to thy power, and take heed to thyself that thou fall not.

42 Give to him that asketh of thee, and from him that would borrow of thee, turn not away. — S. Matt. v.

34 If you lend to them of whom you hope to receive, what thanks have you? for sinners also lend to sinners for to receive as much. — S. Luke vi.

35 ... Do good, and lend; hoping for nothing thereby: and your reward shall be great, and you shall be the sons of the most High; for he is kind to the unthankful and to the evil.

LIBERALITY.

7 WITH the Lord there is mercy: and with him plentiful redemption. — Ps. cxxix.

28 Say not to thy friend: Go, and come again: and to-morrow I will give to thee: when thou canst give at present. — Prov. iii.

20 Do not transgress against thy friend deferring money, nor despise thy dear brother for the sake of gold. — Ecclus. vii.

13 Lose thy money for thy brother and thy friend: and hide it not under a stone to be lost. — Ecclus. xxix.

24 Some distribute their own goods, and grow richer: others take away what is not their own, and are always in want. — Prov. xi.

28 The lips of many shall bless him that is liberal of his bread . . . — Ecclus. xxxi.

5 ... God ... giveth to all men abundantly, and upbraideth not. — S. James i.

9 For you know the grace of our Lord Jesus Christ, that being rich he became poor, for your sakes; that through his poverty you might be rich. — 2 Cor. viii.

17 ... The living God, who giveth us abundantly all things to enjoy. — 1 Tim. vi.

LOVE OF GAIN.

4 Labour not to be rich: but set bounds to thy prudence. — Prov. xxiii.

27 He that is greedy of gain troubleth his own house: but he that hateth bribes shall live. — Prov. xv.

20 ... He that maketh haste to be rich, shall not be innocent. — Prov. xxviii.

22 A man, that maketh haste to be rich, and envieth others, is ignorant that poverty shall come upon him.

20 Hell and destruction are never filled: so the eyes of men are never satisfied. — Prov. xxvii.

11 Substance got in haste shall be diminished: but that which by little and little is gathered with the hand shall increase. — Prov. xiii.

1 Set not thy heart upon unjust possessions ... — Ecclus. v.

10 Be not anxious for goods unjustly gotten: for they shall not profit thee in the day of calamity and revenge.

1 Watching for riches consumeth the flesh, and the thought thereof driveth away sleep. — Ecclus. xxxi.

2 The thinking beforehand turneth away the understanding ...

5 He that loveth gold, shall not be justi-

fied: and he that followeth after corruption, shall be filled with it.

7 Gold is a stumbling-block to them that sacrifice to it: wo to them that eagerly follow after it . . .

8 Wo to you that join house to house and lay field to field, even to the end of the place . . .   Isaias v.

1 Wo to you that devise that which is unprofitable, and work evil in your beds: in the morning light they execute it, because their hand is against God.   Mich. ii.

2 And they have coveted fields, and taken them by violence, and houses have they forcibly taken away: and oppressed a man and his house, a man and his inheritance.

24 No man can serve two masters. For either he will hate the one, and love the other: or he will sustain the one, and despise the other. You cannot serve God and Mammon.   S. Matt. vi.

26 What doth it profit a man, if he gain the whole world, and lose his own soul? . . .   S. Matt. xvi.

21 All seek the things that are their own; not the things that are Jesus Christ's.   Philip. ii.

5 . . . Men corrupted in mind, and who are destitute of the truth, esteeming gain to be piety.   1 Tim. vi.

6 But godliness with contentment is great gain.

Love of Gain.

7 For we brought nothing into this world, and certainly we can carry nothing out.

9 They who will become rich, fall into temptation, and into the snare of the devil, and into many unprofitable and hurtful desires, which drown men in destruction and perdition.

7 But the things that were gain to me, the same I have counted loss for Christ. — Philip. iii.

8 But, indeed, I esteem all things to be but loss, for the excellent knowledge of Jesus Christ my Lord: for whom I have suffered the loss of all things, and count them but as dung, that I may gain Christ.

LOVE TO GOD.

5 THOU shalt love the Lord thy God with thy whole heart, and with thy whole soul, and with thy whole strength. — Deut. vi.

20 ... Love the Lord thy God, and obey his voice, and adhere to him (for he is thy life, and the length of thy days) ... — Deut. xxx.

5 ... Love the Lord your God, and walk in all his ways, and keep all his commandments, and cleave to him, and serve him with all your heart, and with all your soul. — Josue xxii.

11 This only take care of with all diligence, that you love the Lord your God. — Josue xxiii.

15 But if it seem evil to you to serve the Lord, you have your choice: ... but as for me and my house we will serve the Lord. — Josue xxiv.

12 ... All they that love thy name shall glory in thee. — Ps. v.

2 I will love thee, O Lord, my strength. — Ps. xvii.

8 ... Thy name, and thy remembrance are the desire of the soul. — Isaias xxvi.

20 The Lord keepeth all them that love him ... — Ps. cxliv.

94 I am thine, save thou me ... — Ps. cxviii.

3 My soul hath thirsted after the strong living God: when shall I come and appear before the face of God? — Ps. xli.

26 For thee my flesh and my heart hath fainted away: thou art the God of my heart, and the God that is my portion for ever. — Ps. lxxii.

9 ... They that are faithful in love shall rest in him: for grace and peace is to his elect. — Wisd. iii.

14 The love of God is honourable wisdom. — Ecclus. i.

18 ... They that love him will keep his way. — Ecclus. ii.

4 He that loveth God, shall obtain pardon for his sins by prayer, and shall refrain himself from them, and shall be heard in the prayer of days. — Ecclus. iii.

47 ... Many sins are forgiven her, because she hath loved much ... — S. Luke vii.

Love to God.

37 Jesus said to him: Thou shalt love S. Matt.
the Lord thy God with thy whole heart, and xxii.
with thy whole soul, and with thy whole
mind.

38 This is the greatest and the first commandment.

8 ... Thou shalt adore the Lord thy God, S. Luke
and him only shalt thou serve. iv.

21 He that hath my commandments, and S. John
keepeth them: he it is that loveth me, and xiv.
he that loveth me, shall be loved of my
Father: and I will love him, and will manifest myself to him.

37 He that loveth father or mother more S. Matt.
than me, is not worthy of me; and he that x.
loveth son or daughter more than me, is not
worthy of me.

3 If any man love God, the same is known 1 Cor.
by him. viii.

28 And we know that to them that love Rom.
God, all things work together unto good, to viii.
such as according to his purpose are called
to be saints.

9 And this I pray, that your charity may Philip. i.
more and more abound in knowledge and in
all understanding.

17 That Christ may dwell by faith in your Ephes.
hearts: that being rooted and founded in iii.
charity,

18 You may be able to comprehend, with

all the saints, what is the breadth, and length, and height, and depth.

19 To know also the charity of Christ, which surpasseth knowledge, that you may be filled unto all the fulness of God.

1 Be ye therefore followers of God, as most dear children. — Ephes. v.

2 And walk in love, as Christ also hath loved us, and hath delivered himself for us, an oblation and a sacrifice to God, for an odour of sweetness.

5 And the Lord direct your hearts in the charity of God, and the patience of Christ. — 2 Thess. iii.

8 Whom having not seen, you love... — 1 S. Peter i.

21 Keep yourselves in the love of God, waiting for the mercy of our Lord Jesus Christ unto life everlasting. — S. Jude.

7 For God hath not given us the spirit of fear: but of power, and of love, and of sobriety. — 2 Tim. i.

18 Fear is not in charity: but perfect charity casteth out fear, because fear hath pain. And he that feareth, is not perfected in charity. — 1 S. John iv.

19 Let us therefore love God, because God first hath loved us.

20 If any man say, I love God, and hateth his brother; he is a liar. For he that loveth

not his brother, whom he seeth, how can he love God, whom he seeth not?

21 And this commandment we have from God, that he, who loveth God, love also his brother.

LOVE OF INSTRUCTION.

9 ... Teach a just man, and he shall make haste to receive it. Prov. ix.

8 The wise of heart receiveth precepts ... Prov. x.

14 Wise men lay up knowledge ...

14 The heart of the wise seeketh instruction ... Prov. xv.

20 Hear counsel, and receive instruction, that thou mayst be wise in thy latter end. Prov. xix.

22 Knowledge is a fountain of life to him that possesseth it ... Prov. xvi.

18 A man of sense will praise every wise word he shall hear, and will apply it to himself: the luxurious man hath heard it, and it shall displease him ... Ecclus. xxi.

24 Learning to the prudent is as an ornament of gold, and like a bracelet upon his right arm.

18 My son, from thy youth up receive instruction, and even to thy grey hairs thou shalt find wisdom. Ecclus. vi.

15 Wisdom and discipline, and the knowledge of the law are with God. Love and the ways of good things are with him. Ecclus. xi.

LOVE OF RULE.

8 ... HE that taketh authority to himself unjustly, shall be hated. — Ecclus. xx.

1 Be not many masters, my brethren, knowing that you receive the greater judgment. — S. James iii.

MAGISTRATES.*

6 ... TAKE heed what you do: for you exercise not the judgment of man, but of the Lord ... — 2 Paralip. xix.

21 Provide out of all the people able men, such as fear God, in whom there is truth, and that hate avarice ... — Ex. xviii.

22 Who may judge the people at all times ...

22 Let there be equal judgment among you, whether he be a stranger, or a native that offends. — Lev. xxiv.

16 ... Judge that which is just: whether it be one of your country, or a stranger. — Deut. i.

17 There shall be no difference of persons, you shall hear the little as well as the great: neither shall you respect any man's person, because it is the judgment of God ...

18 ... Judge the people with just judgment, — Deut. xvi.

19 And go not aside to either part. Thou shalt not accept person nor gifts: for gifts

* See Justice.

blind the eyes of the wise, and change the words of the just.

3 Neither shalt thou favour a poor man in judgment.   Ex. xxiii.

6 Thou shalt not go aside in the poor man's judgment.

7 Thou shalt fly lying. The innocent and just person thou shalt not put to death: because I abhor the wicked.

15 Thou shalt not do that which is unjust, nor judge unjustly. Respect not the person of the poor, nor honour the countenance of the mighty. But judge thy neighbour according to justice.   Lev. xix.

7 Let the fear of the Lord be with you, and do all things with diligence: for there is no iniquity with the Lord our God, nor respect of persons, nor desire of gifts.   2 Paralip. xix.

3 Judge for the needy and fatherless: do justice to the humble and the poor.   Ps. lxxxi.

4 Rescue the poor; and deliver the needy out of the hand of the sinner.

1 Love justice, you that are the judges of the earth. Think of the Lord in goodness, and seek him in simplicity of heart.   Wisd. i.

MALICE.

5 ... He that rejoiceth at another man's ruin, shall not be unpunished.   Prov. xvii.

17 When thy enemy shall fall, be not glad, and in his ruin let not thy heart rejoice. — Prov. xxiv.

17 Be not pleased with the wrong done by the unjust ... — Ecclus. ix.

28 If one cast a stone on high, it will fall upon his own head: and the deceitful stroke will wound the deceitful. — Ecclus. xxvii.

29 He that diggeth a pit, shall fall into it: and he that setteth a stone for his neighbour, shall stumble upon it: and he that layeth a snare for another, shall perish in it.

30 A mischievous counsel shall be rolled back upon the author, and he shall not know from whence it cometh to him.

4 Wisdom will not enter into a malicious soul, nor dwell in a body subject to sins. — Wisd. i.

15 ... There is no understanding where there is bitterness. — Ecclus. xxi.

6 (Charity) Rejoiceth not in iniquity, but rejoiceth with the truth. — 1 Cor. xiii.

20 Brethren, do not become children in sense, but in malice be children, and in sense be perfect. — 1 Cor. xiv.

MAN REGENERATE AND RENEWED.

3 JESUS answered, and said to him: Amen, amen I say to thee, unless a man be born again, he cannot see the kingdom of God. — S. John iii.

Man Regenerate and Renewed. 283

5 Amen, amen I say to thee, unless a man be born again of water and the Holy Ghost, he cannot enter into the kingdom of God.

6 That which is born of the flesh, is flesh: and that which is born of the Spirit, is spirit.

7 Wonder not, that I said to thee, you must be born again.

12 As many as received him, to them he gave power to be made the sons of God, to them that believe in his name. — S. John i.

13 Who are born, not of blood, nor of the will of the flesh, nor of the will of man, but of God.

5 Not by the works of justice, which we have done, but according to his mercy he saved us, by the laver of regeneration, and renovation of the Holy Ghost. — Titus iii.

6 Whom he hath poured forth upon us abundantly through Jesus Christ our Saviour.

7 ... Every one that loveth is born of God, and knoweth God. — 1 S. John iv.

23 Being born again not of corruptible seed, but incorruptible, by the word of God who liveth and remaineth for ever. — 1 S. Peter i.

29 If you know that he is just; know ye, that every one also, who doth justice, is born of him. — 1 S. John ii.

6 The Lord thy God will circumcise thy heart, and the heart of thy seed: that thou mayst love the Lord thy God with all thy — Deut. xxx.

heart and with all thy soul, that thou mayst live.

26 And I will give you a new heart, and put a new spirit within you: and I will take away the stony heart out of your flesh, and will give you a heart of flesh. *Ezech. xxxvi.*

29 He is a Jew that is one inwardly; and the circumcision is that of the heart, in the spirit, not in the letter: whose praise is not of men, but of God. *Rom. ii.*

15 For in Christ Jesus neither circumcision availeth any thing, nor uncircumcision, but a new creature. *Gal. vi.*

3 Know you not that all we, who are baptized in Christ Jesus, are baptized in his death? *Rom. vi.*

4 For we are buried together with him by baptism into death: that as Christ is risen from the dead by the glory of the Father, so we also may walk in newness of life.

6 Knowing this, that our old man is crucified with him, that the body of sin may be destroyed, and that we may serve sin no longer.

27 For as many of you as have been baptized in Christ, have put on Christ. *Gal. iii.*

17 If then any be in Christ a new creature: the old things are passed away, behold all things are made new. *2 Cor. v.*

21 If so be that you have heard him, and *Ephes. iv.*

have been taught in him, as the truth is in Jesus.

22 To put off, according to former conversation, the old man, who is corrupted according to the desire of error.

23 And be renewed in the spirit of your mind:

24 And put on the new man, who according to God, is created in justice, and holiness of truth.

47 The first man was of the earth, earthly: the second man, from heaven, heavenly.   1 Cor. xv.

49 As we have borne the image of the earthly, let us bear also the image of the heavenly.

1 Therefore, if you be risen with Christ, seek the things that are above; where Christ is sitting at the right hand of God: Coloss. iii.

9 ... Stripping yourselves of the old man with his deeds,

10 And putting on the new, him who is renewed unto knowledge, according to the image of him that created him.

11 Where there is neither gentile nor Jew, circumcision nor uncircumcision, Barbarian nor Scythian, bond nor free: but Christ is all, and in all.

MARRIAGE.

24 A MAN shall leave father and mother, and shall cleave to his wife: and they shall be two in one flesh. — Gen. ii.

15 ... Keep then your spirit, and despise not the wife of thy youth. — Malach. ii.

14 House and riches are given by parents: but a prudent wife is properly from the Lord. — Prov. xix.

3 A good wife is a good portion, she shall be given in the portion of them that fear God, to a man for his good deeds. — Ecclus. xxvi.

4 Rich or poor if his heart is good, his countenance shall be cheerful at all times.

22 He that hath found a good wife, hath found a good thing, and shall receive a pleasure from the Lord ... — Prov. xviii.

26 ... She is a help like to himself, and a pillar of rest. — Ecclus. xxxvi.

6 From the beginning of the creation, God made them male and female. — S. Mark x.

7 For this cause a man shall leave his father and mother; and shall cleave to his wife.

8 And they two shall be in one flesh. Therefore now they are not two, but one flesh.

9 What therefore God hath joined together, let not man put asunder.

18 Every one that putteth away his wife, and marrieth another, committeth adultery: and he that marrieth her that is put away from her husband, committeth adultery.

S. Luke xvi.

10 To them that are married, not I, but the Lord commandeth, that the wife depart not from her husband:

11 And if she depart, that she remain unmarried, or be reconciled to her husband. And let not the husband put away his wife.

1 Cor. vii.

39 A woman is bound by the law as long as her husband liveth: but if her husband die, she is at liberty: let her marry to whom she will: only in the Lord.

40 But more blessed shall she be, if she so remain, according to my counsel: and I think that I also have the Spirit of God.

22 Let women be subject to their husbands, as to the Lord:

Ephes. v.

23 Because the husband is the head of the wife; as Christ is the head of the church. . .

24 Therefore, as the church is subject to Christ, so also let the wives be to their husbands in all things.

25 Husbands, love your wives, as Christ also loved the church, and delivered himself for it:

26 That he might sanctify it . . .

28 So also ought men to love their wives as their own bodies. He that loveth his wife, loveth himself.

29 For no man ever hated his own flesh: but nourisheth and cherisheth it, as also Christ doth the church.

13 Adam was first formed: then Eve.   1 Tim. ii.

14 And Adam was not seduced: but the woman being seduced, was in the transgression.

15 Yet she shall be saved through child-bearing: if she continue in faith and love and sanctification with sobriety.

33 Let every one of you in particular love his wife as himself: and let the wife reverence her husband.   Ephes. v.

18 Wives, be subject to your husbands, as it behoveth in the Lord.   Coloss. iii.

19 Husbands, love your wives, and be not bitter towards them.

1 In like manner also let wives be subject to their husbands: that if any believe not the word, they may be won without the word, by the conversation of the wives,   1 S. Peter iii.

2 Considering your chaste conversation with fear.

3 Whose adorning let it not be the outward plaiting of the hair, or the wearing of gold, or the putting on of apparel:

4 But the hidden man of the heart, in the

incorruptibility of a quiet and meek spirit, which is rich* in the sight of God.

5 For after this manner, heretofore the holy women also, who trusted in God, adorned themselves, being in subjection to their own husbands.

6 As Sara obeyed Abraham, calling him lord: whose daughters you are, doing well, and not fearing any disturbance.

7 Ye husbands, likewise dwelling with them according to knowledge, giving honour to the woman as to the weaker vessel, and as to the coheirs of the grace of life: that your prayers be not hindered.

MEDITATION.

5 Thou shalt love the Lord thy God with thy whole heart, and with thy whole soul, and with thy whole strength. Deut. vi.

6 And these words that I command thee this day, shall be in thy heart.

7 And thou shalt tell them to thy children, and thou shalt meditate upon them sitting in thy house, and walking on thy journey, sleeping and rising.

19 Teach your children that they meditate on them, when thou sittest in thy house, and Deut. xi.

---

* Of great price in the sight of God.

when thou walkest on the way, and when thou liest down and risest up.

20 Thou shalt write them upon the posts and doors of thy house.

37 The Lord also said to Moses: Numb.
38 Speak to the children of Israel, and   xv.
thou shalt tell them to make to themselves fringes* in the corners of their garments, putting in them ribands of blue.

39 That when they shall see them, they may remember all the commandments of the Lord, and not follow their own thoughts and eyes going astray after divers things.

7 Take courage therefore, and be very Josue i.
valiant: that thou mayest observe and do all the law . . .

8 . . . Thou shalt meditate on it day and night, that thou mayest observe and do all things that are written in it: then shalt thou direct thy way, and understand it.

6 I thought upon the days of old: and I   Ps.
had in my mind the eternal years.   lxxvi.

7 And I meditated in the night with my own heart: and I was exercised and I swept my spirit.

47 I meditated also on thy command-   Ps.
ments, which I loved.   cxviii.

---

* The Pharisees enlarged these fringes through hypocrisy, Matt. xxiii. 5, to appear more zealous than other men for the law of God.

97 O how have I loved thy law, O Lord! it is my meditation all the day.

143 Trouble and anguish have found me; thy commandments are my meditation.

148 My eyes to thee have prevented the morning: that I might meditate on thy words.

6 In all thy ways think on him, and he will direct thy steps. — Prov. iii.

5 Evil men think not on judgment: but they that seek after the Lord, take notice of all things. — Prov. xxviii.

22 ... The things that God hath commanded thee, think on them always. — Ecclus. iii.

37 Let thy thoughts be upon the precepts of God, and meditate continually on his commandments: and he will give thee a heart, and the desire of wisdom shall be given to thee. — Ecclus. vi.

15 For the corruptible body is a load upon the soul, and the earthly habitation presseth down the mind that museth upon many things. — Wisd. ix

5 Thus saith the Lord of hosts: Set your hearts to consider your ways. — Aggeus i.

22 Blessed is the man that shall continue in wisdom and shall meditate in his justice, and in his mind shall think of the all seeing eye of God. — Ecclus. xiv.

40 In all thy works remember thy last Ecclus.
end, and thou shalt never sin. vii.

24 Remember the wrath that shall be at Ecclus.
the last day, and the time of repaying when xviii.
he shall turn away his face.

8 For the rest, brethren, whatsoever things Philip.
are true, whatsoever things are modest, what- iv.
soever just, whatsoever holy, whatsoever
lovely, whatsoever of good fame, if there be
any virtue, if any praise of discipline, think
on these things.

2 Looking on Jesus the author and finisher Heb. xii.
of faith, who having joy set before him, endured the cross, despising the shame, and
now sitteth on the right hand of the throne
of God.

3 For think diligently upon him who endured such opposition from sinners against
himself: that you be not wearied, fainting in
your minds.

MEEKNESS AND GENTLENESS.

9 (The Lord) will guide the mild in judg- Ps.
ment: he will teach the meek his ways. xxiv.

11 The meek shall inherit the land, and Ps.
shall delight in abundance of peace. xxxvi.

6 The Lord lifteth up the meek . . . Ps. cxlvi.

4 For the Lord is well pleased with his Ps.
people: and he will exalt the meek unto cxlix.
salvation.

34 ... To the meek he will give grace. Prov. iii.

19 It is better to be humbled with the meek, than to divide spoils with the proud. Prov. xvi.

19 My son, do thy works in meekness, and thou shalt be beloved above the glory of men. Ecclus. iii.

3 Seek the Lord, all ye meek of the earth, you that have wrought his judgment: seek the just, seek the meek: if by any means you may be hid in the day of the Lord's indignation. Sophon. ii.

10 When God arose in judgment, to save all the meek of the earth. Ps. lxxv.

19 The meek shall increase their joy in the Lord, and the poor men shall rejoice in the holy One of Israel. Isaias xxix.

4 Blessed are the meek: for they shall possess the land. S. Matt. v.

29 Take up my yoke upon you, and learn of me because I am meek, and humble of heart; and you shall find rest to your souls. S. Matt. xi.

1 Now I Paul myself beseech you, by the meekness and gentleness of Christ ... 2 Cor. x.

1 ... That you walk worthy of the vocation in which you are called. Ephes. iv.

2 With all humility and mildness, with patience, supporting one another in charity.

21 ... With meekness receive the engrafted word, which is able to save your souls. S. James i.

11 ... Pursue justice, piety, faith, charity, patience, meekness.   1 Tim. vi.

2 ... Showing all mildness towards all men.   Titus iii.

MERCY.

21 ... He that believeth in the Lord, loveth mercy.   Prov. xiv.

6 If thou find as thou walkest by the way, a bird's nest in a tree, or on the ground, and the dam sitting upon the young, or upon the eggs: thou shalt not take her with her young: Deut. xxii.

7 But shalt let her go, keeping the young which thou hast caught that it may be well with thee, and thou mayest live a long time.

4 Thou shalt not muzzle the ox that treadeth out thy corn on the floor.*   Deut. xxv.

7 ... First give the sheep drink, and so lead them back to feed.   Gen. xxix.

14 ... Drink, and I will give thy camels drink also ...   Gen. xxiv.

24 Hast thou cattle? have an eye to them ...   Ecclus. vii.

10 The just regardeth the lives of his beasts: but the bowels of the wicked are cruel.   Prov. xii.

---

* S. Paul understands this of the spiritual labourer in the church of God, who is not to be denied his maintenance. 1 Cor. ix., 8th, 9th, and 10th verses.

13 ... The just are merciful, and show mercy. — Prov. xiii.

3 Let not mercy and truth leave thee, put them about thy neck, and write them in the tables of thy heart. — Prov. iii.

17 A merciful man doth good to his own soul: but he that is cruel casteth off even his own kindred. — Prov. xi.

19 Clemency prepareth life ...

21 ... He that sheweth mercy to the poor, shall be blessed. — Prov. xiv.

22 ... Mercy and truth prepare good things.

3 To do mercy and judgment, pleaseth the Lord more than victims. — Prov. xxi.

21 He that followeth justice and mercy, shall find life, justice, and glory.

9 He that is inclined to mercy, shall be blessed: for of his bread he hath given to the poor. — Prov. xxii.

9 ... Shew ye mercy and compassion every man to his brother. — Zach. vii.

7 Blessed are the merciful: for they shall obtain mercy. — S. Matt. v.

36 Be ye therefore merciful, as your Father also is merciful. — S. Luke vi.

12 Put ye on therefore, as the elect of God, holy, and beloved, the bowels of mercy, benignity, humility, modesty, patience, — Coloss. iii.

13 For judgment without mercy, to him that hath not done mercy. And mercy exalteth itself above judgment. — S. James ii.

MODESTY.

7 LOOK not round about thee in the ways of the city, nor wander up and down in the streets thereof. — Ecclus. ix.

8 Turn away thy face from a woman dressed up, and gaze not about upon another's beauty.

2 Let another praise thee, and not thy own mouth: a stranger, and not thy own lips. — Prov. xxvii.

25 ... There is a shame that bringeth glory and grace. — Ecclus. iv.

19 A holy and shame faced woman is grace upon grace. — Ecclus. xxvi.

MORTIFICATION AND SELF DENIAL.

12 EMBRACE discipline, lest at any time the Lord be angry, and you perish from the just way. — Ps. ii.

30 Go not after thy lusts, and turn away from thine own will. — Ecclus. xviii.

31 If thou give to thy soul her desires, she will make thee a joy to thy enemies.

23 And He said to all: If any man will — S. Luke ix.

come after me, let him deny himself and take up his cross daily, and follow me.

25 . . . He that hateth his life in this world, keepeth it unto life eternal.   S. John xii.

24 They that are Christ's, have crucified their flesh with the vices and concupiscences.   Gal. v.

12 Therefore, brethren, we are debtors, not to the flesh, to live according to the flesh.   Rom. viii.

13 For if you live according to the flesh, you shall die. But if by the Spirit you mortify the deeds of the flesh, you shall live.

25 And every one that striveth for the mastery refraineth himself from all things: and they indeed that they may receive a corruptible crown: but we an incorruptible one.   1 Cor. ix.

26 I therefore so run, not as at an uncertainty: I so fight, not as one beating the air:

27 But I chastise* my body, and bring it into subjection: lest perhaps, when I have preached to others, I myself should become a cast away.

5 Mortify therefore your members which are upon the earth, fornication, uncleanness, lust, evil concupiscence, and covetousness, which is the service of idols.   Coloss. iii.

---

* Here S. Paul shows the necessity of self denial and mortification to subdue the flesh and its inordinate desires.

6 For which things the wrath of God cometh upon the children of unbelief.

14 Put ye on the Lord Jesus Christ, and make not provision for the flesh in its concupiscences. — Rom. xiii.

16 I say then, walk in the spirit, and you shall not fulfil the lusts of the flesh. — Gal. v.

MURDER.

13 THOU shalt not kill. — Ex. xx.

5 ... At the hand of every man, and of his brother, will I require the life of man. — Gen. ix.

6 Whosoever shall shed man's blood, his blood shall be shed: for man was made to the image of God.

14 If a man kill his neighbour on set purpose, and by lying in wait for him: thou shalt take him away from my altar, that he may die. — Ex. xxi.

30 The murderer shall be punished by witnesses: none shall be condemned upon the evidence of one man. — Numb. xxxv.

31 You shall not take money of him that is guilty of blood, but he shall die forthwith.

21 You have heard that it was said to them of old: Thou shalt not kill. And whosoever shall kill shall be in danger of the judgment. — S. Matt. v.

22 But I say to you, that whosoever is

angry with his brother, shall be in danger of the judgment . . .

44 You are of your father the devil, and the desires of your father you will do. He was a murderer from the beginning . . .   S. John viii.

15 . . . And you know that no murderer hath eternal life abiding in himself.   1 S. John iii.

MURMURING.

1 In the meantime there arose a murmuring of the people against the Lord, as it were repining at their fatigue. And when the Lord heard it he was angry . . .   Numb. xi.

29 In the wilderness shall your carcasses lie. All you that were numbered from twenty years old and upward, and have murmured against me.   Numb. xiv.

24 . . . They believed not his word, 25 And they murmured in their tents . . .   Ps. cv.

10 . . . The tumult of murmuring shall not be hid.   Wisd. i.

11 Keep yourselves therefore from murmuring, which profiteth nothing . . .

3 The folly of a man supplanteth his steps: and he fretteth in his mind against God.   Prov. xix.

39 Why hath a living man murmured, man suffering for his sins?   Lament. iii.

13 Your words hath been unsufferable to me, saith the Lord.   Malach. iii.

14 And you have said: What have we spoken against thee? You have said: He laboureth in vain that serveth God, and what profit is it, that we have kept his ordinances, and that we have walked sorrowful before the Lord of hosts?

15 Wherefore now we call the proud people happy, for they that work wickedness are built up, and they have tempted God, and are preserved.

20 O man, who art thou that repliest against God? Shall the thing formed say to him that formed it, why hast thou made me thus? *Rom. ix.*

10 Neither do you murmur: as some of them murmured, and were destroyed by the destroyer. *1 Cor. x.*

16 These are murmurers, full of complaints, walking according to their own desires, and their mouth speaketh proud things, admiring persons for gain's sake. *S. Jude.*

14 Do ye all things without murmurings and hesitations. *Philip. ii.*

NATIONS' HAPPINESS AND WO.

3 If you walk in my precepts, and keep my commandments, and do them, I will give you rain in due seasons. *Lev. xxvi.*

4 And the ground shall bring forth its in-

crease, and the trees shall be filled with fruit.

22 Josue said to the people: You are witnesses, that you yourselves have chosen you the Lord to serve him. And they answered: We are witnesses. — Josue xxiv.

15 ... Happy is that people whose God is the Lord. — Ps. cxliii.

34 Justice exalteth a nation: but sin maketh nations miserable. — Prov. xiv.

14 Where there is no governor, the people shall fall: but there is safety where there is much counsel. — Prov. xi.

5 By the greatness of thy wisdom, and by thy traffic thou hast increased thy strength: and thy heart is lifted up with thy strength. — Ezech. xxviii.

7 ... All iniquity of nations is execrable. — Ecclus. x.

8 A kingdom is translated from one people to another, because of injustices, and wrongs, and injuries, and divers deceits.

18 God hath made the roots of proud nations to wither, and hath planted the humble of these nations.

7 Seek ye the peace of the city, to which I have caused you to be carried away captives: and pray to the Lord for it: for in the peace thereof shall be your peace. — Jer. xxix.

19 By the wrath of the Lord of hosts the land is troubled, and the people shall be as — Isaias ix.

fuel for the fire: no man shall spare his brother.

49 Behold this was the iniquity of Sodom thy sister, pride, fulness of bread and abundance, and the idleness of her and of her daughters: and they did not put forth their hand to the needy, and to the poor. — Ezech. xvi.

10 Because the land is full of adulterers, because the land hath mourned by reason of cursing, the fields of the desert are dried up: and their course is become evil, and their strength unlike. — Jer. xxiii.

32 And thou hast delivered us into the hands of our enemies that are unjust, and most wicked, and prevaricators, and to a king unjust, and most wicked beyond all that are upon the earth. — Daniel iii.

13 And the people are not returned to him who hath struck them, and have not sought after the Lord of hosts. — Isaias ix.

34 And behold, the whole city, [country of the Gerasens] came out to meet Jesus, and when they saw him, they besought him that he would depart from their coasts. — S. Matt. viii.

29 Wo to you Scribes and Pharisees, hypocrites ... — S. Matt. xxiii.

31 You are witnesses against yourselves, that you are the sons of them that killed the prophets.

38 Behold, your house shall be left to you desolate,

39 For I say to you, you shall not see me henceforth till you say: Blessed is he that cometh in the name of the Lord.

22 Pilate saith to them: What shall I do then with Jesus that is called Christ? They say all: Let him be crucified.   S. Matt. xxvii.

24 And Pilate ... taking water washed his hands before the people, saying: I am innocent of the blood of this just man: Look you to it.

25 And the whole people answering, said: His blood be upon us, and upon our children.

OBEDIENCE.

5 IF therefore you will hear my voice, and keep my covenant, you shall be my peculiar possession above all people; for all the earth is mine.   Ex. xix.

7 ... All things that the Lord hath spoken we will do, we will be obedient.   Ex. xxiv.

22 And Samuel said: Doth the Lord desire holocausts and victims, and not rather that the voice of the Lord should be obeyed? For obedience is better than sacrifices: and to hearken rather than to offer the fat of rams.   1 Kings xv.

20 ... Hearken, I beseech thee, to the   Jer. xxxviii.

word of the Lord, which I speak to thee, and it shall be well with thee, and thy soul shall live.

28 The mind of the just studieth obedience ... — Prov. xv.

28 ... An obedient man shall speak of victory. — Prov. xxi.

27 It is good for a man, when he hath borne the yoke from his youth. — Lament. iii.

24 And Joseph rising up from sleep, did as the Angel of the Lord had commanded him. — S. Matt. i.

1 Let every soul be subject to higher powers: for there is no power but from God: and those that are, are ordained of God. — Rom. xiii.

16 Know you not, that to whom you yield yourselves servants to obey, his servants you are whom you obey, whether it be of sin unto death, or of obedience unto justice. — Rom. vi.

7 Be subject therefore to God ... — S. James iv.

19 For as by the disobedience of one man, many were made sinners; so also by the obedience of one many shall be made just. — Rom. v.

19 Your obedience is published in every place ... — Rom. xvi.

21 Being subject one to another in the fear of Christ. — Ephes. v.

9 Moreover we have had fathers of our flesh, for instructors, and we reverenced — Heb. xii.

them: shall we not much more obey the
Father of spirits, and live?

14 As children of obedience, not fashioned   1 S. Peter
according to the former desires of your igno-   i.
rance.

22 Purifying your souls in the obedience
of charity, with a brotherly love, from a sincere
heart love one another earnestly.

51 And (Jesus) went down with them (his   S. Luke
parents) and came to Nazareth : and he was   ii.
subject to them.

8 He humbled himself, becoming obedient   Philip.
unto death : even to the death of the cross.   ii.

13 Be ye subject therefore to every   1 S. Peter
human creature for God's sake . . .   ii.

OBEDIENCE TO CHRIST'S WORD.

37 . . . EVERY one that is of the truth,   S. John
heareth my voice.   xviii.

4 . . . Man liveth not by bread alone but   S. Matt.
by every word that proceedeth out of the   iv.
mouth of God.

24 Whosoever heareth these my words,   S. Matt.
and doeth them, shall be likened to a wise   vii.
man, who built his house upon a rock.

25 And the rain fell, and the floods came,
and the winds blew, and they beat upon that
house, and it fell not: for it was founded
upon a rock.

31 ... If you continue in my word, you shall be my disciples indeed: S. John viii.

32 And you shall know the truth, and the truth shall make you free.

51 Amen, amen, I say to you: If any man keep my word, he shall not see death for ever.

27 My sheep hear my voice: and I know them, and they follow me. S. John x.

48 He that despiseth me, and receiveth not my words, hath one that judgeth him; the word that I have spoken, the same shall judge him in the last day. S. John xii.

49 For I have not spoken of myself, but the Father who sent me, he gave me commandment what I should say and what I should speak.

50 And I know that his commandment is life everlasting. The things therefore that I speak, even as the Father said unto me, so do I speak.

47 He that is of God, heareth the words of God ... S. John viii.

23 ... If any one love me, he will keep my word, and my Father will love him, and we will come to him, and will make our abode with him. S. John xiv.

25 The word of the Lord endureth for ever, and this is the word which by the gospel hath been preached unto you. 1 S. Peter i.

5 ... Bringing into captivity every understanding unto the obedience of Christ. 2 Cor. x.

5 He that keepeth his word, in him in very deed the charity of God is perfected: and by this we know that we are in him. — 1 S. John ii.

1 Therefore ought we more diligently to observe the things which we have heard; lest at any time we should let them slip. — Heb. ii.

16 Let the word of Christ dwell in you abundantly, in all wisdom: teaching and admonishing one another in psalms, hymns, and spiritual canticles, singing in grace in your hearts to God. — Coloss. iii.

OLD AGE.

32 Rise up before the hoary head, and honour the person of the aged man: and fear the Lord thy God. I am the Lord. — Lev. xix.

7 Despise not a man in his old age: for we also shall become old. — Ecclus. viii.

31 Old age is a crown of dignity, when it is found in the ways of justice. — Prov. xvi.

8 Much experience is the crown of old men, and the fear of God is their glory. — Ecclus. xxv.

8 Venerable old age is not that of long time, nor counted by the number of years... — Wisd. iv.

9 A spotless life is old age.

PARDON OF SIN.

11 For thy name's sake, O Lord, thou wilt pardon my sin, for it is great. — Ps. xxiv.

1 My son, hast thou sinned? do so no more: but for thy former sins also pray that they may be forgiven thee. — Ecclus. xxi.

1 Blessed are they whose iniquities are forgiven, and whose sins are covered. — Ps. xxxi.

2 Blessed is the man to whom the Lord hath not imputed sin . . .

25 I am, I am he that blot out thy iniquities for my own sake, and I will not remember thy sins. — Isaias xliii.

18 . . . If your sins be as scarlet, they shall be made as white as snow: and if they be red as crimson, they shall be white as wool. — Isaias i.

1 Be comforted, be comforted, my people, saith your God. — Isaias xl.

22 I have blotted out thy iniquities as a cloud, and thy sins as a mist: return to me, for I have redeemed thee. — Isaias xliv.

18 I saw his ways, and I healed him, and brought him back, and restored comforts to him, and to them that mourn for him. — Isaias lvii.

34 . . . I will forgive their iniquity, and will remember their sin no more. — Jer. xxxi.

6 Behold I will close their wounds and give them health, and I will cure them: and I will reveal to them the prayer of peace and truth. — Jer. xxxiii.

8 And I will cleanse them from all their iniquity, whereby they have sinned against

me: and I will forgive all their iniquities, whereby they have sinned against me, and despised me.

22 I will not remember all his iniquities that he hath done: in his justice which he hath wrought, he shall live. — Ezech. xviii.

13 Blessed is thy name, O God of our fathers: who when thou hast been angry, wilt shew mercy, and in the time of tribulation forgivest the sins of them that call upon thee. — Tobias iii.

2 ... I know that thou art a gracious and merciful God, patient, and of much compassion, and easy to forgive evil. — Jonas iv.

2 Speak ye to the heart of Jerusalem, and call to her: for her evil is come to an end, her iniquity is forgiven: she hath received of the hand of the Lord double for all her sins. — Isaias xl.

1 In that day there shall be a fountain open to the house of David, and to the inhabitants of Jerusalem: for the washing of the sinner, and of the unclean woman. — Zach. xiii.

47 ... Many sins are forgiven her, because she hath loved much. But to whom less is forgiven, he loveth less. — S. Luke vii.

4 Forgive us our sins, for we also forgive every one that is indebted to us. — S. Luke xi.

5 And when Jesus had seen their faith, he saith to the sick of the palsy: Son, thy sins are forgiven thee. — S. Mark ii.

7 ... Who can forgive sins, but God only?
48 ... Thy sins are forgiven thee.   S. Luke vii.
49 ... Who is this that forgiveth sins also?

38 Be it known therefore to you, men brethren, that through him forgiveness of sins is preached to you ...   Acts xiii.

19 For God indeed was in Christ reconciling the world to himself, not imputing to them their sins ...   2 Cor. v.

21 Him, that knew no sin, for us he hath made sin, that we might be made the justice of God in him.

7 ... The blood of Jesus Christ his Son cleanseth us from all sin.   1 S. John i.

2 And he is the propitiation for our sins: and not for ours only, but also for those of the whole world.   1 S. John ii.

14 Blotting out the handwriting of the decree that was against us, which was contrary to us. And he hath taken the same out of the way, fastening it to the cross.   Coloss. ii.

12 I write unto you, little children, because your sins are forgiven you for his name's sake.   1 S. John ii.

14 In whom we have redemption through his blood, the remission of sins.   Coloss. i.

11 ... Go, and now sin no more.   S. John viii.

PATIENCE.

6 BE thou, O my soul, subject to God: for from him is my patience. — Ps. lxi.

29 He that is patient, is governed with much wisdom . . . — Prov. xiv.

18 A passionate man stirreth up strifes: he that is patient appeaseth those that are stirred up. — Prov. xv.

32 The patient man is better than the valiant: and he that ruleth his spirit, than he that taketh cities. — Prov. xvi.

11 The learning of a man is known by patience: and his glory is to pass over wrongs. — Prov. xix.

29 A patient man shall bear for a time, and afterwards joy shall be restored to him. — Ecclus. i.

5 Thou art my patience, O Lord . . . — Ps. lxx.

20 . . . He hath strengthened them that were fainting in patience, and hath appointed to them the lot of truth. — Ecclus. xvii.

11 For I know the thoughts that I think towards you, saith the Lord, thoughts of peace, and not of affliction, to give you an end and patience. — Jer. xxix.

19 In your patience you shall possess your souls. — S. Luke xxi.

15 (The seed) on the good ground, are they who in a good and very good heart, — S. Luke viii.

hearing the word, keep it, and bring forth fruit in patience.

14 ... Be patient towards all men.   1 Thess. v.

12 ... Patient in tribulation ...   Rom. xii.

36 For patience is necessary for you: that, doing the will of God, you may receive the promise.   Heb. x.

4 And patience hath a perfect work: that you may be perfect and entire, failing in nothing.   S. James i.

7 Be patient, therefore, brethren, until the coming of the Lord. Behold, the husbandman waiteth for the precious fruit of the earth: patiently bearing till he receive the early and the latter rain.   S. James v.

8 Be you therefore also patient, and strengthen your hearts: for the coming of the Lord is at hand.

2 I know thy works, and thy labour, and thy patience, and how thou canst not bear them that are evil ...   Apoc. ii.

3 And thou hast patience, and hast endured for my name, and hast not fainted.

12 Here is the patience of the saints, who keep the commandments of God, and the faith of Jesus.   Apoc. xiv.

10 Because thou hast kept the word of my patience, I will also keep thee from the hour of temptation, which shall come upon the whole world to try them that dwell upon the earth.   Apoc. iii.

PATIENT ENDURANCE.

24 ... STAND firm in the lot set before thee, and in prayer to the most high God. Ecclus. xvii.

39 I say to you, not to resist evil: but if one strike thee on thy right cheek, turn to him the other also. S. Matt. v.

40 And if any man will go to law with thee, and take away thy coat, let him have thy cloak also.

41 And whosoever shall force thee to go one mile, go with him other two.

30 Give to every one that asketh thee, and of him that taketh away thy goods, ask them not again. S. Luke vi.

7 Already, indeed, there is plainly a fault* among you, that you have law-suits one with another. Why do you not rather take wrong? why do you not rather suffer yourselves to be defrauded? 1 Cor. vi.

4 Charity is patient, is kind ... 1 Cor. xiii.

20 For you suffer, if a man bring you into bondage, if a man devour you, if a man take from you, if a man be extolled, if a man strike you on the face. 2 Cor. xi.

3 And not only so; but we glory also in Rom. v.

---

* Law-suits can hardly ever be without a fault, on one side or the other; and oftentimes on both sides.

tribulations, knowing that tribulation worketh patience:

4 And patience trial; and trial hope.

11 Strengthened with all might, according to the power of his glory, in all patience and long-suffering with joy. — Coloss. i.

10 Take, my brethren, for an example of suffering evil, of labour and patience, the prophets, who spoke in the name of the Lord. — S. James v.

11 Behold we account them blessed who have endured. You have heard of the patience of Job, and you have seen the end of the Lord, that the Lord is merciful and compassionate.

20 What glory is it, if committing sin and being buffeted for it you endure? But if doing well you suffer patiently; this is thanksworthy before God. — 1 S. Peter ii.

21 For unto this are you called: because Christ also suffered for us, leaving you an example that you should follow his steps.

PAYMENTS AND WAGES.

14 THOU shalt not refuse the hire of the needy, and the poor, whether he be thy brother, or a stranger that dwelleth with thee in the land, and is within thy gates: — Deut. xxiv.

15 But thou shalt pay him the price of

his labour.... lest he cry against thee to the Lord, and it be reputed to thee for a sin.

15 If any man hath done any work for thee, immediately pay him his hire, and let not the wages of thy hired servant stay with thee at all. — Tobias iv.

31 He that oppresseth the poor, upbraideth his maker: but he that hath pity on the poor, honoureth him. — Prov. xiv.

16 He that oppresseth the poor, to increase his own riches, shall himself give to one that is richer, and shall be in need. — Prov. xxii.

22 Do no violence to the poor, because he is poor: and do not oppress the needy in the gate:

23 Because the Lord will judge his cause, and will afflict them that have afflicted his soul.

8 Bow down thy ear cheerfully to the poor, and pay what thou owest, and answer him peaceable words with mildness. — Ecclus. iv.

24 He that offereth sacrifice of the goods of the poor, is as one that sacrificeth the son in the presence of his father. — Ecclus. xxxiv.

25 The bread of the needy, is the life of the poor: he that defraudeth them thereof, is a man of blood.

26 He that taketh away the bread gotten by sweat, is like him that killeth his neighbour.

27 He that sheddeth blood, and he that defraudeth the labourer of his hire, are brothers.

16 The Lord will not accept any person against a poor man, and he will hear the prayer of him that is wronged. — Ecclus. xxxv.

1 Go to now, ye rich men, weep and howl in your miseries, which shall come upon you. — S. James v.

2 Your riches are corrupted: and your garments are moth eaten.

3 Your gold and silver is cankered: and the rust of them shall be for a testimony against you, and shall eat your flesh like fire. You have stored up to yourselves wrath against the last days.

4 Behold the hire of the labourers, who have reaped down your fields, which by fraud has been kept back by you, crieth: and the cry of them hath entered into the ears of the Lord of sabaoth.

PEACE.

18 My people shall sit in the beauty of peace, and in the tabernacles of confidence, and in wealthy rest. — Isaias xxxii.

12 Lord, thou wilt give us peace: for thou hast wrought all our works for us. — Isaias xxvi.

16 I am not troubled, following thee for my pastor, and I have not desired the day of man, thou knowest ... — Jer. xvii.

26 The Lord turn his countenance to thee, and give thee peace. — Numb. vi.

21 Submit thyself then to him, and be at peace: and thereby thou shalt have the best fruits. — Job xxii.

29 For when he granteth peace, who is there that can condemn? ... — Job xxxiv.

10 ... The Lord will bless his people with peace. — Ps. xxviii.

165 Much peace have they that love thy law: and to them there is no stumbling-block. — Ps. cxviii.

7 With them that hated peace I was peaceable ... — Ps. cxix.

7 When the ways of man shall please the Lord, he will convert even his enemies to peace. — Prov. xvi.

19 ... Only love ye truth and peace. — Zach. viii.

17 And the work of justice shall be peace, and the service of justice quietness, and security for ever. — Isaias xxxii.

14 Glory to God in the highest: and on earth peace to men of good will. — S. Luke ii.

9 Blessed are the peace-makers: for they shall be called the children of God. — S. Matt. v.

49 ... Have peace among you. — S. Mark ix.

27 Peace I leave with you, my peace I give unto you: not as the world giveth, do I give unto you. Let not your heart be troubled, nor let it be afraid. — S. John xiv.

18 If it be possible, as much as is in you, having peace with all men. — Rom. xii.

7 And the peace of God, which surpasseth all understanding, keep your hearts and minds in Christ Jesus. — Phil. iv.

14 For he is our peace... — Ephes. ii.

17 And coming, he preached peace to you, that were afar off, and peace to them that were nigh.

16 Now the Lord of peace himself give you everlasting peace in every place. The Lord be with you all. — 2 Thess. iii.

14 Follow peace with all men, and holiness: without which no man shall see God. — Heb. xii.

10 For he that will love life, and see good days... — 1 S. Peter iii.

11 Let him decline from evil, and do good: let him seek after peace, and pursue it.

18 And the fruit of justice is sown in peace, to them that make peace. — S. James iii.

5 Now the God of patience and of comfort grant you to be of one mind one towards another, according to Jesus Christ. — Rom. xv.

3 Grace be with you, mercy, and peace from God the Father, and from Christ Jesus, the Son of the Father, in truth and charity. — 2 S. John i.

PENANCE.

5 LET him do penance for his sin. Lev. v.

22 If we do not penance, we shall fall into the hands of the Lord, and not into the hands of men. Ecclus. ii.

6 Therefore I reprehend myself, and do penance in dust and ashes. Job xlii.

19 After thou didst convert me, I did penance ... Jer. xxxi.

20 I have put off the robe of peace, and have put upon me the sackcloth of supplication, and I will cry to the most High in my days. Baruch. iv.

30 ... Be converted, and do penance for all your iniquities: and iniquity shall not be your ruin. Ezech. xviii.

17 ... Do penance, for the kingdom of heaven is at hand. S. Matt. iv.

8 Bring forth therefore fruits worthy of penance, and do not begin to say, We have Abraham for our father. For I say unto you, that God is able of these stones to raise up children to Abraham. S. Luke iii.

13 Wo to thee, Corozain, wo to thee, Bethsida: for if in Tyre and Sidon had been wrought the mighty works that have been wrought in you, they would have done penance long ago, sitting in sackcloth and ashes. S. Luke x.

3 ... Unless you do penance, you shall all likewise perish. — S. Luke xiii.

7 I say to you ... there shall be joy in heaven upon one sinner that doth penance, more than upon ninety-nine just, who need not penance. — S. Luke xv.

32 I came not to call the just, but sinners to penance. — S. Luke v.

38 Peter said to them: Do penance, and be baptized every one of you in the name of Jesus Christ, for the remission of your sins: and you shall receive the gift of the Holy Ghost. — Acts ii.

20 But (Paul) preached first to them that are at Damascus, and at Jerusalem, and throughout all the country of Judea, and to the Gentiles, that they should do penance, and turn to God, doing works worthy of penance. — Acts xxvi.

9 Now I am glad; not because you were made sorrowful; but because you were made sorrowful unto penance. For you were made sorrowful according to God, that in nothing you should suffer damage by us. — 2 Cor. vii.

PERFECTION.*

1 ... I AM the Almighty God: walk before me, and be perfect. — Gen. xvii.

* See Blessings of God's Servants.

Perfection.

13 Thou shalt be perfect, and without spot before the Lord thy God. — Deut. xviii.

5 Perfect thou my goings in thy paths: that my footsteps be not moved. — Ps. xvi.

8 Keep my precepts and do them. I am the Lord that sanctify you. — Lev. xx.

26 You shall be holy unto me, because I the Lord am holy, and I have separated you from other people, that you should be mine.

21 This people have I formed for myself, they shall show forth my praise. — Isaias xliii.

18 The path of the just, as a shining light, goeth forwards and increaseth even to perfect day. — Prov. iv.

48 Be you therefore perfect, as also your heavenly Father is perfect. — S. Matt. v.

21 If thou wilt be perfect, go sell what thou hast, and give to the poor, and thou shalt have treasure in heaven: and come, follow me. — S. Matt. xix.

40 The disciple is not above his master: but every one shall be perfect, if he be as his master. — S. Luke vi.

12 ... Stand perfect, and full in all the will of God. — Coloss. iv.

10 Proving what is acceptable to God. — Ephes. v.

2 ... If any man offend not in word; the same is a perfect man ... — S. James iii.

13 Therefore take unto you the armour of God, that you may be able to resist in the evil day, and to stand in all things perfect. — Ephes. vi.

12 Not as though I had already attained, or were already perfect: but I follow after, if I may by any means apprehend, wherein I am also apprehended by Christ Jesus. — Philip. iii.

13 Brethren, I do not count myself to have apprehended. But one thing I do: forgetting the things that are behind, and stretching forth myself to those that are before,

14 I press towards the mark, to the prize of the supernal vocation of God in Christ Jesus.

15 Let us therefore, as many as are perfect, be thus minded: and if in anything you be otherwise minded: this also will God reveal to you.

12 That the name of our Lord Jesus may be glorified in you, and you in him, according to the grace of our God, and of the Lord Jesus Christ. — 2 Thess. i.

20 And may the God of peace, who brought again from the dead the great pastor of the sheep, our Lord Jesus Christ, in the blood of the everlasting testament, — Heb. xiii.

21 Fit you in all goodness; that you may do his will; working in you that which is

well-pleasing in his sight, through Jesus Christ; to whom is glory for ever and ever. Amen.]

PERSECUTION.

2 O LORD my God, in thee have I put my trust: save me from all them that persecute me, and deliver me. — Ps. vii.

3 The enemy hath persecuted my soul: he hath brought down my life to the earth. He hath made me to dwell in darkness as those that have been dead of old. — Ps. cxlii.

27 They have persecuted him whom thou hast smitten; and they have added to the grief of my wounds. — Ps. lxviii.

86 ... They have persecuted me unjustly, do thou help me. — Ps. cxviii.

10 Blessed are they that suffer persecution for justice sake: for theirs is the kingdom of heaven. — S. Matt. v.

12 Rejoice, and be exceeding glad: because your reward is very great in heaven: for so they persecuted the prophets, that were before you.

24 The disciple is not above his master, nor the servant above his lord. — S. Matt. x.

25 It is enough for the disciple that he be as his master, and the servant as his lord. If they have called the master of the house

Beelzebub, how much more them of his household?

29 ... Amen I say to you, there is no man who hath left house, or brethren, or sisters, or father, or mother, or children, or lands, for my sake and for the gospel, — S. Mark x.

30 Who shall not receive an hundred times as much, now in this time; houses, and brethren, and sisters, and mothers, and children, and lands, with persecutions: and in the world to come life everlasting.

22 Blessed shall you be when men shall hate you, and when they shall separate you, and shall reproach you, and cast out your name as evil, for the Son of man's sake. — S. Luke vi.

16 And you shall be betrayed by your parents and brethren, and kinsmen and friends: and some of you they will put to death. — S. Luke xxi.

17 And you shall be hated by all men for my name's sake:

18 But a hair of your head shall not perish.

20 Remember my word that I said to you: The servant is not greater than his master. If they have persecuted me, they will also persecute you ... — S. John xv.

3 And these things will they do to you, because they have not known the Father, nor me. — S. John xvi.

Persecution.

34 Do not think I am come to send peace upon earth : I came not to send peace but the sword. — S. Matt. x.

14 Bless them that persecute you : bless, and curse not. — Rom. xii.

35 Who then shall separate us from the love of Christ? shall tribulation? or distress? or famine? or nakedness? or danger? or persecution? or the sword? — Rom. viii.

36 (As it is written:) For thy sake we are put to death, all the day long : We are accounted as sheep for the slaughter.

37 But in all these things we overcome, because of him that hath loved us.

41 And they indeed went from the presence of the council rejoicing, that they were accounted worthy to suffer reproach for the name of Jesus. — Acts v.

12 ... We are persecuted, and we suffer it. — 1 Cor. iv.

13 We are blasphemed, and we entreat: we are made as the refuse of this world, the off-scouring of all even until now.

9 We suffer persecution, but are not forsaken: we are cast down, but we perish not. — 2 Cor. iv.

11 For we who live are always delivered unto death for Jesus's sake: that the life also of Jesus may be made manifest in our mortal flesh.

28 Now we, brethren, as Isaac was, are the children of promise. — Gal. iv.

29 But as then he, that was born according to the flesh, persecuted him, that was after the spirit : so also it is now.

28 And in nothing be ye terrified by the adversaries : which to them is a cause of perdition, but to you of salvation, and this from God. *Philip. i.*

29 For unto you it is given for Christ, not only to believe in him, but also to suffer for him.

4 So that we ourselves also glory in you in the churches of God, for your patience, and faith, in all your persecutions, and tribulations, which you endure. *2 Thess. i.*

5 For an example of the just judgment of God, that you may be counted worthy of the kingdom of God, for which also you suffer.

12 All who will live godly in Christ Jesus, shall suffer persecution. *2 Tim. iii.*

24 By faith Moses, when he was grown up, denied himself to be the son of Pharao's daughter ; *Heb. xi.*

25 Rather choosing to be afflicted with the people of God, than to have the pleasure of sin for a time,

26 Esteeming the reproach of Christ, greater riches than the treasure of the Egyptians. For he looked unto the reward.

1 And therefore we also having so great a cloud of witnesses over our head, laying *Heb. xii.*

aside every weight and sin which surrounds us, let us run by patience to the fight proposed to us.*

4 For you have not yet resisted unto blood, striving against sin.

13 Rejoice, being partakers of the sufferings of Christ; that when his glory shall be revealed, you may also be glad with exceeding joy. — 1 S. Peter iv.

15 But let none of you suffer as a murderer, or a thief, or a railer, or as coveting the goods of others.

16 But if as a Christian, let him not be ashamed; but let him glorify God in that name.

PERSEVERANCE.

16 PERFECT the same which thy right hand hath planted: and upon the son of man whom thou hast confirmed for thyself. — Ps. lxxix.

9 The just man shall hold on his way, and he that hath clean hands shall be stronger and stronger. — Job xvii.

12 Be steadfast in the way of the Lord, and in the truth of thy judgment, and in knowledge, and let the word of peace and justice keep with thee. — Ecclus. v.

13 He that shall persevere to the end, he shall be saved. — S. Matt. xxiv.

* See 2nd and 3rd verses in Example of Christ.

31 ... If you continue in my word, you shall be my disciples indeed. — S. John viii.

58 Therefore, my beloved brethren, be ye steadfast and immoveable, always abounding in the work of the Lord, knowing that your labour is not in vain in the Lord. — 1 Cor. xv.

6 Being confident of this very thing, that he, who hath begun a good work in you, will perfect it unto the day of Christ Jesus. — Phil. i.

13 ... Be not weary in well doing. — 2 Thess. iii.

7 Persevere under chastisement ... — Heb. xii.

8 Look to yourselves, that you lose not the things which you have wrought: but that you may receive a full reward. — 2 S. John i.

21 Keep yourselves in the love of God, waiting for the mercy of our Lord Jesus Christ unto life everlasting. — S. Jude.

10 ... Be thou faithful until death: and I will give thee the crown of life. — Apoc. ii.

5 He that shall overcome, shall thus be clothed in white garments, and I will not blot out his name out of the book of life, and I will confess his name before my Father, and before his Angels. — Apoc. iii.

11 Behold, I come quickly: hold fast that which thou hast, that no man take thy crown.

12 He that shall overcome, I will make him a pillar in the temple of my God; and he shall go out no more: and I will write

upon him the name of my God, and the name of the city of my God, the new Jerusalem, which cometh down out of heaven from my God, and my new name.

PERVERSE MIND.

32 ... I AM come to withstand thee, because thy way is perverse, and contrary to me. — Numb. xxii.

20 A perverse heart is abominable to the Lord: and his will is in them that walk sincerely. — Prov. xi.

31 ... The tongue of the perverse shall perish. — Prov. x.

28 A perverse man stirreth up quarrels ... — Prov. xvi.

20 He that is of a perverse heart, shall not find good ... — Prov. xvii.

15 The perverse are hard to be corrected ... — Eccles. i.

3 Perverse thoughts separate from God ... — Wisd. i.

4 Charity ... dealeth not perversely. — 1 Cor. xiii.

PIETY AND DESIRE OF HOLINESS.

2 As the hart panteth after the fountains of water; so my soul panteth after thee, O God. — Ps. xli.

3 My soul hath thirsted after the strong living God: when shall I come and appear before the face of God?

2 O God, my God, to thee do I watch Ps. lxii.
at break of day. For thee my soul hath
thirsted . . .

25 For what have I in heaven? and be- Ps. lxxii.
sides thee what do I desire upon earth?

8 . . . Thy name and thy remembrance Isaias
are the desire of the soul. xxvi.

9 My soul hath desired thee in the night;
yea, and with my spirit within me in the
morning early I will watch to thee . . .

6 I stretched forth my hands to thee: my Ps. cxlii.
soul is as earth without water unto thee.

1 All you that thirst, come to the waters: Isaias lv.
and you that have no money, make haste,
buy, and eat: come ye, buy wine and milk
without money, and without any price.

6 Blessed are they that hunger and thirst S. Matt.
after justice: for they shall be filled. v.

37 Now on the last great day of the festi- S. John
vity, Jesus stood, and cried out, saying: If vii.
any man thirst, let him come to me, and
drink.

13 . . . He that shall drink of the water S. John
that I shall give him, shall not thirst for iv.
ever.

14 But the water that I shall give him,
shall become in him a fountain of water,
springing up unto everlasting life.

7 . . . Exercise thyself to piety. 1 Tim. iv.

11 . . . In spirit fervent: serving the Lord. Rom. xii.

8 For bodily exercise is profitable to little; but godliness is profitable to all things, having promise of the life that now is, and of that which is to come. —1 Tim. iv.

6 And he said to me: It is done: I am alpha and omega; the beginning and the end. To him that thirsteth, I will give of the fountain of the water of life, freely. —Apoc. xxi.

PLEASURES AND AMUSEMENTS (EVILS OF VAIN).

6 ... And the people sat down to eat and drink, and they rose up to play. —Exod. xxxii.

5 And when the days of their feasting were gone about, Job sent to them (his sons), and sanctified them: and rising up early offered holocausts for every one of them.

For he said: Lest perhaps my sons have sinned, and have blessed* God in their hearts. —Job i.

13 Laughter shall be mingled with sorrow, and mourning taketh hold of the end of joy. —Prov. xiv.

9 Rejoice therefore, O young man, in thy youth, and let thy heart be in that which is good in the days of thy youth, and walk in —Eccles. xi.

---

* "Blessed." For greater horror of the very thought of blasphemy the Scripture uses the word bless to signify its contrary, both here and verse 11, and in the following chapter, verses 5 and 9.

the ways of thy heart, and in the sight of thy eyes: and know that for all these God will bring thee into judgment.

1 I said in my heart: I will go, and abound with delights, and enjoy good things. And I saw that this also was vanity. — Eccles. ii.

10 And whatsoever my eyes desired, I refused them not: and I withheld not my heart from enjoying every pleasure, and delighting itself in the things which I had prepared; and esteemed this my portion, to make use of my own labour.

11 ... I saw in all things vanity, and vexation of mind, and that nothing was lasting under the sun.

5 The heart of the wise is where there is mourning, and the heart of fools where there is mirth. — Ecclus. vii.

32 Take no pleasure in riotous assemblies, be they ever so small: for their contention is continual. — Ecclus. xviii.

15 ... Be first to run home to thy house, and there withdraw thyself, and there take thy pastime. — Ecclus. xxxii.

16 And do what thou hast a mind, but not in sins or proud speech.

14 (The seed) which fell among thorns, are they who have heard, and going their way, are choked with the cares and riches and pleasures of this life, and yield no fruit. — S. Luke viii.

Pleasures and Amusements.

19 ... Soul, thou hast much goods laid up for many years, take thy rest, eat, drink, make good cheer.* — S. Luke xii.

6 She that liveth in pleasures, is dead while she is living. — 1 Tim. v.

1 Know also this, that, in the last days, shall come on dangerous times. — 2 Tim. iii.

2 Men shall be lovers of themselves ...

4 ... And lovers of pleasures more than of God.

13 ... Counting for a pleasure the delights of a day: stains and spots, sporting themselves to excess, rioting in their feasts with you. — 2 S. Peter ii.

POVERTY.

10 Behold I have refined thee, but not as silver, I have chosen thee in the furnace of poverty. — Isaias xlviii.

7 The Lord maketh poor and maketh rich, he humbleth and he exalteth. — 1 Kings ii.

23 Fear not, my son: we lead indeed a poor life, but we shall have many good things if we fear God, and depart from all sin, and do that which is good. — Tobias iv.

16 To the needy there shall be hope ... — Job v.

19 For the poor man shall not be forgotten to the end: the patience of the poor shall not perish for ever. — Ps. ix.

* See following verses in Covetousness.

5 The Lord is in his holy temple, the Lord's throne is in heaven. His eyes look on the poor man . . . Ps. x.

5 God doth not cast away the mighty, whereas he himself also is mighty. Job xxxvi.

6 But he saveth not the wicked and he giveth judgment to the poor.

10 . . . Lord, who is like unto thee? Ps. xxxiv.
Who deliverest the poor from the hand of them that are stronger than he; the needy and the poor from them that strip him.

33 Let the poor see and rejoice . . . Ps. lxviii.

34 For the Lord hath heard the poor: and hath not despised his prisoners.

6 The prayer out of the mouth of the poor shall reach the ears of God, and judgment shall come for him speedily. Ecclus. xxi.

6 By reason of the misery of the needy, and the groans of the poor, now will I arise, saith the Lord. Ps. xi.

I will set him in safety: I will deal confidently in his regard.

17 . . . I the Lord will hear them, I the God of Israel will not forsake them. Isaias xli.

8 Better is a little with justice, than great revenues with iniquity. Prov. xvi.

5 He that despiseth the poor, reproacheth his maker. Prov. xvii.

7 The just taketh notice of the cause of the poor . . . Prov. xxix.

Poverty.

16 He judged the cause of the poor and needy for his own good: was it not therefore because he knew me, saith the Lord? — Jer. xxii.

12 I will leave in the midst of thee a poor and needy people: and they shall hope in the name of the Lord. — Soph. iii.

2 The rich and poor have met one another: the Lord is the maker of them both. — Prov. xxii.

20 And He, lifting up his eyes on his disciples, said: Blessed are ye poor: for yours is the kingdom of God. — S. Luke vi.

21 Blessed are ye that hunger now: for you shall be filled . . .

22 . . . To the poor the gospel is preached. — S. Luke vii.

3 Blessed are the poor in spirit: for theirs is the kingdom of heaven. — S. Matt. v.

20 . . . The foxes have holes, and the birds of the air nests: but the Son of man hath not where to lay his head. — S. Matt. viii.

9 I know thy tribulation and thy poverty, but thou art rich. — Apoc. ii.

PRAISE OF GOD.

22 . . . To God praise with fear.
23 We cannot find him worthily: he is great in strength, and in judgment, and in justice, and he is ineffable. — Job xxxvii.

21 He is thy praise, and thy God . . .   Deut. x.

2 Who shall declare the powers of the   Ps. cv.
Lord! Who shall set forth all his praises!

6 See what he hath done with us, and   Tobias
with fear and trembling give ye glory to him: xiii.
and extol the eternal King of worlds in your
works.

7 As for me I will praise him in the land
of my captivity: because he has shewn his
majesty towards a sinful nation.'

9 I and my soul will rejoice in him.

21 My mouth shall speak the praise of   Ps.
the Lord: and let all flesh bless his holy   cxliv.
name for ever, yea for ever and ever.

11 In God will I praise the word, in the   Ps. lv.
Lord will I praise his speech.

2 The mercies of the Lord I will sing for   Ps.
ever.   lxxxviii.

33 I will sing to the Lord as long as I   Ps. ciii.
live: I will sing praises to my God while I
have my being.

14 The Lord is my strength and my praise: Ps. cxvii.
and he is become my salvation.

19 Open ye to me the gates of justice: I
will go into them and give praise to the Lord.

3 Great is the Lord, and greatly to be   Ps.
praised.   cxliv.

4 Praising I will call upon the Lord: and   Ps.
I shall be saved from my enemies.   xvii.

47 The Lord liveth, and blessed be my

God, and let the God of my salvation be exalted.

7 ... With my will I will give praise to him. — Ps. xxvii.

6 Praise and beauty are before him: holiness and majesty in his sanctuary. — Ps. xcv.

2 Great is the Lord, and exceedingly to be praised in the city of our God, in his holy mountain. — Ps. xlvii.

18 I will give glory to the Lord according to his justice: and will sing to the name of the Lord the most high. — Ps. vii.

2 I will bless the Lord at all times, his praise shall be always in my mouth. — Ps. xxxiii.

3 In the Lord shall my soul be praised; let the meek hear and rejoice.

8 Let the mercies of the Lord give glory to him: and his wonderful works to the children of men. — Ps. cvi.

3 His work is praise and magnificence: and his justice continueth for ever and ever. — Ps. cx.

2 Blessed be the name of the Lord, from henceforth now and for ever. — Ps. cxii.

3 From the rising of the sun unto the going down of the same, the name of the Lord is worthy of praise.

15 For this is God, our God unto eternity, and for ever and ever: he shall rule us for evermore. — Ps. xlvii.

19 Let these things be written unto ano- — Ps. ci.

ther generation : and the people that shall be created shall praise the Lord.

22 That they may declare the name of the Lord in Sion : and his praise in Jerusalem.

6 Hope in God, for I will still give praise to him : the salvation of my countenance, and my God. — Ps. xli.

4 And he put a new canticle into my mouth, a song to our God. — Ps. xxxix.

8 I the Lord this is my name : I will not give my glory to another, nor my praise to graven things. — Isaias xlii.

23 The sacrifice of praise shall glorify me. — Ps. xlix.

12 And they believed his words : and they sing his praises. — Ps. cv.

2 The Lord is my strength and my praise, and he is become salvation to me : he is my God and I will glorify him : the God of my father, and I will exalt him. — Ex. xv.

11 The voice of joy and the voice of gladness, the voice of the bridegroom and the voice of the bride, the voice of them that shall say : Give ye glory to the Lord of hosts, for the Lord is good, for his mercy endureth for ever . . . — Jer. xxxiii.

8 My soul shall praise the Lord even to death. — Ecclus. li.

29 We shall say much, and yet shall want words : but the sum of our words is, He is all. — Ecclus. xliii.

30 What shall we be able to do to glorify him? for the Almighty himself is above all his works.

20 Blessed be the name of the Lord from eternity and for evermore: for wisdom and fortitude are his. — Dan. ii.

34 I Nabuchodonosor do now praise, and magnify, and glorify the King of heaven: because all His works are true, and his ways judgments, and them that walk in pride he is able to abase. — Dan. iv.

18 But we that live bless the Lord from this time now and for ever. — Ps. cxiii.

5 ... I shall go over into the place of the wonderful tabernacle, even to the house of God: with the voice of joy and praise; the noise of one feasting. — Ps. xli.

26 And you shall eat in plenty, and shall be filled: and you shall praise the name of the Lord your God ... — Joel ii.

37 And when he was now coming near the descent of Mount Olivet, the whole multitude of his disciples began with joy to praise God with a loud voice, for all the mighty works they had seen, — S. Luke xix.

38 Saying: Blessed be the king who cometh in the name of the Lord; peace in heaven, and glory on high.

37 ... He hath done all things well ... — S. Mark vii.

53 And they were always in the temple praising and blessing God.   S. Luke xxiv.

25 And at midnight, Paul and Silas praying, praised God. And they that were in prison heard them.   Acts xvi.

17 He that glorieth, let him glory in the Lord.   2 Cor. x.

PRAISE (CALL TO).

9 Lift up your gates, O ye princes, and be ye lifted up, O eternal gates: and the King of Glory shall enter in.   Ps. xxiii.

10 Who is this King of Glory? The Lord of hosts, he is the King of Glory.

35 Let the heavens and the earth praise him; the sea, and every thing that creepeth therein.   Ps. lxviii.

9 Sing to him, yea, sing praises to him: and relate all his wondrous works.   1 Paralip. xvi.

23 Sing ye to the Lord, all the earth: show forth from day to day his salvation.

24 Declare his glory among the gentiles: his wonders among all people.

25 For the Lord is great and exceedingly to be praised.

28 Bring ye to the Lord, O ye families of the nations: bring ye to the Lord glory and empire.

29 Give to the Lord glory to his name, bring up sacrifice, and come ye in his sight: and adore the Lord in holy becomingness.

31 Let the heavens rejoice, and let the earth be glad: and let them say among the nations: The Lord hath reigned.

3 Give glory to the Lord, ye children of Israel, and praise him in the sight of the gentiles.   Tobias xiii.

4 Because he hath therefore scattered you among the gentiles, who know not him, that you may declare his wonderful works, and make them know that there is no other Almighty God besides him.

7 ... Adore him, all you his Angels.   Ps. xcvi.

1 Praise ye the Lord from the heavens: praise ye him in the high places.   Ps. cxlviii.

5 Let every spirit praise the Lord: alleluia.   Ps. cl.

2 You that stand in the house of the Lord, in the courts of the house of our God.   Ps. cxxxiv.

3 Praise ye the Lord, for the Lord is good: sing ye to his name, for it is sweet.

20 ... You that fear the Lord, bless the Lord.

5 Sing to the Lord, O ye his saints: and give praise to the memory of his holiness.   Ps. xxix.

1 Rejoice in the Lord, O ye just: praise becometh the upright.   Ps. xxxii.

1 Praise the Lord, ye children, praise ye the name of the Lord.   Ps. cxii.

2 Blessed be the name of the Lord, from henceforth now and for ever.

3 From the rising of the sun unto the going down of the same, the name of the Lord is worthy of praise.

1 Bring to the Lord, O ye children of God ...   Ps. xxviii.

2 Bring to the Lord glory and honour; bring to the Lord glory to his name; adore ye the Lord in his holy court.

1 Sing ye to the Lord a new canticle: let his praise be in the church of the saints.   Ps. cxlix.

1 Shout with joy to God, all the earth.   Ps. lxv.

2 Sing ye a psalm to his name; give glory to his praise.

5 Exalt ye the Lord our God, and adore his footstool for it is holy.   Ps. xcviii.

1 Sing joyfully to God, all the earth; serve ye the Lord with gladness.   Ps. xcix.

1 O praise the Lord, all ye nations: praise him, all ye people.   Ps. cxvi.

2 For his mercy is confirmed upon us: and the truth of the Lord remaineth for ever.

2 O you of Israel, that have willingly offered your lives to danger, bless the Lord.   Judges v.

3 Hear, O ye kings, give ear, ye princes: it is I, it is I, that will sing to the Lord, I will sing to the Lord the God of Israel.

24 Ye that fear the Lord, praise him: all ye the seed of Jacob, glorify him.   Ps. xxi.

Praise (Call to).

8 O bless our God, ye gentiles: and Ps. lxv.
make the voice of his praise to be heard.

12 Praise the Lord, O Jerusalem: praise Ps.
thy God, O Sion. cxlvii.

1 Praise ye the Lord, because psalm is Ps. cxlvi.
good: to our God be joyful and comely
praise.

7 Sing ye to the Lord with praise: sing
to our God upon the harp.

12 Sing ye to the Lord, who dwelleth in Ps. ix.
Sion: declare his ways among the gentiles.

33 Sing to God, ye kingdoms of the earth: Ps. lxvii.
sing ye to the Lord.

1 Bless the Lord, O my soul: and let all Ps. cii.
that is within me bless his holy name.

22 Bless the Lord, all his works: in every
place of his dominion, O my soul, bless thou
the Lord.

4 O magnify the Lord with me; and let Ps.
us extol his name together. xxxiii.

7 Sing praises to our God, sing ye: sing Ps. xlvi.
praises to our King; sing ye.

8 For God is the king of all the earth:
sing ye wisely.

14 Offer to God the sacrifice of praise: Ps. xlix.
and pay thy vows to the most High.

2 Sing ye a psalm to his name; give glory Ps. lxv.
to his praise.

9 Exalt ye the Lord our God, and adore Ps.
at his holy mountain. xcviii.

2 Sing joyfully to God, all the earth: Ps. xcix.
serve ye the Lord with gladness.

4 Go ye into his gates with praise, into his courts with hymns: and give glory to him.

Praise ye his name: 5 for the Lord is sweet: his mercy endureth for ever, and his truth to generation and generation.

3 Glory ye in his holy name: let the Ps. civ.
heart of them rejoice that seek the Lord.

1 Give glory to the Lord, for he is good: Ps. cvi.
for his mercy endureth for ever.

21 Let the mercies of the Lord give glory to him: his wonderful works to the children of men.

1 Praise ye the Lord from the heavens: Ps.
praise ye him in the high places. cxlviii.

2 Praise ye him all his Angels: praise ye him all his hosts.

11 Kings of the earth and all people: princes and all judges of the earth.

12 Young men and maidens: let the old with the younger, praise the name of the Lord: 13 for his name alone is exalted.

14 The praise of him is above heaven and earth: and he hath exalted the horn of his people.

A hymn to all his saints: to the children of Israel, a people approaching to him. Alleluia.

Praise (Call to).

1 Praise ye the Lord in his holy places: Ps. cl.
praise ye him in the firmament of his power.

2 Praise ye him for his mighty acts: praise ye him according to the multitude of his greatness.

3 Praise him with sound of trumpet: praise him with psaltery and harp.

4 Praise him with timbrel and choir: praise him with strings and organs.

5 Praise him on high sounding cymbals: praise him on cymbals of joy: let every spirit praise the Lord. Alleluia.

1 Come let us praise the Lord with joy: Ps. xciv.
let us joyfully sing to God our Saviour.

12 Rejoice ye just in the Lord: and give Ps. xcvi.
praise to the remembrance of his holiness.

4 ... Praise ye the Lord, and call upon Isaias
his name: make his works known among xii.
the people: remember that his name is high.

5 Sing ye to the Lord, for he hath done great things: shew this forth in all the earth.

6 Rejoice, and praise, O thou habitation of Sion: for great is he that is in the midst of thee, the holy One of Israel.

10 Sing ye to the Lord a new song, his Isai. xlii.
praise is from the ends of the earth: you that go down to the sea, and all that are therein: ye islands, and ye inhabitants of them.

13 Sing ye to the Lord: praise the Lord: because he hath delivered the soul of the poor out of the hand of the wicked. *Jer. xx.*

11 ... Give ye glory to the Lord of hosts, for the Lord is good, for his mercy endureth for ever ... *Jer. xxxiii.*

57 All ye works of the Lord, bless the Lord: praise and exalt him above all for ever. *Dan. iii.*

58 O ye angels of the Lord, bless the Lord: praise and exalt him above all for ever.

59 O ye heavens, bless the Lord: praise and exalt him above all for ever.

60 O all ye waters that are above the heavens, bless the Lord: praise and exalt him above all for ever.

61 O all ye powers of the Lord, bless the Lord: praise and exalt him above all for ever.

62 O ye sun and moon, bless the Lord: praise and exalt him above all for ever.

63 O. ye stars of heaven, bless the Lord: praise and exalt him above all for ever.

64 O every shower and dew, bless ye the Lord: praise and exalt him above all for ever.

65 O all ye spirits of God, bless the Lord: praise and exalt him above all for ever.

66 O ye fire and heat, bless the Lord: praise and exalt him above all for ever.

67 O ye cold and heat, bless the Lord: praise and exalt him above all for ever.

68 O ye dews and hoar frost, bless the Lord: praise and exalt him above all for ever.

69 O ye frost and cold, bless the Lord: praise and exalt him above all for ever.

70 O ye ice and snow, bless the Lord: praise and exalt him above all for ever.

71 O ye nights and days, bless the Lord: praise and exalt him above all for ever.

72 O ye light and darkness, bless the Lord: praise and exalt him above all for ever.

73 O ye lightnings and clouds, bless the Lord: praise and exalt him above all for ever.

74 O let the earth bless the Lord: let it praise and exalt him above all for ever.

75 O ye mountains and hills, bless the Lord: praise and exalt him above all for ever.

76 O all ye things that spring up in the earth, bless the Lord: praise and exalt him above all for ever.

77 O ye fountains, bless the Lord: praise and exalt him above all for ever.

78 O ye seas and rivers, bless the

Lord: praise and exalt him above all for ever.

79 O ye whales, and all that move in the waters, bless the Lord: praise and exalt him above all for ever.

80 O all ye fowls of the air, bless the Lord: praise and exalt him above all for ever.

81 O all ye beasts and cattle, bless the Lord: praise and exalt him above all for ever.

82 O ye sons of men, bless the Lord: praise and exalt him above all for ever.

83 O let Israel bless the Lord: let them praise and exalt him above all for ever.

84 O ye priests of the Lord, bless the Lord: praise and exalt him above all for ever.

85 O ye servants of the Lord, bless the Lord: praise and exalt him above all for ever.

86 O ye spirits and souls of the just, bless the Lord: praise and exalt him above all for ever.

87 O ye holy and humble of heart, bless the Lord: praise and exalt him above all for ever.

88 O Ananias, Azarias, and Misael, bless ye the Lord: praise and exalt him above all for ever. For he hath delivered us from hell,

and saved us out of the hand of death, and delivered us out of the midst of the burning flame, and saved us out of the midst of the fire.

89 O give thanks to the Lord, because he is good: because his mercy endureth for ever and ever.

90 O all ye religious, bless the Lord the God of gods: praise him and give him thanks, because his mercy endureth for ever and ever.

5 Arise, bless the Lord your God from eternity to eternity. — 2 Esdras ix.

41 Now therefore with the whole heart and mouth praise ye him, and bless the name of the Lord. — Ecclus. xxxix.

32 Glorify the Lord as much as ever you can, for he will yet far exceed, and his magnificence is wonderful. — Ecclus. xliii.

33 Blessing the Lord, exalt him as much as you can: for he is above all praise.

34 When you exalt him put forth all your strength, and be not weary: for you can never go far enough.

5 And a voice came out from the throne, saying: Give praise to our God, all ye his servants: and you that fear him, little and great. — Apoc. xix.

6 And I heard as it were the voice of a great multitude, and as the voice of many

waters, and as the voice of great thunders, saying, "Alleluia; for the Lord our God the almighty hath reigned."

7 Let us be glad and rejoice, and give glory to him.

PRAISE TO GOD.

11 Who is like to thee, among the strong, Ex. xv. O Lord? who is like to thee, glorious in holiness, terrible and praise worthy, doing wonders?

2 There is none holy as the Lord is: for 1 Kings there is no other beside thee, and there is ii. none strong like our God.

11 Thine, O Lord, is magnificence, and 1 Paralip. power, and glory, and victory: and to thee xxix. is praise: for all that is in heaven, and in earth, is thine: thine is the kingdom, O Lord, and thou art above all princes.

12 Thine are riches, and thine is glory, thou hast dominion over all, in thy hand is power and might: in thy hand greatness and the empire of all things.

13 Now therefore our God we give thanks to thee, and we praise thy glorious name.

5 ... Blessed be the high name of thy 2 Esdras glory with all blessings and praise. ix.

17 O Lord, thou will open my lips: and Ps. l. my mouth shall declare thy praise.

8 Let my mouth be filled with praise, that I may sing thy glory; thy greatness all the day long. *Ps. lxx.*

23 My lips shall greatly rejoice, when I shall sing to thee: and my soul which thou hast redeemed.

12 I will praise thee, O Lord my God, with my whole heart, and I will glorify thy name for ever. *Ps. lxxxv.*

12 Thou hast turned for me my mourning into joy: thou hast cut my sackcloth, and hast compassed me with gladness: *Ps. xxix.*

13 To the end that my glory may sing to thee, and I may not regret: O Lord, my God, I will give praise to thee for ever.

9 So will I sing a psalm to thy name for ever and ever; that I may pay my vows from day to day. *Ps. lx.*

12 In me, O God, are vows to thee, which I will pay, praises to thee. *Ps. lv.*

8 Bring my soul out of prison, that I may praise thy name. *Ps. cxli.*

175 My soul shall live, and shall praise thee. *Ps. cxviii.*

2 I will give praise to thee, O Lord, with my whole heart: I will relate all thy wonders. *Ps. ix.*

2 I will extol thee, O Lord, for thou hast upheld me: and hast not made my enemies to rejoice over me. *Ps. xxix.*

8 I will freely sacrifice to thee, and will *Ps. liii.*

give praise, O God, to thy name: because it is good.

22 I will also confess to thee: thy truth with the instruments of psaltery: O God, I will sing to thee with the harp, thou holy one of Israel. — Ps. lxx.

15 Thou that liftest me up from the gates of death, that I may declare all thy praises in the gates of the daughters of Sion. — Ps. ix.

2 Every day will I bless thee: and I will praise thy name for ever, yea, for ever and ever. — Ps. cxliv.

17 ... I will sing thy strength, and will extol thy mercy in the morning. — Ps. lviii.

18 Unto thee, O my helper, will I sing, for thou art my God, my defence: my God, my mercy. — Ps. lviii.

5 Thus will I bless thee all my life long: and in thy name will I lift up my hands. — Ps. lxii.

6 Let my soul be filled as with marrow and fatness: and my mouth shall praise thee with joyful lips.

2 My heart is ready, O God, my heart is ready: I will sing, and will give praise, with my glory. — Ps. cvii.

3 Arise, my glory; arise, psaltery and harp: I will arise in the morning early.

4 I will praise thee, O Lord, among the people: and I will sing to thee among the nations.

5 For thy mercy is great above the heavens: and thy truth even unto the clouds.

6 Be thou exalted, O God, above the heavens, and thy glory over all the earth.

1 I will praise thee, O Lord, with my whole heart; in the counsel of the just, and in the congregation. — Ps. cx.

28 My tongue shall meditate thy justice, thy praise all the day long. — Ps. xxxiv.

17 I will sacrifice to thee the sacrifice of praise, and I will call upon the name of the Lord. — Ps. cxv.

14 ... I will always hope; and will add to all thy praise. — Ps. lxx.

13 O Lord my God, I will give praise to thee for ever. — Ps. xxix.

28 Thou art my God and I will praise thee: thou art my God and I will exalt thee. — Ps. cxvii.

I will praise thee because thou hast heard me, and art become my salvation.

7 I will praise thee with uprightness of heart, when I shall have learnt the judgments of thy justice. — Ps. cxviii.

1 I will praise thee, O Lord, with my whole heart: for thou hast heard the words of my mouth. — Ps. cxxxvii.

I will sing praise to thee in the sight of his Angels.

2 I will worship towards thy holy temple, and I will give glory to thy name. For thy

mercy, and for thy truth: for thou hast magnified thy holy name above all.

14 I will praise thee, for thou art fearfully magnified: wonderful are thy works, and my soul knoweth right well. Ps. cxxxviii.

1 I will extol thee, O God, my king: and I will bless thy name for ever, yea, for ever and ever. Ps. cxliv.

2 Every day will I bless thee; and I will praise thy name for ever, yea, for ever and ever.

62 I rose at midnight to give praise to thee; for the judgments of thy justification. Ps. cxviii.

164 Seven times a day I have given praise to thee, for the judgments of thy justice.

171 My lips shall utter a hymn, when thou shalt teach me thy justifications.

175 My soul shall live, and shall praise thee: and thy judgments shall help me.

1 A hymn, O God, becometh thee in Sion. Ps. lxiv.

4 Thou dwellest in the holy place, the praise of Israel. Ps. xxi.

21 ... The poor and needy shall praise thy name. Ps. lxxiii.

5 And they shall speak of the magnificence of the glory of thy holiness and shall tell thy wondrous works. Ps. cxliv.

6 And they shall speak of the might of thy terrible acts: and shall declare thy greatness.

7 They shall publish the memory of the abundance of thy sweetness; and shall rejoice in thy justice.

18 ... Therefore shall people praise thee for ever, yea, for ever and ever. Ps. xliv.

5 Blessed are they that dwell in thy house, O Lord: they shall praise thee for ever and ever. Ps. lxxxiii.

14 Be thou exalted, O Lord, in thy own strength: we will sing and praise thy power. Ps. xx.

10 O Lord our Lord, how admirable is thy name in all the earth. Ps. viii.

11 According to thy name, O God, so also is thy praise unto the ends of the earth: thy right hand is full of justice. Ps. xlvii.

5 ... Let such as love thy salvation say always: the Lord be magnified. Ps. lxix.

11 For the thought of man shall give praise to thee. Ps. lxxv.

6 The heavens shall confess thy wonders, O Lord: and thy truth in the church of the saints. Ps. lxxxviii.

3 Let them give praise to thy great name: for it is terrible and holy. Ps. xcviii.

1 Not to us, O Lord, not to us: but to thy name give glory. Ps. cxiii.

4 May all the kings of the earth give glory to thee: for they have heard all the words of thy mouth. Ps. cxxxvii.

5 And let them sing in the ways of the Lord: for great is the glory of the Lord.

4 Generation and generation shall praise thy works: and they shall declare thy power.   Ps. cxliv.

48 Blessed be the Lord the God of Israel, from everlasting to everlasting: and let all the people say: So be it, so be it.   Ps. cv.

2 We will praise thee, O God: we will praise, and we will call upon thy name. We will relate thy wondrous works.   Ps. lxxiv.

1 O Lord, thou art my God, I will exalt thee, and give glory to thy name ...   Isaias xxv.

19 The living, the living, he shall give praise to thee, as I do this day.   Isaias xxxviii.

14 ... Thou art my praise.   Jer. xvii.

23 To thee, O God of our fathers, I give thanks, and I praise thee: because thou hast given me wisdom and strength ...   Dan. ii.

52 Blessed art thou, O Lord the God of our fathers: and worthy to be praised, and glorified, and exalted above all for ever: and blessed is the holy name of thy glory: and worthy to be praised, and exalted above all in all ages.   Dan. iii.

53 Blessed art thou in the holy temple of thy glory: and exceedingly to be praised, and exceeding glorious for ever.

54 Blessed art thou on the throne of thy kingdom and exceedingly to be praised, and exalted above all for ever.

55 Blessed art thou, that beholdest the depths, and sittest upon the cherubims: and worthy to be praised and exalted above all for ever.

56 Blessed art thou in the firmament of heaven: and worthy of praise, and glorious for ever.

14 Glory to God in the highest.   S. Luke ii.

15 ... Hosanna to the son of David.   S. Matt. vi.

13 ... Hosanna, blessed is he that cometh in the name of the Lord, the king of Israel.   S. John xii.

16 Out of the mouth of infants and sucklings thou hast perfected praise.   S. Matt. xxi.

5 And now glorify thou me, O Father, with thyself, with the glory which I had, with thee, before the world was.   S. John xvii.

4 I have glorified thee on the earth: I have finished the work which thou gavest me to do.

12 I will declare thy name to my brethren: in the midst of the church will I praise thee.   Heb. ii.

11 ... That in all things God may be honoured through Jesus Christ: to whom is glory and empire for ever and ever. Amen.   1 S. Peter iv.

36 For of him, and by him, and in him, are all things: to him be glory for ever. Amen.   Rom. xi.

3 Blessed be the God and Father of our Lord Jesus Christ, who hath blessed us with   Ephes. i.

all spiritual blessings in heavenly places, in Christ.

6 To the praise of the glory of his grace, by which he made us acceptable through his beloved Son.

18 ... To whom be glory for ever and ever. Amen. — 2 Tim. iv.

24 To him, who is able to preserve you without sin, and to present you spotless before the presence of his glory with exceeding joy in the coming of our Lord Jesus Christ, — S. Jude.

25 To the only God our Saviour, through Jesus Christ our Lord, be glory and magnificence, empire and power, before all ages, both now, and for all ages of ages. Amen.

17 To the king of ages, immortal, invisible, the only God, be honour and glory for ever and ever. Amen. — 1 Tim. i.

21 To him be glory in the church, and in Christ Jesus, throughout all generations, world without end. Amen. — Ephes. iii.

8 ... And they rested not day and night, saying: Holy, Holy, Holy, Lord God Almighty, who was, and who is, and who is to come. — Apoc. iv.

11 Thou art worthy, O Lord our God, to receive glory, and honour, and power: because thou hast created all things, and for thy will they were, and have been created.

Praise to God.

12 ... Worthy is the Lamb that was slain, to receive power, and divinity, and wisdom, and strength, and honour, and glory, and benediction. — Apoc. v.

13 And every creature, which is in heaven and on the earth, and under the earth, and such as are in the sea, and the things that are in them: I heard all saying: To him that sitteth on the throne, and to the Lamb, benediction and honour and glory and power for ever and ever.

4 Who shall not fear thee, O Lord, and magnify thy name? For thou only art holy: for all nations shall come, and adore in thy sight, because thy judgments are manifest. — Apoc. xv.

1 ... Alleluia. Salvation, and glory, and power is to our God. — Apoc. xix.

PRAYER TO GOD.

27 Thou shalt pray to Him, and he will hear thee ... — Job xxii.

3 Do not multiply to speak lofty things, boasting: let old matters depart from your mouth: for the Lord is a God of all knowledge, and to him are thoughts prepared. — 1 Kings ii.

23 Far from me be this sin against the Lord, that I should cease to pray for you ... — 1 Kings xii.

14 For the Lord ... will be entreated in favour of his servants. — Ps. cxxxiv.

8 Prayer is good with fasting and alms, more than to lay up treasures of gold. Tobias xii.

11 Know ye that the Lord will hear your prayers, if you continue with perseverance in fastings and prayers in the sight of the Lord. Judith iv.

16 The eyes of the Lord are upon the just: and his ears unto their prayers. Ps. xxxiii.

18 The just cried, and the Lord heard them: and delivered them out of all their troubles.

7 Be subject to the Lord and pray to him. Ps. xxxvi.

15 Call upon me in the day of trouble: I will deliver thee, and thou shalt glorify me. Ps. xlix.

18 Evening and morning, and at noon I will speak and declare: and he shall hear my voice. Ps. liv.

147 I prevented the dawning of the day, and cried: because in thy words I very much hoped. Ps. cxviii.

10 ... In what day soever I shall call upon thee, behold I know thou art my God. Ps. lv.

18 The Lord is nigh unto all them that call upon him: to all that call upon him in truth. Ps. cxliv.

29 The Lord ... will hear the prayers of the just. Prov. xv.

12 ... Who hath called upon him, and he despised him? Ecclus. ii.

Prayer to God.

13 For God ... is a protector to all that seek him in truth.

4 He that loveth God, shall obtain pardon of his sins by prayer, and shall refrain himself from them, and shall be heard in the prayer of days.   Ecclus. iii.

10 Neglect not to pray, and to give alms. Ecclus.vii.

22 Make thy prayer before the face of the Lord, and offend less.   Ecclus. xvii.

22 Let nothing hinder thee from praying always, and be not afraid to be justified even to death : for the reward of God continueth for ever.   Ecclus. xviii.

23 Before prayer prepare thy soul : and be not as a man that tempteth God.

19 ... Pray to the most High, that he may direct thy way in truth.   Ecclus. xxxvii.

1 ... For thy former sins also pray that they may be forgiven thee.   Ecclus. xxi.

20 He that adoreth God with joy, shall be accepted, and his prayer shall approach even to the clouds.   Ecclus. xxxv.

21 The prayer of him that humbleth himself, shall pierce the clouds : and till it come nigh he will not be comforted : and he will not depart till the most High behold.

19 ... Weeping thou shalt not weep, he will surely have pity on thee : at the voice of thy cry, as soon as he shall hear, he will answer thee.   Isaias xxx.

6 ... You that are mindful of the Lord, hold not your peace, — Isaias lxii.

7 And give him no silence till he establish, and till he make Jerusalem a praise in the earth.

7 Every one that calleth upon my name, I have created him for my glory, I have formed him, and made him. — Isaias xliii.

19 I created the fruit of the lips, peace, peace to him that is far off, and to him that is near, said the Lord, and I healed him. — Isaias lvii.

3 Cry to me and I will hear thee: and I will shew to thee great things, and sure things which thou knowest not. — Jer. xxxiii.

22 ... Behold we come to thee: for thou art the Lord our God. — Jer. iii.

19 Arise, give praise in the night, in the beginning of the watches: pour out thy heart like water before the face of the Lord: lift up thy hands to him for the life of thy little children, that have fainted for hunger at the top of all the streets. — Lament. ii.

41 Let us lift up our hearts with our hands to the Lord in the heavens. — Lament. iii.

1 And now, O Lord Almighty, the God of Israel, the soul in anguish, and the troubled spirit crieth to thee. — Baruch iii.

3 For thou remainest for ever, and shall we perish everlastingly?

32 And it shall come to pass, that every — Joel ii.

one that shall call upon the name of the Lord shall be saved . . .

3 And I set my face to the Lord my God, Dan. ix. to pray and make supplication with fasting, and sackcloth, and ashes.

17 Now therefore, O our God, hear the supplication of thy servant, and his prayers: and shew thy face upon thy sanctuary which is desolate, for thy own sake.

1 . . . Lord, teach us to pray . . .   S. Luke xi.

2 And he said to them: When you pray, say: Our Father, &c. . . .*

5 And when you pray, you shall not be as S. Matt. the hypocrites, who love to pray standing in vi. the synagogues, and at the corners of the streets, that they may be seen by men: Amen I say to you, they have received their reward.

6 But thou, when thou shalt pray, enter into thy chamber, and having shut the door, pray to thy Father in secret: and thy Father, who seeth in secret, will reward thee.

7 And when you are praying, speak not much, as the heathens do: for they think that they are heard for their much speaking.

7 Ask, and it shall be given you: seek, S. Matt. and you shall find: knock, and it shall be vii. opened to you.

8 For every one that asketh, receiveth:

* See St. Matt. vi. 9.

and he that seeketh, findeth: and to him that knocketh, it shall be opened.

9 Or what man is there among you, of whom if his son ask bread, will he reach him a stone?

10 Or if he ask a fish, will he reach him a serpent?

11 If you, then, being evil, know how to give good gifts to your children: how much more will your Father who is in heaven, give good things to them that ask him.

19 Again I say to you, that if two of you shall agree upon earth, concerning any thing whatsoever they shall ask, it shall be done for them by my Father who is in heaven. — S. Matt. xviii.

20 For where there are two or three gathered together in my name, there am I in the midst of them.

24 Therefore I say to you, all things whatsoever you ask when ye pray, believe that you shall receive, and they shall come unto you. — S. Mark xi.

25 And when you shall stand to pray: forgive, if you have any thing against any man; that your Father also, who is in heaven, may forgive you your sins.

2 And he said to them: The harvest, indeed, is great, but the labourers are few. Pray ye therefore, the Lord of the harvest, that he send labourers into his harvest. — S. Luke x.

13 If you, being evil, know how to give good gifts to your children, how much more will your Father from heaven give the good Spirit to them that ask him? — S. Luke xi.

1 And he spoke also a parable to them, that we ought always to pray, and not to faint. — S. Luke xviii.

2 Saying: There was a judge in a certain city, who feared not God, nor regarded man.

3 And there was a certain widow in that city, and she came to him, saying: Avenge* me of my adversary.

4 And he would not for a long time. But afterwards he said within himself: Although I fear not God, nor regard man,

5 Yet because this widow is troublesome to me, I will avenge her, lest continually coming, she weary me.

6 And the Lord said: Hear what the unjust judge saith:

7 And will not God avenge his elect who cry to him day and night: and will he have patience in their regard?

8 I say to you that he will quickly avenge them . . .

22 All things whatsoever you shall ask in prayer believing, you shall receive. — S. Matt. xxi.

---

* Avenge—that is, do me justice. It is a Hebraicism.

13 ... Whatsoever you shall ask the Father in my name, that will I do: that the Father may be glorified in the Son. — S. John xiv.

14 If you shall ask me any thing in my name, that I will do.

23 ... Amen, amen, I say to you: if you ask the Father any thing in my name, he will give it you. — S. John xvi.

24 ... Ask, and you shall receive: that your joy may be full.

17 Pray without ceasing. — 1 Thess. v.

21 And it shall come to pass, that whosoever shall call upon the name of the Lord, shall be saved. — Acts ii.

26 Likewise the Spirit also helpeth our infirmity. For we know not what we should pray for as we ought: but the Spirit himself asketh for us with unspeakable groanings. — Rom. viii.

2 Be instant in prayer; watching in it with thanksgiving. — Coloss. iv.

18 By all prayer and supplication praying at all times in the Spirit: and in the same watching with all instance and supplication for all the saints. — Ephes. vi.

1 I desire, therefore, first of all that supplications, prayers, intercessions, and thanksgivings be made for all men: — 1 Tim. ii.

2 For kings, and for all who are in high station: that we may lead a quiet and a peaceful life, in all piety and chastity:

3 For this is good and acceptable in the sight of God our Saviour,

4 Who will have all men to be saved, and to come to the knowledge of the truth.

16 Let us go, therefore, with confidence Heb. iv. to the throne of grace: that we may obtain mercy, and find grace in seasonable aid.

6 Be not solicitous about any thing: but Philip. iv. in everything by prayer and supplication with thanksgiving let your petitions be made known to God.

13 Is any of you sad? Let him pray. S. James v.

5 If any of you want wisdom, let him ask S. James of God, who giveth to all abundantly, and   i. upbraideth not: and it shall be given him.

6 But let him ask in faith, nothing wavering: for he that wavereth is like a wave of the sea, that is moved and carried about by the wind.

7 Therefore, let not that man think that he shall receive any thing of the Lord.

3 You ask, and receive not: because you S. James ask amiss: that you may consume it on   iv. your concupiscences.

16 ... Pray one for another, that you S. James may be saved ...   v.

11 Wherefore also we pray always for you: 2 Thess. that our God would make you worthy of his   i. calling, and fulfil all the good pleasure of his goodness and the work of faith in power.

14 And this is the confidence which we have in him: that whatsoever we shall ask, according to his will, he heareth us. 1 S. John v.

15 And we know that he heareth us whatsoever we ask: we know that we have the petitions which we request of him.

16 He that knoweth his brother to sin a sin which is not unto death, let him ask, and life shall be given to him, who sinneth not to death.

PRESUMPTION.

12 A GENERATION that are pure in their own eyes, and yet are not washed from their filthiness. Prov. xxx.

11 ... And they leaned upon the Lord, saying: Is not the Lord in the midst of us? no evil shall come upon us. Mich. iii.

19 ... I shall have peace, and will walk on in the naughtiness of my heart ... Deut. xxix.

12 Come, let us take wine, and be filled with drunkenness: and it shall be as to-day, so also to-morrow, and much more. Isaias lvi.

3 Say not, how mighty am I? and who shall bring me under for my deeds? for God will surely take revenge. Ecclus. v.

4 Say not: I have sinned, and what harm hath befallen me? for the most High is a patient rewarder.

5 Be not without fear about sin forgiven, and add not sin upon sin.

6 Say not: The mercy of the Lord is great, he will have mercy on the multitude of my sins.

11 Say not: God will have respect to the multitude of my gifts, and when I offer to the most high God, he will accept my offerings. — Ecclus. vii.

11 ... O God, I give thee thanks that I am not as the rest of men, extortioners, unjust, adulterers, as also is this publican. — S. Luke xviii.

12 Let him that thinketh himself to stand, take heed lest he fall. — 1 Cor. x.

PRIDE.

13 A GENERATION, whose eyes are lofty, and their eyelids lifted up on high. — Prov. xxx.

20 The wicked man is proud all his days ... — Job xv.

25 He hath stretched out his hand against God, and hath strengthened himself against the Almighty.

14 Never suffer pride to reign in thy mind, or in thy words: for from it all perdition took its beginning. — Tobias iv.

25 The Lord will destroy the house of the proud ... — Prov. xv.

5 Every proud man is an abomination to the Lord: though hand should be joined to hand, he is not innocent. — Prov. xvi.

18 Pride goeth before destruction: and the spirit is lifted up before a fall.

4 Haughtiness of the eyes is the enlarging of the heart ... — Prov. xxi.

23 Humiliation followeth the proud ... — Prov. xxix.

8 What hath pride profited us? or what advantage hath the boasting of riches brought us? — Wisd. v.

3 The pride of thy heart hath lifted thee up, who dwellest in the clefts of the rocks, and settest up thy throne on high: who sayest in thy heart: Who shall bring me down to the ground? — Abdias i.

14 But all the enemies of thy people that hold them in subjection, are foolish, and unhappy, and proud beyond measure. — Wisd. xv.

30 The congregation of the proud shall not be healed: for the plant of wickedness shall take root in them, and it shall not be perceived. — Ecclus. iii.

4 Seek not of the Lord a pre-eminence, nor of the king the seat of honour. — Ecclus. vii.

7 Pride is hateful before God and men ... — Ecclus. x.

9 ... Why is earth and ashes proud?

14 The beginning of the pride of man, is to fall off from God.

15 Because his heart is departed from him

Pride.

that made him: for pride is the beginning of all sin: he that holdeth it, shall be filled with maledictions, and it shall ruin him in the end.

21 God hath abolished the memory of the proud, and hath preserved the memory of them that are humble in mind.

1 He that toucheth pitch, shall be defiled with it: and he that hath fellowship with the proud, shall put on pride. — Ecclus. xiii.

15 Hear ye, and give ear. Be not proud, for the Lord hath spoken. — Jer. xiii.

9 The Lord of hosts hath designed it, to pull down the pride of all glory, and bring to disgrace all the glorious ones of the earth. — Isaias xxiii.

43 Wo to you Pharisees, because you love the uppermost seats in the synagogues, and salutations in the market-place. — S. Luke xi.

15 And he said to them: You are they who justify yourselves before men, but God knoweth your hearts: for that which is high to men, is an abomination before God. — S. Luke xvi.

14 ... Every one that exalteth himself, shall be humbled ... — S. Luke xviii.

20 ... Be not high-minded; but fear. — Rom. xi.

16 ... Not minding high things, but consenting to the humble ... — Rom. xii.

16 But now you rejoice in your arrogancies. All such rejoicing is wicked. — S. James iv.

2 If any man think that he knoweth any thing, he hath not yet known, as he ought to know. 1 Cor. viii.

7 For who distinguisheth thee? and what hast thou that thou hast not received? And if thou hast received: why dost thou glory, as if thou hadst not received it? 1 Cor. iv.

3 If any man think himself to be something, whereas he is nothing, he deceiveth himself. Gal. vi.

14 But God forbid that I should glory, save in the cross of our Lord Jesus Christ; by whom the world is crucified to me, and I to the world.

18 Not he, that commendeth himself, is approved, but he whom God commendeth. 2 Cor. x.

PROMISES.

35 ... The words that proceed from my mouth I will not make void. Ps. lxxxviii.

3 If you walk in my precepts, and keep my commandments, and do them ... Lev. xxvi.

11 I will set my tabernacle in the midst of you, and my soul shall not cast you off.

12 I will walk among you, and will be your God, and you shall be my people.

30 ... Whosoever shall glorify me, him will I glorify ... 1 Kings ii.

9 And thou shalt know that the Lord thy Deut. vii.

God, he is a strong and faithful God, keeping his covenant and mercy to them that love him, and to them that keep his commandments, unto a thousand generations.

19 ... Hath he said then, and will he not do? hath he spoken, and will he not fulfil? — Numb. xxiii.

56 Blessed be the Lord, who hath given rest to his people Israel, according to all that he promised: there hath not failed so much as one word of all the good things that he promised by his servant Moses. — 3 Kings viii.

2 ... Josue called for all Israel ... and said: ... — Josue xxiii.

14 Behold this day I am going into the way of all the earth, and you shall know with all your mind that of all the words which the Lord promised to perform for you, not one hath failed.

20 O how great is the multitude of thy sweetness, O Lord, which thou hast hidden for them that fear thee! Which thou hast wrought for them that hope in thee, in the sight of the sons of men. — Ps. xxx.

21 Thou shalt hide them in the secret of thy face, from the disturbance of men.

Thou shalt protect them in thy tabernacle from the contradiction of tongues.

2 He that walketh without blemish and worketh justice: — Ps. xiv.

3 He that speaketh truth in his heart, who hath not used deceit in his tongue: nor hath done evil to his neighbour: nor taken up a reproach against his neighbours.

5 ... He that doth these things shall not be moved for ever.

4 The innocent in hands, and clean of heart, who hath not taken his soul in vain, nor sworn deceitfully to his neighbour.   Ps. xxiii.

5 He shall receive a blessing from the Lord, and mercy from God his Saviour.

19 The Lord is nigh unto them that are of a contrite heart: and he will save the humble of spirit.   Ps. xxxiii.

23 The Lord will redeem the souls of his servants: and none of them that trust in him shall offend.

20 The Lord keepeth all them that love him ...   Ps. cxliv.

6 The blessing of the Lord is upon the head of the just ...   Prov. x.

16 The work of the just is unto life ...

18 ... To him that soweth justice, there is a faithful reward.   Prov. xi.

21 ... The seed of the just shall be saved.

2 He that is good shall draw grace from the Lord ...   Prov. xii.

28 In the path of justice is life ...

22 They err that work evil: but mercy and truth prepare good things.   Prov. xiv.

7 When the ways of man shall please the Lord, he will convert even his enemies to peace. — Prov. xvi.

24 The blessing of God maketh haste to reward the just, and in a swift hour his blessing beareth fruit. — Ecclus; xi.

16 The just shall live for evermore: and their reward is with the Lord, and the care of them with the most High. — Wisd. v.

17 Therefore shall they receive a kingdom of glory, and a crown of beauty at the hand of the Lord: for with his right hand he will cover them, and with his holy arm will he defend them.

10 When thou shalt pour out thy soul to the hungry, and shall satisfy the afflicted soul, then shall thy light rise up in darkness, and thy darkness shall be as the noon-day. — Isaias lviii.

11 And the Lord will give thee rest continually, and will fill thy soul with brightness, and deliver thy bones, and thou shalt be like a watered garden, and like a fountain of water whose waters shall not fail.

15 He that walketh in justices, and speaketh truth, that casteth away avarice by oppression, and shaketh his hands from all bribes, that stoppeth his ears lest he hear blood, and shutteth his eyes that he may see no evil. — Isaias xxxiii.

16 He shall dwell on high, the fortifica-

tions of rocks shall be his highness: bread is given him, his waters are sure.

17 His eyes shall see the king in his beauty, they shall see the land far off.

24 And it shall come to pass, that before they call, I will hear: as they are yet speaking, I will hear. Isaias lxv.

3 They that are learned shall shine as the brightness of the firmament: and they that instruct many to justice, as stars for all eternity. Dan. xii.

43 Then shall the just shine as the sun, in the kingdom of their Father. S. Matt. xiii.

23 Well done, good and faithful servant: because thou hast been faithful over a few things, I will set thee over many things; enter thou into the joy of thy Lord. S. Matt. xxv.

29 Every one that hath left house, or brethren, or sisters, or father, or mother, or wife, or children, or lands for my name's sake: shall receive a hundredfold, and shall possess life everlasting. S. Matt. xix.

12 As many as received him, he gave them power to be made the sons of God, to them that believe in his name. S. John i.

36 ... Whither I go, thou canst not follow me now, but thou shalt follow me afterwards. S. John xiii.

3 And if I shall go, and prepare a place for you, I will come again, and will take you S. John xiv.

to myself; that where I am, you also may be.

1 Having, therefore, these promises, dearly beloved, let us cleanse ourselves from all defilement of the flesh and of the spirit, perfecting sanctification in the fear of God. — 2 Cor. vii.

21 Most fully knowing that whatsoever he has promised, he is able also to perform. — Rom. iv.

6 Who will render to every man according to his works. — Rom. ii.

7 To them indeed, who, according to patience in good work, seek glory and honour and incorruption, eternal life.

11 ... Rejoice, be perfect, take exhortation, be of one mind, have peace: and the God of peace and of love will be with you. — 2 Cor. xiii.

8 For the rest, there is laid up for me a crown of justice, which the Lord the just judge will render to me at that day; and not to me only, but to them also who love his coming. — 2 Tim. iv.

23 Let us hold fast the confession of our hope without wavering (for he is faithful that hath promised). — Heb. x.

37 For yet a little while, and a very little while, and he that is to come, will come, and will not delay.

9 There remaineth, therefore, a rest for the people of God. — Heb. iv.

12 Because I will be merciful to their — Heb. viii.

iniquities, and their sins I will remember no more.

2 Grace to you, and peace be fulfilled in the knowledge of God, and of Christ Jesus our Lord.   2 S. Peter i.

20 For all the promises of God are in him, It is: therefore also by him, amen to God.   2 Cor. i.

25 And this is the promise which he hath promised to us, eternal life.   1 S. John ii.

7 ... To him, that overcometh, I will give to eat of the tree of life, which is in the paradise of my God.   Apoc. ii.

17 ... To him, that overcometh, I will give the hidden manna, and will give him a white stone, and in this stone, a new name written, which no man knoweth, but he that receiveth it.

21 To him that shall overcome; I will grant to sit with me in my throne: as I also have overcome, and have sat with my Father in his throne.   Apoc. iii.

PROMISES OF MEN.

14 As clouds, and wind, when no rain followeth; so is the man that boasteth, and doth not fulfil his promises.   Prov. xxv.

3 Keep thy word ...   Ecclus. xxix.

PROSPERITY OF THE WICKED.

24 THE earth is given into the hand of the wicked ...   *Job ix.*

7 Why then do the wicked live, are they advanced, and strengthened with riches?   *Job xxi.*

8 Their seed continueth before them, a multitude of kinsmen, and of children's children in their sight.

9 Their houses are secure and peaceable, and the rod of God is not upon them.

11 Their little ones go out like a flock, and their children dance and play.

12 They take the timbrel and the harp, and rejoice at the sound of the organ.

13 They spend their days in wealth, and in a moment they go down to hell.

14 Who have said to God: Depart from us, we desire not the knowledge of thy ways.

15 Who is the Almighty that we should serve him? and what doth it profit us if we pray to him?

2 Whilst the wicked man is proud, the poor is set on fire.   *Ps. ix.*

3 For the sinner is praised in the desires of his soul: and the unjust man is blessed.

5 ... Thy judgments are removed from his sight: he shall rule over all his enemies.

6 For he hath said in his heart: I shall

not be moved from generation to generation, and shall be without evil.

17 Be not thou afraid, when a man shall be made rich, and when the glory of his house shall be increased.   Ps. xlviii.

18 For when he shall die he shall take nothing away; nor shall his glory descend with him.

20 He shall go into the generations of his fathers: and he shall never see light.

21 Man when he was in honour did not understand: he hath been compared to senseless beasts, and made like to them.

2 But my feet were almost moved; my steps had well nigh slipt.   Ps. lxxii.

3 Because I had a zeal on occasion of the wicked, seeing the prosperity of sinners.

4 For there is no regard to their death, nor is there strength in their stripes.

5 They are not in the labour of men: neither shall they be scourged like other men.

6 Therefore pride hath held them fast: they are covered with their iniquity and their wickedness.

11 And they said: How doth God know? and is there knowledge in the most High?

12 Behold these are sinners; and yet abounding in the world they have obtained riches.

19 How are they brought to desolation? they have suddenly ceased to be: they have perished by reason of their iniquity.

20 As the dream of them that awake, O Lord; so in thy city thou shalt bring their image to nothing.

11 Deliver me, and rescue me out of the Ps. cxliii. hand of strange children: whose mouth hath spoken vanity: and their right hand is the right hand of iniquity.

12 Whose sons are as new plants in their youth: their daughters decked out, adorned round about after the similitude of a temple:

13 Their storehouses full, flowing out of this into that. Their sheep fruitful in young, abounding in their goings forth.

14 Their oxen fat. There is no breach of wall, nor passage, nor crying out in their streets.

15 They have called the people happy, that hath these things: but happy is that people whose God is the Lord.

11 Moab hath been fruitful from his youth, Jer. and hath rested upon his lees: and hath not xlviii. been poured out from vessel to vessel, nor hath gone into captivity: therefore his taste hath remained in him, and his scent is not changed.

9 There is success in evil things to a man Ecclus. xx.

without discipline, and there is a finding that turneth to loss.

1 Thou indeed, O Lord, art just, if I plead with thee, but yet I will speak what is just to thee: Why doth the way of the wicked prosper: why is it well with all them that transgress, and do wickedly? — Jer. xii.

2 Thou hast planted them, and they have taken root: they prosper and bring forth fruit...

3 ... Gather them together as sheep for a sacrifice, and prepare them for the day of slaughter.

13 ... Why lookest thou upon them that do unjust things, and holdest thy peace when the wicked devoureth the man that is more just than himself? — Habac. i.

1 Wo to you that are wealthy in Sion, and to you that have confidence in the mountain of Samaria: ye great men, heads of the people, that go in with state into the house of Israel. — Amos vi.

3 You that are separated unto the evil day: and that approach to the throne of iniquity.

4 You that sleep upon beds of ivory, and are wanton on your couches: that eat the lambs out of the flock, and the calves out of the midst of the herd.

5 You that sing to the sound of the

psaltery: they have thought themselves to have instruments of music like David.

6 That drink wine in bowls, and anoint themselves with the best ointments: and they are not concerned for the affliction of Joseph.

7 ... The faction of the luxurious ones shall be taken away.

30 The wicked man is reserved to the day of destruction, and he shall be brought to the day of wrath. — Job xxi.

14 Therefore hath hell enlarged her soul, and opened her mouth without any bounds, and their strong ones, and their people, and their high and glorious ones shall go down into it. — Isaias v.

24 Wo to you that are rich: for you have your consolation.

25 Wo to you that are filled: for you shall hunger. Wo to you that laugh now: for you shall mourn and weep.

26 Wo to you when men shall bless you: For according to these things did their fathers to the false prophets. — S. Luke vi.

25 ... Son, remember that thou didst receive good things in thy life time, and likewise Lazarus evil things: but now he is comforted, and thou art tormented. — S. Luke xvi.

PRUDENCE.

5 ... Lean not upon thy own prudence. Prov. iii.

10 ... The knowledge of the holy is pru- Prov. ix.
dence.

21 The wise in heart, shall be called pru- Prov. xvi.
dent ...

18 ... The prudent shall look for know- Prov. xiv.
ledge.

5 ... He that regardeth reproofs shall Prov. xv.
become prudent.

19 Meddle not with him that revealeth Prov. xx.
secrets, and walketh deceitfully, and openeth
wide his lips.

14 The eyes of a wise man are in his Eccles.
head ... ii.

20 Detract not the king, no, not in thy Eccles.
thought; and speak not evil of the rich man x.
in thy private chamber: because even the
birds of the air will carry thy voice, and he
that hath wings will tell what thou hast said.

21 Wo to you that are wise in your own Isaias v.
eyes, and prudent in your own conceits.

16 Behold I send you as sheep in the S. Matt.
midst of wolves. Be ye therefore wise as x.
serpents, and simple * as doves.

15 See therefore, brethren, how you walk Ephes. v.
circumspectly, not as unwise.

* Harmless.

7 The end of all approacheth. Be prudent, therefore, and watch in prayers. 1 S. Peter iv.

PURGATORY.

37 ... Restrain not grace from the dead.* Ecclus. vii.

46 It is therefore a holy and wholesome thought to pray for the dead, that they may be loosed from sins.† 2 Mach. xii.

47 That servant who knew the will of his lord, and hath not prepared, and did not according to his will, shall be beaten with many stripes. S. Luke xii.

48 But he that knew not, and did things worthy of stripes, shall be beaten with few stripes.

25 Make an agreement with thy adversary quickly, whilst thou art in the way with him; lest, perhaps, the adversary deliver thee to S. Matt. v.

---

* That is, withhold not from them the benefit of alms, prayers, and sacrifices. Such was the doctrine and practice of the church of God, even in the time of the Old Testament, and the same has always continued from the days of the apostles in the church of the New Testament.

† Here is an evident and undeniable proof of the practice of praying for the dead under the old law, which was then strictly observed by the Jews, and consequently could not be introduced at that time by Judas, their chief and high priest, if it had not been always their custom.

the judge, and the judge deliver thee to the officer, and thou be cast into prison.

26 Amen I say to thee, thou shalt not go out from thence, till thou pay the last farthing.

36 I say unto you, that every idle word* that men shall speak, they shall render an account for it in the day of judgment. — S. Matt. xii.

32 ... He that shall speak against the Holy Ghost it shall not be forgiven him neither in this world, nor in the world to come.†

18 Christ also died once for our sins, the just for the unjust: that he might offer us to God, being put to death indeed in the flesh, but enlivened in the Spirit. — 1 S. Peter iii.

19 In which also coming he preached to those spirits who were in prison.‡

10 He that descended is the same also that ascended above all the heavens, that he might fill all things. — Ephes. iv.

---

* This shews there must be a place of temporal punishment hereafter, where these slighter faults shall be punished.

† From these words S. Augustin and S. Gregory gather, that some sins may be remitted in the world to come: and consequently that there is a purgatory or middle place.

‡ See here a proof of a third place, or middle place of souls: for these spirits in prison, to whom Christ went to preach, after His death, were not in heaven, nor yet in the hell of the damned; because heaven is no prison: and Christ did not go to preach to the damned.

29 What shall they do that are baptized for the dead, if the dead rise not again at all? why are they then baptized for them?   1 Cor. xv.

11 Other foundation no man can lay, but that which is laid; which is Christ Jesus.   1 Cor. iii.

12 Now if any man build upon this foundation, gold, silver, precious stones, wood, hay, stubble:

13 Every man's work shall be made manifest: for the day of the Lord shall declare it, because it shall be revealed in fire: and the fire* shall try every man's work, of what sort it is.

14 If any man's work abide, which he hath built thereupon, he shall receive a reward.

15 If any man's work burn, he shall suffer loss: but he himself shall be saved, yet so as by fire.

---

* The fire of God's judgment "shall try every man's work." And they, whose "works" like "wood, hay, and stubble," cannot abide the fire, shall "suffer loss;" these works being found to be of no value; yet they themselves, having built upon the right "foundation" (by living and dying in the true faith, and in the state of grace, though with some imperfections), "shall be saved, yet so as by fire;" being liable to this punishment, by reason of the "wood, hay, and stubble," which was mixed with their building.

PURITY.

2 I WILL understand in the unspotted way, when Thou shalt come to me. Ps. c.

18 The Lord knoweth the days of the undefiled; and their inheritance shall be for ever. Ps. xxxvi.

17 Never have I joined myself with them that play: neither have I made myself partaker with them that walk in lightness. Tobias iii.

26 Evil thoughts are an abomination to the Lord: and pure words most beautiful shall be confirmed by him. Prov. xv.

11 He that loveth cleanness of heart, for the grace of his lips shall have the king for his friend. Prov. xxii.

5 Give not thy mouth to cause thy flesh to sin . . . Eccles. v.

10 Remove anger from thy heart, and put away evil from thy flesh. For youth and pleasure are vain. Eccles. xi.

20 No price is worthy of a continent soul. Ecclus. xxvi.

21 And as I knew that I could not otherwise be continent, except God gave it, . . . I went to the Lord, and besought him . . . Wisd. viii.

1 O how beautiful is the chaste generation with glory: for the memory thereof is im- Wisd. iv.

Purity.

mortal: because it is known both with God and with men.

2 . . . It triumpheth crowned for ever, winning the reward of undefiled conflicts.

8 Blessed are the clean of heart: for they shall see God.   S. Matt. v.

1 I beseech you, therefore, brethren, by the mercy of God, that you present your bodies a living sacrifice, holy, pleasing to God, your reasonable service.   Rom. xii.

16 Know you not that you are the temple of God, and that the Spirit of God dwelleth in you?   1 Cor. iii.

17 But if any one violate the temple of God: him shall God destroy. For the temple of God is holy: which you are.

19 Or know you not, that your members are the temple of the Holy Ghost, who is in you, whom you have from God; and you are not your own?   1 Cor. vi.

20 For you are bought with a great price. Glorify and bear God in your body.

8 But I say to the unmarried and to the widows: It is good for them if they so continue, even as I.   1 Cor. vii.

28 But if thou take a wife, thou hast not sinned. And if a virgin marry, she hath not sinned: nevertheless, such shall have tribulation of the flesh. But I spare you.

32 . . . He that is without a wife, is solici-

tous for the things that belong to the Lord, how he may please God.

33 But he that is with a wife, is solicitous for the things of the world, how he may please his wife: and he is divided.

34 And the unmarried woman and the virgin thinketh on the things of the Lord: that she may be holy both in body and in spirit. But she that is married thinketh on the things of the world, how she may please her husband.

15 All things are clean to the clean: but to them that are defiled, and to unbelievers, nothing is clean: but both their mind and their conscience are defiled. — Titus i.

11 Dearly beloved, I beseech you as strangers and pilgrims, to refrain yourselves from carnal desires, which war against the soul. — 1 S. Peter ii.

1 And I saw: and, behold, a Lamb stood on Mount Sion, and with him a hundred and forty-four thousand having his name and the name of his Father written on their foreheads. — Apoc. xiv.

2 And I heard a voice from heaven, as the voice of many waters, and as the voice of great thunder: and the voice which I heard, was as of harpers, harping on their harps.

3 And they sang, as it were, a new canticle, before the throne, and before the four

living creatures, and the ancients: and no man could say the canticle, but those hundred forty-four thousand, who were purchased from the earth.

4 ... They are virgins. These follow the Lamb whithersoever he goeth. These were purchased from among men, the first-fruits to God and to the Lamb.

5 And in their mouth was found no lie: for they are without spot before the throne of God.

RELIGIOUS COURAGE.

14 Expect the Lord, do manfully, and let thy heart take courage, and wait thou for the Lord.   Ps. xxvi.

5 His truth shall compass thee with a shield: thou shalt not be afraid of the terror of the night.   Ps. xc.

5 ... In God I have put my trust: I will not fear what flesh can do against me.   Ps. lv.

46 I spoke of thy testimonies before kings: and I was not ashamed.   Ps. cxviii.

25 Be not afraid of sudden fear, nor of the power of the wicked falling upon thee.   Prov. iii.

26 For the Lord will be at thy side, and will keep thy foot that thou be not taken.

1 The wicked man fleeth, when no man   Prov. xxviii.

pursueth: but the just, bold as a lion, shall be without dread.

9 Deliver him that suffereth wrong out of the hand of the proud: and be not faint-hearted in thy soul.   Ecclus. iv.

9 Be not faint-hearted in thy mind.   Ecclus. vii.

16 He that feareth the Lord shall tremble at nothing, and shall not be afraid: for he is his hope.   Ecclus. xxxiv.

14 Fear not, thou worm of Jacob, you that are dead of Israel: I have helped thee, saith the Lord: and thy Redeemer the Holy One of Israel.   Isaias xli.

28 Fear ye not them that kill the body, and are not able to kill the soul . . .   S. Matt. x.

6 . . . I will not fear what man shall do unto me.   Heb. xiii.

14 But if also you suffer any thing for justice sake, blessed are ye. And be not afraid of their terror, and be not troubled.   1 S. Peter iii.

22 And now behold, being bound in the Spirit, I go to Jerusalem: not knowing the things which shall befal me there: Acts xx.

23 Save that the Holy Ghost in every city witnesseth to me, saying: that bands and afflictions wait for me at Jerusalem.

24 But I fear none of these things, neither do I count my life more precious than myself, so that I may consummate my course

and the ministry of the word which I received from the Lord Jesus, to testify the gospel of the grace of God.

10 Fear none of those things which thou shalt suffer . . .   Apoc. ii.

RENOUNCING OURSELVES AND ALL THINGS FOR CHRIST.

16 . . . Let us also go, that we may die with him.   S. John xi.

28 . . . Behold, we have left all things, and have followed thee.   S. Luke xviii.

38 He that taketh not up his cross, and followeth me, is not worthy of me.   S. Matt. x.

25 For whosoever will save his life, shall lose it: and he that shall lose his life for my sake, shall find it.   S. Matt. xvi.

44 The kingdom of heaven is like unto a treasure hidden in a field: which when a man hath found, he hideth, and for joy thereof goeth, and selleth all that he hath, and buyeth that field.   S. Matt. xiii.

45 Again, the kingdom of heaven is like to a merchant seeking good pearls:

46 Who, when he had found one pearl of great price, went his way, and sold all that he had, and bought it.

26 If any man come to me, and hate not* his father and mother, and wife, and children, and brethren, and sisters, yea and his own life also, he cannot be my disciple. — S. Luke xiv.

27 And whosoever doth not carry his cross and come after me, cannot be my disciple.

33 So likewise every one of you that doth not renounce all that he possesseth, cannot be my disciple.

24 Let no man seek his own, but that which is for the welfare of another. — 1 Cor. x.

7 For none of us liveth to himself: and no man dieth to himself. — Rom. xiv.

8 For, whether we live, we live to the Lord; or whether we die, we die to the Lord. Therefore, whether we live, or whether we die, we are the Lord's.

19 ... That I may live to God: with Christ I am nailed to the cross. — Gal. ii.

20 And I live, now not I; but Christ liveth in me. And that I live now in the flesh: I live in the faith of the Son of God, who loved me, and delivered himself for me.

---

* The law of Christ does not allow us to hate even our enemies, much less our parents; but the meaning of the text is, that we must be in that disposition of soul, as to be willing to renounce, and part with everything, how near and dear soever it may be to us, that would keep us from following Christ.

REPENTANCE AND CONTRITION.

29 When thou shalt seek there the Lord thy God, thou shalt find him: yet so, if thou seek him with all thy heart, and all the affliction of thy soul.　Deut. iv.

5 ... The things you say in your hearts, be sorry for them upon your beds.　Ps. iv.

63 That thou mayest remember, and be confounded, and mayest no more open thy mouth because of thy confusion, when I shall be pacified towards thee for all that thou hast done, saith the Lord God.　Ezech. xvi.

9 ... The Lord your God is merciful, and will not turn away his face from you, if you return to him.　2 Paralip. xxx.

19 The Lord is nigh unto them that are of a contrite heart: and he will save the humble of spirit.　Ps. xxxiii.

24 Thou hast mercy upon all, because thou canst do all things, and overlookest the sins of men for the sake of repentance.　Wisd. xi.

20 To the penitent he hath given the way of justice ...　Ecclus. xvii.

4 How good is it, when thou art reproved, to show repentance! for so thou shalt escape wilful sin.　Ecclus. xx.

14 Wash thy heart from wickedness, O Jerusalem, that thou mayest be saved: how long shall hurtful thoughts abide in thee?　Jer. iv.

18 But the soul that is sorrowful for the greatness of evil she hath done, and goeth bowed down, and feeble, and the eyes that fail, and the hungry soul giveth glory and justice to thee the Lord. — Baruch ii.

10 ... Thus you have spoken, saying: Our iniquities, and our sins are upon us, and we pine away in them: how then can we live? — Ezech. xxxiii.

11 As I live, saith the Lord God, I desire not the death of the wicked, but that the wicked turn from his way, and live. Turn ye, turn ye from your evil ways: and why will you die, O house of Israel?

10 And I will pour out upon the house of David, and upon the inhabitants of Jerusalem, the spirit of grace, and of prayers: and they shall look upon me, whom they have pierced: and they shall mourn for him as one mourneth for an only son, and they shall grieve over him, as the manner is to grieve for the death of the first-born. — Zach. xii.

14 And after that John was delivered up, Jesus came into Galilee, preaching the gospel of the kingdom of God, — S. Mark i.

15 And saying: The time is accomplished, and the kingdom of God is at hand: repent, and believe the gospel.

32 This Jesus hath God raised again, whereof all we are witnesses. — Acts ii.

Repentance and Contrition.

37 Now when they had heard these things, they had compunction in their heart, and said to Peter and to the rest of the apostles: What shall we do, men and brethren?

19 Be penitent, therefore, and be converted, that your sins may be blotted out. — Acts iii.

31 Him (Jesus) hath God exalted with his right hand, to be prince and saviour, and give repentance to Israel, and remission of sins. — Acts v.

10 The sorrow that is according to God worketh penance steadfast unto salvation: but the sorrow of the world worketh death. — 2 Cor. vii.

11 For behold this self-same thing, that you were made sorrowful according to God, how great carefulness it worketh in you: yea, defence, yea indignation, yea fear, yea desire, yea zeal, yea revenge . . .

8 Draw nigh to God and he will draw nigh to you . . . — S. James iv.

9 Be afflicted, and mourn, and weep: let your laughter be turned into mourning, and your joy into sorrow.

RESIGNATION.

11 BE still and see that I am God . . . — Ps. xlv.

18 . . . It is the Lord: let him do what is good in his sight. — 1 Kings iii.

33 Thou art just in all things that have come upon us ... — 2 Esdras ix.

21 Naked came I out of my mother's womb, and naked shall I return thither: the Lord gave, and the Lord hath taken away: as it hath pleased the Lord, so is it done: blessed be the name of the Lord. — Job i.

10 ... If we have received good things at the hand of God, why should we not receive evil? ... — Job ii.

7 Be subject to the Lord and pray to him ... — Ps. xxxvi.

27 Now is my soul troubled. And what shall I say? Father, save me from this hour. But for this cause I came unto this hour. — S. John xii.

28 Father, glorify thy name.

11 ... The chalice which my Father hath given me, shall I not drink it? — S. John xviii.

13 Then Paul answered, and said: What do you mean weeping and afflicting my heart? For I am ready not only to be bound, but to die also in Jerusalem for the name of the Lord Jesus. — Acts xxi.

14 The will of the Lord be done.

RESISTANCE TO THE HOLY SPIRIT.

4 ... Who hath resisted him, and hath had peace? — Job ix.

13 They have been rebellious to the light, Job xxiv.
they have not known his ways, neither have
they returned by his paths.

10 But they provoked to wrath, and Isaias
afflicted the spirit of his holy One: and he lxiii.
was turned to be their enemy, and he fought
against them.

5 The Holy Spirit of discipline will flee Wisd. i.
from the deceitful, and will withdraw himself
from thoughts that are without understanding, and he shall not abide when iniquity
cometh in.

9 For it is a people that provoketh to Isaias
wrath, and lying children, children that will xxx.
not hear the law of God.

10 Who say to the seers: See not: and
to them that behold: Behold not for us
those things that are right: speak unto us
pleasant things, see errors for us.

11 Take away from me the way, turn
away the path from me, let the holy One of
Israel cease from before us.

51 You stiff-necked and uncircumcised in Acts vii.
heart and ears, you always resist the Holy
Ghost . . .

19 Extinguish not the Spirit. 1 Thess. v.

30 And grieve not the Holy Spirit of God: Ephes.
whereby you are sealed unto the day of re- iv.
demption.

RESURRECTION.

15 Thou shalt call me, and I will answer thee ...   Job xiv.

25 I know that my Redeemer liveth, and in the last day I shall rise out of the earth.   Job xix.

26 And I shall be clothed again with my skin, and in my flesh I shall see my God.

27 Whom I myself shall see, and my eyes shall behold, and not another: this my hope is laid up in my bosom.

16 God will redeem my soul from the hand of hell, when he shall receive me.   Ps. xlviii.

19 Thy dead men shall live, my slain shall rise again: awake, and give praise, ye that dwell in the dust ...   Isaias xxvi.

1 ... And at that time shall thy people be saved, every one that shall be found written in the book.   Dan. xii.

2 And many of those that sleep in the dust of the earth, shall awake: some unto life everlasting, and others unto reproach, to see it always.

13 But go thou thy ways until the time appointed: and thou shalt rest, and stand in thy lot unto the end of the days.

35 They that shall be accounted worthy of that world and of the resurrection from   S. Luke xx.

Resurrection.

the dead, shall neither be married, nor take wives.

36 Neither can they die any more: for they are equal to the angels, and are the children of God being the children of the resurrection.

28 ... The hour cometh wherein all that are in the graves shall hear the voice of the Son of God. S. John v.

29 And they that have done good things, shall come forth unto the resurrection of life; and they that have done evil, unto the resurrection of judgment.

39 Now this is the will of the Father who sent me: that of all that he hath given me, I should lose nothing, but should raise it up again at the last day. S. John vi.

25 ... I am the resurrection and the life; he that believeth in me, although he be dead, shall live: S. John xi.

8 Why should it be thought a thing incredible, that God should raise the dead? Acts xxvi.

33 And with great power did the apostles give testimony of the resurrection of the Lord Jesus. Acts iv.

5 For if we have been planted together in the likeness of his death, in like manner shall we be of his resurrection. Rom. vi.

9 For to this end Christ died, and rose Rom. xiv.

again; that he might be Lord both of the dead and of the living.

11 And if the Spirit of him, that raised up Jesus from the dead, dwell in you; he that raised up Jesus Christ from the dead, shall quicken also your mortal bodies, because of his Spirit that dwelleth in you. — Rom. viii.

2 ... It hath not yet appeared what we shall be. We know, that, when he shall appear, we shall be like to him: because we shall see him as he is. — 1 S. John iii.

12 And we will not have you ignorant, brethren, concerning them that are asleep, that you be not sorrowful, even as others, who have no hope. — 1 Thess. iv.

13 For if we believe that Jesus died, and rose again, even so them who have slept through Jesus, God will bring with him.

3 For I delivered unto you first of all, which I also received: How that Christ died for our sins according to the Scriptures: — 1 Cor. xv.

4 And that he was buried, and that he rose again the third day according to the Scriptures:

5 And that he was seen by Cephas; and after that by the eleven.

6 Then was he seen by more than five hundred brethren at once: of whom many remain until this present, and some are fallen asleep.

7 After that, he was seen by James, then by all the apostles.

8 And last of all, he was seen also by me, as by one born out of due time.

20 But now Christ is risen from the dead, the first-fruits of them that sleep.

21 For by a man came death, and by a man the resurrection of the dead.

22 And as in Adam all die, so also in Christ all shall be made alive.

35 But some man will say: How do the dead rise again? or with what manner of body shall they come?

36 Senseless man, that which thou sowest is not quickened, except it die first.

37 And that which thou sowest, thou sowest not the body that shall be; but bare grain, as of wheat, or of some of the rest.

38 But God giveth it a body as he will: and to every seed its proper body.

42 So also is the resurrection of the dead. It is sown in corruption, it shall rise in incorruption.

43 It is sown in dishonour: it shall rise in glory. It is sown in weakness: it shall rise in power:

44 It is sown a natural body: it shall rise a spiritual body . . .

50 Now this I say, brethren, that flesh and blood cannot possess the kingdom of

God: neither shall corruption possess incorruption.

51 Behold I tell you a mystery. We shall all indeed rise again: but we shall not all be changed.

52 In a moment, in the twinkling of an eye, at the last trumpet: for the trumpet shall sound, and the dead shall rise again incorruptible: and we shall be changed.

53 For this corruptible must put on incorruption: and this mortal must put on immortality.

54 And when this mortal hath put on immortality, then shall come to pass the saying that is written: Death is swallowed up in victory.

REVENGE.

18 SEEK not revenge, nor be mindful of the injury of thy citizens . . .   Lev. xix.

1 He that seeketh to revenge himself, shall find vengeance from the Lord, and he will surely keep his sins in remembrance.   Ecclus. xxviii.

22 Say not: I will return evil: wait for the Lord, and he will deliver thee.   Prov. xx.

21 If thy enemy be hungry, give him to eat: if he thirst, give him water to drink.   Prov. xxv.

15 Thus saith the Lord God: Because the Philistines have taken vengeance, and   Ezech. xxv.

have revenged themselves with all their mind, destroying and satisfying old enmities:

16 Therefore thus saith the Lord God: Behold I will stretch forth my hand upon the Philistines, and will kill the killers, and will destroy the remnant of the sea-coast.

11 Thus saith the Lord: For three crimes of Edom, and for four I will not convert him: because he hath pursued his brother with the sword, and hath cast off all pity, and hath carried on his fury, and hath kept his wrath to the end. *Amos i.*

54 ... Lord, wilt thou that we command fire to come down from heaven and consume them? *S. Luke ix.*

55 And turning, he rebuked them, saying: You know not of what spirit you are.

38 You have heard that it hath been said: An eye for an eye, and a tooth for a tooth. *S. Matt. v.*

43 You have heard that it hath been said, Thou shalt love thy neighbour, and hate thy enemy.

44 But I say to you, Love your enemies, do good to them that hate you: and pray for them that persecute and calumniate you:

45 That you may be the children of your Father who is in heaven, who maketh his sun to rise upon the good and bad, and raineth upon the just and the unjust.

14 Bless them that persecute you : bless, Rom. xii.
and curse not.

17 To no man rendering evil for evil . . .

19 Not revenging yourselves, my dearly
beloved ; but give place unto wrath, for it is
written : Revenge to me ; I will repay, saith
the Lord.

15 See that none render evil for evil to 1 Thess.
any man : but ever follow that which is good   v.
towards each other, and towards all men.

9 . . . For unto this you are called, that 1 S. Peter
you may inherit a blessing.   iii.

REVILING.

11 BLESSED are you when men shall revile S. Matt.
you, and persecute you, and shall say all   v.
manner of evil against you falsely, for my
sake :

12 Rejoice, and be exceeding glad : because your reward is very great in heaven.

22 But I say to you, that whosoever is
angry with his brother, shall be in danger of
the judgment. And whosoever shall say to
his brother, Raca, shall be in danger of the
council. And whosoever shall say, Thou
fool, shall be in danger of hell fire.

10 . . . Railers . . . shall not possess the 1 Cor. vi.
kingdom of God.

12 . . . We are reviled, and we bless.   1 Cor. iv.

Reviling.

9 Not rendering evil for evil nor railing for railing. 1 S. Peter iii.

14 If you be reproached for the name of Christ, you shall be blessed: for that which is of the honour, glory, and power of God, and that which is his Spirit, resteth upon you. 1 S. Peter iv.

23 (Christ) who when he was reviled, did not revile. 1 S. Peter ii.

9 When Michael the Archangel, disputing with the devil, contended about the body of Moses, he durst not bring against him the judgment of railing speech, but said: The Lord command thee.* S. Jude.

RICHES.

11 TAKE heed, and beware lest at any time thou forget the Lord thy God ... Deut. viii.

12 Lest after thou hast eaten and art filled, hast built goodly houses, and dwelt in them,

13 And shalt have herds of oxen, and flocks of sheep, and plenty of gold and silver, and of all things,

14 Thy heart be lifted up, and thou remember not the Lord thy God, who brought thee out of the land of Egypt, out of the house of bondage.

* Or rebuke thee.

11 ... If riches abound, set not your heart upon them. Ps. lxi.

28 He that trusteth in his riches shall fall ... Prov. xi.

11 The rich man seemeth to himself wise ... Prov. xxviii.

10 Where there are great riches, there are also many to eat them. And what doth it profit the owner, but that he seeth the riches with his eyes? Ecclus. v.

12 There is also another grievous evil which I have seen under the sun: riches kept to the hurt of the owner.

13 For they are lost with very great affliction: he hath begotten a son, who shall be in extremity of want.

14 As he came forth naked from his mother's womb, so shall he return, and shall take nothing away with him of his labour.

1 O death, how bitter is the remembrance of thee to a man that hath peace in his possessions, Ecclus. xli.

2 To a man that is at rest, and whose ways are prosperous in all things ...

3 Gold and silver hath destroyed many, and hath reached even to the heart of kings, and perverted them. Ecclus. viii.

5 Injuries and wrongs will waste riches: and the house that is very rich shall be brought to nothing by pride: so the substance of the proud shall be rooted out. Ecclus. xxi.

30 Riches are good to him that hath no sin in his conscience. Ecclus. xiii.

22 The blessing of the Lord maketh men rich: neither shall affliction be joined to them. Prov. x.

8 Blessed is the rich man that is found without blemish: and hath not gone after gold, nor put his trust in money nor in treasures. Ecclus. xxxi.

9 Who is he, and we will praise him? for he hath done wonderful things in his life.

10 Who hath been tried thereby, and made perfect, he shall have glory everlasting. He that could have transgressed and hath not transgressed: and could do evil things, and hath not done them:

11 Therefore are his goods established in the Lord, and all the church of the saints shall declare his alms.

9 And I say to you: Make to yourselves friends of the mammon of iniquity; that when you shall fail they may receive you into everlasting dwellings . . . S. Luke xvi.

11 If you have not been faithful in the unjust mammon, who will trust you with that which is the true?

23 And Jesus looking round about, saith to his disciples: How hardly shall they who have riches, enter into the kingdom of God! S. Mark x.

24 And the disciples were astonished at

his words. But Jesus again answering, saith to them: Children, how hard is it for them that trust in riches, to enter into the kingdom of God!

25 It is easier for a camel to pass through the eye of a needle, than for a rich man to enter into the kingdom of God.

26 And they wondered the more, saying among themselves: Who then can be saved?

27 And Jesus looking on them, saith: With men it is impossible; but not with God: for all things are possible with God.

19 The cares of the world, and the deceitfulness of riches, and the lusts after other things entering in, choke the word: and it is made fruitless. — S. Mark iv.

17 Charge the rich of this world not to be high-minded, nor to trust in the uncertainty of riches, but in the living God (who giveth us abundantly all things to enjoy); — 1 Tim. vi.

18 To do good; to be rich in good works; to distribute readily; to communicate to others;

19 To lay up in store for themselves a good foundation against the time to come, that they may obtain true life.

9 Let the brother of low condition glory in his exaltation: — S. James i.

10 But the rich, in his being low, because as the flower of the grass shall he pass away.

SADNESS.

38 ... My soul is sorrowful even unto death: stay you here, and watch with me.   S. Matt. xxvi.

13 Is any of you sad? Let him pray ... S. James v.

5 I looked on my right hand, and beheld: and there was no one that would know me.   Ps. cxli.

Flight hath failed me: and there is no one that hath regard to my soul.

11 My life is wasted with grief: and my years in sighs. My strength is weakened through poverty, and my bones are disturbed.   Ps. xxx.

13 I am forgotten as one dead from the heart.

2 Save me, O God: for the waters are come in even unto my soul.   Ps. lxviii.

5 They are multiplied above the hairs of my head, who hate me without cause.

6 Why art thou sad, O my soul? and why dost thou trouble me? Hope in God, for I will still give praise to him: the salvation of my countenance, and my God.   Ps. xli.

25 Grief in the heart of a man shall bring him low, but with a good word he shall be made glad.   Prov. xii.

20 ... As a moth doth by a garment, and a worm by the wood: so the sadness of a man consumeth the heart.   Prov. xxv.

17 The sadness of the heart is every plague ... Ecclus. xxv.

16 ... There is no pleasure above the joy of the heart. Ecclus. xxx.

22 Give not up thy soul to sadness, and afflict not thyself in thy own counsel.

23 The joyfulness of the heart, is the life of a man, and a never failing treasure of holiness: and the joy of a man is length of life.

24 Have pity on thy own soul, pleasing God, and contain thyself: gather up thy heart in his holiness: and drive away sadness far from thee.

25 For sadness hath killed many, and there is no profit in it.

26 Envy and anger shorten a man's days, and pensiveness will bring old age before the time.

27 A cheerful and good heart is always feasting ...

SAINTS.

36 GOD is wonderful in his saints: the God of Israel is he who will give power and strength to his people. Blessed be God. Ps. lxvii.

1 And the Lord said to Moses: Behold I have appointed thee the god of Pharao: and Aaron thy brother shall be thy prophet. Exodus vii.

17 Hath not the Lord made the saints to declare all his wonderful works, which the Lord almighty hath firmly settled to be established for his glory? — Ecclus. xlii.

9 And there are some, of whom there is no memorial . . . — Ecclus. xliv.

10 But these were men of mercy, whose godly deeds have not failed.

15 Let the people shew forth their wisdom, and the church declare their praise.

16 Henoch pleased God, and was translated into paradise, that he may give repentance to the nations.

17 Noe was found perfect, just, and in the time of wrath he was made a reconciliation.

35 I will protect this city, and will save it for my own sake, and for the sake of David my servant. — Isaias xxxvii.

35 Take not away thy mercy from us for the sake of Abraham thy beloved, and Isaac thy servant, and Israel thy holy one. — Dan. iii.

5 Afflicted in few things, in many they shall be well rewarded: because God hath tried them, and found them worthy of himself. — Wisd. iii.

6 As gold in the furnace he hath proved them, and as a victim in a holocaust he hath received them, and in time there shall be respect had to them.

7 The just shall shine, and shall run to and fro like sparks among the reeds.

8 They shall judge nations, and rule over people, and their Lord shall reign for ever.

28 And Jesus said to them: (His Apostles) Amen I say to you, that you, who have followed me, in the regeneration, when the Son of man shall sit on the seat of his majesty, you also shall sit on twelve seats judging the twelve tribes of Israel. — S. Matt. xix.

28 And God indeed hath set some in the church, first apostles, secondly prophets, thirdly doctors, after that miracles, then the graces of healings, helps, governments, kinds of tongues, interpretations of speeches. — 1 Cor. xii.

14 And the multitude of men and women that believed in the Lord was more increased: — Acts v.

15 Insomuch that they brought forth the sick into the streets, and laid them on beds and couches, that when Peter came, his shadow at the least might overshadow any of them, and they might be delivered from their infirmities.

16 ... Sick persons, and such as were troubled with unclean spirits; who were all healed.

20 But yet rejoice not in this, that spirits are made subject unto you: but rejoice in this, that your names are written in heaven. — S. Luke x.

26 He that shall overcome, and keep my works unto the end, to him I will give power over the nations; *Apoc. ii.*

27 And he shall rule them with the rod of iron; and as the vessel of a potter they shall be broken;

28 Even as I received from my Father: and I will give him the morning-star.

SAINTS (COMMUNION OF).

11 ... HOLY FATHER, keep them in thy name, whom thou hast given me: that they may be one, as we also are. *S. John xvii.*

21 That they all may be one, as thou, Father, in me, and I in thee: that they also may be one in us: that the world may believe that thou hast sent me.

22 And the glory which thou hast given me, I have given to them: that they may be one, as we also are one.

5 So we being many, are one body in Christ, and each one members one of another. *Rom. xii.*

12 For as the body is one, and hath many members: and all the members of the body, whereas they are many, yet are one body: so also is Christ. *1 Cor. xii.*

13 For in one Spirit were we all baptized into one body, whether Jews or Gentiles,

whether bond or free: and in one Spirit we have all been made to drink.

14 For the body also is not one member, but many.

20 But now there are many members indeed, yet one body.

26 And if one member suffer any thing, all the members suffer with it: or if one member glory, all the members rejoice with it.

27 Now you are the body of Christ, and members of member.

17 Because the bread is one, all we, being many, are one body, who partake of that one bread. 1 Cor.

28 There is neither Jew, nor Greek: there is neither bond, nor free: there is neither male, nor female. For you are all one in Christ Jesus. Gal. iii.

11 And some, indeed, he gave to be apostles,* and some prophets, and others evangelists, and others pastors and teachers, Ephes. iv.

12 For the perfection of the saints, for the work of the ministry, unto the edification of the body of Christ:

13 Till we all meet in the unity of faith, and of the knowledge of the Son of God,

* Verses 11 and 13—"Some apostles"—"Until we all meet." Here it is plainly expressed, that Christ has left in His church a perpetual succession of orthodox pastors and teachers, to preserve the faithful in unity and truth.

Saints (Communion of). 417

unto a perfect man, unto the measure of the age of the fulness of Christ.

16 From whom the whole body, compacted and fitly joined together by what every joint supplieth, according to the operation in the measure of every part, making increase of the body, unto the edifying of itself in charity.

8 ... And the four and twenty ancients fell down before the Lamb, having every one of them harps, and golden vials full of odours, which are the prayers of the saints. *Apoc. v.*

22 But you are come to Mount Sion, and to the city of the living God, the heavenly Jerusalem, and to the company of many thousands of angels, *Heb. xii.*

23 And to the church of the first-born, who are written in heaven, and to God the judge of all, and to the spirits of the just made perfect,

24 And to Jesus the Mediator of the new testament ...

3 That which we have seen and have heard, we declare unto you; that you also may have fellowship with us, and our fellowship may be with the Father, and with his Son Jesus Christ. *1 S. John i.*

SALVATION.

18 Love God all thy life, and call upon him for thy salvation.   Ecclus. xiii.

39 The salvation of the just is from the Lord, and he is their protector in the time of trouble.   Ps. xxxvi.

155 Salvation is far from sinners; because they have not sought thy justifications.   Ps. cxviii.

17 Israel is saved in the Lord with an eternal salvation: you shall not be confounded, and you shall not be ashamed for ever.   Isaias xlv.

1 ... Fear not, I have redeemed thee, and called thee by thy name: thou art mine.   Isaias xliii.

11 I am, I am the Lord: and there is no saviour besides me.

8 ... My salvation shall be for ever, and my justice from generation to generation.   Isaias li.

9 ... Salvation shall be to them that fear my name ...   Mich. vi.

13 Enter ye in at the narrow gate, for wide is the gate, and broad is the way that leadeth to destruction, and many there are who go in thereat.   S. Matt. vii.

14 How narrow is the gate, and strait is the way that leadeth to life; and few there are who find it!

33 Seek ye therefore first the kingdom of God, and his justice ...   S. Matt. vi.

22 ... He that shall persevere unto the end, he shall be saved.   S. Matt. x.

12 ... The kingdom of heaven suffereth violence, and the violent bear it away.   S. Matt. xi.

42 But one thing is necessary.   S. Luke x.

69 ... Lord, to whom shall we go? thou hast the words of eternal life.   S. John vi.

3 Now this is eternal life: That they may know thee, the only true God, and Jesus Christ, whom thou hast sent.   S. John xvii.

23 ... Christ is the head of the church. He is the saviour of his body.   Ephes. v.

12 ... With fear and trembling work out your salvation ...   Philip. ii.

10 For therefore we labour and are reviled, because we hope in the living God, who is the Saviour of all men, especially of the faithful.   1 Tim. iv.

9 For God hath not appointed us unto wrath, but unto the purchasing of salvation by our Lord Jesus Christ.   1 Thess. v.

9 Christ died for us: much more therefore being now justified by his blood, shall we be saved from wrath through him.   Rom. v.

9 Being consummated, he became to all that obey him, the cause of eternal salvation.   Heb. v.

3 How shall we escape, if we neglect so great savation? ...   Heb. ii.

3 Blessed be the God and Father of our 1 S. Peter
Lord Jesus Christ, who according to his i.
great mercy, hath regenerated us unto a
lively hope, by the resurrection of Jesus
Christ from the dead,

4 Unto an inheritance incorruptible, and
undefiled, and that cannot fade, reserved in
heaven for you,

5 Who, by the power of God, are kept by
faith unto salvation ready to be revealed in
the last time.

6 Wherein you shall greatly rejoice, if
now you must be for a little time made sorrowful in divers temptations.

9 ... Blessed are they that are called to Apoc.
the marriage supper of the Lamb. And he xix.
saith to me: These words of God are true.

SATAN.

4 AND the serpent said to the woman, Gen. iii.
No, you shall not die the death.

5 ... You shall be as gods, knowing
good and evil.

1 And Satan rose up against Israel: and Paralip.
moved David to number Israel. xxi.

6 Now on a certain day when the sons of Job i.
God* came to stand before the Lord, Satan
also was present among them.

* This passage represents to us in a figure: 1st, The restless

7 And the Lord said to him: Whence comest thou? and he answered and said: I have gone round about the earth, and walked through it.

8 And the Lord said to him: Hast thou considered my servant Job?...

9 And Satan answering said: Doth Job fear God in vain?

11 But stretch forth thy hand a little, and touch all that he hath, and see if he blesseth* thee not to thy face.

1 Jesus was led by the spirit into the desert to be tempted by the devil. — S. Matt. iv.

17 The seventy-two returned with joy, saying: Lord, the devils are subject to us in thy name. — S. Luke x.

18 And he said to them: I saw satan like lightning falling from heaven.

31 And the Lord said: Simon, Simon, behold satan hath desired to have you that he may sift you as wheat. — S. Luke xxii.

3 And satan entered into Judas who was surnamed Iscariot, one of the twelve.

26 ... And when (Jesus) had dipped the — S. John xiii.

endeavours of Satan against the servants of God: 2nd, That he can do nothing without God's permission: 3rd, That God doth not permit him to tempt them above their strength; but assists them by His divine grace in such a manner, that the vain efforts of the enemy only serve to illustrate their virtue and increase their merit.

* See note to Job i. 5th v., in Pleasures (Evils of Vain).

bread, he gave it to Judas Iscariot, the son of Simon.

27 And after the morsel, satan entered into him . . .

44 You are of your father the devil, and S. John
the desires of your father you will do. He   viii.
was a murderer from the beginning, and he
stood not in the truth; because truth is not
in him. When he speaketh a lie, he speaketh
of his own: for he is a liar, and the father
thereof.

14 . . . Satan himself transformeth him- 2 Cor. xi.
self into an angel of light.

7 Lest the greatness of the revelations 2 Cor. xii.
should exalt me, there was given me a sting
of my flesh, an angel of satan to buffet me.

20 The God of peace crush satan under Rom.
your feet speedily.   xvi.

27 Give not place to the devil . . .   Ephes. iv.

11 Put you on the armour of God, that   Ephes.
you may be able to stand against the deceits vi.
of the devil.

7 . . . Resist the devil and he will fly 1 S. James
from you.   iv.

8 . . . Your adversary the devil, as a roar- 1 S. Peter
ing lion, goeth about seeking whom he may v.
devour.

9 Whom resist ye, strong in faith . . .

8 He that committeth sin is of the devil: 1 S. John
for the devil sinneth from the beginning. iii.

9 That great dragon was cast out, that old serpent, who is called the devil and satan, who seduceth the whole world; and he was cast unto the earth, and his angels were thrown down with him.

Apoc. xii.

9 ... And the devil who seduced them was cast into the pool of fire and brimstone, where both the beast

Apoc. xx.

10 And the false prophet shall be tormented day and night for ever and ever.

SCANDAL.

24 Do not so, my sons: for it is no good report that I hear, that you make the people of the Lord to transgress.

1 Kings ii.

14 ... Take away the stumbling-blocks out of the way of my people.

Isaias lvii.

1 Hear ye this, O priests, and hearken, O ye house of Israel, and give ear, O house of the king: for there is a judgment against you, because you have been a snare to them whom you should have watched over, and a net spread upon Thabor.

Osee v.

2 And you have turned aside victims, into the depth: and I am the teacher of them all.

41 Whosoever shall scandalize* one of

S. Mark ix.

---

* That is, put a stumbling-block in their way, and cause them to fall into sin. See following verses St. Mark ix. 42 to 47, inclusive, chap. Hell.

these little ones that believe in me; it were better for him that a mill-stone were hanged about his neck, and he were cast into the sea.

7 Wo to the world because of scandals. For it must needs be that scandals come: but nevertheless wo to that man by whom the scandal cometh.   S. Matt. xviii.

41 The son of man shall send his Angels, and they shall gather out of his kingdom all scandals, and them that work iniquity.   S. Matt. xiii.

13 Let us not therefore judge one another any more. But judge this rather, that you put not a stumbling-block, or a scandal in your brother's way.   Rom. xiv.

3 Let not him, that eateth, despise him that eateth not: and he that eateth not, let him not judge him that eateth ...

20 Destroy not the work of God for meat. All things, indeed, are clean: but it is evil for that man who eateth with offence.

21 It is good not to eat flesh, and not to drink wine, nor anything whereby thy brother is offended, or scandalized, or made weak.

12 Now when you sin thus against the brethren, and wound their weak conscience, you sin against Christ.   1 Cor. viii.

13 Wherefore if meat scandalize my brother, I will never eat flesh, lest I should scandalize my brother.

SCORN AND CONTEMPT.

4 ... The simplicity of the just man is laughed to scorn. — Job xii.

3 The wicked man when he is come into the depth of sins, contemneth: but ignominy and reproach follow him. — Prov. xviii.

32 Every mocker is an abomination to the Lord ... — Prov. iii.

12 He that despiseth his friend is mean of heart ... — Prov. xi.

20 ... The foolish man despiseth his mother. — Prov. xv.

15 ... In the way of scorners is a deep pit. — Prov. xiii.

21 He that despiseth his neighbour, sinneth ... — Prov. xiv.

14 ... No man can correct, whom he hath despised. — Eccles. vii.

10 Cast out the scoffer, and contention shall go out with him, and quarrels and reproaches shall cease. — Prov. xxii.

12 Laugh no man to scorn in the bitterness of his soul: for there is one who humbleth and exalteth, God who seeth all. — Ecclus. vii.

34 He shall scorn the scorners ... — Prov. iii.

26 Despise not a just man that is poor, and do not magnify a sinful man that is rich. — Ecclus. x.

6 Despise not a man that turneth away from sin, nor reproach him therewith: remember that we are all worthy of reproof. — Ecclus. viii.

7 Despise not a man in his old age; for we shall also become old.

31 Mockery and reproach are of the proud, and vengeance as a lion shall lie in wait for him. — Ecclus. xxvii.

28 ... God hath shewed to me, to call no man common or unclean. — Acts x.

17 But you, my dearly beloved, be mindful of the words which have been spoken before by the apostles of our Lord Jesus Christ, — S. Jude,

18 Who told you, that in the last time there should come mockers, walking according to their own desires in ungodliness.

SCRUPLES.

1 At that time Jesus went through the corn on the sabbath: and his disciples being hungry, began to pluck the ears, and to eat. — S. Matt. xii.

2 And the Pharisees seeing them, said to him: Behold thy disciples do that which is not lawful to do on the sabbath days.

3 But he said to them: Have you not read what David did when he was hungry, and they that were with him:

4 How he entered into the house of God,

and did eat the loaves of proposition, which it was not lawful for him to eat, nor for them that were with him, but for the priests only?

5 Or have ye not read in the law, that on the sabbath-days the priests in the temple break the sabbath, and are without blame?

6 But I tell you that there is here a greater than the temple.

7 And if you knew what this meaneth: I will have mercy, and not sacrifice: you would never have condemned the innocent.

8 For the son of man is Lord even of the sabbath.

10 ... And they asked him, saying: Is it lawful to heal on the sabbath-days?

15 Ye hypocrites, doth not every one of you on the sabbath-day loose his ox or his ass from the manger, and lead them to water?   S. Luke xiii.

16 And ought not this daughter of Abraham, whom satan hath bound, lo, these eighteen years, be loosed from this bond on the sabbath-day?

12 ... It is lawful to do a good deed on the sabbath-days.   S. Matt. xii.

2 Why do thy disciples transgress the tradition of the ancients? For they wash not their hands when they eat bread.   S. Matt. xv.

11 Not that which goeth into the mouth

defileth a man : but what cometh out of the mouth, this defileth a man.

19 From the heart come forth evil thoughts, murders, adulteries, fornications, thefts, false testimonies, blasphemies.

20 These are the things that defile a man. But to eat with unwashed hands doth not defile a man.

42 Wo unto you, Pharisees, because you tithe mint and rue and every herb : and pass over judgment, and the charity of God. Now these things you ought to have done, and not to leave the other undone.   S. Luke xi.

24 Blind guides, who strain out a gnat and swallow a camel.   S. Matt. xxiii.

10 Now therefore why tempt you God, to put a yoke upon the necks of the disciples, which neither our fathers nor we have been able to bear?   Acts xv.

13 ... Arise, Peter, kill, and eat.   Acts x.

14 But Peter said : Far be it from me ; for I never did eat anything that is common and unclean.

15 And the voice spoke to him again the second time : That which God hath cleansed, do not thou call common.

14 I know, and am confident, in the Lord Jesus, that nothing is unclean of itself ...   Rom. xiv.

32 You shall know the truth, and the truth shall make you free.   S. John viii.

36 If therefore the son shall make you free, you shall be free indeed.

SEEK GOD.

12 Sow for yourselves in justice, and reap in the month of mercy, break up your fallow ground: but the time to seek the Lord is, when he shall come that shall teach you justice. — Osee x.

19 Give therefore your hearts and your souls, to seek the Lord your God: and arise, and build a sanctuary to the Lord God ... — 1 Paralip. xxii.

33 ... Seek ye God, and your soul shall live. — Ps. lxviii.

9 ... If thou seek him, thou shalt find him: but if thou forsake him, he will cast thee off for ever. — 1 Paralip. xxviii.

22 ... The hand of our God is upon all them that seek him in goodness ... — 1 Esdras viii.

4 Seek ye the Lord, and be strengthened: seek his face evermore. — Ps. civ.

6 Seek ye the Lord, while he may be found: call upon him, while he is near. — Isaias lv.

8 ... He that seeketh, findeth ... — S. Matt. vii.

6 ... He that cometh to God, must believe that he is, and is a rewarder to them that seek him. — Heb. xi.

SELF-DELUSION.

12 There is a way which seemeth just to a man: but the ends thereof lead to death. — Prov. xiv.

8 ... I am become rich, I have found me an idol: all my labours shall not find me the iniquity that I have committed. — Osee xii.

21 Not every one that saith to me, Lord, Lord, shall enter into the kingdom of heaven: but he that doeth the will of my Father, who is in heaven, he shall enter into the kingdom of heaven.

22 Many will say to me in that day: Lord, Lord, have we not prophesied in thy name, and cast out devils in thy name, and done many miracles in thy name?

23 And then will I profess unto them, I never knew you: depart from me, you that work iniquity. — S. Matt. vii.

46 Why call you me Lord, Lord: and do not the things which I say? — S. Luke vi.

20 Herod feared John, knowing him to be a just and holy man: and kept him, and when he heard him, did many things: and he heard him willingly. — S. Mark vi.

18 Take heed therefore how you hear. For whosoever hath, to him shall be given; and whosoever hath not, that also which he — S. Luke viii.

thinketh he hath, shall be taken away from him.

24 Strive to enter by the narrow gate; for many, I say to you, shall seek to enter, and shall not be able.

25 But when the master of the house shall be gone in, and shall shut the door, you shall begin to stand without, and knock at the door, saying: Lord, open to us; and he answering shall say to you, I know you not whence you are:

26 Then you shall begin to say: We have eaten and drunk in thy presence, and thou hast taught in our streets.

27 And he shall say to you: I know you not whence you are: depart from me all ye workers of iniquity.'

S. Luke xiii.

3 For when they shall say, peace and security; then shall sudden destruction come upon them...

1 Thess. v.

22 Be ye doers of the word, and not hearers only, deceiving your own selves.

S. James i.

17 Because thou sayest: I am rich, and made wealthy, and I have need of nothing; and thou knowest not, that thou art wretched, and miserable, and poor, and blind, and naked.

18 I counsel thee to buy of me gold fire-tried, that thou mayest be made rich; and mayest be clothed in white garments, that

Apoc. iii.

the shame of thy nakedness may not appear: and anoint thy eyes with eye-salve, that thou mayest see.

SELFISHNESS.

9 ... Am I my brother's keeper? — Gen. iv.

11 ... All have turned aside into their own way, every one after his own gain, from the first even to the last. — Isaias lvi.

10 Who is there among you, that will shut the doors, and will kindle the fire on my altar gratis? I have no pleasure in you, saith the Lord of hosts: and I will not receive a gift of your hands. — Malach. i.

25 ... He that loveth his life shall lose it ... — S. John xii.

4 I have sinned ... What is that to us? look thou to it. — S. Matt. xxvii.

1 ... In the last days shall come dangerous times. — 2 Tim. iii.

2 Men shall be lovers of themselves ...

21 For all seek the things that are their own; not the things that are Jesus Christ's. — Philip. ii.

17 He that hath the substance of this world, and shall see his brother in need, and shall put up his bowels from him: how doth the charity of God abide in him? — 1 S. John iii.

SELF-WILL AND OBSTINACY.

17 ... And hearing the commandments of the Lord, they did all things contrary. *Judges ii.*

8 ... Yield yourselves to the Lord, and come to his sanctuary, which he hath sanctified for ever: serve the Lord the God of your fathers, and the wrath of his indignation shall be turned away from you. *2 Paralip. xxx.*

12 But my people heard not my voice: and Israel hearkened not to me. *Ps. lxxx.*

13 So I let them go according to the desires of their heart: they shall walk in their own inventions.

33 And they have turned their backs to me, and not their faces: when I taught them early in the morning, and instructed them, and they would not hearken to receive instruction. *Jer. xxxii.*

3 O Lord, thy eyes are upon truth: thou hast struck them, and they have not grieved: thou hast bruised them, and they have refused to receive correction: they have made their faces harder than the rock, and they have refused to return. *Jer. v.*

24 They hearkened not, nor inclined their ear: but walked in their own will, and in the perversity of their wicked heart: and went backward and not forward. *Jer. vii.*

28 .:. This is a nation which hath not hearkened to the voice of the Lord their God, nor received instruction: faith is lost, and is taken away out of their mouth.

5 Why then is this people in Jerusalem turned away with a stubborn revolting? they have laid hold on lying, and have refused to return. Jer. viii.

21 I spoke to thee in thy prosperity: and thou saidst: I will not hear: this hath been thy way from thy youth, because thou hast not heard my voice. Jer. xxii.

24 Because I called, and you refused: I stretched out my hand, and there was none that regarded. Prov. i.

1 The man that with a stiff neck despiseth him that reproveth him, shall suddenly be destroyed: and health shall not follow him. Prov. xxix.

4 Be not as your fathers, to whom the former prophets have cried, saying: Thus saith the Lord of hosts: Turn ye from your your evil ways, and from your wicked thoughts: but they did not give ear, neither did they hearken to me, saith the Lord. Zach. i.

11 They would not hearken, and they turned away the shoulder to depart: and they stopped their ears, not to hear. Zach. vii.

10 They kept not the covenant of God: and in his law they would not walk. Ps. lxxvii.

10 And especially them who walk after 2 S. Peter ii.

the flesh in the lust of uncleanness, and despise government, audacious, self-willed, they fear not to bring in sects, blaspheming.

SERVANTS.

15 ... THE wise servant shall prosper in his dealings, and his way shall be made straight. — Prov. xiv.

5 Servants, be obedient to them that are your lords according to the flesh, with fear and trembling, in the simplicity of your heart, as to Christ. — Ephes. vi.

6 Not serving to the eye, as it were pleasing men, but as the servants of Christ, doing the will of God from the heart,

7 With a good will serving, as to the Lord, and not to men:

8 Knowing that whatsoever good thing any man shall do, the same shall he receive from the Lord, whether he be bond or free.

22 Servants, obey in all things your masters according to the flesh, not serving to the eye, as pleasing men, but in simplicity of heart, fearing God. — Coloss. iii.

23 Whatsoever you do, do it from the heart, as to the Lord, and not to men:

24 Knowing that you shall receive of the Lord the reward of inheritance. Serve ye the Lord Christ.

25 For he that doeth an injury shall receive for that which he hath done unjustly; and there is no respect of persons with God.

1 Whosoever are servants under the yoke, let them count their masters worthy of all honour, lest the name and doctrine of the Lord be blasphemed. 1 Tim. vi.

2 But they who have believing masters, let them not despise them, because they are brethren; but serve them the rather, because they are faithful and beloved, who are partakers of the benefit.

9 Exhort servants to be obedient to their masters, in all things pleasing, not contradicting, Titus ii.

10 Not defrauding, but in all things showing good fidelity, that they may adorn the doctrine of God our Saviour in all things.

18 Servants, be subject to your masters with all fear, not only to the good and gentle, but also to the froward. 1 S. Peter ii.

19 For this is thanks-worthy, if for conscience towards God, a man endure sorrows, suffering wrongfully.

20 For what glory is it, if, sinning and being buffeted for it, you endure? But if, doing well, you suffer patiently; this is thanks-worthy before God.*

* See 21st verse in Patient Endurance.

SICKNESS.

25 You shall serve the Lord your God, that I may bless your bread and your waters, and may take away sickness from the midst of thee.   Exod. xxiii.

39 See ye that I alone am, and there is no other God besides me: I will kill and I will make to live: I will strike, and I will heal, and there is none that can deliver out of my hand.   Deut. xxxii.

12 Asa fell sick in the nine and thirtieth year of his reign, of a most violent pain in his feet, and yet in his illness he did not seek the Lord, but rather trusted in the skill of the physicians.   2 Paralip. xvi.

13 And he slept with his fathers : and he died.

14 God speaketh once, and repeateth not the self same thing the second time.   Job xxxiii.

17 That he may withdraw a man from the things he is doing, and may deliver him from pride,

18 Rescuing his soul from corruption : and his life from passing to the sword.

19 He rebuketh also by sorrow in the bed, and he maketh all his bones to wither.

20 Bread becometh abominable to him in his life, and to his soul the meat which before he desired.

18 Their soul abhorred all manner of meat: and they drew nigh even to the gates of death.   Ps. cvi.

19 And they cried to the Lord in their affliction: and he delivered them out of their distresses.

20 He sent his word, and healed them...

3 O Lord my God, I have cried to thee, and thou hast healed me.   Ps. xxix.

2 ... A grievous sickness maketh the soul sober.   Ecclus. xxxi.

15 He that sinneth in the sight of his Maker, shall fall into the hands of the physician.   Ecclus. xxxviii.

11 His bones shall be filled with the vices of his youth, and they shall sleep with him in the dust.   Job xx.

1 ... Take order with thy house, for thou shalt die, and not live.   Isaias xxxviii.

12 My generation is at an end, and it is rolled away from me, as a shepherd's tent. My life is cut off, as by a weaver: whilst I was yet but beginning, he cut me off: from morning even to night thou wilt make an end of me.

14 I will cry like a young swallow, I will meditate like a dove: My eyes are weakened looking upward: Lord, I suffer violence, answer thou for me.

15 What shall I say, or what shall he

answer for me, whereas he himself hath done it? I will recount to thee all my years in the bitterness of my soul.

5 ... I have heard thy prayer, I have seen thy tears: and behold I have healed thee ... — 4 Kings xx.

13 ... The Lord also hath taken away thy sin; thou shalt not die. — 2 Kings xii.

1 Honour the physician for the need thou hast of him: for the most High hath created him. — Ecclus. xxxviii.

2 For all healing is from God ...

3 The skill of the physician shall lift up his head, and in the sight of great men he shall be praised.

4 The most High hath created medicines out of the earth, and a wise man will not abhor them.

6 The virtue of these things is come to the knowledge of men, and the most High hath given knowledge to men, that he may be honoured in his wonders.

7 By these he shall cure and shall allay their pains ...

9 My son, in thy sickness neglect not thyself, but pray to the Lord, and he shall heal thee.

10 Turn away from sin, and order thy hands aright, and cleanse thy heart from all offence.

11 Give a sweet savour, and a memorial of fine flour, and make a fat offering, and then give place to the physician.

12 For the Lord created him: and let him not depart from thee, for his works are necessary.

13 For there is a time when thou must fall into their hands.

35 And Jesus went about all the cities, and towns, ... healing every disease, and every infirmity.   S. Matt. ix.

14 Behold thou art made whole; sin no more, lest some worse thing happen to thee.   S. John v.

3 ... Lord, behold, he whom thou lovest is sick.   S. John xi.

8 ... Only say the word, and my servant shall be healed.   S. Matt. viii.

16 ... All that were sick he healed.

38 ... Who went about doing good, and healing all that were oppressed by the devil, for God was with him.   Acts x.

14 Is any man sick among you? Let him bring in the priests of the church, and let them pray over him, anointing him with oil in the name of the Lord.   S. James v.

15 And the prayer of faith shall save the sick man: and the Lord shall raise him up: and if he be in sins, they shall be forgiven him.

SILENCE.

14 THE Lord will fight for you, and you shall hold your peace. — Exod. xiv.

15 ... In silence and in hope shall your strength be. — Isaias xxx.

19 In the multitude of words there shall not want sin: but he that refraineth his lips is most wise. — Prov. x.

27 He that setteth bounds to his words, is knowing and wise... — Prov. xvii.

28 Even a fool, if he will hold his peace, shall be counted wise: and if he close his lips, a man of understanding.

14 If thou have understanding, answer thy neighbour: but if not, let thy hand be upon thy mouth, lest thou be surprised in an unskilful word, and be confounded. — Ecclus. v.

15 Be not full of words in a multitude of ancients... — Ecclus. vii.

5 ... He that hateth babbling extinguisheth evil. — Ecclus. xix.

7 Rehearse not again a wicked and harsh word, and thou shalt not fare the worse.

28 ... There is one that holdeth his peace, he is wise.

8 He that useth many words shall hurt his own soul... — Ecclus. xx.

31 ... The silent and wise man shall be Ecclus.
honoured. xxi.

9 Hear in silence, and for thy reverence Ecclus.
good grace shall come to thee. xxxii.

10 Young man, scarcely speak in thy own
cause.

11 If thou be asked twice, let thy answer
be short.

12 In many things be as if thou wert ignorant, and hear in silence andwithal seeking.

26 It is good to wait with silence for the Lament.
salvation of God. iii.

20 The Lord is in his holy temple: let all Habac.
the earth keep silence before him. ii.

32 And they bring to him one deaf and S. Mark
dumb: and they besought him that he would vii.
lay his hand upon him.

34 And looking up to heaven, he groaned,
and said to him: Ephepheta, which is, Be
thou opened.

19 ... Let every man be swift to hear, S. James
but slow to speak ... i.

SIMPLICITY.

20 God will not cast away the simple, nor Job viii.
reach out his hand to the evil doer.

7 He will protect them that walk in sim- Prov. ii.
plicity.

32 ... And his communication is with Prov. iii.
the simple.

Simplicity.

3 The simplicity of the just shall guide them...   Prov. xi.

1 Better is the poor man, that walketh in his simplicity, than a rich man that is perverse in his lips and unwise.   Prov. xix.

7 The just that walketh in his simplicity, shall leave behind him blessed children.   Prov. xx.

19 ... I would have you to be wise in good, and simple in evil.   Rom. xvi.

2 ... Not walking in craftiness ...   2 Cor. iv.

7 If we walk in the light, as he also is in the light: we have fellowship one with another, and the blood of Jesus Christ his Son cleanseth us from all sin.   1 S. John i.

9 For the fruit of the light is in all goodness, and justice, and truth.   Ephes. v.

1 Wherefore, laying aside all malice, and all guile, and dissimulations, and envies, and all detractions.   1 S. Peter ii.

2 As new-born infants, desire the rational milk without guile; that thereby you may grow unto salvation.

SIN.

6 ... Why art thou angry? and why is thy countenance fallen?   Gen. iv.

7 If thou do well, shalt thou not receive? but if ill, shall not sin forthwith be present at the door? but the lust thereof shall be

under thee, and thou shalt have dominion over it.

46 ... There is no man who sinneth not ...   3 Kings viii.

6 ... He that loveth iniquity hateth his own soul.   Ps. x.

23 ... Know ye that your sin shall overtake you ...   Numbers xxxii.

6 All the days of thy life have God in thy mind: and take heed thou never consent to sin, nor transgress the commandments of the Lord our God.   Tobias iv.

13 Who can understand sins? from my secret ones, cleanse me, O Lord. | Ps. xviii.

14 And from those of others spare thy servant ...

14 Blessed is the man that is always fearful: but he that is hardened in mind, shall fall into evil.   Prov. xxviii.

1 ... He that contemneth small things, shall fall by little and little.   Ecclus. xix.

1 Behold the hand of the Lord is not shortened that it cannot save, neither is his ear heavy that it cannot hear.   Isaias lix.

2 But your iniquities have divided between you and your God, and your sins have hid his face from you that he should not hear.

3 For your hands are defiled with blood, and your fingers with iniquity: your lips

have spoken lies, and your tongue uttereth iniquity.

15 And truth hath been forgotten: and he that departed from evil, lay open to be a prey; and the Lord saw, and it appeared evil in his eyes, because there is no judgment.

25 ... Your sins have withholden good things from you. Jer. v.

4 Behold all souls are mine: as the soul of the father, so also the soul of the son is mine: the soul that sinneth, the same shall die. Ezech. xviii.

29 If thy right eye scandalize* thee, pluck it out and cast it from thee. For it is expedient for thee that one of thy members should perish, rather than thy whole body be cast into hell. S. Matt. v.

30 And if thy right hand scandalize thee, cut it off, and cast it from thee: for it is expedient for thee that one of thy members should perish, rather than thy whole body go into hell.

34 Amen, amen, I say unto you: That whosoever committeth sin, is the servant of sin. S. John viii.

35 Now the servant abideth not in the house for ever: but the son abideth for ever.

* That is, if it be a stumbling-block, or occasion of sin to thee. By which we are taught to fly the immediate occasions of sin, though they be as dear to us, or as necessary, as a hand or an eye.

36 If therefore, the son shall make you free, you shall be free indeed.

2 For we that are dead to sin, how shall we live any longer therein. Rom. vi.

12 Let not sin therefore reign in your mortal body, so as to obey the lusts thereof.

13 Neither yield ye your members as instruments of iniquity unto sin . . .

14 For sin shall not have dominion over you . . .

21 What fruit therefore had you then in those things, of which you are now ashamed? For the end of them is death.

23 The wages of sin, is death . . .

24 Unhappy man that I am, who shall deliver me from the body of this death? Rom. vii.

25 The grace of God by Jesus Christ our Lord . . .

24 Who his own self bore our sins in his body upon the tree; that we, being dead to sins, should live to justice; by whose stripes you were healed. 1 S. Peter ii.

5 And you know that he appeared to take away our sins: and in him there is no sin. 1 S. John iii.

6 Whosoever abideth in him, sinneth not:* and whosoever sinneth hath not seen him, nor known him.

* Viz., mortally.

8 He that committeth sin, is of the devil: for the devil sinneth from the beginning. For this purpose the Son of God appeared, that he might destroy the works of the devil.

17 All iniquity is sin: and there is a sin unto death.   1 S. John v.

4 You have not yet resisted unto blood, striving against sin.   Heb. xii.

SINCERITY OF HEART.

14 Now therefore fear the Lord, and serve him with a perfect and most sincere heart...   Josue xxiv.

2 ... Blessed is the man in whose spirit there is no guile.   Ps. xxxi.

9 He that walketh sincerely, walketh confidentially...   Prov. x.

20 A perverse heart is abominable to the Lord: and his will is in them that walk sincerely.   Prov. xi.

8 Therefore let us feast, not with the old leaven, nor with the leaven of malice and wickedness, but with the unleavened bread of sincerity and truth.   1 Cor. v.

12 For our glory is this, the testimony of our conscience, that in simplicity of heart and sincerity of God, and not in carnal wisdom, but in the grace of God, we have conversed in this world...   2 Cor. i.

22 ... From a sincere heart love one another earnestly. — 1 S. Peter i.

15 That you may be blameless, and sincere children of God, without reproof, in the midst of a crooked and perverse generation: among whom you shine as lights in the world. — Philip. ii.

SINGLENESS OF INTENTION.

1 TAKE heed, that you do not your justice before men, that you may be seen by them: otherwise you shall not have a reward from your Father who is in heaven. — S. Matt. vi.

3 But when thou doest alms, let not thy left hand know what thy right hand doeth.

6 But thou, when thou shalt pray, enter into thy chamber, and having shut the door, pray to thy Father in secret; and thy Father, who seeth in secret, will reward thee.

34 The light of thy body, is thy eye. If thy eye be single, thy whole body will be lightsome; but if it be evil, thy body also will be darksome. — S. Luke xi.

21 He that doeth truth, cometh to the light, that his works may be made manifest, because they are done in God. — S. John iii.

SLOTH.

24 THE hand of the valiant shall bear rule: but that which is slothful, shall be under tribute. — Prov. xii.

16 ... He that neglecteth his own way, shall die. — Prov. xix.

13 Love not sleep, lest poverty oppress thee: open thy eyes, and be filled with bread. — Prov. xx.

19 ... He that followeth idleness, shall be filled with poverty. — Prov. xxviii.

4 The slothful hand hath wrought poverty: but the hand of the industrious getteth riches. — Prov. x.

11 He that tilleth his land shall be satisfied with bread: but he that pursueth idleness is very foolish. — Prov. xii.

19 The way of the slothful is as a hedge of thorns ... — Prov. xv.

15 Slothfulness casteth into a deep sleep, and an idle soul shall suffer hunger. — Prov. xix.

24 The slothful hideth his hand under his arm-pit, and will not so much as bring it to his mouth.

33 Thou wilt sleep a little, thou wilt slumber a little, thou wilt fold thy hands a little to rest: — Prov. xxiv.

34 And poverty shall come to thee as a runner, and beggary as an armed man.

29 ... Linger not in the time of distress. — Ecclus. x.

29 Idleness hath taught much evil.   Ecclus. xxxiii.

26 ... Thou wicked and slothful servant ...   S. Matt. xxv.

28 Take ye away, therefore, the talent from him, and give to him that hath ten talents.

30 And the unprofitable servant cast ye into the exterior darkness. There shall be weeping and gnashing of teeth.

12 ... Become not slothful, but followers of them, who through faith and patience shall inherit the promises.   Heb. vi.

10 ... If any man will not work, neither let him eat.   2 Thess. iii.

11 For we have heard, there are some among you who walk disorderly, working not at all, but curiously meddling.

13 And withal, being idle, they learn to go about from house to house: and are not only idle, but tatlers also, and busy-bodies, speaking things which they ought not.   1 Tim. v.

SPIRITUAL LIFE.*

3 INCLINE your ear, and come to me: hear and your soul shall live.   Isaias lv.

13 ... And you shall know that I am the Lord, when I shall have opened your sepul-   Ezech. xxxvii.

* See Christ our Life, and Union with God.

Spiritual Life.

chres, and shall have brought you out of your graves, O my people.

14 And shall have put my Spirit in you, and you shall live...

175 My soul shall live, and shall praise thee...   Ps. cxviii.

21 As the Father raiseth up the dead, and giveth life; so the Son also giveth life to whom he will.   S. John v.

25 Amen, amen I say unto you, that the hour cometh, and now is, when the dead shall hear the voice of the Son of God; and they that hear shall live.

11 So do you also reckon that you are dead to sin, but alive unto God in Christ Jesus our Lord.   Rom. vi.

13 ... Present yourselves to God as those that are alive from the dead: and your members as instruments of justice to God.

5 ... They that are according to the spirit, mind the things that are of the spirit.   Rom. viii.

45 The first man Adam was made into a living soul: the last Adam into a quickening spirit.   1 Cor. xv.

46 Yet that was not first which is spiritual, but that which is natural: afterwards that which is spiritual.

48 Such as is the earthly, such also are the earthly: and such as is the heavenly, such also are they that are heavenly.

14 ... Rise thou that sleepest, and arise Ephes.
from the dead: and Christ shall enlighten   v.
thee.

25 If we live in the Spirit, let us also walk Gal. v.
in the Spirit.

9 ... God hath sent his only begotten 1 S. John
Son into the world, that we may live by him. iv.

3 For we are the circumcision, who serve Philip.
God in spirit, and glory in Christ Jesus, not iii.
having confidence in the flesh.

13 You, when you were dead in your Coloss.
sins, and the uncircumcision of your flesh: ii.
he hath quickened together with him; forgiving you all offences.

STRANGERS.

3 ... AFFLICT not the stranger ...   Jer. xxii.

21 Thou shalt not molest a stranger nor Ex. xxii.
afflict him, for you know the hearts of strangers: for you also were strangers in the land
of Egypt.

33 If a stranger dwell in your land, and Lev.
abide among you, do not upbraid him.   xix.

34 But let him be among you as one of
the same country: and you shall love him as
yourselves ... I am the Lord your God.

18 (God) ... Loveth the stranger, and Deut.
giveth him food and raiment.   x.

19 And do you therefore love strangers ...

SUPERSTITION.

26 ... You shall not divine nor observe dreams. Lev. xix.

2 ... Be not afraid of the signs of heaven, which the heathens fear. Jer. x.

10 Neither let there be found among you any one ... that consulteth soothsayers, or observeth dreams and omens, neither let there be any wizard. Deut. xviii.

11 Nor charmer, nor any one that consulteth pythonic spirits, or fortune-tellers, or that seeketh the truth from the dead.

12 For the Lord abhorreth all these things ...

21 And turn not aside after vain things, which shall never profit you nor deliver you, because they are vain. 1 Kings xii.

19 And when they shall say to you: Seek of pythons, and of diviners, who mutter in their enchantments: should not the people seek of their God, for the living of the dead? Isaias viii.

2 The man that giveth heed to lying visions, is like to him that catcheth at a shadow, and followeth after the wind. Ecclus. xxxiv.

3 The vision of dreams is the resemblance of one thing to another: as when a man's likeness is before the face of a man.

4 ... What truth can come from that which is false?

5 Deceitful divinations and lying omens, and the dreams of evil doers, are vanity.

6 ... Except it be a vision sent forth from the most High, set not thy heart upon them.

7 For dreams have deceived many, and they have failed that put their trust in them.

11 And you, that have forsaken the Lord, that have forgotten my holy mount, that set a table for fortune, and offer libations upon it.   Isaias lxv.

12 I will number you in the sword, and you shall all fall by slaughter: because I called, and you did not answer: I spoke, and you did not hear: and you did evil in my eyes, and you have chosen the things that displease me.

22 ... Ye men of Athens, I perceive that in all things you are too superstitious.   Acts xvii.

SWEARING.

7 THOU shalt not take the name of the Lord thy God in vain: for the Lord will not hold him guiltless that shall take the name of the Lord his God in vain.   Exod. xx.

15 ... The man that curseth his God, shall bear his sin.   Lev. xxiv.

12 Thou shalt not swear falsely by my name, nor profane the name of thy God. I am the Lord. — Lev. xix.

30 While the ungodly curseth the devil, he curseth his own soul. — Ecclus. xxi.

9 Let not thy mouth be accustomed to swearing: for in it there are many falls. — Ecclus. xxiii.

10 And let not the naming of God be usual in thy mouth, and meddle not with the names of saints, for thou shalt not escape free from them.

11 ... So every one that sweareth, and nameth, shall not be wholly pure from sin.

12 A man that sweareth much, shall be filled with iniquity, and a scourge shall not depart from his house.

13 And if he make it void, his sin shall be upon him: and if he dissemble it, he offendeth double.

14 And if he swear in vain, he shall not be justified: for his house shall be filled with his punishment.

20 The man that is accustomed to opprobrious words, will never be corrected all the days of his life.

15 The speech that sweareth much shall make the hair of the head stand upright: and its irreverence shall make one stop his ears. — Ecclus. xxvii.

33 You have heard that it was said to them of old: Thou shalt not forswear thyself: but shall perform thy oaths to the Lord. — S. Matt. v.

34 But I say to you, not to swear at all, neither by heaven, for it is the throne of God:

35 Nor by the earth, for it is his footstool: nor by Jerusalem, for it is the city of the great king:

36 Neither shalt thou swear by thy head, because thou canst not make one hair white or black.

37 But let your speech be yea, yea: no, no: for whatsoever is more than these, cometh from evil.

20 Whosoever, therefore, sweareth by the altar, sweareth by it, and by all things that are upon it: — S. Matt. xxiii.

21 And whosoever shall swear by the temple, sweareth by it, and by him that dwelleth in it.

22 And he that sweareth by heaven, sweareth by the throne of God, and by him that sitteth thereon.

TALE BEARER.

22 The words of a tale bearer are as it were simple, but they reach to the innermost parts of the belly. — Prov. xxvi.

1 Repeat not the word which thou hast heard, and disclose not the thing that is secret. — Ecclus. xlii.

31 The tale bearer shall defile his own soul, and shall be hated by all: and he that shall abide with him shall be hateful. — Ecclus. xxi.

TEMPERANCE.

13 Let us walk honestly as in the day: not in rioting and drunkenness. — Rom. xiii.

18 Be not drunk with wine, wherein is luxury; but be ye filled with the Holy Spirit. — Ephes. v.

17 The kingdom of God is not meat and drink; but justice and peace, and joy in the Holy Ghost. — Rom. xiv.

31 Therefore, whether you eat or drink, or whatsoever else you do; do all to the glory of God. — 1 Cor. x.

5 For all you are the children of light, and children of the day: we are not of the night, nor of darkness. — 1 Thess. v.

6 Therefore let us not sleep, as others do: but let us watch, and be sober.

7 For they that sleep, sleep in the night; and they that are drunk, are drunk in the night.

8 Let us, who are of the day, be sober, having on the breastplate of faith and charity, and for a helmet, the hope of salvation.

2 That the aged men be sober. — Titus ii.

6 Young men in like manner exhort that they be sober.

5 And you, giving all diligence, join with your faith, virtue; and with virtue, knowledge; — 2 S. Peter i.

6 And with knowledge, abstinence; and with abstinence, patience; and with patience, piety.

TEMPT NOT GOD.

16 Thou shalt not tempt the Lord thy God. — Deut. vi.

2 For he is found by them that tempt him not: and he showeth himself to them that have faith in him. — Wisd. i.

9 Neither let us tempt Christ; as some of them tempted, and perished by serpents. — 1 Cor. x.

18 ... Why do you tempt me, ye hypocrites? — S. Matt. xxii.

TEMPTATION.

29 ... O my God, enlighten my darkness. — Ps. xvii.

30 For by thee I shall be delivered from temptation ...

29 An unjust man allureth his friend: and leadeth him into a way that is not good. Prov. xvi.

27 ... He that loveth danger shall perish in it. Ecclus. iii.

11 Say not: It is through God, that (wisdom) is not with me: for do not thou the things that he hateth. Ecclus. xv.

12 Say not: He hath caused me to err: for He hath no need of wicked men.

21 He hath commanded no man to do wickedly, and he hath given no man license to sin.

1 No evils shall happen to him that feareth the Lord, but in temptation God will keep him, and deliver him from evils. Ecclus. xxxiii.

46 And he said to them: Why sleep you? Arise, pray, lest you enter into temptation. S. Luke xxii.

41 Watch ye, and pray that ye enter not into temptation. The spirit indeed is willing, but the flesh weak. S. Matt. xxvi.

13 Let no temptation take hold on you, but such as is human:* and God is faithful, who will not suffer you to be tempted above that which you are able; but will make also with temptation issue, that you may be able to bear it. 1 Cor. x.

9 They who would become rich, fall into temptation, and into the snare of the devil, 1 Tim. vi.

* Such as is incident to man.

and into many unprofitable and hurtful desires, which drown men in destruction and perdition.

9 The Lord knoweth how to deliver the godly out of temptation ...   2 S. Peter ii.

9 ... My grace is sufficient for thee: for power* is made perfect in infirmity.   2 Cor. xii.

15 We have not a high priest, who cannot have compassion on our infirmities; but one tempted in all things like as we are, yet without sin.   Heb. iv.

18 For in that, wherein he himself hath suffered and been tempted, he is able to succour those also who are tempted.   Heb. ii.

12 Blessed is the man that endureth temptation: for when he hath been proved, he shall receive the crown of life, which God hath promised to them that love him.   S. James i.

13 Let no man, when he is tempted, say that he is tempted of God: for God is not a tempter of evils: and he tempteth no man.

14 But every man is tempted, being drawn away by his own concupiscence, and allured.

15 Then when concupiscence hath conceived, it bringeth forth sin: but sin, when it is completed, begetteth death.

* See note in God our Strength.

THANKSGIVING.

1 I WILL give thanks to thee, O Lord, for thou wast angry with me: thy wrath is turned away, and thou hast comforted me. — Isaias xii.

8 O bless our God, ye Gentiles: and make the voice of his praise to be heard.
9 Who hath set my soul to live. — Ps. lxv.

6 Let the people, O God, confess to thee: let all the people give praise to thee: 7 the earth hath yielded her fruit. — Ps. lxvi.

13 Now therefore, our God, we give thanks to thee, and we praise thy glorious name. — 1 Paralip. xxix.

2 Let us come before his presence with thanksgiving. — Ps. xciv.

2 Bless the Lord, O my soul, and never forget all he hath done for thee.
3 Who forgiveth all thy iniquities; who healeth all thy diseases.
4 Who redeemeth thy life from destruction: who crowneth thee with mercy and compassion. — Ps. cii.

7 I will bless the Lord, who hath given me understanding. — Ps. xv.

4 Thy mercy is better than life: thee my lips shall praise. — Ps. lxii.

18 I will give thanks to thee in a great church... — Ps. xxxiv.

27 Give thanks whilst thou art living, — Ecclus. xvii.

whilst thou art alive and in health thou shalt give thanks, and shalt praise God, and shalt glory in his mercies.

10 Daniel ... knelt down three times a day, and adored, and gave thanks before his God. Dan. vi.

41 ... And Jesus lifting up his eyes said: Father, I give thee thanks that thou hast heard me. S. John xi.

4 I give thanks to my God always for you, for the grace of God that is given you in Christ Jesus. 1 Cor. i.

15 That the grace abounding through many may abound in thanksgiving to the glory of God. 2 Cor. iv.

15 Thanks be to God for his unspeakable gift. 2 Cor. ix.

57 Thanks be to God who hath given us the victory through our Lord Jesus Christ. 1 Cor. xv.

14 ... Who always maketh us to triumph in Christ Jesus ... 2 Cor. ii.

3 I give thanks to my God, in every remembrance of you. Philip. i.

16 (I) Cease not to give thanks for you, making commemoration of you in my prayers. Ephes. i.

20 Giving thanks always for all things, in the name of our Lord Jesus Christ, to God and the Father. Ephes. v.

6 Be not solicitous about any thing: but in every thing by prayer and supplication with Philip. iv.

thanksgiving let your petitions be made known to God.

17 All whatsoever you do in word or in work, do all in the name of the Lord Jesus Christ, giving thanks to God and the Father by him. — Coloss. iii.

7 ... Abounding in him in thanksgiving. — Coloss. ii.

2 Be instant in prayer; watching in it with thanksgiving. — Coloss. iv.

2 ... We give thanks to God always for you all: making a remembrance of you in our prayers without ceasing. — 1 Thess. i.

18 In all things give thanks: for this is the will of God in Christ Jesus concerning you all. — 1 Thess. v.

3 ... We give thanks to God, and the Father of our Lord Jesus Christ, praying always for you. — Coloss. i.

4 Hearing your faith in Christ Jesus, and the love which you have towards all the saints,

5 For the hope that is laid up for you in heaven: which you have heard in the word of the truth of the gospel.

3 We are bound to give thanks always to God for you, brethren, as it is fitting, because your faith groweth exceedingly; and the charity of every one of you towards each other aboundeth. — 2 Thess. i.

12 I give him thanks, who hath strength- — 1 Tim. i.

ened me, even to Christ Jesus our Lord, for that he hath counted me faithful, putting me in the ministry.

9 For what thanks can we return to God for you, in all the joy wherewith we rejoice for you before our God? 1 Thess. iii.

17 We give thee thanks, O Lord God Almighty, who art, and who wast, and who art to come: because thou hast taken to thee thy great power, and thou hast reigned. Apoc. xi.

THEFT.

15 THOU shalt not steal. Exod. xx.

14 Thou shalt not take nor remove thy neighbour's landmark... Deut. xix.

13 Thou shalt not have divers weights in thy bag, a greater and a less. Deut. xxv.

14 Neither shall there be in thy house a greater bushel and a less.

15 Thou shalt have a just and a true weight, and thy bushel shall be equal and true: that thou mayest live a long time upon the land which the Lord thy God shall give thee.

16 For the Lord thy God abhorreth him that doth these things, and he hateth all injustice.

21 ... It is not lawful for us either to Tobias ii.

eat or to touch any thing that cometh by theft.

1 A deceitful balance is an abomination before the Lord: and a just weight is his will.   Prov. xi.

10 Diverse weights and diverse measures, both are abominable before God.   Prov. xx.

7 The robberies of the wicked shall be their downfall, because they would not do judgment.   Prov. xxi.

24 He that stealeth any thing from his father, or from his mother, and saith, This is no sin, is the partner of a murderer.   Prov. xxviii.

24 He that is partaker with a thief, hateth his own soul: he heareth one putting him to his oath, and discovereth not.   Prov. xxix.

10 Be not anxious for goods unjustly gotten: for they shall not profit thee in the day of calamity and revenge.   Ecclus. v.

17 For confusion and repentance is upon a thief...

11 As the partridge hath hatched eggs which she did not lay: so is he that hath gathered riches, and not by right: in the midst of his days he shall leave them, and in his latter end he shall be a fool.   Jer. xvii.

10 You shall have just balances, and a just ephi, and a just bate.   Ezech. xlv.

9 The voice of the Lord crieth to the city...   Mich. vi.

10 As yet there is a fire in the house of

the wicked, the treasures of iniquity, and a scant measure full of wrath . . .

11 Shall I justify wicked balances, and the deceitful weights of the bag?

12 By which her rich men were filled with iniquity, and the inhabitants thereof have spoken lies, and their tongue was deceitful in their mouth.

13 And I therefore began to strike thee with desolation for thy sins.

6 . . . Wo to him that heapeth together that which is not his own? how long also doth he load himself with thick clay?   Habac. ii.

18 . . . Thou shalt not steal . . .   S. Matt. xix.

19 . . . Do not steal . . . do no fraud . . .   S. Mark x.

10 . . . He that is unjust in that which is little, is unjust also in that which is greater.   S. Luke xvi.

12 If you have not been faithful in that which is another's; who will give you that which is your own?

5 Why was not this ointment sold for three hundred pence, and given to the poor?   S. John xii.

6 Now he said this, not because he cared for the poor; but because he was a thief, and having the purse, carried the things that were put therein.

9 . . . Thou shalt not steal . . .   Rom. xiii.

8 But you do wrong and defraud: and that to your brethren.   1 Cor. vi.

9 Know you not that the unjust shall not possess the kingdom of God?

10 ... Nor thieves, nor covetous, nor drunkards, nor railers, nor extortioners shall possess the kingdom of God.

28 He that stole, let him now steal no more: but rather let him labour, working with his hands that which is good, that he may have to give to him who is in need. — Ephes. iv.

25 For he that doeth an injury shall receive for that which he hath done unjustly ... — Coloss. iii.

6 And that no man over-reach, nor circumvent his brother in business: because the Lord is the avenger of all these things, as we have told you before, and have testified. — 1 Thess. iv.

8 He therefore that despiseth these things, despiseth not man, but God.

TIME.

15 We are sojourners before thee, and strangers, as were all our fathers. Our days upon earth are as a shadow, and there is no stay. — 1 Paralip. xxix.

8 The number of the days of men at the most are a hundred years: as a drop of water of the sea are they esteemed: and as a pebble of the sand, so are a few years compared to eternity. — Ecclus. xviii.

5 In the morning I will stand before Ps. v.
thee...

27 Well doth he rise early who seeketh Prov. xi.
good things...

35 And rising very early, going out (Jesus) S. Mark i.
went into a desert place: and there he prayed.

38 And all the people came early in the S. Luke
morning to him in the temple to hear him. xxi.

2 And early in the morning he came again S. John
into the temple, and all the people came to viii.
him, and sitting down he taught them.

4 I must work the works of him that sent S. John
me, whilst it is day: the night cometh when ix.
no man can work.

4 ... I have finished the work which S. John
thou gavest me to do. xvii.

2 ... Behold; now is the acceptable 2 Cor.
time: behold now is the day of salvation. vi.

11 ... It is now the hour for us to rise Rom.
from sleep. For now our salvation is nearer xiii.
than when we believed.

12 The night is past, and the day is at
hand. Let us therefore cast off the works
of darkness, and put on the armour of
light.

10 Therefore, whilst we have time, let us Gal. vi.
do good to all men, but especially to those
who are of the household of faith.

5 Walk with wisdom towards them that Coloss.
are without, redeeming the time. iv.

16 ... Redeeming the time, because the Ephes. v.
days are evil.

TONGUE.

13 Who is the man that desireth life: Ps. xxxiii.
who loveth to see good days?

14 Keep thy tongue from evil, and thy
lips from speaking guile.

3 Do not multiply to speak lofty things, 1 Kings
boasting: let old matters depart from your   ii.
mouth ...

2 I said: I will take heed to my ways: Ps.
that I sin not with my tongue. I have set a xxxviii.
guard to my mouth, when the sinner stood
against me.

3 I was dumb, and was humbled, and
kept silence from good things ...

2 O Lord, deliver my soul from wicked Ps. cxix.
lips, and a deceitful tongue.

12 A man full of tongue shall not be   Ps.
established in the earth ...   cxxxix.

3 Set a watch, O Lord, before my mouth: Ps. cxl.
and a door round about my lips.

6 ... Iniquity covereth the mouth of the Prov. x.
wicked.

31 The mouth of the just shall bring forth
wisdom: the tongue of the perverse shall
perish.

13 For the sins of the lips ruin draweth Prov. xii.
nigh to the evil man ...

14 By the fruit of his own mouth shall a man be filled with good things . . .

19 . . . He that is a hasty witness, frameth a lying tongue.

3 He that keepeth his mouth, keepeth his soul: but he that hath no guard on his speech shall meet with evils.   Prov. xiii.

4 A peaceable tongue is a tree of life: but that which is immoderate, shall crush the spirit.   Prov. xv.

1 It is the part of man to prepare the soul: and of the Lord to govern the tongue.   Prov. xvi.

21 . . . He that is sweet in words shall attain to greater things.

23 The heart of the wise shall instruct his mouth: and shall add grace to his lips.

24 Well ordered words are as a honeycomb: sweet to the soul, and health to the bones.

21 Death and life are in the power of the tongue: they that love it, shall eat the fruits thereof.   Prov. xviii.

23 He that keepeth his mouth and his tongue, keepeth his soul from distress.   Prov. xxi.

28 As a city that lieth open and is not compassed with walls, so is a man that cannot restrain his own spirit in speaking.   Prov. xxv.

7 The spirit of the Lord hath filled the whole world: and that, which containeth all things, hath knowledge of the voice.   Wisd. i.

8 Therefore he that speaketh unjust things cannot be hid, neither shall the chastising judgment pass him by.

9 For inquisition shall be made into the thoughts of the ungodly: and the hearing of his words shall come to God, to the chastising of his iniquities.

37 ... Let not thy lips be a stumbling-block to thee. — Ecclus. i.

38 Watch over them, lest thou fall, and bring dishonour upon thy soul.

34 Be not hasty in thy tongue: and slack and remiss in thy works. — Ecclus. iv.

23 Let the thought of God be in thy mind, and all thy discourse on the commandments of the Highest. — Ecclus. ix.

1 Blessed is the man that hath not slipt by a word out of his mouth, and is not pricked with the remorse of sin. — Ecclus. xiv.

33 Who will set a guard before my mouth, and a sure seal upon my lips, that I fall not by them, and that my tongue destroy me not? — Ecclus. xxii.

7 Hear, O ye children, the discipline of the mouth: and he that will keep it shall not perish by his lips, nor be brought to fall into most wicked works. — Ecclus. xxiii.

16 The tongue of a third person hath disquieted many, and scattered them from nation to nation. — Ecclus. xxviii.

17 It hath destroyed the strong cities of the rich, and hath overthrown the houses of great men.

18 It hath cut in pieces the forces of people, and undone strong nations.

19 The tongue of a third person hath cast out valiant women, and deprived them of their labours.

20 He that hearkeneth to it, shall never have rest, neither shall he have a friend in whom he may repose.

21 The stroke of a whip maketh a blue mark: but the stroke of the tongue will break the bones.

22 Many have fallen by the edge of the sword, but not so many as have perished by their own tongue.

23 Blessed is he that is defended from a wicked tongue, that hath not passed into the wrath thereof, and that hath not drawn the yoke thereof, and hath not been bound in its bands.

24 For its yoke is a yoke of iron: and its bands are bands of brass.

26 Its continuance shall not be for a long time, but it shall possess the ways of the unjust: and the just shall not be burnt with its flame.

27 They that forsake God shall fall into it, and it shall burn in them, and shall not

be quenched, and it shall be sent upon them as a lion, and as a leopard it shall tear them.

28 Hedge in thy ears with thorns, hear not a wicked tongue, and make doors and bars to thy mouth.

29 Melt down thy gold and silver, and make a balance for thy words and a just bridle for thy mouth;

30 And take heed lest thou slip with thy tongue, and fall in the sight of thy enemies who lie in wait for thee, and thy fall be incurable unto death.

21 A wicked word shall change the heart: out of which four manner of things arise, good and evil, life and death: and the tongue is continually the ruler of them.   Ecclus. xxxvii.

34 O generation of vipers, how can you speak good things, whereas you are evil? for out of the abundance of the heart the mouth speaketh.   S. Matt. xii.

36 I say unto you, that every idle word that men shall speak, they shall render an account for it in the day of judgment.

37 For by thy words thou shalt be justified, and by thy words thou shalt be condemned.

18 He who speaketh of himself, seeketh his own glory.   S. John vii.

29 Let no evil speech proceed from your mouth ...   Ephes. iv.

18 But the soul that is sorrowful for the greatness of evil she hath done, and goeth bowed down, and feeble, and the eyes that fail, and the hungry soul giveth glory and justice to thee the Lord. *Baruch ii.*

10 ... Thus you have spoken, saying: Our iniquities, and our sins are upon us, and we pine away in them: how then can we live? *Ezech. xxxiii.*

11 As I live, saith the Lord God, I desire not the death of the wicked, but that the wicked turn from his way, and live. Turn ye, turn ye from your evil ways: and why will you die, O house of Israel?

10 And I will pour out upon the house of David, and upon the inhabitants of Jerusalem, the spirit of grace, and of prayers: and they shall look upon me, whom they have pierced: and they shall mourn for him as one mourneth for an only son, and they shall grieve over him, as the manner is to grieve for the death of the first-born. *Zach. xii.*

14 And after that John was delivered up, Jesus came into Galilee, preaching the gospel of the kingdom of God, *S. Mark i.*

15 And saying: The time is accomplished, and the kingdom of God is at hand: repent, and believe the gospel.

32 This Jesus hath God raised again, whereof all we are witnesses. *Acts ii.*

whole body,
our nativity,

nd of birds,
t, is tamed

tame, a

ther: and
e after the

th proceedeth
ren. these

speak as 1 S. Peter
iv.

of that wor- Tobias
be under iii.
be under
and if it be
el to come

thers were Judith
l, whether viii.

you, that Deut.
xiii.

4 Nor obscenity, nor foolish talking, nor Ephes.
scurrility, which is to no purpose; but rather v.
giving of thanks.

11 And have no fellowship with the unfruitful works of darkness; but rather reprove them.

12 For the things that are done by them in private, it is shameful even to mention.

6 Let your speech be always in grace Col. iv.
seasoned with salt; that you may know how you ought to answer every man.

19 Speaking to yourselves in psalms and Ephes.
hymns, and spiritual canticles, singing, and v.
making melody in your hearts to the Lord.

2 Speak evil of no man . . . Titus iii.

16 Shun profane and vain speeches; for 2 Tim.
they grow much towards impiety: ii.

17 And their speech spreadeth like a cancer . . .

26 If any man think himself to be religious, S. James
not bridling his tongue, but deceiving i.
his own heart, this man's religion is vain.

2 . . . If any man offend not in word; S. James
the same is a perfect man. He is able also iii.
with a bridle to lead about the whole body.

5 The tongue is indeed a little member, and boasteth great things. Behold how small a fire what a great wood it kindleth?

6 And the tongue is a fire, a world of iniquity. The tongue is placed among our

members, which defileth the whole body, and setteth on fire the wheel of our nativity, being set on fire by hell.

7 For every kind of beasts, and of birds, and of serpents, and of the rest, is tamed and hath been tamed by mankind:

8 But the tongue no man can tame, a restless evil, full of deadly poison.

9 By it we bless God and the Father: and by it we curse men, who are made after the likeness of God.

10 Out of the same mouth proceedeth blessing and cursing. My brethren, these things ought not so to be.

11 If any man speak, let him speak as the words of God.   1 S. Peter iv.

TRIALS.

21 THIS every one is sure of that worshippeth thee, that his life, if it be under trial, shall be crowned: and if it be under tribulation it shall be delivered: and if it be under correction, it shall be allowed to come to thy mercy.   Tobias iii.

21 ... Be mindful how our fathers were tempted that they might be proved, whether they worshipped their God truly.   Judith viii.

3 ... The Lord your God trieth you, that   Deut. xiii.

it may appear whether you love him with all your heart, and with all your soul, or no.

2 And thou shalt remember all the way through which the Lord thy God hath brought thee for forty years through the desert, to afflict thee and to prove thee, and that the things that were in thy heart might be made known, whether thou wouldst keep his commandments or no. Deut. viii.

3 He afflicted thee with want, and gave thee manna for thy food, which neither thou nor thy fathers knew : to show that not in bread alone doth man live, but in every word that proceedeth from the mouth of God.

4 Thy raiment, with which thou wast covered, hath not decayed for age, and thy foot is not worn, lo this is the fortieth year.

5 That thou mayst consider in thy heart, that as a man traineth up his son, so the Lord thy God hath trained thee up.

22 They must remember how our father Abraham was tempted, and being proved by many tribulations, was made the friend of God. Judith viii.

23 So Isaac, so Jacob, so Moses, and all that have pleased God, passed through many tribulations remaining faithful.

24 But they that did not receive the trials with the fear of the Lord, but uttered

their impatience, and the reproach of their murmuring against the Lord,

25 Were destroyed by the destroyer, and perished by serpents.

13 Because thou wast acceptable to God, it was necessary that temptation should prove thee. — Tobias xii.

3 As silver is tried by fire, and gold in the furnace: so the Lord trieth the hearts. — Prov. xvii.

1 Son, when thou comest to the service of God, stand in justice and in fear, and prepare thy soul for temptation. — Ecclus. ii.

2 Humble thy heart, and endure: incline thy ear, and receive the words of understanding: and make not haste in the time of clouds.

3 Wait on God with patience: join thyself to God, and endure, that thy life may be increased in the latter end.

4 Take all that shall be brought upon thee: and in thy sorrow endure, and in thy humiliation keep patience.

5 For gold and silver are tried in the fire, but acceptable men in the furnace of humiliation.

6 Believe God, and he will recover thee: and direct thy way, and trust in him . . .

2 My brethren, count it all joy, when you shall fall into divers temptations: — James i.

3 Knowing that the trying of your faith worketh patience.

4 And patience hath a perfect work: that you may be perfect and entire, failing in nothing.

TROUBLES OF LIFE.

1 THE life of man upon earth is a warfare . . . — Job vii.

1 Man born of a woman, living for a short time, is filled with many miseries. — Job xiv.

12 . . . Surely in vain is any man disquieted. — Ps. xxxviii.

2 . . . All is vanity. — Eccles. i.

23 Cast thy care upon the Lord, and he shall sustain thee: he shall not suffer the just to waver for ever. — Ps. liv.

13 Give us help from trouble: for vain is the salvation of man. — Ps. lix.

2 Our God is our refuge and strength: a helper in troubles, which have found us exceedingly. — Ps. xlv.

17 The troubles of my heart are multiplied: deliver me from my necessities. — Ps. xxiv.

6 Better is a handful with rest, than both hands full with labour, and vexation of mind. — Eccles. iv.

7 Surely man passeth as an image: yea, and he is disquieted in vain. He storeth — Ps. xxxviii.

up: and he knoweth not for whom he shall gather these things.

1 Unless the Lord build the house, they labour in vain that build it. Unless the Lord keep the city, he watcheth in vain that keepeth it.   Ps. cxxvi.

10 I have seen the trouble, which God hath given the sons of men to be exercised in it.   Eccles. iii.

26 God hath given to a man that is good in his sight, wisdom and knowledge, and joy: but to the sinner he hath given vexation, and superfluous care, to heap up and to gather together, and to give it to him that hath pleased God; but this also is vanity, and a fruitless solicitude of the mind.   Eccles. ii.

8 There is but one: and he hath not a second, no child, no brother, and yet he ceaseth not to labour, neither are his eyes satisfied with riches, neither doth he reflect, saying: For whom do I labour, and defraud my soul of good things? in this also is vanity, and a grievous vexation.   Eccles. iv.

1 Great labour is created for all men, and a heavy yoke is upon the children of Adam . . .   Eccles. xl.

2 Their thoughts, and fears of the heart, their imagination of things to come, and the day of their end:

3 From him that sitteth on a glorious

throne, unto him that is humbled in earth and ashes:

4 From him that weareth purple, and beareth the crown, even to him that is covered with rough linen: wrath, envy, trouble, unquietness, and the fear of death, continual anger, and strife.

8 Such things happen to all flesh, from man even to beast, and upon sinners are sevenfold more.

1 Let not your heart be troubled. You believe in God, believe also in me. *S. John xiv.*

7 And to you who are troubled, rest with us when the Lord Jesus shall be revealed from heaven with the angels of his power. *2 Thess. i.*

TRUST IN GOD.

7 CASTING all your care upon him, for he hath care of you. *1 S. Peter v.*

6 Offer up the sacrifice of justice, and trust in the Lord... *Ps. iv.*

15 Although he should kill me, I will trust in him. *Job xiii.*

13 ... Blessed are all they that trust in him. *Ps. ii.*

5 Blessed is the man whose trust is in the name of the Lord: and who hath not had regard to vantities, and lying follies. *Ps. xxxix.*

Trust in God.

23 The Lord will redeem the souls of his servants: and none of them that trust in him shall offend. — Ps. xxxiii.

8 ... The children of men shall put their trust under the covert of thy wings. — Ps. xxxv.

3 Trust in the Lord, and do good, and dwell in the land, and thou shalt be fed with its riches. — Ps. xxxvi.

5 Commit thy way to the Lord, and trust in him, and he will do it.

8 In God is my salvation and my glory: he is the God of my help, and my hope is in God. — Ps. lxi.

9 Trust in him, all ye congregation of people: pour out your hearts before him: God is our helper for ever.

9 It is good to trust in the Lord, rather than to trust in princes. — Ps. cxvii.

20 ... He that trusteth in the Lord is blessed. — Prov. xvi.

9 They that trust in him, shall understand the truth ... — Wisd. iii.

40 ... There is no confusion to them that trust in thee. — Dan. iii.

31 Be not solicitous therefore, saying: What shall we eat, or what shall we drink, or wherewith shall we be clothed? — S. Matt. vi.

32 For after all these things do the heathen seek. For your Father knoweth that you have need of all these things.

33 Seek ye therefore first the kingdom of God, and his justice, and all these things shall be added unto you.

34 Be not therefore solicitous for to-morrow; for the morrow will be solicitous for itself. Sufficient for the day is the evil thereof.

11 And when they shall bring you into the synagogues, and to magistrates and powers, be not solicitous how or what you shall answer, or what you shall say.   S. Luke xii.

12 For the Holy Ghost shall teach you in the same hour what you must say.

TRUST IN MAN VAIN.

2 ... You are all troublesome comforters.   Job xvi.

10 Vain are the sons of men, the sons of men are liars in the balances: that by vanity they may together deceive.   Ps. lxi.

13 O grant us help from trouble: for vain is the help of man.   Ps. cvii.

2 ... Put not your trust in princes: in the children of men, in whom there is no salvation.   Ps. cxlv.

26 He that trusteth in his own heart, is a fool ...   Prov. xxviii.

5 Thus saith the Lord: Cursed be the man that trusteth in man, and maketh flesh   Jer. xvii.

his arm, and whose heart departeth from the Lord.

9 We had in ourselves the answer of death, that we should not trust in ourselves, but in God who raiseth the dead.   2 Cor. i.

TRUTH.

8 BEHOLD thou hast loved truth ...   Ps. l.

3 ... O Lord, thy eyes are upon truth ...   Jer. v.

24 O love the Lord, all ye his saints: for the Lord will require truth ...   Ps. xxx.

3 Let not mercy and truth leave thee, put them about thy neck, and write them in the tables of thy heart.   Prov. iii.

12 God loveth mercy and truth ...   Ps. lxxxiii.

19 The lip of truth shall be steadfast for ever ...   Prov. xii.

5 The just shall hate a lying word.   Prov. xiii.

25 A faithful witness delivereth souls ...   Prov. xiv.

6 By mercy and truth iniquity is redeemed ...   Prov. xvi.

24 For thy soul be not ashamed to say the truth.   Ecclus. iv.

10 ... Truth will return to them that practise her.   Ecclus. xxvii.

19 ... Love ye truth and peace.   Zach. viii.

16 These then are the things which you shall do: speak ye truth every one to his

neighbour: judge ye truth and judgment of peace in your gates.

8 And he said: Surely they are my people, children that will not deny: so he became their saviour. — Isaias lxiii.

18 ... He that seeketh the glory of him that sent him, he is true; and there is no injustice in him. — S. John vii.

21 He that doth truth, cometh to the light, that his works may be made manifest, because they are done in God. — S. John iii.

14 ... We have spoken all things to you in truth ... — 2 Cor. vii.

8 We can do nothing against the truth; but for the truth. — 2 Cor. xiii.

15 But doing the truth in charity, we may in all things grow up in him who is the head, Christ. — Ephes. iv.

25 ... Speak ye the truth every man with his neighbour: for we are members one of another.

8 ... Walk then as children of the light: — Ephes. v.

9 For the fruit of the light is in all goodness, and justice, and truth.

14 Stand therefore, having your loins girt about with truth ... — Ephes. vi.

18 My little children, let us not love in word, nor in tongue, but in deed and in truth. — 1 S. John iii.

19 In this we know that we are of the truth ...

UNBELIEVERS.

13 Thou say'st: What doth God know? Job xxii, and he judgeth as it were through a mist.

14 The clouds are his covert, and he doth not consider our things, and he walketh about the poles of heaven.

15 Who is the Almighty, that we should Job xxi serve him? and what doth it profit us if we pray to him?

1 The fool hath said in his heart: There is Ps. xiii. no God. They are corrupt, and are become abominable in their ways: there is none that doth good, no not one.

5 ... Say not before the angel: There is Eccles. v no providence: lest God be angry at thy words, and destroy all the works of thy hands.

15 Wo to them that are faint-hearted, who Ecclus. believe not God: and therefore shall not be ii. protected by him.

9 ... If you will not believe, you shall Isaias not continue. vii.

4 Behold, he that is unbelieving, his soul Hab. ii. shall not be right in himself: but the just shall live in his faith.

2 I have spread forth my hands all the Isaias day to an unbelieving people, who walk in lxv.

a way that is not good after their own thoughts.

8 ... When the Son of man cometh, shall he find, think you, faith on earth? S. Luke xviii.

16 ... He that believeth not, shall be condemned. S. Mark xvi.

31 ... If they hear not Moses and the prophets, neither will they believe if one rise again from the dead. S. Luke xvi.

14 ... And he upbraided them with their incredulity and hardness of heart, because they did not believe them who had seen him after he was risen again. S. Mark xvi.

25 ... O foolish, and slow of heart to believe in all things which the prophets have spoken. S. Luke xxiv.

18 ... He that doth not believe, is already judged: because he believeth not in the name of the only begotten Son of God. S. John iii.

19 And this is the judgment: because the light is come into the world, and men loved darkness rather than the light: for their works were evil.

20 For every one that doth evil hateth the light, and cometh not to the light, that his works may not be reproved.

24 Therefore I said to you, that you shall die in your sins: for if you believe not that I am he, you shall die in your sin. S. John viii.

16 My doctrine is not mine, but his that sent me. — S. John vii.

17 If any man will do the will of him: he shall know of the doctrine, whether it be from God, or whether I speak of myself.

36 He that believeth in the Son, hath life everlasting: but he that believeth not the Son, shall not see life, but the wrath of God abideth in him. — S. John iii.

47 He that is of God heareth the words of God. Therefore you hear them not, because you are not of God. — S. John viii.

23 He that hateth me, hateth my Father also. — S. John xv.

48 He that despiseth me, and receiveth not my words, hath one that judgeth him; the word that I have spoken, the same shall judge him in the last day. — S. John xii.

24 He that loveth me not, keepeth not my words. And the word which you have heard is not mine, but the Father's who sent me. — S. John xiv.

27 ... Be not faithless, but believing. — S. John xx.

18 For the word of the cross, to them indeed that perish, is foolishness: but to them that are saved, that is, to us, it is the power of God. — 1 Cor. i.

23 But we preach Christ crucified, unto the Jews indeed a stumbling-block, and unto the gentiles, foolishness.

8 And a stone of stumbling, and a rock of scandal to them that stumble at the word, neither do believe, whereunto also they are set.   1 S. Peter ii.

3 If our gospel be also hid; it is hid to them that are lost.   2 Cor. iv.

4 In whom the god of this world hath blinded the minds of unbelievers, that the light of the gospel of the glory of Christ, who is the image of God, should not shine unto them.

18 And to whom did he swear that they should not enter into his rest; but to them that were incredulous?   Heb. iii.

19 And we see that they could not enter in, because of unbelief.

25 See that you refuse not him that speaketh. For if they escaped not who refused him that spoke upon earth, much more shall not we, that turn away from him that speaketh to us from heaven.   Heb. xii.

3 ... In the last days there shall come deceitful scoffers, walking after their own lusts,   2 S. Peter iii.

4 Saying: Where is his promise, or his coming? For since the time that the fathers slept, all things continue as they were from the beginning of the creation.

8 But of this one thing, be not ignorant, my beloved, that one day with the Lord is

as a thousand years, and a thousand years as one day.

10 But these men blaspheme whatsoever things they know not: and what things soever they naturally know, like dumb beasts, in these they are corrupted.   S. Jude.

18 The wrath of God is revealed from heaven, against all ungodliness and injustice of these men that detain the truth of God in injustice: Rom. i.

19 Because that which is known of God is manifest in them. For God hath manifested it unto them.

20 For the invisible things of him, from the creation of the world, are clearly seen, being understood by the things that are made: his eternal power also and divinity: so that they are inexcusable.

21 Because that, when they knew God, they have not glorified him as God, or given thanks: but became vain in their thoughts, and their foolish heart was darkened.

4 . . . Denying the only Sovereign Ruler, and our Lord Jesus Christ.   S. Jude i.

23 Whosoever denieth the Son, the same hath not the Father.   1 S. John ii.

18 But the so...
greatness of evil s...
bowed down, and ...
fail, and the hungr...
justice to thee the L...

10 ... Thus you
Our iniquities, and our
we pine away in then
live?

11 As I live, saith the
not the death of the w...
wicked turn from his wa...
ye, turn ye from your e...
will you die, O house of I...

10 And I will pour out ...
David, and upon the inh...
salem, the spirit of grace. ...
and they shall look upon ...
have pierced; and they shall ...
as one mourneth for an only ...
shall grieve over him, as the
grieve for the death of the first.

14 And after that John was
Jesus came into Galilee, preach...
of the kingdom of God,

15 And saying: The time
plished, and the kingdom of God
repent, and believe the gospel.

32 This Jesus hath God r...
whereof all we are witnesses.

UNION WITH GOD.*

24 (HENOCH) walked with God and was Gen. v.
in no more: because God took him.

21 ... Lo, the kingdom of God is within S. Luke
u. xvii.

23 ... If any one love me, he will keep S. John
word, and my Father will love him, and xiv.
will come to him, and will make our abode
in him.

26 I have made known thy name to them, S. John
will make it known: that the love, xvii.
wherewith thou hast loved me, may be in
, and I in them.

And not for them only do I pray, but
them also who through their word shall
eve in me:

... That they also may be one in
..

Mind the things that are above, not the Coloss.
s that are upon the earth. iii.
For you are dead; and your life is hid
Christ in God.

No man hath seen God at any time. 1 S. John
love one another, God abideth in us, iv.
is charity is perfected in us.

In this we know that we abide in him,

* See Christ our Life and Spiritual Life.

UNHOLY FEAR.

24 And Saul said to Samuel: I have sinned because I have transgressed the commandment of the Lord, and thy words, fearing the people, and obeying their voice. — 1 Kings xv.

11 For whom hast thou been solicitous and afraid, that thou hast lied, and hast not been mindful of me, nor thought of me in thy heart? for I am silent, and as one that seeth not, and thou hast forgotten me. — Isaias lvii.

7 Hearken to me, you that know what is just, my people who have my law in your heart: fear ye not the reproach of men, and be not afraid of their blasphemies. — Isaias li.

12 ... Who art thou, that thou shouldst be afraid of a mortal man, and of the son of man, who shall wither away as grass.

13 And thou hast forgotten the Lord thy maker, who stretched out the heavens, and founded the earth: and thou hast been afraid continually all the day at the presence of his fury who afflicted thee, and had prepared himself to destroy thee: where is now the fury of the oppressor?

UNION WITH GOD.*

24 (HENOCH) walked with God and was seen no more: because God took him. Gen. v.

21 ... Lo, the kingdom of God is within you. S. Luke xvii.

23 ... If any one love me, he will keep my word, and my Father will love him, and we will come to him, and will make our abode with him. S. John xiv.

26 I have made known thy name to them, and will make it known; that the love, wherewith thou hast loved me, may be in them, and I in them. S. John xvii.

20 And not for them only do I pray, but for them also who through their word shall believe in me:

21 ... That they also may be one in us ...

2 Mind the things that are above, not the things that are upon the earth. Coloss. iii.

3 For you are dead; and your life is hid with Christ in God.

12 No man hath seen God at any time. If we love one another, God abideth in us, and his charity is perfected in us. 1 S. John iv.

13 In this we know that we abide in him,

* See Christ our Life and Spiritual Life.

and he in us; because he hath given us of his Spirit.

16 ... God is charity: and he that abideth in charity, abideth in God, and God in him.

23 ... He that confesseth the Son, hath the Father also.   1 S. John ii.

24 ... If that abide in you, which you have heard from the beginning, you also shall abide in the Son and in the Father.

4 You are of God, little children, and have overcome him (anti-Christ). Because greater is he that is in you, than he that is in the world.   1 S. John iv.

12 ... If we love one another, God abideth in us, and his charity is perfected in us.

13 In this we know that we abide in him, and he in us; because he hath given us of his Spirit.

9 Whosoever revolteth, and continueth not in the doctrine of Christ, hath not God. He that continueth in the doctrine, the same hath both the Father and the Son.   2 S. John i.

20 And we know that the Son of God is come: and he hath given us understanding, that we may know the true God, and may be in his true Son ...   1 S. John v.

4 By whom he hath given us most great and precious promises: that by these you   2 S. Peter i.

may be made partakers of the divine nature: flying the corruption of that concupiscence which is in the world.

UNJUST MAN.

15 Thou shalt not do that which is unjust, nor judge unjustly ... — Lev. xix.

1 ... Deliver me from the unjust and deceitful man. — Ps. xlii.

2 The unjust hath said within himself, that he would sin: there is no fear of God before his eyes. — Ps. xxxv.

4 The words of his mouth are iniquity and guile: he would not understand that he might do well.

28 ... The unjust shall be punished, and the seed of the wicked shall perish. — Ps. xxxvi.

12 ... Evils shall catch the unjust man unto destruction. — Ps. cxxxix.

30 Strive not against a man without cause, when he hath done thee no evil. — Prov. iii.

6 ... The unjust shall be caught in their own snares. — Prov. xi.

15 He that justifieth the wicked, and he that condemneth the just, both are abominable before God. — Prov. xvii.

UNSELFISHNESS.

31 And returning to the Lord (Moses) Ex. xxxii.
said: I beseech thee: this people hath sinned
a heinous sin, and they have made to themselves gods of gold: either forgive them this
trespass,

32 Or if thou do not, strike me out of the book that thou hast written.

17 And David said to God: Am not I he 1 Paralip.
that commanded the people to be num- xxi.
bered? It is I that have sinned: it is I
that have done the evil: but as for this flock
what hath it deserved? O Lord my God,
let thy hand be turned, I beseech thee, upon
me, and upon my father's house: and let
not thy people be destroyed.

16 In this we have known the charity of 1 S. John
God, because he hath laid down his life for iii.
us: and we ought to lay down our lives for
the brethren.

25 ... He that hateth his life in this S. John
world, keepeth it unto life eternal. xii.

1 Now we that are stronger, ought to bear Rom.
the infirmities of the weak, and not to please xv.
ourselves.

3 For Christ did not please himself ...

24 Let no man seek his own, but that 1 Cor. x.
which is for the welfare of another.

Unselfishness.

33 As I also in all things please all men, not seeking that which is profitable to myself, but to many, that they may be saved.

3 For I wished myself to be an anathema from Christ,* for my brethren, who are my kinsmen according to the flesh. — Rom. ix.

15 And I most gladly will spend and be spent myself for your souls: although loving you more, I be loved less. — 2 Cor. xii.

16 But be it so . . .

5 (Charity) . . . seeketh not her own . . . — 1 Cor. xiii.

15 And Christ died for all: that they also, who live, may not now live to themselves, but unto him who died for them and rose again. — 2 Cor. v.

4 Each one not considering the things that are his own, but those that are other men's. — Philip. ii.

11 . . . They loved not their lives unto death. — Apoc. xii.

VANITY OR VAIN GLORY.

8 REMOVE far from me vanity, and lying words. — Prov. xxx.

---

* The apostle's concern and love for his countrymen the Jews was so great that he was willing to suffer even an anathema, or curse, for their sake: or any evil that could come upon him, without his offending God.

37 Turn away my eyes that they may not behold vanity...   Ps. cxviii.

12 A vain man is lifted up into pride, and thinketh himself born free like a wild ass's colt.   Job xi.

3 They have spoken vain things every one to his neighbour: with deceitful lips, and with a double heart have they spoken.   Ps. xi.

8 He that is vain and foolish, shall be exposed to contempt.   Prov. xii.

12 Hast thou seen a man wise in his own conceit? there shall be more hope of a fool than of him.   Prov. xxvi.

2 Let another praise thee, and not thy own mouth: a stranger, and not thy own lips.   Prov. xxvii.

2 Extol not thyself in the thoughts of thy soul like a bull: lest thy strength be quashed by folly.   Ecclus. vi.

29 Extol not thyself in doing thy work...   Ecclus. x.

2 Praise not a man for his beauty, neither despise a man for his look.   Ecclus. xi.

4 Glory not in apparel at any time, and be not exalted in the day of thy honour: for the works of the Highest only are wonderful, and his works are glorious, and secret, and hidden.

8 A sinner is caught in his own vanity, and the proud and the evil speakers shall fall thereby.   Ecclus. xxiii.

18 Wo to you that draw iniquity with cords of vanity. — Isaias v.

23 Thus saith the Lord: Let not the wise man glory in his wisdom, and let not the strong man glory in his strength, and let not the rich man glory in his riches: — Jer. ix.

24 But let him that glorieth glory in this, that he understandeth and knoweth me, for I am the Lord that exercise mercy, and judgment, and justice in the earth: for these things please me, saith the Lord.

17 This then I say and testify in the Lord: that henceforward you walk not as also the gentiles walk, in the vanity of their mind. — Ephes. iv.

26 Let us not be made desirous of vain glory, provoking one another, envying one another. — Galat. v.

VOCATION (RELIGIOUS).

1 AND the Lord said to Abram: Go forth out of thy country, and from thy kindred, and out of thy father's house, and come into the land which I shall show thee. — Gen. xii.

9 Here am I: for thou didst call me... — 1 Kings iii.

10 ... Speak, Lord, for thy servant heareth.

5 Blessed is he whom thou hast chosen, and taken to thee: he shall dwell in thy courts. — Ps. lxiv.

1 ... Fear not, for I have redeemed thee, and have called thee by thy name: thou art mine. — Isaias xliii.

16 And passing by the sea of Galilee, he (Jesus) saw Simon and Andrew his brother, casting nets into the sea (for they were fishermen). — S. Mark i.

17 And Jesus said to them: Come after me, and I will make you to become fishers of men.

18 And immediately, leaving their nets, they followed him.

19 And going on from thence a little farther, he saw James the son of Zebedee, and John his brother, who also were mending their nets in the ship:

20 And forthwith he called them. And leaving their father Zebedee in the ship with his hired men, they followed him.

27 And after these things he went forth, and saw a publican named Levi, sitting at the receipt of custom, and he said to him: Follow me. — S. Luke v.

28 And leaving all things, he rose up and followed him.

38 Now the man, out of whom the devils were departed, besought him that he might be with him. But Jesus sent him away, saying: — S. Luke viii.

39 Return to thy house, and tell how

great things God hath done to thee. And he went through the whole city, publishing how great things Jesus had done to him.

59 But he said to another: Follow me. And he said: Lord, suffer me first to go, and bury my father.

S. Luke ix.

60 And Jesus said to him: Let the dead bury their dead: but go thou, and preach the kingdom of God.

61 And another said: I will follow thee, Lord, but let me first take my leave of them that are at my house.

62 Jesus said to him: No man putting his hand to the plough, and looking back, is fit for the kingdom of God.

17 And when he was gone forth into the way, a certain man running up and kneeling before him, asked him, Good Master, what shall I do that I may receive life everlasting?

S. Mark x.

19 Thou knowest the commandments, Do not commit adultery, do not kill, do not steal, bear not false witness, do no fraud, honour thy father and mother.

20 But he answering, said to him: Master, all these things I have observed from my youth.

21 And Jesus looking on him, loved him, and said to him: One thing is wanting unto thee: go, sell whatsoever thou hast, and give

to the poor, and thou shalt have treasure in heaven: and come, follow me.

22 Who being struck sad at that saying, went away sorrowful: for he had great possessions.

12 And it came to pass in those days, that he (Jesus) went out into a mountain to pray, and he passed the whole night in the prayer of God.   S. Luke vi.

13 And when day was come, he called unto him his disciples; and he chose twelve of them (whom also he named Apostles).

16 You have not chosen me: but I have chosen you; and have appointed you, that you should go, and should bring forth fruit: and your fruit should remain: that whatsoever you shall ask of the Father in my name, he may give it you.   S. John xv.

19 ... Follow me.   S. John xxi.

21 ... Lord, and what shall this man do?

22 Jesus saith to him: So I will have him to remain till I come, what is it to thee? follow thou me.

29 ... We ought to obey God rather than men.   Acts. v.

12 I give him thanks, who hath strengthened me, even to Christ Jesus our Lord, for that he hath counted me faithful, putting me in the ministry.   1 Tim. i.

15 ... It is good for me to die, rather   1 Cor. ix.

Vocation (Religious).

than that any one should make void my glory.

16 For if I preach the gospel: it is no glory* to me : for a necessity lieth upon me : for wo is unto me if I preach not the gospel.

17 For if I do this thing willingly, I have a reward ...

8 To me, the least of all the saints, is given this grace, to preach among the gentiles the unsearchable riches of Christ. — Ephes. iii.

VOWS.

27 ... Thou shalt pay thy vows. — Job xxii.

28 Any thing that is devoted to the Lord, whether it be man, or beast, or field, shall not be sold, neither may it be redeemed. Whatsoever is once consecrated shall be holy of holies to the Lord. — Lev. xxvii.

3 If any man make a vow to the Lord, or bind himself by an oath : he shall not make his word void, but shall fulfil all that he promised. — Numb. xxx.

21 When thou hast made a vow to the Lord thy God, thou shalt not delay to pay it : because the Lord thy God will require it. And if thou delay, it shall be imputed to thee for a sin.

22 If thou wilt not promise, thou shalt be without sin. — Deut. xxiii.

* That is, I have nothing to glory of.

23 But that which is once gone out of thy lips, thou shalt observe, and shalt do as thou hast promised to the Lord thy God, and hast spoken with thy own will and with thy own mouth.

8 The victims of the wicked are abominable to the Lord: the vows of the just are acceptable. Prov. xv.

25 It is ruin to a man . . . after vows to retract. Prov. xx.

1 Speak not any thing rashly, and let not thy heart be hasty to utter a word before God. For God is in heaven, and thou upon earth: therefore let thy words be few. Eccles. v.

3 If thou hast vowed any thing to God, defer not to pay it: for an unfaithful and foolish promise displeaseth him: but whatsoever thou hast vowed, pay it:

4 And it is much better not to vow, than after a vow not to perform the thing promised.

18 Paul when he had stayed yet many days, taking his leave of the brethren, sailed thence into Syria, having shorn his head in Cenchra. For he had a vow. Acts xviii.

WAR.

10 IF at any time thou come to fight against a city, thou shalt first offer it peace. Deut. xx.

11 If they receive it, and open the gates

to thee, all the people that are therein, shall be saved, and shall serve thee paying tribute.

9 ... O you that of your own good will offered yourselves to danger, bless the Lord.   Judges v.

13 The remnants of the people are saved, the Lord hath fought among the valiant ones.

7 Behave like men, and take courage: be not afraid nor dismayed for the king of the Assyrians, nor for all the multitude that is with him: for there are many more with us than with him.   2 Paralip. xxxii.

8 For with him is an arm of flesh: with us the Lord our God, who is our helper, and fighteth for us.

11 ... Lord there is no difference with thee, whether thou help with few, or with many: help us, O Lord our God: for with confidence in thee, and in thy name we are come against this multitude. O Lord, thou art our God, let not man prevail against thee.   2 Paralip. xiv.

4 ... What is this confidence wherein thou trustest?   Isaias xxxvi.

5 Or with what counsel or strength dost thou prepare for war? ...

18 Designs are strengthened by counsels: and wars are to be managed by governments.   Prov. xx.

6 Because war is managed by due ordering: and there shall be safety where there are many counsels.   Prov. xxiv.

1 All things have their season, and in their times all things pass under heaven. — Eccles. iii.

8 ... A time of war, and a time of peace.

19 The success of war is not in the multitude of the army, but strength cometh from heaven. — 1 Mach. iii.

6 And you shall hear of wars, and rumours of wars. See that ye be not troubled. For these things must come to pass, but the end is not yet. — S. Matt. xxiv.

WAR (AGGRESSIVE).

5 SIMEON and Levi brethren: vessels of iniquity, waging war. — Gen. xlix.

· 6 Let not my soul go into their counsel, nor my glory be in their assembly: because in their fury they slew a man, and in their self-will they undermined a wall.

7 Cursed be their fury because it was stubborn: and their wrath because it was cruel ...

5 ... Joab ... shed the blood of war in peace, and put the blood of war on his girdle that was about his loins, and in his shoes that were on his feet. — 3 Kings ii.

6 ... Let not his hoary head go down to hell in peace.

8 The word of the Lord came to me saying: Thou hast shed much blood, and — 1 Paralip. xxii.

fought many battles, so thou canst not build a house to my name, after shedding so much blood before me.

8 In the strength of thy arm thou didst possess the land, and being the most mighty thou holdest it.   Job xxii.

10 Therefore art thou surrounded with snares, and sudden fear troubleth thee.

12 Wo to him that buildeth a town with blood, and prepareth a city by iniquity.   Habac. ii.

9 Come and behold ye the works of the Lord: what wonders he hath done upon earth.   Ps. xlv.

10 Making wars to cease even to the end of the earth. He shall destroy the bow, and break the weapons: and the shield he shall burn in the fire.

31 ... Scatter thou the nations that delight in wars.   Ps. lxvii.

1 From whence are wars and contentions among you? Are they not hence, from your concupiscences, which war in your members.   S. James iv.

WATCHING.

23 With all watchfulness keep thy heart . . .   Prov. iv.

18 ... Because the Lord is the God of judgment: blessed are all they that wait for him.   Isaias xxx.

42 Watch ye therefore, because ye know not what hour your Lord will come.   S. Matt. xxiv.

38 Watch ye, and pray that you enter not into temptation. The spirit indeed is willing, but the flesh is weak.   S. Mark xiv.

35 Let your loins be girt, and lamps burning in your hands,   S. Luke xii.

36 And you yourselves like to men who wait for their lord, when he shall return from the wedding: that when he cometh, and knocketh, they may open to him immediately.

37 Blessed are those servants, whom the Lord, when he cometh, shall find watching. Amen I say to you, that he will gird himself, and make them sit down to meat, and passing will minister to them.

38 And if he shall come in the second watch, or come in the third watch, and find them so, blessed are those servants.

44 Wherefore be you also ready, because at what hour you know not, the Son of man will come.   S. Matt. xxiv.

35 Watch ye (for you know not when the lord of the house cometh: at even, or at midnight, or at the cock-crowing, or in the morning).   S. Matt. xiii.

36 Lest, coming on a sudden, he find you sleeping.

37 And what I say to you I say to all: Watch.

13 Watch ye, stand fast in the faith, do manfully, and be strengthened. — 1 Cor. xvi.

7 The end of all approacheth. Be prudent therefore, and watch in prayers.' — 1 S. Peter iv.

8 Be sober and watch: because your adversary the devil, as a roaring lion, goeth about, seeking whom he may devour. — 1 S. Peter v.

2 Be watchful and strengthen the things that remain, which are ready to die. For I find not thy works full before my God. — Apoc. iii.

3 ... If then thou shalt not watch; I will come to thee as a thief, and thou shalt not know at what hour I will come to thee.

15 Behold, I come as a thief. Blessed is he that watcheth... — Apoc. xvi.

WICKED (CHARACTER OF).

4 THE wicked are alienated from the womb, they have gone astray from the womb, they have spoken false things. — Ps. lvii.

20 ... The heart of the wicked is nothing worth. — Prov. x.

9 The way of the wicked is an abomination to the Lord... — Prov. xv.

28 ... The mouth of the wicked overfloweth with evils.

27 The wicked man diggeth evil, and in his lips is a burning fire. — Prov. xvi.

4 ... The lamp of the wicked is sin. — Prov. xxi.

27 ... The wicked loathe them that are in the right way. — Prov. xxix.

3 The evil of their hands they call good ... — Mich. vii.

20 The wicked are like the raging sea, which cannot rest, and the waves thereof cast up dirt and mire. — Isaias lvii.

7 Their feet run to evil, and make haste to shed innocent blood: their thoughts are unprofitable thoughts: wasting and destruction are in their ways. — Isaias lix.

8 They have not known the way of peace, and there is no judgment in their steps: their paths are become crooked to them: every one that treadeth in them, knoweth no peace.

3 They have bent their tongue, as a bow, for lies, and not for truth: they have strengthened themselves upon the earth, for they have proceeded from evil to evil, and me they have not known, saith the Lord. — Jer. ix.

6 ... Through deceit they have refused to know me, saith the Lord.

20 For every one that doth evil hateth the light, and cometh not to the light, that his works may not be reproved. — S. John iii.

28 And as they liked not to have God in their knowledge; God delivered them up to — Rom. i.

a reprobate sense, to do those things which are not convenient,

29 Being filled with all iniquity, malice, fornication, avarice, wickedness, full of envy, murder, contention, deceit, malignity, whisperers.

30 Detracters, hateful to God, contumelious, proud, haughty, inventors of evil things, disobedient to parents,

31 Foolish, dissolute, without affection, without fidelity, without mercy.

32 Who, having known the justice of God, did not understand that they, who do such things, are worthy of death : and not only they that do them, but they also that consent to them that do them.

18 Having their understanding darkened, being alienated from the life of God through the ignorance that is in them, because of the blindness of their hearts. *Ephes. iv.*

2 ... Lovers of themselves, covetous, haughty, proud, blasphemers, disobedient to parents, ungrateful, wicked, *2 Tim. iii.*

3 Without affection, without peace, slanderers, incontinent, unmerciful, without kindness,

4 Traitors, stubborn, puffed up, and lovers of pleasures more than of God.

13 Evil men and seducers shall grow worse and worse : erring, and driving into error.

16 They profess that they know God: Titus i. but in their works they deny him; being abominable, and incredulous, and to every good work reprobate.

WICKED (END OF THE).

10 Let us have pity on the wicked, but he will not learn justice: in the land of the saints he hath done wicked things, and he shall not see the glory of the Lord.   Isaias xxvi.

23 God hath given him place for penance, and he abuseth it unto pride: but his eyes are upon his ways.   Job xxiv.

27 The heavens shall reveal his iniquity, and the earth shall rise up against him.   Job xx.

28 The offspring of his house shall be exposed, he shall be pulled down in the day of God's wrath.

29 This is the portion of a wicked man from God, and the inheritance of his doings from the Lord.

8 He that soweth iniquity, shall reap evils, and with the rod of his anger he shall be consumed.   Prov. xxii.

25 As a tempest that passeth, so the wicked shall be no more.   Prov. x.

22 The death of the wicked is very evil: and they that hate the just shall be guilty.   Ps. xxxiii.

7 When the wicked man is dead, there shall be no hope any more... Prov. xi.

19 And they shall fall after this without honour, and be a reproach among the dead for ever: for he shall burst them puffed up and speechless, and shall shake them from the foundations, and they shall be utterly laid waste: they shall be in sorrow and their memory shall perish. Wisd. iv.

20 They shall come with fear at the thought of their sins, and their iniquities shall stand against them to convict them.

1 Then shall the just stand with great constancy against those that have afflicted them, and taken away their labours. Wisd. v.

2 These seeing it, shall be troubled with terrible fear...

3 Saying within themselves, repenting, and groaning for anguish of spirit: These are they, whom we had some time in derision, and for a parable of reproach.

4 We fools esteemed their life madness, and their end without honour.

5 Behold, how they are numbered among the children of God, and their lot is among the saints.

6 Therefore we have erred from the way of truth, and the light of justice hath not shined unto us, and the sun of understanding hath not risen upon us.

7 We wearied ourselves in the way of iniquity and destruction, and have walked through hard ways, but the way of the Lord we have not known.

8 What hath pride profited us? or what advantage hath the boasting of riches brought us?

9 All those things are passed away like a shadow, and like a post that runneth on.

13 So we also being born, forthwith ceased to be: and have been able to show no mark of virtue: but are consumed in our wickedness.

14 Such things as these the sinners said in hell:

15 For the hope of the wicked is as dust, which is blown away with the wind, and as a thin froth which is dispersed by the storm: and a smoke that is scattered abroad by the wind: and as the remembrance of a guest of one day that passeth by.

11 Wo to the wicked unto evil: for the reward of his hands shall be given him.   Isaias iii.

18 Wo to them that desire the day of the Lord: to what end is it for you? the day of the Lord is darkness and not light.   Amos v.

20 Shall not the day of the Lord be darkness, and not light: and obscurity, and no brightness in it?

17 For acting wickedly against the laws of God doth not pass unpunished. — 2 Mach. iv.

11 Thy pride is brought down to hell, thy carcass is fallen down: under thee shall the moth be strewed, and worms shall be thy covering. — Isaias xiv.

41 ... Depart from me, you cursed, into everlasting fire which was prepared for the devil and his angels. — S. Matt. xxv.

46 And these shall go into everlasting punishment ...

49 So shall it be at the end of the world. The angels shall go out, and shall separate the wicked from among the just. — S. Matt. xiii.

50 And shall cast them into the furnace of fire: there shall be weeping and gnashing of teeth.

15 ... The kingdom of this world is become our Lord's and his Christ's, and he shall reign for ever and ever. — Apoc. xi.

18 ... And thy wrath is come, and the time of the dead, that they should be judged, and that thou ... shouldest destroy them that have corrupted the earth.

8 But the fearful, and unbelieving, and the abominable, and murderers, and whoremongers, and sorcerers, and idolaters, and all liars, they shall have their portion in the pool burning with fire and brimstone, which is the second death. — Apoc. xxi.

WILL OF GOD.

6 ... Lord, what wilt thou have me to do? — Acts ix.

26 ... I am ready, let him do that which is good before him. — 2 Kings xv.

14 As for me, my prayer is to thee, O Lord; for the time of thy good pleasure, O God. — Ps. lxviii.

10 Teach me to do thy will, for thou art my God. — Ps. cxlii.

15 ... If thou thyself dost not go before, bring us not out of this place. — Ex. xxxiii.

8 Then said I, Behold! I come. 9 In the head of the book it is written of me that I should do thy will:
O my God, I have desired it, and thy law in the midst of my heart. — Ps. xxxix.

10 ... Thy will be done on earth as it is in heaven. — S. Matt. vi.

34 Jesus saith to them: my meat is to do the will of him that sent me, that I may perfect his work. — S. John iv.

17 If any man will do the will of him: he shall know of the doctrine, whether it be of God, or whether I speak of myself. — S. John vii.

21 Not every one that saith to me, Lord, Lord, shall enter into the kingdom of — S. Matt. vii.

heaven: but he that doth the will of my
Father, who is in heaven.

30 ... My judgment is just: because I   S. John
seek not my own will, but the will of him   v.
that sent me.

50 Whosoever shall do the will of my   S. Matt.
Father, that is in heaven, he is my brother,   xii.
and sister, and mother.

39 ... O my Father, if it be possible, let   S. Matt.
this chalice pass from me. Nevertheless,   xxvi.
not as I will, but as thou wilt.

42 ... O my Father, if this chalice may
not pass away except I drink it, thy will be
done.

19 Wherefore let them also that suffer   1 S. Peter
according to the will of God, commend   iv.
their souls in good deeds to the faithful
Creator.

14 And this is the confidence which we   1 S. John
have towards him: That, whatsoever we   v.
shall ask according to his will, he heareth
us.

17 Wherefore become not unwise, but un-   Ephes. v.
derstanding what is the will of God.

9 That he might make known unto us the   Ephes. i
mystery of his will.

13 For it is God who worketh in you   Philip. ii
both to will and to accomplish, according to
his good will.

20 And may the God of peace ...   Heb. xiii

21 Fit you in all goodness, that you may do his will.

12 ... That you may stand perfect and full in all the will of God.   Coloss. iv.

3 For this is the will of God, your sanctification ...   1 Thess. iv.

17 And the world passeth away, and the concupiscence thereof. But he that doth the will of God, abideth for ever.   1 S. John ii.

WISDOM.

12 WHERE is wisdom to be found, and where is the place of understanding?   Job xxviii.

13 Man knoweth not the price thereof, neither is it found in the land of them that live in delights.

24 The path of life is above for the wise ...   Prov. xv.

6 The Lord giveth wisdom ...   Prov. ii.

10 If wisdom shall enter into thy heart, and knowledge please thy soul:

11 Counsel shall keep thee, and prudence shall preserve thee.

7 Be not wise in thy own conceit: fear God and depart from evil.   Prov. iii.

13 Blessed is the man that findeth wisdom and is rich in prudence:

15 She is more precious than all riches:

and all the things that are desired, are not to be compared with her.

17 Her ways are beautiful ways, and all her paths are peaceable.

18 She is a tree of life to them that lay hold on her: and he that shall retain her is blessed.

12 I wisdom dwell in counsel, and am present in learned thoughts. Prov. viii.

13 The fear of the Lord hateth evil: I hate arrogance, and pride, and every wicked way, and a mouth with a double tongue.

14 Counsel and equity is mine, prudence is mine, strength is mine.

15 By me kings reign, and lawgivers decree just things.

17 I love them that love me: and they that in the morning early watch for me, shall find me.

32 ... Blessed are they that keep my ways.

33 Hear instruction and be wise, and refuse it not.

34 Blessed is the man that heareth me, and that watcheth daily at my gates, and waiteth at the posts of my doors.

35 He that shall find me, shall find life, and shall have salvation from the Lord:

36 But he that shall sin against me, shall hurt his own soul. All that hate me love death.

33 The fear of the Lord, is the lesson of wisdom . . .   Prov. xv.

7 And if a man love justice: her labours have great virtues: for she teacheth temperance, and prudence, and justice, and fortitude, which are such things as men can have nothing more profitable in life.   Wisd. viii.

16 To think therefore upon her, is perfect understanding: and he that watcheth for her, shall quickly be secure.   Wisd. vi.

17 For she goeth about seeking such as are worthy of her, and she sheweth herself to them cheerfully in the ways, and meeteth them with all providence.

18 For the beginning of her is the most true desire of discipline.

19 And the care of discipline is love: and love is the keeping of her laws: and the keeping of her laws is the firm foundation of incorruption.

20 And incorruption bringeth near to God.

21 Therefore the desire of wisdom bringeth to the everlasting kingdom.

25 The root of wisdom is to fear the Lord: and the branches thereof are long lived.   Ecclus. i.

33 Son, if thou desire wisdom, keep justice, and God will give her to thee.

7 . . . Foolish men shall not see her: for she is far from pride and deceit.   Ecclus. xv.

8 Lying men shall not be mindful of her: but men that speak truth shall be found with her, and shall advance, even till they come to the sight of God.

2 Who will set scourges over my thoughts, and the discipline of wisdom over my heart, that they spare me not in their ignorances, and that their sins may not appear: Ecclus. xxiii.

3 Lest my ignorances increase, and my offences be multiplied, and my sins abound . . .

15 There is a wisdom that aboundeth in evils . . . . Ecclus. xxi.

6 For the wisdom of the flesh is death: but the wisdom of the spirit is life and peace. Rom. viii.

7 Because the wisdom of the flesh is an enemy to God: for it is not subject to the law of God, neither can it be.

21 . . . The world by wisdom knew not God . . . 1 Cor. i.

2 I judged not myself to know any thing among you, but Jesus Christ, and him crucified. 1 Cor. ii.

3 In whom are hid all the treasures of wisdom and knowledge. Coloss. ii.

18 Let no man deceive himself: if any man among you seem to be wise in this world, let him become a fool, that he may be wise. 1 Cor. iii.

19 For the wisdom of this world is foolishness with God ...

1 ... Knowledge puffeth up :* but charity edifieth.   1 Cor. viii.

6 Howbeit we speak wisdom among the perfect: yet not the wisdom of this world, neither of the princes of this world, that come to nought.   1 Cor. ii.

5 If any of you want wisdom, let him ask of God, who giveth to all abundantly, and upbraideth not : and it shall be given him.   S. James i.

13 Who is a wise man, and endued with knowledge among you? Let him show, by a good conversation, his work in the meekness of wisdom.   S. James iii.

WORD OF GOD.

3 ... Not in bread alone doth man live, but in every word that proceedeth from the mouth of God.   Deut. viii.

18 Lay up these my words in your hearts and minds, and hang them for a sign on your hands, and place them between your eyes.   Deut. xi.

19 Teach your children that they meditate on them, when thou sittest in thy house, and when thou walkest on the way, and when thou liest down and risest up.

* Knowledge without charity and humility serveth only to puff persons up.

9 ... Thou shalt teach them to thy sons Deut. iv.
and to thy grandsons.

11 Thy words have I hidden in my heart, Ps.
that I may not sin against thee. cxviii.

18 Open thou my eyes: and I will consider the wondrous things of thy law.

162 I will rejoice at thy words, as one that hath found great spoil.

105 Thy word is a lamp to my feet, and a light to my paths.

130 The declaration of thy words giveth light: and giveth understanding to little ones.

133 Direct my steps according to thy word: and let no iniquity have dominion over me.

13 Be meek to hear the word, that thou Ecclus.
mayest understand: and return a true answer v.
with wisdom.

16 Search ye diligently in the book of the Isaias
Lord, and read. xxxiv.

16 Thy words were found, and I did eat Jer. xv.
them, and thy word was to me a joy and gladness of my heart: for thy name is called upon me, O Lord God of hosts.

29 Are not my words as a fire, saith the Jer. xxiii.
Lord: and as a hammer that breaketh the rock in pieces.

6 I have manifested thy name to the men S. John
whom thou hast given me out of the world. xvii.

Thine they were, and to me thou gavest them: and they have kept thy word.

14 I have given them thy word . . .

17 Sanctify them in truth. Thy word is truth.

28 . . . Blessed are they who hear the word of God, and keep it. — S. Luke xi.

45 Then he opened their understanding, that they might understand the scriptures. — S. Luke xxiv.

32 And they said one to the other: Was not our heart burning within us, whilst he spoke in the way, and opened to us the scriptures?

31 These are written that you may believe that Jesus is the Christ the Son of God: and that believing you may have life in his name. — S. John xx.

30 . . . Thinkest thou that thou understandest what thou readest? — Acts viii.

31 How can I, unless some man show me? . . .

35 Then Philip opening his mouth, and beginning at this scripture,* preached unto him Jesus.

20 . . . No prophecy of scripture is made by private interpretation. — 2 S. Peter i.

16 . . . In which are certain things hard to be understood, which the unlearned and — 2 S. Peter iii.

---

* Isaias liii. 7.

unstable wrest, as they do also the other scriptures, to their own destruction.

22 Be ye doers of the word, and not hearers only, deceiving your own selves. — S. James i.

4 For what things soever were written, were written for our learning: that through patience and comfort of the scriptures we might have hope. — Rom. xv.

15 From thy infancy thou hast known the holy scriptures, which can instruct thee to salvation, by faith which is in Christ Jesus. — 2 Tim. iii.

16 All scripture,* inspired of God, is profitable to teach, to reprove, to correct, to instruct in justice,

17 That the man of God may be perfect, furnished to every good work.

11 If any man speak, let him speak as the words of God . . . — 1 S. Peter iv.

1 My little children, these things I write to you that you may not sin . . . — 1 S. John ii.

2 For if the word, spoken by angels, became steadfast, and every transgression and — Heb. ii.

* Every part of divine Scripture is certainly profitable for all these ends. But, if we would have the whole rule of Christian faith and practice, we must not be content with those Scriptures which Timothy knew from his infancy, that is, with the Old Testament alone; nor yet with the New Testament, without taking along with it the traditions of the apostles, and the interpretation of the church, to which the apostles delivered both the book and the true meaning of it.

disobedience received a just recompense of reward:

3 How shall we escape if we neglect so great salvation? which having begun to be declared by the Lord, was confirmed unto us by them that heard him.

WORK.

15 AND the Lord God took man, and put him into the paradise of pleasure, to dress it, and to keep it. — Gen. ii.

19 In the sweat of thy face shalt thou eat bread till thou return to the earth, out of which thou was taken... — Gen. iii.

23 And the Lord God sent him out of the paradise of pleasure, to till the earth from which he wast taken.

16 ... Arise then, and be doing, and the Lord will be with thee. — 1 Paralip. xxii.

11 ... If thou be diligent, thy harvest shall come as a fountain, and want shall flee far from thee. — Prov. vi.

4 ... The hand of the industrious getteth riches. — Prov. x.

4 ... The soul of them that work, shall be made fat. — Prov. xiii.

23 In much work there shall be abundance: but where there are many words, there is oftentimes want. — Prov. xiv.

10 Whatsoever thy hand is able to do, do it earnestly ...   Eccles. ix.

16 Hate not laborious works, nor husbandry ordained by the most High.   Ecclus. vii.

35 I have shewed you all things, how that so labouring you ought to support the weak ...   Acts xx.

17 ... Provide things good, not only in the sight of God, but also in the sight of men.   Rom. xii.

11 Use your endeavour to be quiet, that you do your own business, and work with your own hands, as we commanded you; and that you walk honestly towards them that are without; and that you want nothing of any man's.   1 Thess. iv.

12 We labour, working with our own hands ...   1 Cor. iv.

8 Neither did we eat any man's bread for nothing, but in labour and in toil we worked night and day, lest we should be chargeable to any of you.   2 Thess. iii.

9 Not as if we had not power; but that we might give ourselves a pattern to you to imitate us.

10 For also, when we were with you, we declared this to you: that, if any man will not work, neither let him eat.

11 For we have heard that there are some among you who walk disorderly, working not at all, but curiously meddling.

12 Now we charge them that are such, and beseech them by the Lord Jesus Christ, that, working with silence they would eat their own bread.

3 ... His servants shall serve him.   Apoc. xxii.

WORLD.

10 HE was in the world, and the world was made by him, and the world knew him not.   S. John i.

3 O ye sons of men, how long will you be dull of heart? why do you love vanity, and seek after lying?   Ps. iv.

2 Why do you spend money for that which is not bread, and your labour for that which doth not satisfy you? ...   Isaias lv.

12 Yea and they have counted our life a pastime, and the business of life to be gain, and that we must be getting every way, even out of evil.   Wisd. xv.

4 ... They trust in a mere nothing, and speak vanities ...   Isaias lix.

4 Riches make many friends: but from the poor man, even they whom he had, depart.   Prov. xix.

6 Many honour the person of him that is mighty, and are friends of him that giveth gifts.

7 The brethren of the poor man hate

him: moreover his friends have departed far from him.

28 The rich man spoke, and all held their peace, and what he said they extol even to the clouds. — Ecclus. xiii.

29 The poor man spoke, and they say: Who is this? and if he stumble, they will overthrow him.

30 . . . Poverty is very wicked,' in the mouth of the ungodly.

25 . . . Wo to you that laugh now: for you shall mourn and weep. — S. Luke vi.

26 Wo to you when men shall bless you: for according to these things did their fathers to the false prophets.

44 How can you believe, who receive glory one from another: and the glory which is from God alone, you do not seek. — S. John v.

26 What doth it profit a man, if he gain the whole world and lose his own soul? . . . — S. Matt. xvi.

30 . . . The prince of this world cometh, and in me he hath not any thing. — S. John xiv.

18 If the world hate you, know ye that it hated me before you. — S. John xv.

19 If you had been of the world: the world would love its own: but because you are not of the world, but I have chosen you out of the world, therefore the world hateth you.

24 . . . But now have they both seen and hated both me and my Father.

25 . . . They have hated me without cause.

33 These things have I spoken to you, that in me you may have peace. In the world you shall have distress : but have confidence ; I have overcome the world.   S. John xvi.

5 And now glorify thou me, O Father, with thyself, with the glory which I had with thee, before the world was.   S. John xvii.

9 . . . I pray not for the world, but for them whom thou hast given me, because they are thine :

14 I have given them thy word : and the world hath hated them, because they are not of the world : as I also am not of the world.

15 I do not ask that thou take them away out of the world, but that thou preserve them from evil.

16 They are not of the world : as I also am not of the world.

18 As thou hast sent me into the world, I also have sent them into the world.

25 Just Father, the world hath not known thee : but I have known thee : and these have known, that thou hast sent me.

2 Be not conformed to this world : but be reformed in the newness of your mind, that you may prove what is the good, and the acceptable, and the perfect will of God.   Rom. xii.

World.

18 While we look not at the things which are seen, but at the things which are not seen. For the things which are seen, are temporal: but the things which are not seen, are eternal. — 2 Cor. iv.

3 Grace be to you and peace from God the Father, and from our Lord Jesus Christ. — Gal. i.

4 Who gave himself for our sins, that he might deliver us from this present wicked world, according to the will of God and our Father.

10 Do I now persuade men, or God? Or do I seek to please men? If I yet pleased men, I should not be the servant of Christ.

4 Know you not that the friendship of this world, is the enemy of God? Whosoever, therefore, will be a friend of this world, becometh an enemy of God. — S. James iv.

13 Let us go forth therefore to him without the camp; bearing his reproach.* — Heb. xiii.

14 For here we have no permanent city: but we seek one to come.

15 Love not the world, nor those things which are in the world. If any man love the world, the charity of the Father is not in him. — 1 S. John ii.

* That is, bearing His cross. It is an exhortation to them to be willing to suffer with Christ, reproaches, persecutions, and even death, if they desire to partake of the benefits of His suffering for man's redemption.

16 For all that is in the world, is the concupiscence of the flesh, and the concupiscence of the eyes, and the pride of life, which is not of the Father, but is of the world.

17 In this is the charity of God perfected with us, that we may have confidence in the day of judgment: because as he is, we also are in this world. — 1 S. John iv.

4 Whatsoever is born of God, overcometh the world: and this is the victory that overcometh the world, our faith. — 1 S. John v.

5 Who is he that overcometh the world, but he that believeth that Jesus is the Son of God?

YOUTH.

10 ... Youth and pleasure are vain. — Eccles. xi.

1 Remember thy Creator in the days of thy youth, before the time of affliction come, and the years draw nigh of which thou shalt say: They please me not. — Eccles. xii.

5 The things that thou hast not gathered in thy youth, how shalt thou find them in thy old age? — Eccles. xxv.

16 The just that is dead, condemneth the wicked that are living, and youth soon ended, the long life of the unjust. — Wisd. iv.

Youth.

13 Being made perfect in a short space, he fulfilled a long time.

14 For his soul pleased God: therefore he hastened to bring him out of the midst of iniquities: but the people see this, and understand not, nor lay up such things in their hearts.

ZEAL.

33 ... I WILL not eat till I tell my message ...   Gen. xxiv.

12 ... Behold! I give (Phineas) the peace of my covenant,   Numb. xxv.

13 And the covenant of the priesthood for ever shall be both to him and his seed, because he hath been zealous for his God, and hath made atonement for the wickedness of the children of Israel.

139 My zeal hath made me pine away: because my enemies forgot thy words.   Ps. cxviii.

158 I beheld the transgressors, and I pined away; because they kept not thy word.

50 I have a baptism, wherewith I am to be baptized: and how am I straitened until it be accomplished?   S. Luke xii.

13 And the pasch of the Jews was at hand, and Jesus went up to Jerusalem: S. John ii.

14 And he found in the temple those that

sold oxen and sheep and doves, and the changers of money sitting.

15 And when he had made as it were a scourge of little cords, he drove them all out of the temple, the sheep also and the oxen, and he poured out the changers' money; and the tables he overthrew.

16 And he said to them that sold doves: Take these things hence; and make not the house of my Father a house of traffic.

17 And his disciples remembered that it was written: The zeal of thy house hath eaten me up.

18 Be zealous for that which is good in a good thing always ...   Gal. iv.

19 Whereas I was free as to all, I made myself the servant of all: that I might gain more persons.   1 Cor. ix.

20 And I became to the Jews a Jew, that I might gain the Jews.

22 To the weak I became weak, that I might gain the weak. I became all things to all men, that I might save all.

23 And I do all things for the gospels' sake: that I may be made partaker thereof.

24 Know you not that they that run in the race, all run indeed, but one receiveth the prize? so run that you may obtain.

10 Therefore I endure all things for the sake of the elect, that they also may obtain   2 Tim. ii.

the salvation, which is in Christ Jesus, with heavenly glory.

13 Who is he that can hurt you, if you be zealous of good ?   1 S. Peter iii.

14 But if you have bitter zeal, and there be contentions in your hearts ; glory not, and be not liars against the truth.   S. James iii.

15 For this is not wisdom, descending from above ; but is earthly, sensual, diabolical.

15 I know thy works, that thou art neither cold, nor hot. I would thou wert cold, or hot: Apoc. iii.

16 But because thou art lukewarm, and neither cold, nor hot, I will begin to vomit thee out of my mouth.

19 Those whom I love, I rebuke and chastise. Be zealous, therefore, and do penance.

INDEX.

	Page
Acknowledgment of Sin	1
Affliction	4
Almsgiving	11
Ambition	18
Angels	20
Anger	22
Avoid Evil Companionship	24
Backsliders	28
Blessed Virgin	30
Blessings of God's Servants	35
Blessings of God's Teaching	38
Calling (General)—see Vocation (Religious)	40
Calumny	42
Carnal Mind	43
Charity, or Love to Neighbour	45
Charity to Neighbour (Further Duties and Counsels of)	50
Children (Duties of)	53
Childhood (Duties towards)	56
Christ our Life	57

Index. 535

	Page
Church (Pastors)	61
Church (Duties of the Faithful)	70
Commandments	75
Confidence in God	83
Content	84
Contention	85
Conversion	87
Covetousness	91
Death	95
Deceit and Lying	101
Despair	103
Detachment	104
Detraction	104
Discouragement	107
Disobedience	108
Divine Threatenings	109
Duty towards Rulers	117
Envy	118
Example of Christ	120
Excuses in Sins	125
Exhortation to Kings and Princes	126
,, Masters	128
,, Men	129
,, Parents	129
,, Priests	132
,, Women	136
Faith	138
Family Union	142
Fasting	143
Fatherless and Widows	145
Fear of God	149

	Page
Flattery	153
Fools	155
Forgiveness of Injuries	157
Fraternal Reproof	160
Fraternal Sympathy	162
Friendship	163
General Precepts and Exhortation	166
God...	171
God (Compassion of)	175
,, Creator	177
God's Hatred	180
God's Love	182
God (Mercy of)	186
,, (Presence of)	188
God our Protector	189
,, (Providence of)	190
God our Strength	192
,, (Truth of)	194
Good Counsel	195
Good Example and Edification	197
Good Works	198
Grace	202
Hatred	205
Hatred of Reproof	207
Hatred of Sin	208
Heaven	209
Hell	214
Holiness of Conduct	215
Holy Communion	218
Holy Joy	225
Holy Spirit Indwelling	227
Hope	231

Index.

	Page
Hospitality	233
Human Respect	234
Humility	236
Hypocrisy	239
Ignorance of God	242
Ignorance of and Uncertainty of Future Events	244
Indiscretion	245
Ingratitude	246
Ingratitude to God	246
Innocence	249
Intemperance	249
Jesus Saviour	252
Judge not...	257
Just Judgments of God	259
Justice	264
Last Judgment	264
Lending and Borrowing	269
Liberality	272
Love of Gain	273
,, to God	275
,, of Instruction	279
,, of Rule	280
Magistrates	280
Malice	281
Man Regenerate and Renewed	282
Marriage	286
Meditation	289
Meekness and Gentleness	292
Mercy	294
Modesty	296

	Page
Mortification and Self-Denial	296
Murder	298
Murmuring	299
Nation's Happiness and Wo	300
Obedience	303
Obedience to Christ's Word	305
Old Age	307
Pardon of Sin	307
Patience	311
Patient Endurance	313
Payments and Wages	314
Peace	316
Penance	319
Perfection	320
Persecution	323
Perseverance	327
Perverse Mind	329
Piety and Desire of Holiness	329
Pleasures and Amusements (Evils of Vain)	331
Poverty	333
Praise of God	335
Praise (Call to)	340
Praise to God	350
Prayer to God	359
Presumption	368
Pride	369
Promises	372
Promises of Men	378
Prosperity of the Wicked	379
Prudence	384
Purgatory	385

Index.

	Page
Purity	388
Religious Courage	391
Renouncing ourselves and all things for Christ	393
Repentance and Contrition	395
Resignation	397
Resistance to the Holy Spirit	398
Resurrection	400
Revenge	404
Reviling	406
Riches	407
Sadness	411
Saints	412
Saints (Communion of)	415
Salvation	418
Satan	420
Scandal	423
Scorn and Contempt	425
Scruples	426
Seek God	429
Self-Delusion	430
Selfishness	432
Self-will and Obstinacy	433
Servants	435
Sickness	437
Silence	441
Simplicity	442
Sin	443
Sincerity of Heart	447
Singleness of Intention	448
Sloth!	449
Spiritual Life	450
Strangers	452
Superstition	453

	Page
Swearing ...	454
Tale Bearer	456
Temperance	457
Tempt not God...	458
Temptation	458
Thanksgiving ...	461
Theft	464
Time	467
Tongue ...	469
Trials	475
Troubles of Life	478
Trust in God	480
Trust in Man Vain	482
Truth	483
Unbelievers	485
Unholy Fear	490
Union with God	491
Unjust Man	493
Unselfishness	494
Vanity or Vain Glory	495
Vocation (Religious) ...	497
Vows	501
War	502
War (Aggressive)	504
Watching...	505
Wicked (Character of)	507
Wicked (End of the) ...	510
Will of God	514
Wisdom ...	516
Word of God	520

Index.

	Page
Work	524
World	526
Youth	530
Zeal	531

THE END.

R. WASHBOURNE, 18A, PATERNOSTER ROW, LONDON.

[ADVERTISEMENT.]

Foolscap 8vo., 550 pp., cloth, 5s.

MAXIMS
OF THE
KINGDOM OF HEAVEN.

Extract and Notices of the Press.

"A collection of passages from the Holy Scriptures put into my hands by the Compiler to carry through the Press. I could not but gladly avail myself of the opportunity, which a friend thus presented to me, of having a share, however small, in a work directed in so pious a spirit towards the promotion among Catholics of an habitual reverent meditation, upon the Sacred Words of Him who spoke 'as man never did speak.'"—J. H. N.

"The contents of the volume are simply texts from Scripture arranged under heads, so as to bring passages of the same import together for the purposes of reflection and meditation. We have no doubt that this carefully compiled work will be found highly useful."—*The Month.*

"The collection is one calculated to do much good by familiarizing us with words of Holy Writ, and assisting us to apply them practically to ourselves and to our needs. Besides this, the work will prove useful as being one in which may be found collected passages on particular subjects for introducing into sermons, or for similar purposes."—*Westminster Gazette.*

"A most invaluable help and guide to meditation, bears the Imprimatur of the Archbishop of Westminster, as well as a short Introductory Notice, to which are attached the well-known initials J. H. N. With such testimonials it would not only be useless, but also presumptuous in us to say more in favour of such a praiseworthy compilation."—*The Tablet.*

"The work is one of an eminently devout kind. The Maxims are very carefully selected, exceedingly well-arranged, and are not only Catholic and devotional in themselves, but are eminently calculated to promote the study of the sacred books from which they have been gathered. This work only requires to be known in order to find a place amongst the devotional books of every English-spoken Catholic."—*The Weekly Register.*

London: R. WASHBOURNE, 18A, PATERNOSTER ROW.

BOOKS PUBLISHED BY R. WASHBOURNE.

Life of S. Francis of Assisi. Fcap. 8vo., cloth, 3s.

Annals of the Tractarian Movement, from the year 1842 to 1860. By E. G. K. Browne, late Protestant Curate of Bawdsey, Suffolk. *Fourth Edition.* 8vo., cloth 4s.

Anglican Orders. By the Very Rev. John Canon Williams. *Second Edition.* Crown 8vo., cloth, 3s. 6d.

Anglican Prejudices Examined by the Written Word. 18mo., cloth, 1s.

Bishop Challoner's "Grounds of the Catholic Doctrine." 18mo., cloth, 4d.

Catholic Biographical Library.
>   **His Holiness Pope Pius IX.** 1s. 6d.
>   **His Eminence Cardinal Wiseman.** 1s.
>   **The Count de Montalembert.** 6d.

Bishop Milner's Devotion to the Sacred Heart. 32mo., wrapper, 3d.; cloth, 6d.; gilt, 1s.

The Little Office of the Immaculate Conception, in Latin and English. By the Very Rev. Provost Husenbeth, D.D. Pocket size, 6d.

The Life of our Lord Commemorated in the Mass; a Method of assisting at the Holy Sacrifice. By Edward G. Bashawe, Priest of the Oratory of St. Philip Neri. 32mo., 3d., cloth 4d., roan 1s., imitation morocco 1s. 6d., calf or morocco 2s. 6d.

Following of Christ. Edited by the Right Rev. Dr. Challoner. Pocket Edition, 1s., roan 2s., imitation morocco 2s. 6d., calf or morocco 4s. 6d.

Crusade against Drunkenness. By the Rev. Fr. Richardson. 1d.
>   **Little by Little, or the Penny Bank.**
>   **Rainy Day—Guild of Our Lady.** 2d.

₊ *A large Reduction to Priests, using Numbers.*

London: R. WASHBOURNE, 18A, PATERNOSTER ROW.

R. WASHBOURNE'S CATALOGUE.

JULY 1872.

New Books.

The Confessional Unmasked; or the Revelations. A Farce in Two Acts. Adapted from "Shandy Maguire," by San Columbano. *In the Press.*

The Reverse of the Medal. A Drama in Four Acts, for young ladies. Translated from the French. *In the Press.*

Ernscliff Hall: or, Two Days Spent with a Great-Aunt. A Drama in Three Acts, for young ladies. Translated from the French. *In the Press.*

Filiola. A Drama in Four Acts, for young ladies. Translated from the French. *In the Press.*

Maxims of the Kingdom of Heaven. New and enlarged Edition. *In the Press.*

Margarethe Verflassen. A Picture from the Catholic Church. Translated from the German by Mrs. Smith Sligo. Fcap. 8vo. 3s.; gilt, 3s. 6d.

Chats about the Rosary: or, Aunt Margaret's Little Neighbours. By Skelton Yorke. Fcap. 8vo. 3s.

Sancti Alphonsi Doctoris Officium Parvum—Novena and Little Office in honour of St. Alphonsus Liguori. Fcap. 8vo. 1s.; cloth, 2s.; cloth bevilled, red edges, 3s.

Contemplations on the Most Holy Sacrament of the Altar, drawn from the Sacred Scriptures. 18mo. 2s.

The Hawthorn. A Magazine of Essays, Sketches, and Reviews. Monthly, 8vo., price 1s.

R. Washbourne, 18a, Paternoster Row, London.

Life of Our Lord Commemorated in the Mass; a Method of Assisting at the Holy Sacrifice. By Edward G. Bagshawe, Priest of the Oratory of St. Philip Neri. 32mo. 3d.; cloth, 4d.; roan, 1s.; French morocco, 1s. 6d.; calf or morocco, 2s. 6d.

"In following and uniting with the Priest as he recites the prayers of the Missal, Fr. Bagshawe's 'Life of our Lord' will prove a great help."—*Tablet*.

Conversion of the Teutonic Race—Conversion of the French and the English. By Mrs. Hope. Edited by the Rev. Fr. Dalgairns. Crown 8vo. 6s.

Sequel to the Conversion of the Teutonic Race—St. Boniface and the Conversion of Germany. By Mrs. Hope, with a Preface by the Rev. Father Dalgairns. Crown 8vo. 6s.

The Life of the Blessed Virgin. Translated from the French of Orsini by the Very Rev. Dr. Husenbeth. Illustrated. Crown 8vo. 3s. 6d.

Devotion to Our Lady in North America. By the Rev. Xavier Donald Macleod. 8vo. 7s. 6d.

A General Catechism of the Christian Doctrine. By the Right Rev. Dr. Poirier, Bishop of Roseau, West Indies. 18mo. 9d.

Monastic Legends. By E. G. K. Browne. 8vo 6d.

A Homely Discourse; Mary Magdalen. Cr. 8vo. 6d.

On the Spirit in which Scientific Studies should be pursued, with Remarks on the Darwinian Theory of Evolution. By Mr. George Richardson. 8vo. 6d.

Diary of a Confessor of the Faith. 12mo. 1s.

Following of Christ. Small pocket edition, with initial letters (old style). 1s.; roan, 2s.; French morocco, 2s. 6d.; calf or morocco, 4s.

Manual of Catholic Piety. A Selection of Fervent Prayers, Pious Reflections and Solid Instructions adapted to every state of life. Green border edition. French mor., 3s. 6d.; calf or mor., 5s.

Men and Women of the English Reformation, from the days of Wolsey to the death of Cranmer. By S. H. Burke. 2 vols. crown 8vo., 13s.

"It contains a great amount of curious and useful information, gathered together with evident care."—*Dublin Review.* "Interesting and valuable. The author has hit on the true way of writing history attractively, by making it a series of biographies connected together and mutually interdependent."—*Tablet.* "The author produces evidence that cannot be gainsayed."—*Universe.* "Full of interest, and very temperately written."—*Church Review.* "Able, fairly impartial, and likely to be of considerable value to the student of history. Replete with information."—*Church Times.* "The book supplies many hitherto unknown facts of the times of which it is a history."—*Church Opinion.* "A clever and well-written historical statement of facts concerning the chief actors of our so-called Reformation."—*The Month.* "Ought to find, as it deserves, many readers."—*Weekly Register.* "Its author gives us the honest truth, relies upon none but the most authentic documents." —*Belfast Northern Star.* "Mr. Burke's enthralling Biographical Dictionary."—*Illustrated Review.* "It is, in truth, the only dispassionate record of a much contested epoch we have ever read." —*Cosmopolitan.* "It is very interesting, and though written in the Roman interest, it seems on the whole fair and tolerably trustworthy." *Church Times.* "It is so forcibly, but truthfully written, that it should be in the hands of every seeker after truth."—*Catholic Opinion.*—"On all hands admitted to be one of the most valuable historical works ever published."—*Nation.*

Washbourne's Edition of the "Garden of the Soul," in medium-sized type. Cloth 9d.; roan, 1s.; with rims and clasp, 1s. 6d. French morocco, 2s.; with rims and clasp, 2s. 6d. French morocco extra, 2s. 6d.; with rims and clasp, 3s. Calf or morocco, 4s.; with rims and clasp, 5s. 6d. Calf or morocco extra, 5s.; with rims and clasp, 6s. 6d. Velvet, with rims and clasp, 8s. and 10s. 6d. Russia, antique, with clasp, 12s. 6d. Ivory, 15s. and 21s. The above can be had with Epistles and Gospels, 6d. extra. The Epistles and Gospels in cloth, 6d.

"This is one of the best editions we have seen of one of the best of all our Prayer Books. It is well printed in clear large type, on good paper."—*Catholic Opinion.* "A very complete arrangement of this which is emphatically the Prayer Book of every Catholic household. It is as cheap as it is good, and we heartily recommend it."—*Universe.*

Religious Reading.

Complete Works of Saint John of the Cross. Translated from the original Spanish by David Lewis, Esq., M.A. 2 vols. 8vo. 21s. cash.

Meditations of the Veni Sancte Spiritus. 1s. or 9d. cash.

Louise Lateau, the Ecstatica of Bois d'Haine. Her Life, Stigmata, and Ecstacies. By Dr. Lefebvre. Translated from the French by T. S. Shepard. Fcap. 8vo. 2s. Cheap edition, 6d.

Spiritual Works of Louis of Blois, Abbot of Liesse. Edited by John Edward Bowden, Priest of the Oratory of St. Philip Neri. Fcap. 8vo. 3s. 6d; red edges, 4s.

"No more important or welcome addition could have been made to our English ascetical literature than this little book. The writings of Blosius are especially suited for popular reading. It is a model of good translation. Conscientiously faithful to the original, it is at the same time excellent English. The translator has succeeded even in transferring the sweet, earnest style of the author into our own language, without any trace of Latinism."—*Dublin Review.* "This handy little volume will certainly become a favourite. We do not hesitate, therefore, strongly to recommend these well-chosen selections from the works of the great spiritual writer of Blois."—*Tablet.* "Elegant and flowing."—*Weekly Register.* "Most useful of meditations."—*Catholic Opinion.*

Heaven Opened by the Practice of Frequent Confession and Communion. By M. l'Abbé Favre. Translated from the French, carefully revised by a Father of the Society of Jesus. Second Edition. Fcap. 8vo. 3s. 6d. ; red edges, 4s.

"This beautiful little book of devotion. We may recommend it to the clergy as well as to the laity."—*Tablet.* "The treatment of the subject is so clear as to be intelligible to all, whilst the simplicity and methodical arrangement of its contents are beyond all praise. It is filled with quotations from the Holy Scriptures, the Fathers, and the Councils of the Church, and thus will be found of material assistance to the clergy, as a storehouse of doctrinal and ascetical authorities on the two great sacraments of Holy Eucharist and Penance."—*Weekly Register.* "A work on the most important subject of Christian faith and practice."—*Church Herald.*

One Hundred Pious Reflections. Extracted from Alban Butler's "Lives of the Saints." 18mo. cloth, red edges, 2s.; cheap edition, 1s.

"A happy idea. The author of 'The Lives of the Saints' had a way of breathing into his language the unction and force which carries the truth of the Gospel into the heart. As to commending the little work, though the name of Alban Butler commends itself, yet I shall not fail to draw attention to the usefulness of this selection."—*Letter to the Editor from* THE RIGHT REV. DR. ULLATHORNE, BISHOP OF BIRMINGHAM. "Well selected, sufficiently short, and printed in good bold type."—*Tablet.* "Nothing could be better. Good, sound practical reflections."—*Church Herald.*

Following of Christ. Small pocket edition, with initial letters (old style). 1s.; roan, 2s; French morocco, 2s. 6d.; calf or morocco, 4s.

The Book of Perpetual Adoration; or, the Love of Jesus in the most Holy Sacrament of the Altar. By Mgr. Boudon. Edited by the Rev. J. Redman, D.D. Fcap. 8vo. 3s. *In the Press.*

Cistercian Order: its Mission and Spirit. Comprising the Life of S. Robert of Newminster, and the Life of S. Robert of Knaresborough. By the author of "Cistercian Legends." Crown 8vo. 3s. 6d.

The Monitor of the Association of Prayer. Monthly, 1d. Subscription 1s. 6d. a year, post free. Notices, 6s. 1000. Prints, 7s. 6d. 1000. Zelator's Cards, 10s. 1000.

Cistercian Legends of the 13th Century. Translated from the Latin by the Rev. Henry Collins. 3s.

"A number of interesting records of Cistercian sanctity and cloistral experience, which remind us forcibly of the illustrations in the 'Christian Perfection of Rodriguez.'"—*Dublin Review.* "A casquet of jewels. We commend them to all our readers, and most of all to Religious."—*Weekly Register.* "Most beautiful legends, full of deep spiritual reading."—*Tablet.* "Well translated, and beautifully got up."—*Month.* "A compilation of anecdotes, full of heavenly wisdom."—*Catholic Opinion.*

Holy Readings. Short Selections from well-known Authors. By J. R. Digby-Beste, Esq. 32mo. cloth, 2s.; cloth, red edges, 2s. 6d.; roan, 3s.; morocco, 5s. [See "Catholic Hours," p. 16.]

Conversion of the Teutonic Race : Conversion of the Franks and the English. By Mrs. Hope, author of "Early Martyrs." Edited by the Rev. Father Dalgairns. Crown 8vo. 6s.

"It is good in itself, possessing considerable literary merit ; it fills up a blank, which has never yet been occupied, to the generality of readers ; and lastly, and beyond all, it forms one of the few Catholic books brought out in this country which are not translations or adaptations."—*Dublin Review.* "It is a great thing to find a writer of a book of this class so clearly grasping, and so boldly setting forth truths, which, familiar as they are to scholars, are still utterly unknown —or, worse than unknown, utterly misconceived—by most of the writers of our smaller literature."—*Saturday Review.* "It bids fair to be a very valuable book . . . . Mrs. Hope has compiled an original history, which gives constant evidence of great erudition, and sound historical judgment. The latter part of the volume, which gives us a capital sketch of the first Christian centuries of our own race, has a special claim on our attention, and the subject is well arranged. We trust to see the work become very popular."—*Month.* "This is a most taking book : it is solid history and romance in one."—*Catholic Opinion.* "It is carefully, and in many parts beautifully written."—*Universe.*

Sequel to the Conversion of the Teutonic Race—St. Boniface, and the Conversion of Germany. By Mrs. Hope. Edited, with a Preface, by the Rev. Fr. Dalgairns. Crown 8vo. 6s.

St. Peter; his Name and his Office as set forth in Holy Scripture. By T. W. Allies. *Second Edition.* Revised. Crown 8vo. 5s.

"A standard work. There is no single book in English, on the Catholic side, which contains the Scriptural argument about St. Peter and the Papacy so clearly or conclusively put."—*Month.* "An admirable volume."—*The Universe.* "This valuable work." —*Weekly Register.* "There is in this volume, written in a pure style, with a clear and logical arrangement of its arguments, much which will afford agreeable reading to every lover of truth and learning."—*Belfast Weekly Observer.* "A second edition, with a new and very touching preface."—*Dublin Review.*

Dr. Pusey's Eirenicon considered in Relation to Catholic Unity. By H. N. Oxenham. *Second Edition.* 8vo. 2s. 6d.

BY THE POOR CLARES OF KENMARE.

Jesus and Jerusalem; or, the Way Home. A book for Spiritual Reading. Fcap. 8vo. 4s. 6d.

Meditations for Advent and Easter. Fcap. 8vo. 3s. 6d.

The Spouse of Christ—Vol. I.—her Privileges and her Duties. Crown 8vo. 7s. 6d. Vol. II.—her Duties and her Privileges. *In preparation.*

The Ecclesiastical Year. Fcap. 4s. 6d.; calf, 6s. 6d.

Visits to the Crib, 6d.; The Living Crib, 2d.; How to Spend a Holy Lent, 4d.; Child's Book for Lent, 4d.; Little Book of the Lovers of the Heart of Jesus Crucified, 4d.; Month of Reparation to the Heart of Love, 4d.; Child's Month of the Sacred Heart, 4d.; Association of Our Lady of the Sacred Heart, 6d.

Synodi Diœceseos Suthwarcensis ad ejusdem erectione anno 1850 ad finem anni 1868 habitæ. 8vo. cloth, 7s. 6d.; 1869-70, 1s.

Sancti Alphonsi Doctoris Officium Parvum—Novena and Little Office in honour of St. Alphonsus. Fcap. 8vo. 1s.; cloth, 2s.; cloth extra, 3s.

"It will be very popular amongst those who have a devotion to the last made Doctor of the Church. The Hymns in the English portion of the book are thoroughly devotional, and expressed in the choicest and most poetical language."—*Weekly Register.*

Great Truths in Little Words. By Fr. Rawes. 6d.

Diary of a Confessor of the Faith. 12mo. 1s.

A New Miracle at Rome; through the Intercession of Blessed John Berchmans. 2d.

Cure of Blindness; through the Intercession of Our Lady and St. Ignatius. 2d.

The Directorium Asceticum; or, Guide to the Spiritual Life. By Scaramelli. Translated and Edited at St. Beuno's College. 4 vols. crown 8vo. 24s.

Annals of the Tractarian Movement, from 1842 to 1867. By E. G. K. Browne. 2s. 6d.; cloth, 4s.

Eight Short Sermon Essays. By Dr. Redmond. 1s.
Non Possumus; or, the Temporal Sovereignty of the Popes, and the Roman Question. By Father Lockhart. 1s.
Secession or Schism. By Fr. Lockhart. 6d.
Who is the Anti-Christ of Prophecy? By the Rev. Fr. Lockhart. 1s.
The Communion of Saints; or, the Catholic Doctrine concerning and in relation to the Blessed Virgin, the Angels, and Saints. By Father Lockhart. 1s.; cloth, 1s. 6d.
The Church of England and its Defenders. By the Rev. W. R. Bernard Brownlow. 8vo. 6d.
The Jesuits and their Accusers. 2d.
Nationalities. By W. Chadson. 8vo. 3d.
Anti-Janus. A Reply to Janus; or, the Pope and the Council. By Dr. Hergenröther. Translated by Prof. Robertson. Crown 8vo. 6s.
The Knight of the Faith. By the Rev. Dr. Laing.
1. A Favourite Fallacy about Private Judgment and Inquiry. 1d.
2. Catholic not Roman Catholic. 4d.
3. Rationale of the Mass. 1s.
4. Challenge to the Churches of England, Scotland, and all Protestant Denominations. 1d.
5. Absurd Protestant Opinions concerning *Intention*, and Spelling Book of Christian Philosophy. 4d.
Professor Robertson's Lectures on Modern History and Biography. Crown 8vo. cloth, 6s.

BY THE PASSIONIST FATHERS.

The School of Jesus Crucified. 3s. 6d.; morocco, 5s.
The Manual of the Cross and Passion. 32mo. 2s. 6d.
The Manual of the Seven Dolours. 32mo. 1s. 6d.
The Christian Armed. 32mo. 1s. 6d.; mor. 3s. 6d.
Guide to Sacred Eloquence. 2s.
Week sanctified by Devotion to the Sacred Heart. 1d.

The Old Religion; or, how shall we find Primitive Christianity? By Rev. Fr. Lockhart. 8vo. 5s.

BY DR. MANNING, ARCHBISHOP OF WESTMINSTER.

Confidence in God. Fcap. 1s.; cloth, 1s. 6d.
Grounds of Faith. Fcap. 8vo., 1s.
Temporal Sovereignty of the Popes. Fcap. 8vo. 1s.; cloth, 1s. 6d.

Religious Instruction.

The Catechism of Christian Doctrine. Approved for the use of the Faithful in all the Dioceses of England and Wales. Large type edition, printed on superfine paper, in a neat wrapper, 68 pages. Price 1d.; cloth, 2d.

The Catechism, Illustrated with Passages from the Holy Scriptures. Arranged by the Rev. J. B. Bagshawe, with Imprimatur. Crown 8vo. 2s. 6d.

"An excellent idea. The very thing of all others that is needed by many under instruction."—*Tablet.* "We hope that it will produce the desired effect upon teachers as well as learners."—*Catholic Opinion.* "It is a book which will do incalculable good. Our priests will hail with pleasure so valuable a help to their weekly instructions in the Catechism, while in schools its value will be equally recognised."—*Weekly Register.* "A work of great merit."—*Church Herald.* "We can hardly wish for anything better, either in intention or in performance."—*The Month.* "Very valuable."—*Dublin Review.*

A First Sequel to the Catechism. By the Rev. J. Nary. 32mo. 1d.

"It will recommend itself to teachers in Catholic schools as one peculiarly adapted to the use of such children as have mastered the Catechism, and yet have nothing else to fall back upon for higher religious instruction. It will be found a great assistance as well to teachers as to pupils who belong to the higher standards in our Catholic poor schools."—*Weekly Register.*

Dr. Butler's *First* Catechism, ½d.; *Second* Catechism, 1d.; *Third* Catechism, 1½d.

Dr. Doyle's Catechism, 1½d.

Fleury's Historical Catechism. Large edition, 1½d.

Lessons on the Christian Doctrine, 1d.

A General Catechism of the Christian Doctrine. By the Right Rev. Dr. Poirier, Bishop of Roseau, West Indies. 18mo. 9d.

Bible History for the use of Catholic Schools and Families. By the Rev. R. Gilmour. Beautifully Illustrated. 2s.

Catechism made Easy. A Familiar Explanation of "The Catechism of Christian Doctrine." By the Rev. H. Gibson. To be completed in 3 vols. Fcap. 8vo. cloth. Vol. I., 3s. 6d.

A Dogmatic Catechism. By Frassinetti. Translated from the original Italian by the Oblate Fathers of St. Charles. With a Preface by His Grace the Archbishop of Westminster. Fcap. 8vo. 3s.

"We give a few extracts from Frassinetti's work, as samples of its excellent execution."—*Dublin Review.* "Needs no commendation."—*Month.* "The Preface written by the Archbishop of Westminster in hearty approval, is a sufficient recommendation. It will be found useful not only to catechists, but also for the instruction of converts from the middle class of society."—*Tablet.*

The Grounds of Catholic Doctrine. By Dr. Challoner. Large type edition. 18mo. cloth, 4d.

Testimony; or, the Necessity of Enquiry as to Religion. By Henry John Pye, M.A. 4d.; for distribution, 20s. a hundred; cloth, 6d.

"Mr. Pye is particularly plain and straightforward."—*Tablet.* "It is calculated to do much good. We recommend it to the clergy, and think it a most useful work to place in the hands of all who are under instruction."—*Westminster Gazette.* "A thoroughly searching little pamphlet."—*Universe.* "A clever little pamphlet. Each point is treated briefly and clearly."—*Catholic Opinion.*

Protestant Principles Examined by the Written Word. Originally entitled, "The Protestant's Trial by the Written Word." *New edition.* 18mo. 1s.

"An excellent book."—*Church News.* "A good specimen of the concise controversial writing of English Catholics in the early part of the seventeenth century."—*Catholic Opinion.* "A little book which might be consulted profitably by any Catholic."—*Church Times.* "A clever little manual."—*Westminster Gazette.* "A useful little volume."—*The Month.* "An excellent little book."—*Weekly Register.* "A well-written and well-argued treatise."—*Tablet.*

R. Washbourne, 18a, Paternoster Row, London.

Origin and Progress of Religious Orders, and Happiness of a Religious State. Being chiefly selections in English, by Patrick Mannock, from a Work written in Latin, by Fr. Jerome Platus, S.J., 1632. Fcap. 8vo. 2s. 6d.

"The whole work is evidently calculated to impress any reader with the great advantages attached to a religious life."—*Weekly Register.*

Form of Association for Children of Mary in the World. 32mo. 1d.

"Will be found very useful in Missions where the Association is established."—*Tablet.*

The Young Catholic's Guide to Confession and Holy Communion. By Dr. Kenny. *Third edition.* Paper, 4d.; cloth, 6d.; cloth, red edges, 9d.

"Admirably suited to the purpose for which it is intended."—*Weekly Register.* "One of the best we have seen. The instructions are clear, pointed, and devout, and the prayers simple, well constructed, and sufficiently brief. We recommend it to our readers."—*Church News.*

A Rule of Life. By St. Charles Borromeo. 18mo. 6d.

Intentions for Mass and Holy Communion. By the Poor Clares of Kenmare. 18mo. 2s. 6d.

Practical Counsels for Holy Communion. By Mgr. de Ségur. Translated for children. 18mo. cloth, 6d.; gilt, 1s.

Anglican Orders. By the Very Rev. Canon Williams. *Second Edition.* Crown 8vo. 3s. 6d.

A Letter to George Augustus Simcox, Esq. By One who has lately been received into the Church. 6d.

Rome, Purgatory, Indulgences, Idolatry, &c. By the Rev. Dr. Green. 8vo. 6d.

The Rule of the Third Order of St. Francis. 18mo. 1s.

The Christian Teacher, comprising the Ven. de la Salle's "Twelve Virtues of a Good Master." 18mo. roan, 1s. 8d.

Christian Politeness. By the Ven. de la Salle. 18mo. cloth, 1s.

Duties of a Christian. By the Ven. de la Salle. 2s.

R. Washbourne, 18a, Paternoster Row, London.

The Monks of Iona and the Duke of Argyll. By the Rev. J. Stewart M'Corry, D.D. 8vo. 3s. 6d.
The Rainy Day, and Guild of Our Lady. By the Rev. Fr. Richardson. 2d.
Little by Little; or, the Penny Bank. By the Rev. Fr. Richardson. 1d.
The Catechism of the Council. By a Doctor of Canon Law. 2d.
Auricular Confession: Dogmatical, Historical, and Practical. By the Rev. Dr. Melia. 18mo. 1s. 6d.
Saturday Night Association in Honour of Our Lady. By the Rev. K. Digby-Beste. 3d.
Blue Scapular: Its Objects, Excellency, and Advantages. By a Catholic Priest. 1d.

Lives of Saints.

Life of St. Boniface, and the Conversion of Germany. By Mrs. Hope. Edited, with a Preface, by the Rev. Father Dalgairns. Cr. 8vo. 6s.
The Life of St. Francis of Assisi. Translated from the Italian of St. Bonaventure by Miss Lockhart. With a Preface by His Grace the Archbishop of Westminster. Fcap. 8vo. cloth, 2s. and 3s.; gilt, 4s.

"It is beautifully translated."—*Catholic Opinion*. "A most interesting and instructive volume."—*Tablet*. "This is a first-rate translation by one of the very few persons who have the art of translating as if they were writing an original work."—*Dublin Review*.

Life of St. Charles Borromeo. By the Rev. Father Richards. 18mo. 6d.
The Glory of St. Vincent de Paul. By the Most Rev. Dr. Manning, Archbishop of Westminster. 1s.
Life of Pope Pius IX. 6d.
Martyrdom of the Archbishop of Paris. See the "Catholic Calendar and Church Guide for 1872." Price 4d.

Catholic Glories of the Nineteenth Century. Pius IX., Cardinal Wiseman, and Count de Montalembert. By G. White. Crown 8vo. 2s. 6d.

His Holiness Pope Pius IX.: from his Birth to the Centenary of St. Peter, 1867. By George White. Cloth, red edges, 1s. 6d.

His Eminence Cardinal Wiseman; with full account of his Obsequies; Funeral Oration by Archbishop Manning, &c. 1s.; cloth, red edges, 1s. 6d.

Count de Montalembert; his Life and Writings. By George White. 6d.

BY THE POOR CLARES OF KENMARE.

Life and Revelations of St. Gertrude. Cr. 8vo. 7s. 6d.
Spirit of St. Gertrude. 18mo. 2s. 6d.
Life of St. Aloysius. 6d.
Life of St. Joseph, 6d.; cloth, 9d.
Life of St. Patrick, 6d.; cloth, 9d.
Life of St. Patrick. Illustrated by Doyle. 4to. 20s.

Life of St. Patrick. 12mo. gilt, 1s.
The Holy Isle; or the Life of St. Bridget, and other Saints of Ireland. 12mo. gilt, 1s.
Panegyric of St. Patrick. By the Rev. Dr. M'Corry. 6d.
Insula Sanctorum: the Island of Saints. Fcap. 8vo. 1s.; cloth, 2s.

"The author brings forward much historical testimony, and we must say that he proves his point."—*Tablet.* "This spirited little *Noli me tangere.*"—*Dublin Review.*

Life of Fr. de Ravignan. Crown 8vo. 9s.
Life of Mgr. Weedall. By Dr. Husenbeth. 7s. 6d.
The Conversion of Ratisbonne. Translated from the French, by M. E. J. 18mo. 6d.

DR. NEWMAN'S LIVES OF THE ENGLISH SAINTS.

Life of St. Augustine of Canterbury. 12mo. 3s. 6d.
Life of St. German. 12mo. cloth, 3s. 6d.
Life of Stephen Langton. 12mo. cloth, 2s. 6d.

R. Washbourne, 18a, Paternoster Row, London.

Memoir of the Rt. Rev. Dr. Grant. See "The Catholic Calendar and Church Guide for 1871." 4d.
Pictorial Lives of Twelve Saints. 6d.; cloth, 1s.
The Life of Rev. Fr. Pallotti. By the Rev. Dr. Melia. Crown 8vo. 4s.

Our Lady.

Devotion to Our Lady in North America. By the Rev. Xavier Donald Macleod. 8vo. 7s. 6d.

"The work of an author than whom few more gifted writers have ever appeared among us. It is not merely a religious work, but it has all the charms of an entertaining book of travels. We can hardly find words to express our high admiration of it."—*Weekly Register.*

The History of the Blessed Virgin Mary, Mother of God, completed by the Traditions of the East, the Writings of the Holy Fathers, and the Private History of the Hebrews. By the Abbé Orsini. Translated from the French by the Very Rev. F. C. Husenbeth, D.D. Crown 8vo. 3s. 6d.

"A very learned and very pious work, and gathers up the ancient legends about our Blessed Lady in a most pleasing manner."—*Month.* "A really charming reproduction in an English garb of Orsini's standard work. It is illustrated with many exquisite woodcuts after the ancient masters. The binding is very handsome."—*Catholic Opinion.*

A Devout Exercise in Honour of the Blessed Virgin Mary. A Daily Devotion in honour of the Ever Blessed Virgin Mother of God, from the Psalter and Prayers of S. Bonaventure. In Latin and English, with Indulgences applicable to the Holy Souls. 32mo. 1s.

Simple Explanations concerning the Co-operation of the Most Holy Virgin in the work of Redemption. By Père Jeanjacquot. 3s. or 2s. 3d., cash.

Our Blessed Lady of Lourdes. By F. C. Husenbeth, D.D. Fcap. 8vo. 1s.; cloth, 2s.

The Blessed Virgin's Root traced in the Tribe of Ephraim. By the Rev. F. H. Laing, D.D. 8vo. 10s. 6d.

The Little Office of the Immaculate Conception. In Latin and English. By the Very Rev. Dr. Husenbeth. 32mo. 4d. ; cloth, 6d. ; roan, 1s.; calf or morocco, 2s. 6d.

Some account of the Definition of the Immaculate Conception. 12mo. 6d.

Our Lady's Lament, and the Lamentation of St. Mary Magdalene. Edited from the original MSS., &c., by C. E. Tame. 16mo. 2s.

Our Lady's Month ; or, Short Lessons for the Month of May and the Feasts of Our Lady. By the Rev. A. P. Bethell. 18mo. 1s.; with Frontispiece, 1s. 6d.

Month of Mary for Interior Souls. By M. A. Macdaniel. 18mo. 2s. ; cloth, 2s. 6d.

The Child's Month of May. By the Poor Clares of Kenmare. 6d. ; cloth, 1s.

Visits to the Altar of Mary. By the Poor Clares of Kenmare. 1s. ; cloth, 1s. 6d.

The Virgin Mary. By the Rev. Dr. Melia, P.S.M. 8vo. 11s. 3d. cash.

Prayers.

The Lily of St. Joseph ; a little Manual of Prayers and Hymns for Mass. Price 2d. ; cloth, 3d. ; or with gilt lettering, 4d. ; more strongly bound, 6d. ; or with gilt edges, 8d.; roan, 1s.; French morocco, 1s. 6d. ; calf, or morocco, 2s. ; gilt, 2s. 6d.

"It supplies a want which has long been felt ; a prayer-book for children, which is not a childish book, a handy book for boys and girls, and for men and women too, if they wish for a short, easy-to-read, and devotional prayer-book."—*Catholic Opinion.* " A very complete prayer-book. It will be found very useful for children and for travellers."—*Weekly Register.* "A neat little compilation, which will be specially useful to our Catholic School-children. The hymns it contains are some of Fr. Faber's best."—*Universe.*

Occasional Prayers for Festivals. By Rev. T. Barge. 32mo. 4d. and 6d. ; gilt, 1s.

Washbourne's Edition of the "Garden of the Soul," in medium-sized type (small type as a rule being avoided). Cloth, 9d.; roan, gilt edges, 1s.; with rims and clasp, 1s. 6d. French morocco, 2s.; with rims and clasp, 2s. 6d. French morocco, extra, 2s. 6d.; with rims and clasp, 3s. Calf or morocco, 4s.; with rims and clasp, 5s. 6d. Calf or morocco extra, 5s.; with rims and clasp, 6s. 6d. Velvet, with rims and clasp, 8s. and 10s. 6d. Russia, antique, with clasp, 12s. 6d. Ivory, 15s. and 21s. The above can be had with Epistles and Gospels, 6d. extra. The Epistles and Gospels, in cloth, 6d.

Garden of the Soul, in large type. Roan, gilt edges, 2s.; French morocco, 3s., clasp and rims, 4s.; French morocco, antique, 3s. 6d.; calf, 4s. 6d.; morocco, 6s.; roan, sprinkled edges, with Epistles and Gospels, 2s.

Illustrated Manual of Prayers. 32mo., 3d.; cloth, 4d.

Key of Heaven. Very large type edition, 1s.

Catholic Hours: a Manual of Prayer, including Mass and Vespers. By J. R. Digby-Beste, Esq. 32mo. cloth, 2s; red edges, 2s. 6d.; roan, 3s.; morocco, 5s.

Novena to St. Joseph. By A. J. V. Translated by M. A. Macdaniel. To which is added a Pastoral of the late Right Rev. Dr. Grant. 32mo. 4d.; cloth, 6d.

"All seasons are fitting in which to make Novenas to St. Joseph, for which reason this little work will be found very serviceable at any time."—*Weekly Register.* "A useful little manual; we recommend it cordially."—*Westminster Gazette.*

Devotions to St. Joseph. 1s. per 100.

Devotion to St. Joseph as Patron of the Catholic Church. 2d.

Gahan's Catholic Piety. 32mo. roan, gilt edges, 1s.; roan, gilt, 1s. 6d., with rims and clasp, 2s.; imitation ivory, rims and clasp, 2s. 6d.; velvet rims and clasps, 3s. 6d.

Sacred Heart of Jesus offered to the Piety of the Young engaged in Study. By Rev. A. Deham, S.J. 6d.

Pleadings of the Sacred Heart. 18mo., 1s.

"It is a complete little Manual of Devotion to the Sacred Heart, and as such will be valued by Catholics of every age and station."—*Tablet*.

Treasury of the Sacred Heart. A new Manual of Catholic Devotion, with Epistles and Gospels. 18mo. cloth, red edges, 3s. 6d.

Little Treasury of the Sacred Heart. 32mo. cloth, gilt edges, 2s. ; French morocco, 2s. 6d.

Devotions to Sacred Heart of Jesus. By the Rt. Rev. Dr. Milner. *New Edition*. To which is added Devotions to the Immaculate Heart of Mary. 3d. ; cloth, 6d. ; gilt, 1s.

An Act of Consecration to the Sacred Heart of Jesus. By the Rev. C. Bennett. 1d. ; 6s. per 100.

Manual of Devotions in Honour of Our Lady of Sorrows. Compiled by the Clergy at St. Patrick's, Soho. 18mo. 1s. ; cloth, red edges, 1s. 6d.

St. Angela's Manual : a Book of Devout Prayers and Exercises for Female Youth. Compiled and translated from approved sources. Fcap. 8vo. cloth, 2s. ; calf, 3s. 6d.

A New Year's Gift to our Heavenly Father ; or, Dedication of the First Hours of the Year, Quarter, Month, or Week to God. 2d. ; cloth, 4d.

Devotions for Mass. Very large type, 2d.

Memorare Mass. By the Poor Clares of Kenmare, 2d.

Fourteen Stations of the Holy Way of the Cross. By St. Liguori. Large type edition, 1d.

Litany of Resignation. 1s. per 100.

Indulgenced Prayers. 1s. per 100.

Intentions for Indulgences. 6d. per 100.

Prayers for the Dying. 1s. per 100.

R. Washbourne, 18a, Paternoster Row, London.

Paroissien Romain. Various editions. Prices 8d., 1s., 1s. 6d., 2s. 6d., 3s. 6d., 4s., 4s. 6d., 5s., 6s., 7s., 8s. 6d., 10s. 6d.

Manual of Prayer, Key of Heaven, Catholic Piety, Miniature Prayer Book. Size, 3¼ inches by 2½, each, cloth, 6d.; cape, 1s.; imitation ivory rims and clasp, 2s. 6d.; calf, 2s. 6d.; morocco, with clasp, 3s.; with rims and clasp, 4s. 6d.; with tuck, 4s. 6d.; velvet, rims and clasp, 4s.; Russia leather, 10s. 6d.; ivory, 7s. 6d., 10s. 6d., 15s., 18s. The same books, with red border round pages, calf, 6s. 6d.; morocco, with clasp, 7s., or with tuck, 8s.

Manual of Catholic Piety, containing a selection of Fervent Prayers, Pious Reflections, and Solid Instructions, adapted to every State of Life. Green border edition. French mor., 3s. 6d.; mor., 5s.

Catholic Psalmist: or, Manual of Sacred Music, containing Vespers in Latin and English; Chants, Hymns, and Litanies; Instructions for Choirs, &c., with an Appendix, including the Gregorian Chants for High Mass, Processions, Holy Week, &c. Compiled by C. B. Lyons, Hon. Member of the Pontifical Academy of St. Cecilia, Rome. Fcap. 8vo. cloth, red edges, 4s.

Catholic Choir Manual: containing Vespers for all the Sundays and Festivals of the year, Hymns and Litanies, &c. Compiled by C. B. Lyons. Fcap. 8vo. cloth, red edges, 1s.

The Rosary for the Souls in Purgatory, *with Indulgenced Prayer.* 6d., 9d., 1s. and 1s. 6d. each. Medals separately, 1d. each, 9s. gross. Prayers separately, 1d. each, 1s. per 100.

Church Hymns. By J. R. Digby-Beste, Esq. 6d.

Ordo Administrandi Sacramenta. *Prior Park Edition.* 32mo. roan, 1s.

Rome, &c.

Two Years in the Pontifical Zouaves. A Narrative of Travel, Experience, and Residence, in the Roman States. By Joseph Powell, Z.P. With Engravings by Sergeant Collingridge, Z.P. 8vo. 5s.

"Will be read with attention and approval."—*Weekly Register.* "It affords us much pleasure, and deserves the notice of the Catholic public."—*Tablet.* "Familiar names meet the eye on every page, and as few Catholic circles in either country have not had a friend or relative at one time or another serving in the Pontifical Zouaves, the history of the formation of the corps, of the gallant youths, their sufferings, and their troubles, will be valued as something more than a contribution to modern Roman history."—*Freeman's Journal.* "Highly interesting."—*Catholic Opinion.* "An interesting book, well got up."—*Month.* "Excellent."—*Dublin Review.*

Personal Recollections of Rome. By W. J. Jacob, Esq., late of the Pontifical Zouaves. 8vo. 1s. 6d.

"An interesting description of the Eternal City."—*Tablet.* "All will read it with pleasure, and many to their profit."—*Register.*

The Rule of the Pope-King, Weighed by Facts and Figures. By the Rev. E. R. Martin. 6d.

The Roman News-Letter, Jan. 8, to Aug. 16. 1s. 6d.

The Crusader, with which is incorporated "The Roman News-Letter," the Official Organ of the League of St. Sebastian. A journal devoted to the Restoration of the Temporal Power of the Pope. Published fortnightly, price 1d. Yearly subscription, 1 copy, 3s. 6d.; 2 copies, 5s. 6d.; 3 copies, 8s., payable in advance.

Report of the League of St. Sebastian. 6d.

The Victories of Rome. By the Rev. K. Digby-Beste, of the Oratory. 6d.

The Years of Peter. A Poem. By an Ex-Papal Zouave. 6d.

Defence of the Roman Church against Fr. Gratry. By Dom Gueranger. Translated by the V. Rev. Canon Woods, with a Preface by the V. Rev. Prior Vaughan, O.S.B. 6d.

Tales and Poetry.

Margarethe Verflassen. Translated from the German by Mrs. Smith Sligo. Fcap. 8vo. 3s. ; gilt, 3s. 6d.

Chats about the Rosary ; or, Aunt Margaret's Little Neighbours. By Skelton Yorke, author of " Hilda." Fcap. 8vo. 3s.

"The style of the book is pleasing, and has a slightly allegorical tone. There is scarcely any devotion so calculated as the Rosary to keep up a taste for piety in little children, and we must be grateful for any help in applying its lessons to the daily life of those who already love it in their unconscious tribute to its value and beauty."—*Month.* "We do not know of a better book for reading aloud to children, it will teach them to understand and to love the Rosary."—*Tablet.* "A graceful little book, in fifteen chapters, on the Rosary, illustrative of each of the mysteries, and connecting each with the practice of some particular virtue."—*Catholic Opinion.*

The People's Martyr, a Legend of Canterbury. 4s.

Lord Dacre of Gilsland. A Tale of England in the days of Queen Elizabeth. Crown 8vo. 5s.

Cloister Legends : or, Convents and Monasteries in the Olden Time. *Second Edition.* Cr. 8vo. 4s.

"Deeply interesting and edifying."—*Weekly Register.* "A charming book of tales of the olden time."—*Catholic Opinion.* "A charming volume."—*Universe.* "The stories are very well told." *The Month.*

Ned Rusheen ; or, Who Fired the First Shot. By the Poor Clares of Kenmare. Crown 8vo. 6s.

The Last of the Catholic O'Malleys. A Tale. By M. Taunton. 18mo. cloth, 2s.

"A sad and stirring tale, simply written, and sure to secure for itself readers."—*Tablet.* "Deeply interesting. It is well adapted for parochial and school libraries."—*Weekly Register.* "A very pleasing tale."—*The Month.*

Sir Ælfric and other Tales. By the Rev. G. Bampfield. 18mo. 6d. ; cloth, 1s. ; gilt, 1s. 6d.

"Beautifully and touchingly written."—*Tablet.*

Keighley Hall and other Tales. By Elizabeth King. 18mo. 6d.; cloth, 1s. ; gilt, 1s. 6d. ; or, separately, Keighley Hall, Clouds and Sunshine, The Maltese Cross, 3d. each.

"Written by a loyal member of the true Church."—*Tablet.*

Adolphus ; or, the Good Son. 18mo. gilt, 6d.

Nicholas ; or, the Reward of a Good Action. 6d.

Nina and Pippo ; or, the Lost Children of Mount St. Bernard. 18mo. gilt, 6d.

A Broken Chain. An Episode of the French Revolution. 18mo. gilt, 6d.

The Baker's Boy, the Life of General Drouot ; or, the Results of Industry. 18mo. gilt, 6d.

"All prettily got up, artistically illustrated, and pleasantly-written. Better books for gifts and rewards we do not know."—*Weekly Register.* "We can thoroughly recommend them."—*Tablet.*

Tales and Sketches. By Charles Fleet. 8vo. cloth, 2s. and 2s. 6d. ; cloth, gilt, 3s. 6d.

"Pleasingly-written, and containing some valuable hints. There is a good deal of nice feeling in these short stories."—*Tablet.* "Well written; they will be found innocent as well as pleasant reading."—*Weekly Register.*

The Three Elizabeths. By A. M. Stewart. Crown 8vo. cloth, 3s. 6d. ; gilt edges. 4s. 6d.

Alone in the World. By the above Author. Crown 8vo. cloth, 3s. 6d. and 4s. 6d.

Shakespeare's Plays. Abridged and Revised for the use of Schools. By Rosa Baughan. 8vo. 4s. 6d.

Shakespeare's Tragedies. Abridged and Revised for the use of Schools. By Rosa Baughan. 8vo. 4s. 6d.

Poems. By H. N. Oxenham. *Third Edition.* 8vo. 3s. 6d.

The Convent Prize Book. A Selection of Verses on the Festivals of the Church, Feasts of the Blessed Virgin, Festivals of the Principal Saints, and Miscellaneous Poems. By the author of "Geraldine." Fcap. 8vo. 2s. 6d. ; gilt, 3s. 6d.

An Epitome of the Fall, Redemption, and Exaltation of Man. Cloth, 6d. and 1s.

R. Washbourne, 18a, Paternoster Row, London.

Educational.

General Questions in History, Chronology, Geography, the Arts, &c. By A. M. Stewart. 4s. 6d.

"To parents and teachers, we most warmly recommend it, as a safe and instructive book to be placed in the hands of the young."—*Belfast Northern Star*.

Catechism of the History of England. By Ellen Chapman. Cloth, 1s.

History of Modern Europe. With a Preface by the Very Rev. Mgr. Weathers, D.D. 12mo. cloth, 5s.; gilt, 6s.; roan, 5s. 6d.

A Chronological Sketch of the Kings of England from the Conquest to the Present Reign; and the Kings of France, from the Accession of Hugh Capet to the Present Time. With Anecdotes for the use of Children. By H. M. L. Cr. 8vo. 2s. 6d.; or separately, England, 1s. 6d., France, 1s. 6d.

"Admirably adapted for teaching young children the elements of English and French history."—*Tablet*. "A very interesting contribution."—*Church Herald*. "A very useful little publication."—*Weekly Register*. "An admirably arranged little work for the use of children."—*Universe*.

Lingard's History of England. 10 vols. Cloth, 21s. cash.

History of England. By W. Mylius. 12mo. 3s. 6d.

The Illustrated History of Ireland. By the Poor Clares of Kenmare. With Illustrations by Doyle. 8vo. 10s.; gilt, 11s.

The Patriots' History of Ireland. By the Poor Clares of Kenmare. 18mo. cloth, 2s.; cloth gilt, 2s. 6d.

History of Ireland. By T. Young. 18mo. cloth, 2s. 6d.

An Abridgment of Ecclesiastical History. In Question and Answer. 32mo. cloth, 9d.

Bell's Modern Reader and Speaker; a Selection of Poetry and Prose from the Writings of Eminent Authors, preceded by the Principles of Elocution. 12mo. cloth, 3s. 6d.

Une Corbeille des Fleurs. 12mo. cloth, 2s.

The Catholic Alphabet of Scripture Subjects. Price, on a sheet, plain, 1s.; coloured, 2s.; mounted on linen, to fold in a case, 3s. 6d.; varnished, on linen, on rollers, 4s.

"This will be hailed with joy by all young children in Catholic schools, and we should gladly see it placed conspicuously before the eyes of our little ones."—*Catholic Opinion.* "Will be very welcome in the infant school."—*Weekly Register.*

Extracts from the Fathers and other Writers of the Church. 12mo. cloth, 4s. 6d.

Poor School Committee Reading Books. Primer, 1½d.; Book I., 2d.; II., 5d.; III., 8d.; IV., 1s.

Standard Series. Primer, 4d. (Part I. of Primer, 1½d.); I., 6d.; II., 7d.; III., 10d.; IV., 1s.; V. and VI., 1s. 4d.

Religious Reading Books. 1. for Standards I. and II., 9d.; 2. for Standards III. and IV., 10d.; 3. for Standards V. and VI., 1s. 6d.

The Irish Board Reading Books. I., ½d. nett; II., 4d.; Sequel I., 4d.; Sequel II., 4d.; III., 8d.; IV., 9d.; V., 9d. Arithmetic, 4d., larger, 9d.; Grammar, 4d.; Geography, 4d.; Book-Keeping, 6d.

Christian Brother's Reading Books. 1st, 3d.; 2nd, 8d.; 3rd, 1s. 6d.; 4th, 2s. Historical Class Book, 3s. 1st Spelling, 4d.; 2nd, 1s. 1st Geography, 4d.; 2nd, 9d.; 3rd, 2s. 6d. 1st Grammar, 4d.; 2nd, 9d. Arithmetic, 1s. 4d.

Chambers', Grayston and Birkby's, and any other Standard Books supplied. *See School Catalogue.*

Brickley's Standard Table Book, ½d.

Washbourne's Multiplication Table on a sheet, 3s. per 100. Specimen sent for 1d. stamp.

Irish Varieties. By J. Gaskin. Illustrated with Chromo-Lithographs. Crown 8vo. cloth, 6s.

The Crucifixion. Coloured, on black ground. Size 20 in. by 27 in. Price 2s.

R. Washbourne, 18a, Paternoster Row, London.

Music.

Mass of the Holy Child Jesus, and Ave Maria for unison and congregational singing, with organ accompaniment, composed for the Church of the Oratory. By W. Schulthes. 6s. for 3s., with allowance for numbers to choirs. *For use at Low Mass, the Kyrie and Glorie will fill up the time to the Credo. All the other movements are kept in the proper limits. The Mass is especially adapted for Children and Congregational use. It has the advantage of being kept in the proper compass for all voices.*

The Vocal Part may be had separately, in 18mo., at 4d. each, or 22s. 6d. cash per 100; or bound in cloth, at 6d. each, or 33s. 6d. cash per 100.

"A mass both useful and pleasing. The music is quite in the modern idiom, and tinged with the individuality of the talented composer."—*Weekly Register.*

The **Ave Maria** of this Mass can be had for Four Voices, with the Ingressus Angelus. 2s. 6d. for 1s. 3d.

Ne projicias me a facie Tua. Motett for Four Voices. (T.B.) By Wilhelm Schulthes. 2s. 6d. for 1s. 3d.

"A very effective offertory. The sudden change from the key of E minor to that of E major is very telling. The piece contains some grand harmonies, and is very singable and melodious."—*Weekly Register.* "This is a really solid, as well as beautiful composition, and worthy of the pen of its well-known and talented composer. We recommend it as an Offertory piece suitable for Penitential Seasons in churches where men's voices alone are employed."—*Tablet.*

Recordare. Oratio Jeremiæ Prophetæ. By W. Schulthes. 2s. for 1s.

Six Litany Chants. By F. Leslie. 6d.

A separate Catalogue of FOREIGN Books, Educational Books, Books for the Library or for Prizes, supplied; also a Catalogue of School and General Stationery, a Catalogue of Secondhand Books, and a Catalogue of Crucifixes and other Religious Articles.

R. WASHBOURNE, 18A, PATERNOSTER ROW.

www.ingramcontent.com/pod-product-compliance
Lightning Source LLC
Chambersburg PA
CBHW031935290426
44108CB00011B/566